THE WORLD'S

GREATEST

UNEXPLAINED
MYSTERIES

THE
WORLD'S
GREATEST
UNEXPLAINED
MYSTERIES

Bounty
Books

This collection first published in 2014 by Bounty Books,
a division of Octopus Publishing Group Ltd,
Endeavour House, 189 Shaftesbury Avenue,
London WC2H 8JY
www.octopusbooks.co.uk

An Hachette UK company
www.hachette.co.uk

The material in this book originally appeared in three separate
titles:
The World's Greatest Mysteries by Gerry Brown
The World's Greatest UFO Encounters by Nigel Cawthorne
The World's Greatest Secrets by Allan Hall

ISBN: 978-0-753727-77-5

Printed and bound by CPI Group (UK) Ltd, Croydon, CR0 4YY

Contents

THE WORLD'S
GREATEST
UNEXPLAINED
MYSTERIES

Chapter One

CRIME & INTRIGUE

Some of the most sinister and upsetting mysteries we have to face are those when people suddenly go missing, for no apparent reason and leaving behind them precious little for investigators to go on. Even more sinister, perhaps, are the methods of occultism and psychic clairvoyance, used either to find missing persons or criminals in hiding, or abused by their practitioners, in order to commit dastardly acts . . .

Suzy Lamplugh

On Monday 28 July 1986, Suzy Lamplugh made an entry in her business diary. It read: '12.45. Mr Kipper, 37 Shorrolds Road, O/S'.

For 25-year-old Suzy, the summons to get out of doors and meet a perfect stranger must have been a welcome opportunity to have a break from her busy office routine at Sturgis Estate Agents in Fulham Road, west London, where she had worked for 16 months.

The diary note was a simple shorthand reminder to herself. Suzy, a young, ambitious and hard-working estate agent negotiator, was due to meet a client outside that address at the appointed time. The property – a furnished three-storey terraced house – had come on to the books a few days before. The asking price was £128,000 and a successful sale would have meant a tidy commission bonus for the eager young estate agent.

Suzy had spent a wasteful and frustrating morning taking phone calls from potential clients who just wanted to compare house prices with those of rival estate agents, making her own calls to friends, trying to locate her pocket diary and a postcard she had lost before the previous weekend, and notifying her bank manager about her cheque book which had been misplaced at the same time.

But nothing distracted her from her meeting with Mr Kipper. That appointment seemed like a real sales prospect. Mr Kipper could be a serious potential purchaser.

Just before her lunch break she strode over to the desk of Mark Gurdon, the office manager, and collected the keys to the house in Shorrolds Road. The Ford Fiesta car supplied by her employers was parked just outside the office. It would take only three or four minutes for Suzy to drive to her appointment. The office manager expected Suzy would be gone just long enough to show her potential customer around the property before heading back to the office. She would probably bring back a sandwich to eat at her desk, because she was always keen to be there, ready to answer any calls that might lead to more sales and more commission bonuses.

Suzy took only her purse with her, leaving her handbag behind. Then she left the office and drove away to become the subject of the biggest and most puzzling missing persons mystery which has ever baffled the experts at New Scotland Yard.

Missing estate agent Suzy and (inset) 37 Shorrolds Road.

It was only a few hours before her friends and colleagues at the estate agent's began to become concerned about Suzy's absence. At first Mark Gurdon was simply irritated that Suzy seemed to be taking too much time over her visit to the terraced house. He assumed there might be unforeseen complications with the client, possibly caused by lengthy on-the-spot nego-tiating over the price for the property. But if that had been the case, she should have returned immediately to the office, where she could have taken advice and hammered out any financial details.

He strolled over to Suzy's desk and checked her diary entry. By late afternoon he had become worried. It was unlike Suzy to take long, unauthorized lunch breaks. He decided to check for himself. With another of Suzy's colleagues he drove round to the vacant property. There was no sign of Suzy or her car. But as the two estate agents prepared to leave Shorrolds Road, next door neighbour 58-year-old unemployed bachelor Harry Riglin asked them: 'Are you looking for the young couple?'

Riglin confirmed that Suzy had indeed been at the house with a young man. He had thought they looked like a nice, prosperous young couple as they stood outside and looked up admiringly at the house. The kind of people he would have liked as neighbours.

Mark Gurdon returned to his office. He checked his file of clients. They had never done business before with a 'Mr Kipper'. The mystery client may have only phoned that morning and by sheer chance Suzy had taken the call; or he may have stepped into the office at any time in the past few days after seeing a property in the window display which had caught his eye.

Gurdon's next call was to Suzy's mother, 54-year-old swimming teacher and slimming counsellor Diana Lamplugh, at her home in East Sheen, a few miles away. Gurdon asked if Suzy had skipped work to have lunch with her mother, but Mrs Lamplugh had not seen her daughter since she had paid a visit to her family the day before.

Increasingly worried, Gurdon then began to phone the casualty depart-ments of local hospitals. He went to Fulham police station to report his young sales agent's disappearance, but couldn't afford the time to wait in the lengthy queue at the desk. He hurried off to an appointment with a client, checked Shorrolds Road again, and returned to his office.

Six hours after Suzy had last been seen, Gurdon phoned Fulham police station and spoke to PC Duncan Parker. Immediately, Missing Person Report FF584/1/54 was filed. Next, an urgent call was made to the home of Detective Inspector Peter Johnstone, the officer on call for emergencies, instructing him to take charge of the investigation.

Detective Inspector Johnstone was, at the time, heading the hunt for the murderer of an elderly London woman who had been raped and strangled the week before. When he heard the first details of Suzy's disappearance, he feared he had another murder case on his hands.

Missing persons reports at London police stations fall into two categories: 'active' and 'inactive'. Inactive files cover those whose overwhelming family, career or financial problems seem to give them some melancholy but logical reason for dropping out of sight, cutting off all contact with those closest to them.

But the case of Suzy Lamplugh definitely fell into the 'active' category. For this was a well-adjusted, normal, happy young woman. She had gone for a lunchtime appointment leaving her handbag behind at her office, obviously expecting to return. There was no apparent reason for Suzy Lamplugh to vanish, unless she had been the victim of foul play.

Johnstone quickly ordered local police officers to go to Suzy's own home – a two-bedroomed flat in Putney – and smash their way in if need be. He wanted to make sure that Suzy had not become unwell that day and had simply gone home to sleep off a sudden bout of illness; or that the missing estate agent had not suddenly lost her heart in a mad moment of passion with the mysterious Mr Kipper and had taken him home with her.

At Suzy's flat there was no sign of her or her flatmate, 25-year-old advertising executive Nick Bryant. He was still at work, unaware of Suzy's disappearance.

In Suzy's neat and orderly bedroom lay the material for a dress; there was a partially completed sleeve beside the sewing machine her mother had lent her. There were no signs of a struggle; nor of any visitors; nor of any empty wardrobes, which might have hinted at Suzy running away.

At the same time, two detectives forced their way into the unoccupied 'House for Sale' in Shorrolds Road. There were no clues there either.

Throughout London, a general alert was flashed to all mobile patrols and beat bobbies to locate Suzy's Ford Fiesta, registration number B396 GAN. A 'grid search' was organized, marking off the immediate vicinity of Shorrolds Road into squares, so that every road and side-street could be checked out for signs of Suzy or her car.

Detectives began to build up a picture of Suzy, her friends, her contacts, her boyfriends, her business associates. They found nothing sinister whatsoever. In fact, the picture they had was of a wholesome, beautiful girl-next-door type, who could have been anyone's daughter, sister or friend.

Suzy was a go-ahead, strong-willed girl, the second oldest child of the Lamplugh family, with an older brother and two younger sisters. She had overcome the handicap dyslexia, the inability to read letters and numbers properly, which also afflicted her mother and her brother and sisters. Sufferers from dyslexia see script and text only as a confusing jumble of letters. With

11

the patient help and support of her father, 55-year-old solicitor Paul Lamplugh, Suzy had learned to read and had successfully passed her exams.

After leaving school, Suzy had trained and qualified as a beautician, and went to work in the floating beauty salon of the *Queen Elizabeth II* luxury cruise ship. On board the liner she was known to her shipmates as 'H', because she insisted on being called by her full name and was constantly telling the crew and passengers that her name was 'Susannah – with an H!'?

She had cruised the world and dreamed of settling down in South Africa with a boyfriend she had met on board, but back on dry land, practical and ambitious Suzy had buckled down to hard work as an estate agent, eventually buying her own £70,000 flat in Putney, just south of the river Thames and near to her parents' home.

Although she had lived independently away from home for six years, she visited her parents regularly. In fact, she had been to see her parents the night before she went missing. Just before she kissed them goodbye, Suzy had summed up her own easy-going vitality. 'Life is for living,' she told them.

Mr Riglin, the neighbour who had seen the young couple viewing the house at Shorrolds Road, was able to give police an accurate description of Suzy as she was last seen: 5ft 6in tall, pretty, medium-built with blond streaked hair, wearing a peach blouse, black jacket and grey skirt with high-heeled shoes.

The detectives grilled Riglin at length about Suzy's companion, the man now known to everyone on the case as 'Mr Kipper'. He was a couple of inches taller than Suzy, aged between 25 and 30. He was handsome, slimly built, clean shaven and looked prosperous and wealthy in his neatly tailored dark business suit.

At home in East Sheen, Suzy's parents were frantic with worry. Her father, Paul, travelled to Fulham, anxious to witness for himself the massive police effort now being mounted to locate his daughter. Meanwhile, Diana Lamplugh waited at home by the telephone, hoping against hope that Suzy would call her. Even a message from a kidnapper demanding a ransom would have been welcome.

Offering what little help he could, Paul Lamplugh joined two detectives in their patrol car and toured the streets of west London, hoping to spot his daughter among the happy crowds of young people sipping drinks in wine bars or queueing for cinema seats. He had only been in the patrol car a few minutes when he heard the radio message announcing the first clue to Suzy's disappearance. The Ford Fiesta car she had driven that day had been found in Stevenage Road, a quiet residential street. It was a little over a mile from the vacant property where Suzy had met Mr Kipper and in the opposite direction from the route she would have taken to return to the office.

By now, it was 10 p.m., and Detective Inspector Johnstone decided that a full forensic examination would have to wait until daylight. In the meantime, careful not to accidentally wipe out any fingerprints or disturb any microscopic hairs or fibres invisible to the naked eye, the police inspected the abandoned car as closely as they dared.

The Ford Fiesta had been parked at a slight angle to the kerb and the rear end of the car was partially blocking the entrance to a garage. It had been dumped there by someone in a hurry; the handbrake had been left in the off position.

The driver's door was unlocked, but the passenger door was firmly secure, suggesting that only one person had been driving the car. On the back shelf they could clearly see Suzy's straw hat.

The police meticulously opened the driver's door and prised up the back shelf to check the boot of the car. It was empty. But in the rack of the door, they found a purse.

Then they found the most intriguing clue of all: the driver's seat, which would normally have been moved forward in the position closest to the steering wheel for a girl like Suzy, had been pushed back several notches. It seemed likely that the car had been driven to its final parking place by someone several inches taller than Suzy; possibly a man; probably Mr Kipper.

There the clues stopped.

Since the disappearance of Suzy Lamplugh there have been reports of her being seen alive in many different locations, from London nightspots to the sun-soaked beaches of Spanish and Greek holiday resorts. The release of a photo-fit impression of the shadowy figure of Mr Kipper produced a flood of calls to the police, but no solid leads.

In the search for Suzy, the biggest ever mounted by New Scotland Yard, more than 26,000 separate index cards were filed on computer, detailing every aspect of Suzy's life and those of her friends, family and almost everyone who had come in contact with her.

In the busy sales offices of estate agents throughout London, worried staff began to change their carefree office routines. Before any male customers were fixed up with appointments with young female negotiators with a prospect of buying property, they were asked to call in at the office where colleagues could discreetly make a note of their description and the number of the vehicle they drove.

Potential buyers making telephone appointments were asked for contact numbers and business addresses, where their identities could be verified before any female negotiator was despatched to meet them.

Nine months after Susannah Jane Lamplugh disappeared with the mysterious Mr Kipper, a remembrance service was held at her family's local church,

All Saints, East Sheen. Everyone who attended wore bright clothes and buttonhole flowers, like at a wedding. It was a celebration of the life of the young estate agent, they were told. They heard of the launch of the Suzy Lamplugh Trust, a charity dedicated to making life safer and less fearful for young career girls.

And they heard Paul Lamplugh say of his daughter: 'While we do not believe that Suzy is alive, we do not believe she is dead. That is the paradox.'

Helen Smith

As a former detective with the Leeds police force in Yorkshire, Ron Smith was no stranger to seeing the bodies of victims of violent death. But he had to steel his courage to near breaking point on the night of Saturday 26 May 1979, when he was led into the mortuary of the Baksh Hospital in Jeddah, Saudi Arabia. The body he had come to view was not that of some faceless stranger – it was the body of his own daughter, Helen.

Ron Smith had been living with the grief of his daughter's death since he had received a phonecall a week earlier telling him that 23-year-old Helen had died tragically in an accident in Jeddah, falling from a balcony of a block of flats where she had gone to a party.

Choking back his emotions, the ex-policeman, now a successful businessman, had flown to the Middle East, where Helen had been working as a nurse since the Baksh Hospital had opened 15 months earlier. He simply wanted to bring her body home for burial.

Sympathetic Foreign Office officials who met him in the Saudi capital could offer him little comfort. In an attempt to explain the circumstances surrounding Helen's death, they escorted him to the local prison to meet Richard Arnot, the English senior surgeon at Baksh Hospital.

Arnot was awaiting trial for breaching the strict Saudi Muslim law banning alcohol. He had hosted the drinks party at which Helen had died.

Arnot could only outline briefly that Helen had died as a result of a fall from the balcony of his sixth-floor flat in the hospital complex. There had been a lot of heavy, illegal drinking at the party and another party guest, a 31-year-old Dutchman, Johannes Otten, had also been killed in a 70-foot tumble from the same balcony. Arnot claimed he had slept through the fatal drama, and knew none of the details.

The distressed father brushed aside diplomatic objections and demanded to see the body of his dead daughter. When mortuary attendant Subi Bakir drew back the shroud over Helen's body, Ron Smith began to have doubts about the authorities' simple explanation for her death. Helen's body showed some signs of internal bleeding but, apart from this, there was no evidence of the massive injuries one would normally expect to see in someone who had crashed from a great height on to the solid concrete forecourt outside the block of flats.

Ron Smith was soon convinced that his daughter's death was not a simple accident, but a bizarre murder mystery. He set out on a dogged crusade of investigation and inquiry which was still unresolved a decade later. In fact, the mystery of his daughter's death may *never* be explained.

The official Saudi police report accepted Helen Smith's death as a tragic accident. But when Ron Smith gave them the results of his own detective work – five days spent interviewing hospital staff who knew the background to the events leading up to Doctor Arnot's wild drinks party – they began to change their minds.

On 2 June, Saudi government pathologist Dr Ali Kheir carried out a detailed post mortem examination on the body. He found no evidence of fractures of the neck, shoulder blades or spine. As Ron Smith prepared to fly home to England, he was assured that police were now treating his daughter's death as a murder enquiry.

A year later, when he had only received evasive answers from the Saudi Government and British Foreign Office diplomats about the progress of the murder investigation, Ron Smith was informed that heavy punishments for the hosts of the party and some of their guests had been ordered by the Serious Crimes Court: three German guests at the party suffered no further penalties; two other Germans were sentenced to 30 lashes each; Richard Arnot was sentenced to a year in prison and 80 lashes for consuming alcohol and allowing his wife Penny to commit adultery with a party guest, New Zealand-born deep sea diver Tim Hayter. Mrs Arnot and Hayter were also sentenced to 80 lashes, to be administered in front of a crowd. But there were no charges against anyone in relation to Helen Smith's death.

After five months in prison, the Arnots and their party friends were all released on bail.

In June 1980, Ron Smith decided his only hope of unravelling the mystery of the fatal drinks party lay in uncovering the facts before a British court. He

Dr and Mrs Arnot and (inset) Nurse Helen Smith.

flew to Jeddah, collected his daughter's body and returned to Leeds. There he petitioned acting coroner Mr Miles Coverdale for an inquest.

Coroners can, if they wish, conduct inquests into the death of any British subject anywhere in the world, but Mr Coverdale ruled that the death had taken place outside his jurisdiction and would, therefore, not conduct an inquest. He did, however, agree to carry out his legal obligation to commission an official autopsy, which was carried out by Home Office pathologist Dr Michael Green, at Leeds University. The coroner later announced that the autopsy report confirmed that Helen had suffered injuries consistent with a fall from a height, and an inquest would not be necessary.

But Ron Smith claimed the autopsy report was full of inaccuracies. He found, for instance, references to 'bruises to the face that were consistent with slaps and punches'. He saw this as proof that Helen had been severely beaten, and possibly even murdered, before her body was thrown over the balcony, or placed there by her murderer to make it look as if she and the Dutch guest, Johannes Otten, had both fallen to their deaths.

A month after his report, Dr Green, the pathologist, admitted in a newspaper interview: 'If I was to say Helen Smith's death was an accident, I would be a liar. My conscience would not allow me to say so.'

The interview led to a storm of publicity about the mystery death, and public interest was suddenly aroused. Ron Smith, who had already travelled to Holland to consult the family of Johannes Otten, then hired one of Europe's most respected pathologists to carry out another post mortem.

In December 1980, Danish Professor Jorgen Dalgaard conducted his own autopsy, with Dr Green also present. Professor Dalgaard's report, submitted three months later, uncovered an injury unnoticed until then: a wound covering the whole of the left side of the scalp. He concluded that the wound could have caused bleeding inside the brain leading to Helen falling unconscious or possibly even dying before she sustained any of the other injuries.

It wasn't until March 1982, after a long and bitter legal battle, that two High Court judges ruled that an inquest should be held into Helen's death. The inquest finally opened before a jury in Leeds in November 1982. It was to be a costly hearing, with witnesses flown in from around the world. Dr Richard Arnot, now divorced, had to travel from Australia. His ex-wife, the party hostess Penelope Arnot, announced her marriage to an American journalist and was no longer subject to a subpoena from a British court. And Tim Hayter – another vital witness – did not attend the inquest either.

The evidence of the witnesses at the inquest was a tale of drunkenness and confusion. The party had been organized as a farewell gesture for New Zealander Hayter, who had become a friend of the Arnots' when he had offered to teach the doctor and his wife scuba diving.

At the party there had been five German salvage experts working on a Saudi contract. One German witness said that their hosts, the Arnots, had provided liberal supplies of whisky for the party and had invited Helen because she worked at the hospital with Dr Arnot and often acted as a babysitter for their children. Salvage worker Martin Fleischer testified that they had all helped themselves to large quantities of drink, risking harsh penalties under Saudi law, which strictly prohibits alcohol even for foreign residents and guest workers.

Some time after the party was already under way, Helen arrived and chatted and mingled with the guests. Later still, Doctor Arnot turned up, although his wife had already been acting as a generous hostess.

Dr Arnot went to bed around 2 a.m. leaving his guests to continue the party. Fleischer added that he and his German friends had drifted away shortly afterwards and returned to their digs on board a floating accommodation barge in Jeddah Harbour. When he and his workmates left, Helen and Johannes, Tim Hayter and Mrs Arnot, and a French guest, Jacques Texier, a marine biologist, were still drinking and enjoying the party.

Fleischer had only been in bed for a couple of hours when he was shaken awake by a terrified and trembling Tim Hayter, who told him that there had been a tragedy at the party. Hayter claimed that Helen and Johannes had fallen to their deaths from the balcony while having sex.

Dr Arnot told the court that he had only spent three hours at the party before leaving for a tour of the hospital to check on patients who had undergone surgery earlier that day. When he returned, around 2 a.m., tired and weary, he had gone to bed. He had slept soundly until his wife woke him around 5.30 a.m. to tell him, 'something terrible has happened. Helen and Johannes have fallen from the balcony.'

He had gone down to the forecourt and saw Helen's body crumpled at the foot of the building. But he didn't see any signs of violence on her body. Johannes Otten's body was a few feet away. He was not lying on the forecourt, but was slumped across a set of low pointed railings, his legs gruesomely impaled by the sharp spikes. His trousers were missing and he was wearing only a pair of underpants.

In the street, Arnot found Otten's passport and some private papers. Otten's trousers were never found. There was no sign of them inside the Arnots' flat, and the doctor said he presumed that some passing heartless thief had stolen the trousers from the corpse and thrown away the passport.

Dr Arnot admitted that his next concern, as a matter of urgency, was to get back inside his flat and try to hide all evidence of illicit alcohol.

Frenchman Jacques Texier was able to add more detail. He said he had seen Helen and Otten out on the balcony when he had gone into the kitchen to make himself a sandwich. When it was pointed out to him that the kitchen window looked out on to a different balcony, he changed his evidence, saying he had seen them from another window.

At about 3 a.m. he had asked Mrs Arnot if he could stay the night at the flat, because he did not want to wake up the official at the French Embassy who had offered him a bed for the night. Penelope Arnot agreed, and after the German guests had left Texier stretched out on a sofa. He did not notice where Helen Smith and Johannes Otten had gone, but he was wakened from his sleep around 5 a.m. by the unmistakeable sound of Mrs Arnot and Tim Hayter making passionate love in the room beside him. Later, all three of them had gone into the kitchen to make coffee. When they strolled unsuspectingly out on to the balcony, they were startled to see the two bodies beneath them.

The inquest also heard from witness Dr Hag Abdel Rachman, a gynae-cologist who lived in the same block of flats. He had been wakened by the building's night porter and told there were two bodies outside the block. Dr Rachman said: 'I went to investigate and saw the man hanging upside down on an iron bar. The girl was on the ground, wearing a blue dress and no underwear, there was no blood or indications of violence.'

Dr Rachman gave one vital piece of evidence which left all the other witnesses puzzled. He testified he had knocked on Doctor Arnot's door after the discovery, and the surgeon opened it quickly, saying: 'If you mean that event down the building, I know about that, leave it to me and I will deal with it.' There was a lot of noise coming from the flat and, behind Dr Arnot, the gynaecologist saw a mystery man – a white, short man with a beard – who was never identified by any of the party guests.

The inquest jury retired for eight hours to consider the evidence. After their deliberations they still could not say that Helen's death was an accident, nor could they decide if she had been murdered. Eventually, they returned an open verdict.

Ron Smith remained convinced that all the medical evidence pointed to his daughter having been beaten unconscious, possibly resisting rape, and being placed under the balcony to make it look as if she had fallen to her death. There was evidence that her sternum, or chest bone, had been fractured, perhaps by violent chest massage in an attempt to revive her. Johannes Otten may have been thrown to his death on the railings to silence him.

Helen Smith took her camera to the party. She carried her camera everywhere and was constantly taking photographs. Yet, when the Saudi police recovered it from the death flat, they told Ron Smith there was no film in it. Helen, they said, had taken her camera to the party but hadn't bothered to load it. Another camera in the flat that fateful night belonged to Martin

Fleischer; but when he developed the film he found that all the frames were double-exposed.

No evidence remains of the mystery guest at the party, the white, short, bearded man.

A decade after her death, Helen Smith's body was still in the mortuary in Leeds. Her father's struggle to find out how his daughter died continues undiminished and relentless.

After the inquest, which still proclaimed his Helen's death a mystery, Ron Smith said: 'Honesty and justice will prevail. Everything will be resolved in God's good time.'

Oscar Mike

When Aer Lingus Flight 712 departed from Cork in Ireland for London's Heathrow Airport on Sunday 24 March 1968, it should have been a routine journey lasting little more than an hour and 20 minutes.

On board the Viscount turbo-prop airliner were four crew members and 57 passengers. At the controls was 35-year-old Captain Bernard O'Beirne, one of the airline's most senior pilots, with over 6,600 hours of flying to his credit. More than 1,600 of the hours listed in his pilot's log book had been spent flying Viscounts, considered to be one of the world's safest and most carefully engineered aircraft. O'Beirne's co-pilot, 22-year-old First Officer Paul Heffernan, had 900 hours flying experience on the same type of tried and tested four-engined airliner.

The weather was cloudless and Captain O'Beirne assured his passengers they should enjoy a pleasant, smooth flight. But, half an hour later, the Viscount, codenamed Echo India Alpha Oscar Mike, was a tangled mass of wreckage sinking under the waves in the Irish Sea, and Flight 712 entered the history books as one of the most baffling aviation mysteries ever.

Despite a detailed technical examination of the crumpled remains of the airliner, dredged from the bottom of the sea, and the painstaking analysis of the last frantic and garbled radio messages from Captain O'Beirne, no real answer has ever been found to the riddle of the disaster which left Oscar Mike spinning helplessly to its doom. There was no evidence of a structural or mechanical defect which could have led to the crash; there were no signs of a fire or explosion and no indication of metal fatigue; the weather in the area at the time was good; there were no other aircraft in the vicinity, and the possibility of a collision with a flock of birds was ruled out because Oscar Mike had been flying so high. The only spine-chilling theory, supported by the accounts of eye witnesses, is that Oscar Mike was blown from the sky by a glowing red, supersonic, unidentified flying object.

Within five minutes of take-off from Cork Airport in south-west Ireland, at 11.32 a.m. on a perfect spring morning, the Viscount was climbing up smoothly through the 7000 feet level. Local Air Traffic Controllers gave Captain O'Beirne clearance to continue his ascent to 17,000 feet and advised him of his course for Tuskar Rock, the craggy prominence with its flashing lighthouse off the Irish coast in the Saint George's Channel, separating Ireland from Wales. The cabin crew prepared to serve a light snack to the passengers, who included more than a score of enthusiastic Swedish anglers happily swapping tales of the salmon they had caught during their week-long expedition in the lakes and rivers of Killarney. The anglers were due to catch a connecting flight at London to take them on the last leg of their journey.

With the sight of Tuskar Rock slipping smoothly beneath him, the Captain steered Oscar Mike along the air corridor towards his next landfall, barely 50 miles away, at Strumble Head on the rocky Welsh coast. Twenty-five minutes into the flight, Oscar Mike's radio made a routine check call, reporting that the aircraft was expected to cross over the Welsh mainland within the next six minutes. Everything was going perfectly to schedule.

Two minutes later the master Air Traffic Control for Irish flights, at Shannon on the west coast, radioed the Viscount and instructed Captain O'Beirne to switch his frequency to London Air Traffic Control at Heathrow to be picked up and guided by his new controller.

Captain O'Beirne was calm and unruffled. He acknowledged the message by repeating, confidently, '131.2' – the frequency for the control tower operators who were awaiting his arrival in London just 50 minutes later.

Then disaster, unexpected and violent, shook Oscar Mike from its flight deck to its tailplane. The Shannon Air Traffic Controller no longer had responsibility for monitoring Flight 712 and he turned his attention to other flights inside Irish airspace. Meanwhile, at the radio and radar centre in London, the controllers were busy plotting the paths of dozens of flights heading for Heathrow that day.

The crew of one transatlantic flight were already reporting their position to the control room and Captain O'Beirne should have followed procedure by

21

waiting for that conversation to end before he came on the air to announce his own presence entering the London air traffic zone. Instead, he broke into the other radio transmission. His message to London simply said: 'Echo India Alpha Oscar Mike, with you.' There was no sound of urgency or distress, but his call irritated the controllers because it partially blotted out the other aircraft already reporting their positions. They waited for Oscar Mike to repeat his check call when the airwaves were clear.

Only eight seconds later the next report came. This time it was frantic and desperate, distorted by a roaring and screaming noise in the background. Captain O'Beirne was gasping as he wrestled with the controls and yelled into his radio: 'Twelve thousand feet, descending, spinning rapidly.'

The controllers could hardly believe their ears. Two other listeners heard the heart-rending distress call from Oscar Mike: the pilot of the transatlantic flight, nearing the English coast, and the flight crew of Aer Lingus 362, Oscar Mike's sister aircraft. Both pilots acted independently, checking with London Traffic Control to make sure that the emergency message had been received clearly. The London controller made repeated attempts to contact the stricken aircraft. There was no reply.

But Oscar Mike was still airborne. Captain O'Beirne, struggling with the controls, had turned his aircraft away from the forbidding mountains around the Welsh coast and he was already retracing his flight path back across the Irish Sea. Perhaps he thought he had a slim chance of bringing the Viscount safely down on the smooth, sandy beaches near Rosslare, back on the Irish coast, just over the horizon.

The anxious listeners got no clue. There was only baffling and ominous radio silence from Oscar Mike.

With fear mounting, the pilot of the other Aer Lingus flight, bound from Dublin to Bristol, aborted his approach to his destination and sped north towards Strumble Head, Oscar Mike's last reported position, to begin an immediate search. Unbeknownst to him, however, the final moments of the fatal drama were being played out 30 miles to the west of him.

At 12.10 p.m., a deckhand on board the German cargo ship *Metric*, steaming southbound through St George's Channel, ten miles off Rosslare, thought he saw a large bird close by suddenly whirl from the sky and plunge into the sea. He thought no more about it. At the same time another witness, walking along the shore near Greenore Point, heard a roaring splash, and saw a column of water rising from the sea just off the Tuskar lighthouse.

The routine flight of Oscar Mike had ended in tragedy, less than an hour after it had begun.

Within a few minutes of the time Flight 712 had been due to land at Heathrow Airport with its crew and passengers, a major search and rescue operation had been mounted across the width of the Irish Sea, with aircraft, helicopters and high speed launches hunting for a clue to the disappearance of Oscar Mike. By nightfall, when the search was called off without success, the news of the disaster was broadcast. At home, watching television reports of the missing Viscount, the lunchtime beachcomber remembered the giant water splash he had seen off Tuskar Rock and phoned his local police station.

As a general appeal for all shipping to watch out for wreckage or survivors was broadcast on the marine shipping frequencies, the deckhand on the cargo ship *Metric* thought of the silver bird he had seen splashing into the sea. Could it have been an aircraft, its size distorted by distance? Thinking the worst, he radioed search headquarters.

The following day, using the approximate bearings supplied by the two witnesses, the search was resumed. Within a few hours floating wreckage had been sighted, having drifted less than six miles from Tuskar Rock. Over the course of the next few days, 14 bodies and more cabin wreckage was found. There were no survivors.

It took two more months for the bulk of the wreckage of Oscar Mike to be located, lying in 39 fathoms of water. The job of recovering the sunken aircraft and beginning an exhaustive examination of the mass of twisted metal began immediately. Accident investigators began to piece together a grim jigsaw puzzle of the remains of Oscar Mike in a deserted hangar at the headquarters of the Irish Air Force at Casement Aerodrome, Baldonnel.

Most of the twisted fuselage, wings and engines of the Viscount were recovered, but the tail plane sections and elevators were missing. One small section of elevator spring tab, a small control needed to trim the aircraft in flight, was found six months after the crash, entangled in seaweed on the coast of Rosslare, seven miles from the scene of the crash. The small metal flap couldn't have floated. Had it fallen off from the wrecked tail section as Captain O'Beirne tried to make a landing on the beach?

In the meantime, other eye witnesses had come forward with evidence, turning the disaster from an unexplained accident into a mystery of deadly intrigue. During the late morning on the day of the Viscount crash, hundreds of devout Roman Catholics in the small seaside parishes around Rosslare had been going to and from the celebration of Mass in their local churches. The first Mass, which had begun at 10 a.m. had finished and now the church bells were calling the faithful to 11 o'clock Mass. The precise timings of the church services and the ringing of the chapel bells had etched the events into the memories of the witnesses with reliable accuracy.

In the official accident investigation report published two years after the crash, the identity of these witnesses is masked by code numbers which refer to their sworn affidavits of evidence. None of the witnesses had noticed the uneventful flight of Oscar Mike as it passed overhead. But they all heard and saw strange sounds and sights in the sky a few minutes later.

Shortly after the Viscount flew over Tuskar Rock, bound for the Welsh coast, ten witnesses near the village of Broadway, three miles inland, heard loud cracking noises and rolling explosions in the air, like peals of thunder. Four witnesses saw a high-speed object in the air, its wings bright red and its tail glowing 'as if on fire' as it streaked out to sea towards Wales. Another witness saw it turn sharply in mid-air 'as if fired out of the clouds'. A witness ten miles away from Broadway, across the sweeping Ballyteige Bay, saw the same object 'enveloped in a small dark cloud which travelled along with the aeroplane, swirling'. This was followed by a bang, which died away 'like thunder'.

The evidence of the witnesses is all technically consistent with a supersonic flying machine, trailing clouds of turbulent air from its wings and leaving a wake of booming shock waves as it streaks through the sound barrier.

The investigators turned immediately to the possibility that Oscar Mike had been struck by an air-to-air missile or had collided with a military jet fighter, but checks with Britain's Royal Air Force, the only operator of supersonic aircraft over the Irish Sea, only deepened the mystery. No RAF jets were in the area at the time and none had been reported missing. The only missile firing range near the flight path of Oscar Mike, the Ministry of Defence rocket range at Aberporth in Wales, had been closed that Sunday.

Government officials in Dublin made approaches to the NATO military powers to check the flights of supersonic aircraft. The answer came back that no jets had been operational anywhere near Oscar Mike. They even asked the Soviet Navy if any of their aircraft carriers had been prowling undetected around the southern stretches of the Atlantic where it reaches into the Irish Sea. They drew a blank.

In the final dossier, which drew a veil of mystery over the fate of Oscar Mike, the Irish government's official accident investigator, R W O'Sullivan, confirmed: 'There is not enough evidence available on which to reach a conclusion of reasonable probability as to the initial cause of this accident.' But he did reveal that only one theory, even though 'improbable', covers all the bizarre unexplained elements in the accounts of the Viscount crash.

In his report, R W O'Sullivan admitted the possibility that: 'While Viscount EI-AOM was in normal cruising flight at 17,000 feet, and within six minutes of reaching Strumble Head, another aircraft, which could have been a manned or unmanned aeroplane or a missile, passed in close proximity, possibly even colliding with the tail of the Viscount, causing an upset before control was finally lost.'

Hitler and the Occult

When Adolf Hitler set out to conquer Europe and build an empire he predicted would last a thousand years, it seemed to military tacticians that he had put his faith in the strength of his armoured tank divisions and the swift striking power of the Luftwaffe bombers. At the massed rallies of his fanatical followers in the giant stadium in Nuremburg, the crazed dictator entranced hundreds of thousands of his countrymen into believing that he had built an invincible war machine. Even when the tide of war turned against the Nazis – when the Russians began to repulse the sweeping attack of the Germans and the Allies liberated Occupied Europe – Hitler was still convinced that, through some miraculous intervention, he would triumph in the end.

As the Third Reich crumbled around the Führer's ears, and he still insisted that a miracle would save Germany from total collapse and devastation, his own generals began to wonder about Hitler's state of mind. Had he launched the Second World War not through his confidence in military strength, but in the belief that he could achieve victory using black magic, by appealing to the occult and holy mysticism?

Hitler had begun his obsession with the occult when he was a teenager. He had been deeply, and perversely, moved by a performance of Wagner's opera, *Rienzi*, which tells the tale of the rise and fall of a Roman Tribune. The young Hitler saw the opera as a metaphor for the destiny of his own nation and plunged himself into the composer's romantic world of Germanic myth and fantasy. He began to study the occult and a few years later, in 1909, the young Austrian became a follower of the eccentric religious leader Dr Jorg Lanz von Leibenfels. This former monk had abandoned his Christian religion and had formed a new cult in a run-down castle on the banks of the Danube. Here, he preached magic, occultism and race mysticism.

Soon after this, Hitler became struck by the power of a particular religious legend, which was to become an obsession and may have even led to his suicide more than 30 years later.

In the summer of 1912, Viennese economist Dr Walter Stein, an expert in early Byzantine and Medieval art, purchased a second-hand copy of an edition of *Parsifal* from an occult bookseller in his home town. The book was a 13th-century romance about the Holy Grail, the cup from which Jesus drank wine during the last supper. Throughout the Middle Ages, legends abounded about the whereabouts of the Holy Grail as well as another powerful religious relic – the Holy Lance. In the margins of the slim volume he had bought, Dr Stein found pencilled notes made by the previous owner. They were mostly rambling little comments on mythology, the occult and the power of racial superiority of those descended from the Crusaders and Teutonic knights. Intrigued, Dr Stein asked the bookseller to put him in contact with the previous owner ... and soon came face to face with the young Adolf Hitler.

Hitler amazed and intrigued Stein with his knowledge of ancient myths; but he also puzzled him by his sinister belief in the magical powers of the Holy Lance. Hitler had seen the Lance in the Hofburg Museum in Vienna. According to the tales handed down since medieval times, this was the actual weapon used by a Roman soldier to pierce the side of Jesus as he lay dying on the Cross. The Roman had experienced an ecstatic vision in which he realized that he had thrust the weapon into the body of God himself. From that moment, the Lance gained magical powers.

There were at least two other sharpened iron blades in existence reputed to be the actual weapon used during the Crucifixion – one in the Vatican and one in a Paris museum. But Hitler was particularly fascinated with the Hapsburg Lance, which had been passed down to the Austrian royalty from a long line of conquerors and military leaders. The Holy Lance of Hapsburg could be traced back to Antioch, in the Middle East, where it was discovered by Crusaders besieged by Saracens in the city. German folk legend claimed that the Lance was carried by the Emperor Charlemagne through 47 victorious military campaigns, and that it had endowed him with powerful magic. In fact, it was said Charlemagne died immediately after letting the Lance slip from his grasp. Later it was wielded by the Saxon king Heinrich, who drove the Poles out of eastern Germany. It was then passed down to the 12th-century conqueror Frederick Barbarossa, who had triumphed over the forces of Italy and driven the Pope himself into exile.

Hitler told Stein how he had been overcome when he saw the Lance on display in the museum in Vienna. He explained: 'I slowly became aware of a mighty presence around it. I sensed a great destiny awaited me and I knew beyond contradiction that the blood in my veins would one day become the Folk Spirit of my people.'

But the Lance remained firmly in the security of the museum for the next 25 years, during which Hitler's belief in magic and mysticism was to become more and more deeply rooted.

It was more than a decade later when Hitler, then the aspiring leader of the Nazi movement, decreed that his whole terrible political philosophy should be symbolized by one fearful mystic design – the swastika. The sign of the 'crooked cross' had long been a good luck symbol in the Hindu religion, where it represented the life-giving rays of the sun, and in Viking mythology it had portrayed the Hammers of Thor, the god of thunder and war. It had been resurrected in late 19th-century Germany by Guido von List, a religious leader who led his followers in pagan rituals and the worship of old Nordic gods. Finally, it was adopted by Hitler, who wanted a bold, instantly recognizable symbol to rival that of the Communists' hammer and sickle.

By the early 1930s, Hitler had already bemused many of his top aides by his childlike belief in mysticism. His Armaments Minister, Albert Speer, recalled a bizarre incident in October 1933, when Hitler was laying the foundation stone of the Museum of German Art in Munich. As the Führer tapped the stone into place, the silver hammer he was using shattered into fragments. Hitler recoiled in horror and told Speer it was an omen that powerful evil was about to strike. Hitler spent three months in abject torment until, in January 1934, the architect of the Museum, Paul Ludwig Troost, suddenly died. Even though Troost had been a close friend, Hitler gloated: 'The curse is now lifted; it was Troost who was meant to die, not me.'

That same year, Hitler had appointed Heinrich Himmler as the deputy leader of the Nazi movement. He watched in satisfaction as Himmler began to persecute Jews and Christians alike. Himmler drew up plans to outlaw all religions except the new Nazism, banning festivals such as Christmas and Easter and replacing them with his own neo-pagan rituals. Only one thing troubled Hitler about his depraved and ambitious deputy: Himmler claimed to be the reincarnation of Heinrich, the founder of the Saxon royal dynasty, and a previous owner of the Holy Lance of the Hapsburgs.

One of the Führer's closest confidants, Hermann Rauschning, wrote of Hitler: 'He wakes up at night, screaming and in convulsions. He calls out for help and appears to be half paralysed. He is seized with panic that makes him tremble until the bed shakes. He utters confused and unintelligible sounds, gasping as if on the point of suffocation.'

But all Hitler's hidden fears and insecurity seemed to vanish on 14 March 1938, when, as Chancellor of all Germany, he addressed a rally in the Heldenplatz in Vienna and announced that he was about to absorb Austria into the Nazi empire. As he finished his speech, his soldiers quietly entered the museum behind him. All the regalia of the Hapsburg monarchy, including the precious Holy Lance, was seized and carried off to St Catherine's Church in Nuremberg, the spiritual home of the Nazi movement.

Flushed with victory, and reassured by his possession of the Holy Lance, Hitler plunged Europe into war the following year.

For the first four years it seemed as if Hitler and his forces were truly invincible. Even experienced Prussian generals, the aristocratic backbone of the German Army, became almost convinced that Hitler possessed super-human powers. He directed one successful campaign after another, relying on a mere hunch or intuition which he refused to share with anyone else. They watched in dismay as his deputy, Himmler, held councils of war from his headquarters – a rebuilt medieval fortress in Westphalia, where the vast banqueting hall was laid out with 13 thrones, for the Deputy Führer and his 12 closest 'apostles'. And they were even more bemused when Hitler himself set up the 'Occult Bureau' in Berlin, employing favoured astrologers and psychics to help him direct the war.

Soon, the military planning sessions with the Chiefs of Staff were being postponed and interrupted while the impatient generals waited for their Führer to consult fortune tellers before important battlefield decisions could be made. As the lightning advances of the German armies were halted, entrenched and forced back, Hitler insisted on having more and more detailed personal horoscopes drawn up for him before he could decide on the next course of action.

Navy chiefs were constantly overruled and had their orders counter-manded by one of Hitler's closest occult advisers, architect Ludwig Straniak. Straniak, an amateur occultist who redirected the Navy's battleships through-out the Atlantic, claimed that he could detect the presence of warships by 'dowsing' over maps and sensing the locations of ships by psychic vibrations. He had impressed the Führer once by dangling a pendulum over an admiralty chart and pinpointing the position of the pocket battleship *Prinz Eugen*, then on a secret mission. After that episode, the German admirals were not in a position to argue with him, and they were often forced to send futile fleets off to do battle in totally empty seas.

In London, Hitler's reliance on astrology and black magic was well known to Prime Minister Winston Churchill and his wartime Cabinet. They even established their own tongue-in-cheek department of astrology and occult to try to guess the psychic advice Hitler would be given, and to react accordingly. One of their advisers was Walter Stein, the occult and medieval art expert who had escaped from Nazi Germany. Stein still had vivid memories of his encounter with the young Hitler, and he was able to predict how the Führer would respond to the prophecies of his mystic advisers.

By the spring of 1945, it seemed as if no power on earth could save the doomed Third Reich. But even as the Allied forces advanced across the Rhine and through Germany and the Russian troops began pounding at Berlin itself, the Führer was still predicting some perverse, supernatural, miracle would turn the fortunes of war. In October 1944, when Nuremberg was pounded by heavy Allied bombing, far from evacuating the civilian population, he ordered it instead to be reinforced by 22,000 SS troops, 100

Panzer tanks and 22 regiments of artillery. Next, he gave orders that the Hapsburg regalia, including the Holy Lance, should be moved from St Catherine's Church to a specially constructed vault.

In April 1945 the liberating American Thunderbird Division reached the outskirts of Nuremberg and began battering at the defences. It took four days, but on 20 April – Hitler's 56th birthday – the Americans finally achieved their objective. When they began the interrogation of the prisoners, a wounded and embittered SS officer revealed to his captors how he had sacrificed thousands of his men, on the Führer's orders, to ensure that the Holy Lance was not captured.

The Americans immediately began a search to locate the holy relic. Ten days later, 'C' Company of the US Army's Third under the command of Lieutenant William Horn tore their way through the rubble and reached the twisted steel doors leading to the vault. Shoving aside the shattered brickwork, Lt Horn reached out and grabbed the Holy Lance. The foot-long blade was bound with gold wire which held a rusting nail – one of the nails which, the legend insisted, had been used to fasten Jesus to the cross.

That night as the Lieutenant returned to his command headquarters with the sacred relic, now the property of the US Government, Adolf Hitler put his pistol to his head and killed himself in fatal despair. It was 30 April, the end of the Hitler nightmare. It was also Walpurgis Night, the most celebrated event in the pagan calendar, the high feast of the Powers of Darkness.

Amelia Earhart

W hen aviation pioneer Amelia Earhart roared off into the skies on 1 June 1937, she may have carried a guilty secret with her. The darling girl of the air, who had become the first woman to fly solo across the Atlantic and the first pilot ever to fly solo from Hawaii to California, was determined to add one more flying record to her list of achievements.

Amelia was willing to risk her life to make the first flight around the world by the longest possible route – the closest course to the equator, a distance of

27,000 miles. She was confident that she had the flying skill to make the gruelling journey and that her twin-engined Lockheed Electra 10-E aircraft was mechanically tough and reliable enough to carry her through the worst of the weather the Earth's tropics would throw at her.

But determined and self-sufficient though she was, Amelia Earhart could not hope to smash the world record again on initiative and guts alone. She needed help from friends in high places to make her record attempt possible.

There were certainly many powerful and important people who saw that cooperation with Amelia Earhart could pay dividends to suit all parties. Earhart would have to enlist the aid of the best technical experts at the Lockheed aircraft builders and the vast resources of the United States Navy for her enterprise. Without them, the project was doomed to failure.

Normally, the American aircraft builders would have been only too willing to promote and sponsor any move by Earhart to get herself in the record books once more. Her exploits of daring marathon flights had captured the headlines and the country's imagination, and had helped to convince a hesitant public that travel by commercial airline was becoming a safe and commonplace event. They helped to sell hundreds of small airliners to more and more new operators each year.

But in 1937, the planemakers had different priorities. Their production lines were producing fewer civilian aircraft and were being increasingly heavily committed to turning out combat planes for the US Army Air Corps and the US Navy. Washington was nervously eyeing the expansion of Japanese military ambitions in the Pacific and they had themselves begun a growing programme of rearming and updating the squadrons of America's own flying forces.

During the First World War, Japan had occupied the Marshall, Caroline and Mariana Islands and had managed to retain these under a League of Nations mandate. In 1934, the Japanese began isolating the islands from their Pacific neighbours. Both America and Japan had agreed, at the Naval Treaty Conference in Washington in 1923, that military construction of the Pacific islands occupied by either side should be strictly banned. Now American strategists believed the Japanese were secretly preparing their captive islands as giant munitions dumps, communications bases and airfields for an attack on the US controlled Pacific islands – or even the American mainland – in defiance of all the guarantees they had given the League of Nations.

The Americans themselves had launched a defensive military build-up in the Pacific, aimed mainly at developing radio facilities to control a series of direction-finding stations strung out across the ocean to detect any large movements of aircraft. The War Department had entered into a secret partnership with Pan American Airways to build a series of direction-finding

Amelia Earhart – she vanished mysteriously in the Pacific.

bases on Midway and Wake Island, under the guise of providing navigation facilities for the airline's trans-oceanic flights across the Pacific.

The years of hidden preparation by the Japanese were to climax in 1941, with their surprise attack on Pearl Harbour. Even by 1937, the troubled skies over the Pacific were no place for amateur pilots to tax strained diplomatic relations by making trail-blazing publicity stunts in their aircraft. Amelia Earhart, however, was no unknown amateur. She had served as a lecturer and counsellor at the Purdue Research Foundation at Purdue University in Lafayette, Indiana; and the Foundation openly admitted its aims were to conduct aviation research 'with particular reference to National Defense'. The research unit was also in receipt of government grants backed by the US War Department, and the Foundation openly admitted it was providing the money to buy the Lockheed Electra for Earhart, for the scientific purpose of testing and improving radio direction-finding equipment.

In her eagerness to claim the glory for new achievements in flying history, Amelia had originally wanted to go one step further. She planned to fly the Pacific from east to west and carry out the first mid-air refuelling, using specially adapted US Navy planes. But the War Department ruled out her plan as too risky. Instead, they proposed an alternative, which would provide them with a strategic military bonus.

Amelia, they suggested, should be provided with a safe landing and refuelling stop in the middle of the vast ocean. The place they chose was remote Howland Island, only a few degrees north of the Equator and less than 600 miles from the Japanese-controlled Marshall Islands. Work began immediately on the construction of an airstrip and fuel dump, while suspicious Japanese warships patrolled around Howland on spying missions. Any muted protests from the Japanese were countered with outraged indignation on the part of the Americans, who explained that the airbase on the tiny speck of land, only three-quarters of a mile long and half a mile wide, was essential for the safety of the daring woman air pioneer.

In the meantime, Amelia continued with the preparations for her record-breaking flight and her aircraft was flown to Lockheed's private factory for special modifications. Amelia's technical supervisor, Paul Mantz, tried to monitor all the changes, but even he was unaware that Lockheed's chief specialist in its latest top-secret radio gear, Joseph Gurr, was detailed to fit experimental direction-finding equipment inside the plane.

On 17 March, Amelia set out on the first leg of the trip. But this proved only to be a disastrous false start after the first 2,410 miles, from San Francisco to Honolulu, had been covered. On take-off from Honolulu, overburdened with the weight of 1,100 US gallons of fuel and two navigators, the Electra crashed and its undercarriage collapsed.

Amelia sat down to an urgent conference with her technical advisors and her husband, George Palmer Putnam, and changed her plans completely. The flight would now circumnavigate the globe from west to east. With the help of prevailing winds on the new route, she would be able to dispense with the weight of one navigator and give herself some margin of safety. (The delay in her plans also gave the US Navy and the Army Air Corps a valuable breathing space in which to instal more and more secret defence equipment on Howland Island.)

On 1 June, Earhart started again from scratch. By this time her aircraft was bristling with a bewildering array of low and high frequency radio equipment and direction-finders.

There can be little doubt that, as she took off, Amelia may have realized that she had already become a pawn in the deadly mock war games the US military chiefs were planning in the Pacific. But for Amelia, her one goal was the successful achievement of her round-the-world trip. If her plane was being used as some kind of military flying test bed, it was a small price to pay for the chance to circle the globe. The flight was publicized every step of the way, with cheering crowds to greet her as she touched down, rested, refuelled and took off again from the various airfields in South America, Africa, Asia and Australia.

A month after her voyage had begun, her navigator, Captain Frederick Noonan, strapped himself into the cockpit behind her and the pair prepared for take-off from Lae, in New Guinea, for the riskiest part of the flight. Their course was to go over a stretch of the Pacific never crossed by an aircraft before – the 2,556 miles from the coast of New Guinea to Howland Island. It was the major leg of the flight across open water. The next stop should have been Honolulu, then Oakland in San Francisco Bay and finally home in triumph to Lafayette, Indiana.

The flight plan between Lae and Howland island was also the most crucial part of the journey for the US Navy's warship *Ontario* and the Coastguard cutter USS *Itasca*, supposedly acting as safety and rescue standby vessels, but secretly using Earhart's Electra as a 'target' plane to check and test their direction-finding equipment. As Amelia took off, the American radio operator in Lae, Harry Balfour, received a weather forecast on his radio and teleprinter from the US Navy Fleet base at Pearl Harbour. Although he called the information through to Earhart and her navigator several times, he received no reply.

Just five hours after his transmission, at 3 p.m., Balfour picked up Amelia's voice, clear and unflustered. All seemed to be going well. Two hours later the pilot radioed again, this time reporting that adverse weather conditions were forcing her to lose height and speed. But she was still unconcerned.

In mid-ocean, on board the warship *Ontario*, navigation officer Lieutenant Horace Blakeslee, who had estimated the plane should be overhead at 10 p.m., failed to make radio contact, although one of his deck officers thought he heard the sound of an aircraft overhead. The *Ontario*'s searchlights were switched on full, but heavy rain clouds had blotted out the sky. The warship, low on fuel supplies, was soon forced to return to base on a nearby island, and to leave the task of locating Amelia and her plane to the Coast Guard vessel *Itasca* almost 1,000 miles further along the course, off Howland Island. As the *Ontario* turned away, a land-based radio operator on Nauru island to the north picked up a broadcast from her, reporting the words: 'A ship in sight ahead.'

In the early hours of the morning, at 2.45 a.m., the radio room of the *Itasca* heard Amelia's voice on the radio again. The only part of the message they could understand was: 'Cloudy weather ... cloudy.' On the island itself, a top-secret high frequency radio direction-finder failed to track the location of the transmissions.

An hour later Amelia broadcast again, forlornly reporting overcast weather and asking the Coastguard ship to contact her on a new radio frequency. Again, they failed to locate her or raise her on the radio. Throughout the night they heard sporadic plaintive calls from Amelia Earhart, fragments of weary speech, but despite all their high-powered equipment they still could not reach her.

At 8.43 a.m. came Amelia's final message, frantic and desperate. She gave a confusing, wide-ranging compass position, which could have put her any-where on a line stretching hundreds of miles both north or south of Howland Island. Then, all contact was lost for good, and soon the massive, but fruitless search began.

President Franklin Roosevelt personally ordered the battleship USS *Colorado* from Hawaii to steam full-speed to the search area with its three catapult-launched spotter aircraft. The following day he instructed the aircraft carrier USS *Lexington* and three destroyers to set off on a ten-day voyage from the west coast of America to join the search.

Nervous US Navy senior brass, who had secretly organized the seemingly innocent Earhart flight as an experimental trial, now began to complain they were 'spending millions of dollars and disrupting Navy training schedules to search for a couple of stunt fliers'.

There were a spate of heartless and cruel hoax calls from American radio hams, claiming that they had picked up distress messages from Amelia. Some claimed she was 'injured but alive' and quoted her call sign – KHAQQ.

On 5 July newspaper stories reported that a radio message had been picked up from Amelia by the Pan American Airways bases on Midway and Wake

Island. The message indicated that Amelia had been forced down several miles south-east of Howland, near the Phoenix Islands. War Department chiefs rushed to deny the reports, afraid that the Japanese might learn of the existence and power of these covert radio installations. For two weeks, an entire task force of US warships and planes scoured more than 150,000 square miles of the Pacific, skirting the Japanese-held islands to the north.

Then, speculation erupted among the more sceptical and scandal-hungry Americans that Amelia Earhart had been on a mission for the Government and had landed safely on Howland Island, in order to give the War Department an excuse to send warships and aircraft to spy on the Japanese war preparations in the Pacific. There were reports that US pilots, supposedly engaged in the search for their public heroine, had returned to base with aerial photographs of Japanese bases.

The rumours persisted for almost a year. One newspaper in Oakland, California, began a series of articles about Earhart's disappearance. Their first issue claimed that the woman pilot had been lost because the direction-finding equipment on Howland had been supplied with the wrong kind of batteries and had failed the moment it was switched on. But Washington soon put a stop to this, and no further articles were published.

Amelia Earhart and Captain Noonan were never seen again. Three years later, after the attack on Pearl Harbour and the overwhelming carnage of the war in the Pacific, the fate of the two fliers paled into insignificance until, as America fought back against the Japanese and began to drive them westward across the ocean, the mystery of Amelia Earhart slowly began to unravel.

Then it suddenly deepened again. In 1944, the victorious US forces captured the Marshall Islands from the Japanese. During routine interrogation, Vice Admiral Edgar Cruise was told by a native interpreter that two American fliers, a man and a woman, had been brought to the islands by Japanese captors in 1937. The couple had been transferred to the grim Garapon Prison at Japanese military headquarters in Saipan in the Mariana Islands. The woman was dispirited and broken. After only a few months in the hellish conditions of the military torture centre, she died of dysentery. Her male companion, of no further use to his interrogators, was executed.

Twenty years later, in 1964, two former US Marines, who had served in the Pacific, announced publicly that they had recovered the remains of Amelia Earhart and Frederick Noonan from unmarked graves on Saipan in July 1944 and had transferred them back to the United States for burial. But the US Marine Corps still refuses to confirm or deny their stories.

And so, the mystery remains. Was Amelia Earhart an intrepid espionage agent who gave her life to help her country develop its air defences? Did she die an unsung heroine with her brave navigator in the squalor of a

Japanese prison camp? Is she buried in a secret grave back in her American homeland with the location of her final resting place known only to a handful of military intelligence officials? Or was she simply an enthusiastic amateur glory-seeker who didn't care who organized and subsidized her daring exploits, just as long as she made the headlines?

The unemotional answer may lie in a report in a small Australian newspaper, published a year after her disappearance. The Sydney newspaper claimed that the United States had secretly informed the Australian Government, their Pacific ally, of their plans to monitor Amelia's last flight as cover for its preparations for war. The US War Department, which made great propaganda of the treachery of the Japanese sneak attack on Pearl Harbour, had refused to admit that it had duped her into a peacetime spying mission. The newspaper claimed the last distress signal had, in fact, come from the location of the Phoenix Islands, but the search squadrons used it as an excuse to turn north and spy on the potential enemy.

The paper concluded: 'Sentiment comes second to Secret Service.'

The Psychic Detectives

Even the most puzzling of murder mysteries usually yield, in the end, to patient, plodding detective work. The breakthrough can often come when the murderer makes a slip-up, giving himself or herself away, when a nosy neighbour makes an anonymous phone call to the local police station, or when villains argue among each other and turn to betrayal. Sometimes a mundane piece of police routine, a random check on parking tickets, or another tedious interview with a witness to check an insignificant detail can bring spectacular results. Even, in very rare cases, when every avenue has been explored and the secrets remain, a case can be cracked by a policeman's illogical hunch, or an investigator's unexplained instinct, which leads to the vital piece of evidence to unravel an apparently baffling, insoluble crime.

But when all else has failed, when the trail has gone cold and the case is marked 'UNSOLVED', is there one last hope? Is it possible for supernatural sleuths, psychic detectives, to see beyond the limited horizons of tangible evidence? Is it possible they can succeed in prising hidden clues from spiritual vibrations at the scene of a crime simply from the feel of inanimate objects, such as clothes or a cold weapon? Can people have 'visions', provoked by a lifeless photograph, or from the testimony of dead victims beyond the grave?

Most police forces scoff at the idea of accepting the help of psychic detectives, especially in serious cases such as murder. Often, they have to cope with cranks and deranged amateurs who plague them with tip-offs and bizarre theories. Usually there is no time for them to be taken seriously. Occasionally, after a case is cracked, the detectives allow themselves the satisfaction of revealing how so-called gifted psychics proved to be as worthless and as troublesome as any other time-wasting crackpots.

It is a brave psychic who risks his reputation publicly by making predictions in a murder case. Unlike seances and stage shows, where their apparently supernatural powers are often aided by collusion and harmless amateur psychology, meddling in an unsolved crime usually leads to charlatans being exposed. But often, police forces have to bow to pressure to lend a polite, if disbelieving, ear to psychics when distraught relatives plead with them to leave no stone unturned, when public opinion is crying out for some sign of progress or when a higher authority makes it known that a favoured clairvoyant should be consulted.

Such was the case in the investigations of the baffling Jack the Ripper murders in East London in 1888.

Robert James Lees was a celebrated spiritualist, whose psychic powers were reckoned to be so outstanding that Queen Victoria consulted him when he was only 13 years old. Other consultations and private royal seances followed, and Lees's reputation soared. So, when Lees approached the police investigating the Jack the Ripper murders, and explained the importance of his royal patronage, they could not show him the door of their Whitechapel police station as quickly as they might have wished. Queen Victoria had, herself, been bombarded with petitions from the fearful women residents of the East End of London as well as the worthy businessmen of the City area adjacent to the scenes of the horrific unsolved murders in Whitechapel. So, when James Lees claimed that he had suffered a harrowing psychic vision of one of the murders being committed, he was treated with some consideration and referred to senior officers.

Lees described the villain known as Jack the Ripper as a man wearing a dark tweed suit and a light coloured overcoat which he used to cover up his bloodstained shirt. Details of Lees's visions were duly noted. The clairvoyant admitted he was so shaken by the experience that he had gone abroad afterwards to France for a brief holiday to calm his nerves. A few weeks later, when he returned to London, he had another experience. As he boarded a horse-drawn omnibus at Shepherd's Bush in west London, he came face to face with the very man he had seen in his visions of the murders.

Lees had blurted out his fears to the other astonished passengers, including the suspect and the suspect's wife. The couple only laughed loudly at him as Lees fled from the omnibus and grabbed a passing policeman. The sceptical police officer returned to the top deck of the omnibus with Lees, where the laughter of the mystery suspect and his wife soon turned to indignation. While Lees and the policeman argued about whether to arrest the man on the unsupported word of the clairvoyant, the suspect and his wife slipped away, hailed a passing cab and galloped off into the London traffic.

Lees was devastated, but his tormented visions of the Ripper murders didn't end there. A short time later he arrived at Scotland Yard again, having had another vision, in which one of the Ripper's victims had her ears cut off. This time, Scotland Yard had to take him seriously. The police had received a gloating letter from the Ripper warning that he would slash the ears off his next victim. They had kept the contents of the letter secret. Even more important, they had just discovered the body of the Ripper's fourth victim, prostitute Catherine Eddowes, and the mutilations were exactly as Lees had described in his vision.

Lees then told them of a further vision he had had which seemed to match, in great detail. It was of the murder of Mary Kelly, whose disembowelled body had been found in a shabby lodging house in Miller's Court, right in the heart of Ripper territory.

It was at that point that Scotland Yard decided to carry out an experiment to test Lees's psychic abilities. That night, they took him close to the scene of the killing, a small alley which led to the door of the murdered woman's four-shillings-a-week lodgings. Their plan was to use Lees as a 'psychic bloodhound' to pick up the trail of the murderer. He set off through the side-streets and, in the early hours of the morning, the psychic led them to number 74 Brook Street, in Mayfair.

Seventy-four Brook Street was only a few miles away from the squalid slums of the East End, but a million miles away in terms of the social spectrum. The elegant mansion was the home of Sir William Gull, personal physician to Queen Victoria and her son the Prince of Wales. Gull had been created a Baronet by the grateful Queen 16 years earlier, when he had saved the life of the Prince of Wales by successfully treating him for a potentially fatal bout of typhoid. By now, Gull was a frail 70-year-old, partially paralysed from a stroke he had suffered a year before the murders began.

Lees pointed at the gates to the mansion and declared: 'There is your murderer – the man you are looking for.'

Even though their curiosity had been aroused by the clairvoyant's unshakeable assurance that he had tracked down Jack the Ripper, the police decided to wait until daylight before rousing Sir William from his untroubled slumber. The next morning, during a delicate and respectful interrogation, Sir William's wife admitted that her husband experienced occasional lapses of memory and had come home several times late at night with bloodstains on his clothes. Sir William explained these away as symptoms of the crippling effects of his stroke and the frequent nosebleeds he suffered. There were no further questions for the eminent doctor, and the Ripper murders ceased as abruptly as they had begun.

Mary Kelly was the last of the Ripper's victims. There were no more murders after the night that psychic James Lees turned up on the doorstep of Sir William Gull and named the Queen's doctor as Jack the Ripper. Sir William died 14 months later, after another stroke which left him completely crippled. And James Lees died in 1931, taking with him to his grave the secrets of his ghastly psychic visions of the Ripper.

However, in 1970, when medical historian Dr William Stowell examined Sir William Gull's private papers, the mystery surfaced once more. In an article in the journal *The Criminologist*, Dr Stowell claimed that Gull spent many lonely nights lurking in the darkened alleys of the East End. He also claimed that Sir William Gull may have been part of a conspiracy to cover up for another Ripper suspect, His Royal Highness Prince Albert Victor, Duke of Clarence and nephew of Queen Victoria. The Duke had been one of Sir William's patients and, according to Dr Stowell, may have committed at least one of the Ripper murders in a fit of syphilitic insanity, while Sir William Gull carried out others to raise a smokescreen and distract attention away from his royal patient.

Did James Lees really have visions of the royal doctor murdering the Whitechapel prostitutes? Or had he picked up more earthly clues from his own association with the royal family? Were his suspicions of Sir William based on psychic nightmares which revealed the truth to him, or did he point the finger at Sir William because he had listened in to gossip spread by members of the royal family, who suspected that one of their own inner circle may have been Jack the Ripper?

The mystery still remains.

There was certainly no gossip or insider information to help the psychic detectives who rushed to identify the beast responsible for the ghastly series of Yorkshire Ripper murders in the north of England between 1975 and 1980.

Doris Stokes (l) and the real 'Yorkshire Ripper', Peter Sutcliffe (r).

The murders made the headlines worldwide and sparked off one of the most baffling, frustrating and costly murder hunts in British police history.

The deaths of 13 women, most of them prostitutes but also a couple of respectable housewives and a young student, brought unsolicited help from psychics, astrologers and cranks who bombarded the hard-pressed police. Many of them claimed to have experienced detailed psychic visions revealing the identity of the Yorkshire Ripper, but the Yorkshire police tried to ignore their offers of information, putting their faith in the more tried and trusted police methods. They conducted thousands of interviews with witnesses and potential suspects, and launched a massive computer file, sifting through the few vague clues and countless hours of dedicated work by undercover detectives and beat policemen.

There were some apparently promising leads to the identity of the Ripper: a series of letters claiming to be from the murderer and a tape recording of the voice of a man with a strong north-eastern accent, mocking the police and boasting they would never bring him to justice for his crimes.

As a matter of routine, the tape recording was carefully examined by forensic scientists and voice analysis experts, and played to broadcasters at a press conference in the hope that someone would recognize the man's voice. No one knew, except, of course the perverted author of the tape, whether or not it was a cruel hoax. In fact, it was only much later that they discovered it had, indeed, been a false lead; but the tape was enough to spark off even more spurious information and tip-offs, which succeeded only in increasing the frustration and sense of hopelessness of the overworked detectives.

At the height of Ripper hysteria, in July 1979, the police were confronted by an astonishing story in a national Sunday newspaper. The article was illustrated by a vivid artist's impression of 'The Yorkshire Ripper', based on a psychic vision experienced by medium Doris Stokes. The fame of Mrs Stokes had spread throughout Britain as a result of her sell-out public seances. The newspaper report contained startlingly detailed information which she claimed had been psychically formed in her mind after she had listened to the tapes of the fake murderer. She claimed, confidently, that he was 5ft 8in tall, was called Johnnie or Ronnie, had a scar below his left eye and a balding patch which he tried to disguise by brushing his long, mousey hair over it. He was clean shaven, his surname began with the letter 'M' and he had received psychiatric treatment in a mental hospital. He lived in a street named Berwick, or Bewick.

This information, Mrs Stokes insisted, had been passed to her in a psychic trance when she had 'contacted' the Ripper's dead mother, a woman called Molly, or Polly.

The psychic floodgates were opened. Dutch psychic detective Gerard Croiset agreed with Mrs Stokes, and added the intriguing details that the Ripper walked with a limp because of a damaged right knee and lived in a block of service flats over a garage in Sunderland.

Clairvoyant Patrick Barnard disagreed with both of them. His own psychic vision was dramatically different, but equally specific. A week after the Ripper killed Leeds student Jacqueline Hill, in November 1980, Barnard revealed in the *Southend Evening Echo* how, in a psychic vision, he had looked down on the Yorkshire Ripper 'as if from my bedroom window'. He described the scene graphically:

'. . . On the shoulders of his black duffel coat were the white letters RN. It seemed as if he was walking out of a submarine dockyard. I felt I was in Scotland and I got the impression he was working on a nuclear submarine. Wouldn't that explain everything? A crewman on a sub, at sea for months at a time, while police are chasing their own tails looking for him ashore?'

Barnard also revealed that in his vision he saw an abandoned railway coach in a siding, where the Ripper changed his clothes after each murder before returning to his home – the top flat in a run-down grey house overlooking a railway tunnel.

Murder squad detectives suffered the spate of psychic clues and tips in stoic silence until, on 2 January 1981, the Yorkshire Ripper was arrested.

He was not mousey-haired with a scar and a balding patch; he was dark haired with a full beard. He was not called Johnnie or Ronnie. He didn't live in Berwick or Bewick Street, and he had never received psychiatric treatment. He wasn't a submariner; he didn't walk with a limp, he never frequented abandoned railway coaches, nor did he live in a house above a tunnel. His name was Peter – Peter Sutcliffe. He was a truck driver, who lived in a quiet suburban home in Bradford with his wife.

Sutcliffe had been captured as a result of plodding routine work. A police patrol keeping watch in the red-light district of Sheffield had spotted him sitting in a parked car with a known prostitute. A routine check, through the Police National Computer, had shown that the licence number plates of the car didn't match the registration details of the vehicle.

At the local police station to which he was taken, Peter Sutcliffe gave no hint he was a murderer. It was only while he was being routinely questioned about possible vehicle licensing offences that one of the traffic officers who had arrested him remembered that he had allowed Sutcliffe one brief favour: he had let him get out of his car and urinate out of sight in the shadows, behind a roadside fuel tank.

The officer had no psychic visions, no revelations in trances; no shadowy glimpses into the unknown; but he had a hunch, a policeman's mysterious sixth sense. He returned to the scene and found a blood-stained hammer in the shadows where Sutcliffe had relieved himself.

When the officer brought the evidence back to the police station, Peter Sutcliffe quietly began to unburden himself about his catalogue of horrific crimes, in a confession which went on until the early hours of the morning.

The Yorkshire Ripper was unmasked not by psychic detectives, but by the intuition of a suspicious policeman.

Chapter Two

MYSTERIES OF NATURE

In these days of high-technology, nature has still held back some of its most precious secrets. The animal world, for instance, is a constant source of wonder, with its tales of werewolves, flying fish and living fossils. In addition, we still have a long way to go to get to the bottom of *human* mysteries, such as miracle healing and the inexplicable relationships between identical twins ...

Werewolves

Werewolves, half-man, half-wolf, have played a horrifying role in mythology and superstition. They are the spine-chilling, bloodthirsty villains of scores of horror movies, men turned into raging monsters, covered with coarse hair, with fangs for teeth, and slashing claws for fingernails. But are werewolves just a figment of the imagination, the products of the fevered delusions of poor peasants, the superstitious dwellers of the thickly wooded forests of medieval Europe and Asia? Or did they actually exist? And are there still men, and women, who can be transformed into snarling monsters who shun the light and attack with fang and claw to rip at human flesh?

Amazingly, scientific and medical evidence shows that werewolves may not be creatures of myth, but ordinary men and women – and even blue-blooded royalty – who have actually developed some of the characteristics and ferocity of wolves.

Tales of werewolves go deep back into history. Herodotus, the Greek historian in the fifth century BC, wrote of explorers returning from the settlements around the Black Sea with tales of local natives who could transform themselves, by magic, into wolves. Two centuries later the Roman administrator Pliny described how transformation into a wolf was punishment for anyone foolish enough to try to placate an angry god with a human sacrifice. According to Pliny, the victim would be taken to a distant river and forced to swim to the far shore. If he survived the freezing water, he reached the other shore only to be transformed into a werewolf, where he would roam the forests in the company of other packs of werewolves for a period of nine years. If the werewolf resisted the temptation to eat human flesh during that time, he would be changed back to his original form and allowed to rejoin his fellow humans.

Other myths and legends grew and grew. Men born on Christmas Eve were said to be more likely to become werewolves. It was also said that there were men who inherited the curse of the werewolf, passed on down through the generations from father to son as a punishment for some terrible sin committed in the past. Some men became a werewolf by choice, because they used the magic of the Devil to give them the power to change shape and to go about their evil deeds. And there were the benevolent werewolves, the poor unfortunates who could not help but change into beasts during the full moon, but who were bitterly ashamed of their involuntary weakness and who struggled to keep their guilty secret from friends and family.

The terror that the wolf struck into medieval man can easily be imagined. Packs of ferocious wolves roamed around the woodlands of most of the northern hemisphere and even the hot, dusty plains of India. Hunting in groups, they were a predatory menace to other wild animals, livestock herds, and man himself if they became bold.

By the end of the 16th century, wolves had been hunted to extinction in England, and within 200 years had been eliminated throughout the rest of the British Isles. But they were still prowling freely in the rest of Europe, where fear of the wolf showed itself in folklore, such as the cautionary tale of Little Red Riding Hood, the innocent girl lured to a grisly encounter in a woodland cottage by a cunning wolf.

During the 16th century, when the European colonies in North America were being settled, Henry VIII was on the English throne and Galileo was making his first astronomical studies with his newly invented telescope, France was in the midst of a religious frenzy where the mere accusation of being a werewolf resulted in thousands of innocent people being hanged or burned at the stake, along with other unfortunates charged with being witches and wizards. In one period of just over 100 years, between 1520 and 1630, there were 30,000 trials of werewolves in France. Most of those found guilty were quickly executed by their fearful fellow countrymen. Luckily, by the end of the 16th century, a growing sense of doubt about the strength of superstitious belief, as well as a feeling of communal guilt, led to more lenient treatment of 'werewolves'. After all, most of them were simply tormented and mentally deranged peasants, afflicted by lycanthropy, the belief that they could be transformed into werewolves.

An example of lycanthropy occurred in 1598 in Caude, northern France, when villagers stumbled across the half-gnawed body of a boy. They gave chase to two wolves that ran off as they approached. Searching a nearby wood, they discovered Jacques Rollet, a half-wild peasant who suffered from mental illness. He was almost naked, with a long hair and a straggling beard and claw-like nails which were clotted with blood and human remains.

The young boy had not been his first victim. At his trial, Rollet admitted to the judges that he believed himself to be a wolf and he confessed to several charges of killing and eating young children. He was sentenced to death, but the legal authorities in Paris commuted his sentence to life imprisonment and he was kept in a madhouse.

A few years later, the pathetic figure of 13-year-old Jean Grenier appeared in court in Bordeaux as a self-confessed werewolf. Jean was mentally retarded and his face was dominated by a large, misshapen jaw, which jutted out and

Half man, half wolf, werewolves are a horrifying sight.

revealed pointed, sharp teeth. He had been startled by some young shep-
herdesses as he prowled among their flocks, and he had terrified them by
telling how he had made a pact with the Devil to turn himself into a
werewolf. When one of the girls was attacked a few days later by a creature
with red hair and sharp claws, the townsfolk scoured the fields and forests
until they tracked down Jean Grenier. In court the pathetic teenager stuck to
his tale of a meeting with the Devil, in which he had sold his soul in exchange
for a magic ointment and a shred of wolf's pelt which would turn him into a
werewolf any time he wished.

There was no doubt that the boy was deranged, but equally little doubt
that he had been responsible for several murderous attacks on children who
had been killed and eaten. On 6 September 1603, Jean Grenier was found
guilty of multiple murder while acting under the influence of lycanthropy.
He was ordered to be held for the rest of his life in the Franciscan Friary of St
Michael the Archangel. When the monks led their new prisoner to the Friary,
he dropped on all fours and ravenously tore into scraps of raw, stale meat he
found in their kitchens.

Jean Grenier lived only another seven years, howling at the full moon,
unkempt and unwashed, still utterly convinced that the Devil had turned him
into a werewolf.

With the near extinction of the wolf in Europe, the scourge of lycanthropy
looked as if it might die out. Surprisingly, it surfaced again in modern times
when Hollywood film makers hit on reviving the myth. In a new genre of
horror movies, the werewolf and the human vampire were portrayed as 'up-
to-date' demons.

In 1975, the myth of the werewolf so aroused one disturbed English
teenager that he committed suicide. The 17-year-old apprentice carpenter
from Eccleshall, Staffordshire, had become obsessed by studies of the occult,
and had attended a number of seances in the hope of 'contacting' his dead
father. At one of these morbid sessions, he revealed to a friend that he had
become possessed by the Devil.

A few nights later, the teenager telephoned his friend again. By this time,
the delusion of lycanthropy had taken an overwhelming hold of his imagination. His friend later told an inquest: 'He told me his face and hands were
changing colour and that he was turning into a werewolf. He would go quiet
and then start growling.'

The young carpenter's body was found near the village crossroads by the
postman next morning. He had thrust a knife into his own heart.

Although an attack of lycanthropy had plunged that particular teenager
into fatal depression, it had a different effect on 43-year-old building worker
Bill Ramsay of Southend, Essex. Ramsay went into a frenzied rampage in the

local police station in July 1987, after he had driven himself there in a state of wild agitation. Inside the police station, he suffered a mental blackout, and fought a four-hour battle with eight terrified policemen. One officer was scratched across the face as Ramsey arched his fingers like claws. Others were hurled across the yard as they tried to restrain him. He was partly subdued when a doctor gave him a double dose of powerful sedative, but then he smashed his head through a one-and-a-half-inch-thick wooden hatch in the door of a detention room and had to be cut free by firemen.

Chief Superintendent Charles Harper described the scene: 'The man was snarling, his lips were turned back and he held his hands rigid like claws. He seemed possessed of extraordinary strength and attacked the men with a ferocity that was frightening to all who observed him.'

Ramsey was ordered by the local magistrates to be detained for 28 days for medical tests. At Runwell Hospital, near his home, he admitted: 'This has happened to me three times in six years. I do bare my teeth, I do drool at the mouth. I do snap and snarl and howl. I go on all fours, and my hands turn like claws. I display some tremendous strength and do incredible things, but I never seem to hurt myself. Why it happens, I don't know. I only know what people tell me happened afterwards. I just act like an animal. It's just a freak form of temporary insanity. The only thing that seems to affect me is walking into a church. I feel strange in churches. I can't explain it.'

There are a number of rational scientific explanations which appear to give some clues to the mystery of lycanthropy. According to medieval superstition, a man who survived a wolf bite would later become a werewolf himself. The suspicion grew from the fact that the majority of those bitten by wolves would, within a few days, begin to suffer a horrific transformation. They would get fevered convulsions, their facial muscles would tighten into spasms which bared their teeth. Then they would fly into wild fevered fits and begin to foam at the mouth. This was usually followed by collapse, and then death.

These are symptoms known only too well to modern doctors as the clinical effects of rabies. Most wild wolf packs are infected with the virus, and those animals savage enough to attack men are also most likely to be suffering from the disease themselves.

However, not all recorded cases of men behaving like mad animals were caused by a bite from a rabid wolf. The potent medicines of the day included extracts from plants and animals, such as mushrooms or toads. These could often cause wild fantasies, including the delusions of turning into an animal. Even the grain storage methods caused the spread of the fungus ergot, which produces a natural version of the drug LSD, lysergic acid diethylamide. Many 'werewolves' were merely experiencing the wild horrors of 'bad acid trips'.

Some could also have been sufferers of the rare disease porphyria. The disease causes mental confusion, which can border on madness, excessive growth of hair, contraction of the muscles to reveal the teeth, and a necessity to hide in dark places, away from the sunlight which the sufferers find too painful. Sufferers also experience a need to take blood from others, to replace the constituents missing in their own system.

There is nothing demonic about porphyria. It is an inherited metabolic disease, once known as the 'Royal Disease', because its victims included Mary Queen of Scots, James I and George III. In King George III, the disease was so pronounced that his fits of madness and his bizarre, ranting behaviour almost brought the government of the country to a halt. His wild delusions about his own powers in stemming the disaffections among the British colonies in America, was said to have provoked the American War of Independence.

Although George III reigned for 60 years, for the last decade of his life, when his insanity became permanent and reduced him to behaving like a degenerate animal, his son, George, had to rule for him as Prince Regent from 1811 until his death in 1820.

It seems remarkable to think that America might still be British had it not been for a king who, by medieval definition, was a mad werewolf!

Miracle Healing

In these days of high technology, medical science discovers more and more wonder-drugs daily. These drugs seem to hold out the promise of curing the few remaining unconquered diseases and ailments in the world today. Each year, billions of pounds are spent on research to find yet more ways of keeping the human body fit and healthy. In such a climate of scientific progress, faith healers appear to be an anomaly. But as the numbers of drugs increase, so do the number of people who seem unaffected by their potency. Many incurable and dying patients put aside cynicism and turn to that last hope, the chance of a miracle cure.

It is not difficult for Christians to forsake the clinical methods of drugs and surgery, for Jesus himself was one of the best-documented faith healers of all time, with more than 40 miraculous cures, ranging from curing the lame and crippled to helping the mentally ill achieve full recovery. He cured lepers and made the blind see. All these incidents are recorded in graphic detail in the New Testament.

According to the Bible, Christ's Apostles were imbued with the same powers, and believers have no doubt that the power of prayer can sometimes effect a cure when conventional methods have proved useless.

Sometimes it is individuals who appear to have these strange gifts; but certain places have also become renowned for their mysterious healing properties and have become popular places of pilgrimage for those who are desperate for help. Springs, wells and rivers are often associated with miracle cures, like the Shrine of the Madonna of the Baths of Scafati in Italy, St Moritz in Switzerland and Grisy in France.

The most famous is the little town of Lourdes in south-west France, a favourite haven for the hopeful. In 1858 a 14-year-old peasant girl, Bernadette Soubirous, claimed to have had a series of visions of the Virgin Mary over a six-month period. The visions, she explained, revealed to her the existence of a hidden spring in an underground grotto which she was told had miraculous curative powers.

The visions were declared authentic by the Pope in 1862, and the cult of Our Lady of Lourdes has become one of the most fervent of the Roman Catholic Church. Now, more than three million people make the pilgrimage every year, seeking help. And for at least a few of them, the relief they seek so devoutly seems to be given. Crippled limbs are made strong again, diseases conquered, tumours vanish.

One well-documented cure dates from the 1970s. Three-year-old Frances Burnes from Glasgow, Scotland, was flown to the shrine by her mother, Deirdre, after surgeons diagnosed malignant cancer and gave her just weeks to live. Little Frances bathed in the waters. A few days later, when she returned to the hopsital in Glasgow where she was expected to die, she began to make an amazing recovery. Within three weeks, doctors could find no trace of the carcinoma which had racked her little body with pain. A month later Frances was back at playschool with the classmates who thought they would never see her again. Her specialist doctor at Yorkhill Hospital, a Protestant surgeon who held no religious faith in the powers of the Lourdes Shrine, admitted: 'There are cases of spontaneous remission, or cure, of malignant cancers, but we don't know why some patients suddenly recover against all the odds. We can accept that the powerfully-charged religious atmosphere around a place of pilgrimage can sometimes have an effect on the personality of a patient and give them a desire to fight their illness. This positive attitude, born of religious faith, can only help if it gives a seriously ill

The Grotto at Lourdes is lined with crutches and other offerings.

patient a renewed vigour and determination, a will to live. None of this can have been a factor in the case of little Frances. She is only a little child and couldn't have been swayed by religious fervour. The odds against her enjoying a spontaneous cure are thousands to one. These events are not entirely unknown. But the odds against this happening immediately after a visit to Lourdes are incalculable. We have no explanation. In medical terms we can only call it a miracle.'

Religious inspiration has been credited as the source of most dramatic cures which have baffled doctors using tried-and-tested clinical techniques. But other specialists in faith healing claim that, apart from physical injury, most disabilities and illnesses have their source deep inside the human mind.

Charismatic healer Phineas Parkhurst Quimby, from Maine, USA, founded his New Thought healing movement in the last century after claiming spectacular results from meditation and mesmerism and laying his hands on trusting patients. Quimby believed that all physical illnesses were basically symptoms of disorders of the mind, and his New Thought movement taught that effective cures would follow as soon as the patient learned to heal himself, or herself, by the power of positive thinking. There is little doubt that Quimby goaded and encouraged seriously ill patients into positive mental attitudes to conquer a wide range of illnesses.

One of his young students, Mary Baker Eddy, took his philosophy of psycho-medicine one step further, and in doing so relieved the patients of the need to rely on their own inner mental resources to give them strength to cure themselves. She fused the principles of New Thought with her own intensely religious beliefs and founded the Christian Science sect, which proclaimed that disease was an illusion created by man and that sufferers could be cured of their ailments simply by the power of prayer.

French healer Emil Coue, who was a qualified chemist, had carefully studied the apparent success of the practitioners of Mesmerism, who cured the sick by putting them in deep hypnotic trances and laying hands upon them, insisting that a form of 'animal magnetism' transferred a mysterious healing force between them and their patients. In Nancy, France, during the 1880s, Coue conducted his own unorthodox, and somewhat cynical, experiments. To carefully selected groups of patients, referred to him by qualified doctors with prescriptions for powerful medicines, Coue secretly dispensed ineffective doses of coloured water. He noticed, to his delight, that the patients who were treated with coloured water, especially those suffering from ulcers and nervous diseases, recovered more fully than those who followed the doctors' recommended course of drugs.

To Coue, the answer was obvious. His experimental patients were not being helped by animal magnetism or the power of prayer to God. All he had done was to stimulate their own imaginations into believing that they were taking medicines that would cure them. He called his new techniques 'auto-suggestion', and devoted the rest of his life to teaching the sick to cure themselves simply by imagining that their illness would vanish. His slogan, designed to reinforce the imagination of the patient, was simple and stunningly effective. Many thousands were cured by chanting Coue's incant-ation: 'Every day, in every way, I get better and better.'

In the 1930s, when conventional medicine was still firmly based on the belief that all disease and illness had an organic cause beyond the patient's control, two young British doctors hit upon an apparently rational, psycho-logical answer to the phenomenon of Coue's cures by auto-suggestion. Doctors William Evans and Clifford Hoyle of the London Hospital were conducting carefully-documented clinical trials of different brands of new drugs for the painful heart muscle disorder, angina. To ensure that the effects of the new drugs were accurately proved without any irrational effects of auto-suggestion or positive thinking, they split their guinea pig patients into two groups. They told all the patients they were giving them the new drugs, but one group was given simple bicarbonate of soda without their know-ledge. To the amazement of the two doctors, the group being treated with bicarbonate of soda showed the most dramatic improvement. It was exactly the same effect that Coue had witnessed on his early patients whose prescriptions had been made up with nothing more than coloured water.

The outcome of these unbiased tests was reluctantly accepted into the techniques of conventional medicine as the 'placebo' effect, literally meaning a treatment which does nothing clinically, but puts the patient in a happier frame of mind. Doctors now accept that many patients are susceptible to the placebo effect, but since harmless medicines do nothing to tackle the root cause of disease, it is dangerous to use it as a form of treatment.

But if belief, faith, or even a happier state of mind only lull a patient into a false sense of wellbeing, how can doctors explain the apparently astonishing cures recorded by healers who seem to be able to conquer advanced clinical symptoms in seriously ill patients?

Psychic Matthew Manning was just a teenager with no apparent appreci-ation of art when the artist Pablo Picasso died in April 1973. A few months after Picasso died, however, Manning found he could sit at an easel and produce vivid works of art in exactly Picasso's style, claiming that the dead artist's spirit was guiding his brush from beyond the grave. The following year he published his first book, with remarkable drawings faithfully executed in the style of other dead artists, including Aubrey Beardsley, Leonardo Da Vinci and Paul Klee. Manning insisted they were not his works, but the psychically transmitted drawings and paintings of the dead artists.

It was not until 1977 that Manning discovered he also had a mysterious gift for miraculous healing. When the young English psychic submitted to a series of rigorous tests at the Mind Science Foundation in San Antonio, Texas, he was found to be able to alter the electrical resistance of human skin and to accelerate the death of certain types of cancer cells simply by touch and concentrating his mind.

Manning's first attempt at healing a stricken patient was almost his last. He was asked to treat a woman dying of cancer. She was jaundiced and vomiting, and she couldn't eat. 'I just held her in my hands and tried to influence the cancer cells the way I had done in the laboratory tests,' he later explained. 'Nothing happened. I left, telling her I would come back to try again, but I felt a sense of complete failure. When I returned six hours later, she was out of bed. Her temperature was normal, her nausea was gone and she amazed the nurses by eating a meal.'

That night, however, the woman died. It was two years before Manning tried to heal anyone again. Later, though, he took it up once more, not only in private sessions in hospital wards and scientific laboratory experiments, but also by going on international 'healing tours'. During a public healing tour of West Germany in 1981, Manning encouraged doctors to examine his patients both before and after his psychic healing sessions. The doctors reported an immediate 95 per cent improvement in the patients treated by Manning. In Bremen, orthopaedic surgeon Dr Thomas Hansen verified that the psychic healer had taken only ten minutes to relieve the excruciating arthritic pain in one woman's shoulder, a feat which could not have been achieved by orthodox treatment. In Freiburg, Manning even invited the wife of independent consultant Dr Otto Ripprich to submit to his healing forces. Frau Ripprich had been unable to straighten her right arm for several months following crippling nerve and muscle damage sustained in an accident. After five minutes of treatment from Manning, she was able to straighten her arm, fully outstretched, to the amazement of her husband.

Not all miracle cures have been achieved by the mysterious forces of the mind or by the laying on of hands. 'Miracle' healer Jose Arigo had no medical knowledge, but his astonishing cures through his violently crude methods of surgery and his bizarre medicinal concoctions baffled the medical authorities of Brazil throughout the '50s and '60s. Arigo discovered his own awesome powers when he was summoned to the bedside of the dying wife of a friend, together with other members of the family who were preparing to mourn her impending death. Suddenly overcome, he seized a kitchen knife and plunged it into the woman's body. From the gaping wound he dragged out a tumour the size of a grapefruit. He dropped the knife and the tumour into the kitchen sink, horrified by what he had done. A doctor was quickly summoned and he confirmed that the bloody mass in the sink was indeed a uterine tumour. To everyone's amazement, the patient claimed she felt no pain from the impromptu 'operation' and there was no bleeding from the wound. She recovered fully, but Jose Arigo, still reeling in confusion, had no memory of the incident. Later, he told the woman's family that he had sensed he had been taken over by the spirit of a doctor he called Adolphus Fritz, who had died in 1918.

As word of the incident spread, hundreds of incurable patients began to gather at Arigo's house in the small town of Congonhas do Campo. Most of them happily submitted to the rough surgery of the healer, who often simply thrust them against a wall and cut away at their flesh with an unsterilized penknife which he later wiped on his shirt. For other patients, he would simply glance at them for a few seconds and then write a prescription for apparently conflicting doses of medicines, freely available from their local chemists. After following Arigo's instructions, the patients found themselves completely recovered.

As Arigo's fame spread, so did official curiosity about his methods, and he was sent to jail in 1956 for practising medicine without a licence. He served only a few months in prison until the President of Brazil, impressed by the petitions of Arigo's grateful patients, gave him a pardon.

In 1964 he was arrested and jailed again on the same charges, but was allowed out of prison awaiting the results of his legal appeal to a State Court. The Appeal Judge, Fillipe Immesi, decided he would be better able to judge the case if he paid an unannounced visit to Arigo's home to witness for himself a session of surgery. When he arrived, Arigo recognized him, and even asked him to assist in an operation he was about to perform on an elderly woman almost blinded by cataracts in both her eyes. The judge, who held the patient's head steady, reported later: 'I saw him pick up what looked like a pair of nail scissors. He wiped them on his shirt and used no disinfectant of any kind. Then I saw him cut straight into the cornea of the patient's eye. She never moved a muscle, although she was conscious all the time. The cataract was out in a matter of seconds. The district attorney and I were speechless, amazed. Then Arigo said some kind of prayer as he held a piece of cotton in his hand. A few drops of liquid suddenly appeared on the cotton and he wiped the woman's eye with it. She was completely cured.'

Arigo's case was reviewed by the Federal Supreme Court, and the charges against him were dropped.

Even when he was not practising mysterious surgery, where his rusty knives left no scars or bleeding, Arigo performed miraculous cures by prescribing dangerous doses of chemical mixtures. In the case of a woman patient brought to him, riddled with cancer and suffering the effects of a colostomy operation performed because a tumour blocked her colon, Arigo ordered her to take powerful overdoses of medicine which should have proved fatal. During the consultation, Arigo just nodded towards his patient without asking about her medical history, while her husband, a German-born Brazilian, spoke to Arigo in his native tongue. Arigo, apparently under the influence of 'Dr Fritz', replied in fluent German. Then, Dr Jose Hortencia de Madeiros, a specialist at the Sao Paulo State Institute of Cardiology, anxiously administered the massive doses of the drugs prescribed by Arigo. Within a week the woman had begun to recover, and on her third visit to the psychic surgeon Arigo insisted she was totally cured. He told her to have the painful and uncomfortable colostomy operation reversed. The surgeons who later opened her abdomen to restore her severed colon could find no trace of the cancer which had threatened her life.

When Jose Arigo died in a car crash in 1971, he took the secrets of his mysterious surgical miracles and the shadowy identity of 'Dr Fritz' with him to the grave. He had always insisted that he himself had no surgical skill or training. Indeed, on the one occasion when Arigo plucked up the courage to watch a film of himself carrying out surgery with a rusty fish-gutting knife, he turned white and fainted!

The Disappearance of the Dinosaurs

Powerful and ferocious, armour-plated and unassailable, the dinosaurs towered above the other creatures on the face of the earth. With scales and claws, fangs and toughened muscles, these gigantic reptiles had evolved over millions of years to become the undisputed masters of all prehistoric life forms.

With flesh-eating dinosaurs roaming freely in almost every region of the Earth's single, global land-mass, man could never have evolved or survived.

The span of the Dinosaur Age is almost beyond our comprehension. Consider, for a moment, that 225 million years ago the dinosaurs reigned supreme, flourishing for a further 160 million years, while our own ape-like ancestors only appeared on Earth as recently as two million years ago; and modern man has only been around for a brief 50,000 years.

Somehow, in one mysterious cataclysm, the dinosaurs died out. On the evolutionary time scale of the history of the Earth, they vanished overnight. The disaster, which wiped out the dinosaurs and three-quarters of every other species on Earth, tipped the evolutionary scale in favour of small rodent-like mammals that grew and developed into dwarf monkeys, apes and, eventually, the human race.

Only one remnant of the Dinosaur Age still slithers through living experience of life on Earth – the crocodile; and even the largest crocodile is a puny creature compared to the giant dinosaur reptiles, such as the 325-tonne *Brontosaursus*, which grazed on vegetation, or the flesh-eating *Tyrannosaurus rex*, the largest carnivore that has ever lived – 16 metres tall, 12 metres long and weighing 7 tonnes. With a great armour-plated head one-and-a-half metres long, and a gaping mouth filled with double rows of razor-sharp teeth, *Tyrannosaurus rex* ripped apart and fed on almost every other species of living creature, from the sub-tropical jungles of prehistoric England to the swampy marshlands which are now the prairies of North America.

The dinosaurs themselves evolved, like all life forms, from early sea creatures. Great upheavals in the Earth's crust led to climatic changes. The oceans began to recede and a great landmass began to break the surface of the waters. As the Earth became drier, some sea creatures made the transition to land by evolving lungs and primitive limbs, to enable them to spend some time foraging for food along the newly emerging shorelines. Some looked like giant tadpoles, with a third eye growing in the centre of their foreheads. This third eye is believed to have allowed them to see clearly in air, just as their other two eyes were adjusted to underwater vision. In time, the two eyes grew to develop perfect 'clear air' vision and the lungs took over from gills to allow the new land creatures to survive completely out of water. The third eye became useless – but it has not vanished entirely from the life forms which grew from these primitive amphibians. Even today, hidden inside the human brain is the pineal gland, the size of a pea, which is the hereditary remains of the third eye.

But long before man's ancestors appeared on the face of the Earth, the air-breathing reptiles had spawned the dinosaurs. During the Mesozoic Era, from 225 million years ago until 65 million years ago, the adaptable and versatile species of dinosaurs ranged from the flesh-eating *Compsognathus*, about the size of a chicken, to the gargantuan *Brontosaurus*.

The dinosaurs were refined by the forces of nature until it seemed nothing could replace them on the evolutionary scale. Then, suddenly, they disappeared – so completely that, until 200 years ago, men had no idea that such huge creatures had ever walked on the face of the planet.

The first partial remains of a dinosaur were found by a farmer in a field near Cuckfield, Sussex in 1822. The dinosaur's teeth seemed to resemble those of the present day iguana, so it was immediately dubbed *Iguanadon*. But, as more and more of the skeleton was uncovered and pieced together, early archaeological scientists realized that it was like no other creature.

The remains were soon matched up with other finds in the plains of North America, where the first enormous limbs of the *Brontosaurus* were being unearthed; and slowly, incredulous scientists, now called palaeontologists, began to piece together the colossal jigsaw puzzle of the dinosaurs. It wasn't long before they began to ponder the mystery of how these seemingly invulnerable creatures met their sudden end.

In the late 18th century, German quarrymen began to unearth fossils of giant marine molluscs, great spiral shellfish called ammonites which grew as much as 4 metres in diameter. The ammonites had died out at the same time as the dinosaurs; so had most types of primitive plant life.

Theories about the cause of the death of the dinosaurs abound. Some scientists say that a gradual change in the Earth's climate killed off the vegetation – the staple food of some dinosaurs – while the carnivorous dinosaurs became disorientated and sluggish, unable to protect their eggs from tiny, more adaptable predators. However, the dinosaurs had survived, adapted and flourished during other periods of climatic upheaval. Hence, it must have been some far more violent and sudden incident that caused them to perish entirely.

The first clues to a possible answer came in 1974, when Dr Louis Alvarez of the University of California carried out tests on a layer of clay gathered from a site in Italy. The clay, he quickly discovered, contained levels of the element iridium more than 30 times greater than he would have expected to find. Apart from a volcanic rift, the only event that could have spread so much of the earth's iridum into the atmosphere, Dr Alvarez decided, was the impact of a meteor ripping into the planet's crust.

Although tiny meteorites are constantly bombarding Earth, only about 200 have ever been big enough to penetrate the atmosphere. Some of these have left craters on the ground, which have survived to this day; but a meteor capable of powdering the Earth with an instant sprinkling of iridium strong enough to wipe out the dinosaurs, would have to have been at least six miles across, releasing the energy of a billion Hiroshima nuclear bombs, leaving a crater at least a mile deep and several miles wide.

Surely, such a massive dent in the crust of the planet could not remain hidden. Besides, if such a huge meteor had struck a landmass, it would not

Why did the dinosaurs suddenly die out?

only have released iridium, but billions of tons of powdered rock and dust which would have plunged the Earth into total darkness for many years, wiping out all life. Since some life forms did survive virtually undamaged and the process of evolution continued, the meteor theory could no longer stand undisputed.

It was Dr Alvarez's colleague, the astronomer Fred Whipple, who came up with the only plausible answer. What if a meteor, or possibly even an asteroid, had plunged into the sea instead of land? The effects would have been different, but equally catastrophic for the dinosaurs. In addition to the dust thrown into the air, a thick blanket of steam would have billowed round the globe in a cloud miles thick. The oceans would have boiled furiously at the point of impact, and a surge of warm water would have been sent up, encircling the planet. This black, choking envelope of smoky mist would have killed off enough plant life to starve the fish-eating dinosaurs of food. And, as the dust settled and the swirling steam remained, the humidity would have overwhelmed the land-living dinosaurs and wiped them out.

In the oceans, only the creatures of the coolest deep would survive. And on land, only small, furry mammals with highly-developed metabolic systems would be able to cope and remain relatively unscathed. The little rodents, the ancestors of man, would have also been able to feed on the eggs and the flesh of the enormous dinosaurs, who were rendered helpless and vulnerable to the elements.

A meteor or asteroid large enough to cause a gaping rupture in the fabric of life would still be expected to have left some sort of mark. For instance, it may have formed an island, embedded in the floor of the ocean and rising above its waters. Yet, there is no geological evidence of such an interplanetary 'bullet' lodged in the skin of the Earth. Hence, according to Dr Whipple, the meteor must have splashed down into the Pacific Ocean, burying itself in the moving plate of the Earth's crust, which would have carried it steadily eastwards over the millenia until it became crushed against the continent of North or South America. Then, like all the other debris of the floor of the Pacific, it would have been forced down underneath the continental ridge until it became swallowed into the molten core of the Earth itself, ready to spew out again in the form of molten lava, forming new land to give more life to the inhabitants of the planet it so nearly completely destroyed.

Identical Twins

For most parents, the birth of twins is a double blessing. Sharing the same life cycle in their early years, it's only natural that twins should become patterned to look and act like each other. What doting mother can resist the temptation to dress twin children in identical clothes, to feed them the same diets, to offer them the same toys and playthings, to make sure that they attend the same school, staying in the same classroom and undergoing the same experiences as they grow up inseparably together? Small wonder, then, that many twins are conditioned by their upbringing and their environment to lead very similar lives.

But what happens if twins are separated at birth, if they are brought up independently by different families, miles apart in surroundings which are totally dissimilar? Amazingly, even if twins grow up totally unaware of each other's existence, scientific research has shown that separated twins can lead uncannily parallel lives. Some studies even suggest that identical twins, two babies who are born of the same egg in the womb, may act like one individual person occupying two bodies at the same time.

The vast majority of human births are the result of a single egg released from the female ovaries and fertilized by a single male sperm. In one case in 80, two eggs are released at the same time, and each one is fertilized by a separate male sperm. The result is non-identical twin children. Although they share the same moment of conception and the same birthday, the children are no more alike than brothers and sisters born at different times to the same mother and father.

In even rarer cases, a single egg is fertilized and undergoes a remarkable transformation. Instead of doubling and redoubling in size to become a collection of cells that develop into a single baby, the solitary fertilized egg splits into two and grows into identical twins.

Twins may look uncannily alike, but nature ensures there are subtle differences to set them apart. Even twins who seem to be physical doubles of each other have different fingerprints – although their fingerprints are often a mirror image of each other, perfectly reproduced but reversed. However, sometimes a pair of twins seem so alike, they appear to have duplicate personalities. It is this that is one of nature's most baffling mysteries.

Twins Freda and Greta Chaplin were at the centre of a bizarre court case in York in 1980 when they appeared before magistrates accused of harassing their next-door neighbour, truck driver Ken Iveson. The 38-year-old twins had hounded Mr Iveson for 15 years, waiting outside the glass factory where he worked, shouting abuse at him and hitting him with their identical handbags. The distressed women could not explain their fixation over the long-suffering Mr Iveson. They did not seem to know why they continued to follow him and taunt him. Astonishingly, they answered the court's questions in perfect synchronization, speaking simultaneously, as one person. Whenever Freda prepared to talk, Greta would form exactly the same words, apparently at the same moment.

The court was told the extraordinary story of their life as identical twins who seemed to think and act almost as one being. As teenagers, they were so alike in the way they dressed and acted and moved in perfect harmony that local children called them 'witches' and threw stones at them in the street. Some adults spat on them, some crossed to the other side of the street to avoid having to face them.

Examined by psychiatrists, the Chaplin twins were given a pair of grey coats, identical except for varying sets of green and grey buttons. The twins cut the buttons off the coats and swopped them over until they each had the same set of mixed grey and green buttons. Supplied with two different pairs of gloves, they simply took a glove each and wore the resulting ill-matched pairs instead.

But when given two different bars of soap, the twins could not see any easy way out of the dilemma. Having spent a lifetime of eating identical food and wearing identical clothes, they both burst uncontrollably into tears when faced with the prospect of having to use different soap. Then, at the same instant, they both found a solution to the problem. They cut the soap bars in half and shared them.

Interviewing Greta and Freda, psychiatrists found themselves listening to an unbelievably outlandish 'stereo' conversation, with both of the women speaking in word-perfect unison. Greta and Freda explained simultaneously: 'We are so close that we are really one person. We know exactly what each other is thinking because we are just one brain.'

The lonely women, who still lived with their excessively overbearing and protective parents, seemed to have only one pleasure, a ritual obsession with cleanliness. They used 14 bars of soap and three large bottles of shampoo each week, bathing together, grooming each other and washing each other's hair.

The twins were discharged by the magistrates and left the court hand in hand to begin a new life together, as residents of a local hostel for the mentally disturbed, although there was no evidence that they were maladjusted.

The ability of the Chaplin twins to speak in unison is rare, but psychologists have studied cases of an even more unusual phenomenon – idioglossia –

Twins Hans and Gernard Fischer – 'mirror images of each other'.

where identical twins develop their own highly complex language which is totally incomprehensible to any outsider.

Twins Grace and Virginia Kennedy, born in Columbus, Georgia, in 1970 baffled their parents when they began to speak in an apparently alien language when they were only 17 months old. As the children grew older they used only two English words: 'Mommy' and 'Daddy'. Every other conversation was held only between themselves, without anyone else able to understand a word. They even gave themselves their own names. Grace called herself 'Poto' and Virginia named herself 'Cabenga'. They only responded to these names, and they refused to speak English, although they could obviously converse, share a joke and make themselves perfectly understood to each other in their own secret language.

At the age of seven the twins were moved to the speech therapy unit of the Children's Hospital in San Diego, California, where experts tape-recorded their conversations. There were few clues in the unidentifiable dialogue of 'Poto' and 'Cabenga'. Analysts thought they could detect jumbled phrases of

German and English. Perhaps, thought the analysts, this was learned unconsciously from their German-born mother, who was bilingual, and their grandmother, who only spoke in her native German tongue. But the complex grammar, using totally unrecognizable nouns, verbs and adjectives, defeated them.

After a year of speech training, the twins suddenly abandoned their secret language and lapsed into clear English. Excitedly, the speech therapists began to ask them to translate the phrases of their unique code. The girls looked at them blankly. From that day on they spoke only English and remained silent about the hidden meanings of their private language.

But if living and growing together leads twins to think and act as one, what can explain the amazing coincidences in the lives of twins who live apart?

In Piqua, Ohio, in 1939, twin brothers were born to an unmarried mother. They were adopted by different families and raised without knowing of each other's existence. Adoptive parents Jess and Lucille Lewis in Lima, Ohio, were told that the twin brother of their new son had died. The same story was told to the Springer family 80 miles away in Dayton in another part of the state. Six years later, when Mrs Lewis completed the long adoption procedure, she told court officials she had called her son James. 'You can't do that,' they warned. 'His twin brother is actually alive – and *he* is called James.'

It was nearly 40 years before James Lewis tracked down his missing twin brother James Springer and arranged a meeting. Both men were astonished that their lives had developed along inexplicably similar patterns. They had both grown up with adoptive brothers called Larry. Both had identical interests and weaknesses in the same school subjects, and they both owned dogs called 'Troy'. They had both married women called Linda, had both divorced them and both had subsequently remarried women called Betty.

Their first sons had each been named James Alan. They had taken their families each year to the same small Florida holiday resort, staying at hotels on the same beach. James Lewis and James Springer both worked as pump attendants in petrol stations, and they had worked as assistants for the same chain of hamburger restaurants.

Independently of each other, they had both volunteered to serve their communities in different parts of Ohio as part-time deputy sheriffs and, unknown to each other, they both immersed themselves in the hobbies of carpentry and technical drawing.

Medically and physically they had shared the same history. Each was 6ft tall and weighed 180 pounds. They had suffered tension headaches and migraines at the same times in their lives and had recovered from the symptoms at the same age. They had experienced identical heart problems and other ailments at the same periods in their lives.

The case of the 'Twin Jims' sparked off an intensive research programme headed by psychologist Thomas Bouchard at the University of Minnesota. Bouchard undertook a detailed comparison of more than 30 cases of identical twins separated at birth and raised independently.

Long-lost twins who had been reunited were flown to the American clinic to take part in the research. They included Mrs Jean Hamilton of Paisley, Scotland, who had been separated from her twin Mrs Irene Reid, raised 400 miles away in Market Harborough, Leicestershire. On examination, both women were found to suffer from mild vertigo and claustrophobia. They had led scout packs as youth workers and had identical careers with the same cosmetics company. They both had a strong aversion to water, so much so that on visits with their families to the seaside they had the same unusual habit of sitting on the beach with their backs to the water.

Bouchard also examined the cases of Mrs Bridget Harrison of Leicester and Mrs Dorothy Lowe of Blackburn. Identical twins, they had been separated since their birth in 1943. Both women had married within a year of each other. One had named her son Richard Andrew; the other had called her son Andrew Richard. Both women had studied piano to the same level of tuition, and had passed the same music exams. Both had kept diaries for just one year, in 1960, buying the same type of diary from the same printer, and they had faithfully made entries for exactly the same number of days before giving up and abandoning their daily notes.

But the most unaccountable case of separated twins who had led totally opposed lives was that of Oscar Stohy and Jack Yufe. They had grown up thousands of miles apart, but shared the same personality quirks and foibles. They fidgeted with rubber bands they absent-mindedly wound round their wrists. They liked to dip buttered toast into their coffee. They read magazines beginning with the back cover and finishing at the front. They had the same weird sense of humour, which included the practical joke of pretending to collapse in a fit of sneezing in crowded lifts to scare their fellow passengers into fits of hysteria.

At first it seemed as if the differences between the twins could not have been more pronounced. They were separated in Trinidad in the Caribbean in 1933 when their parents quarrelled and became estranged. Jack Yufe had stayed in Trinidad, raised by his father, a Jewish merchant. He had religiously studied the Jewish scriptures and regularly attended the synagogue, and became an enthusiastic King's Scout. He spoke only English. His twin brother Oscar had been taken to Germany by his mother when their parents had parted. Tutored in the propaganda-ridden schools of the Third Reich, he had become an ardent Nazi worshipper and a junior member of the Hitler Youth. He spoke only German. When the twins met for the first time since infancy, at the airport in Minnesota 46 years later, they were almost identically dressed, with wire-rimmed rectangular spectacles, blue shirts with epaulettes, and sporting short clipped moustaches.

Unable to understand each other's language, the Jew and the Nazi embraced each other silently with tears in their eyes, two halves of nature in a most astonishing double act; identical twins reunited and made into one complete person again.

Fishfalls

For timber worker John Lewis the sudden shower of rain on 9 February 1859, at the sawmill at Mountain Ash, Glamorgan, Wales, meant that he had to pack away his tools and take shelter until the weather cleared. As he ran through the puddles of rainwater to reach the cover of the tool shed, he felt himself being pelted by a stream of objects falling from the clouds. Then, as he pulled the brim of his hat tighter over his head for protection, he found himself standing in the middle of a downpour of live, wriggling fish.

The brim of his hat was filled with fish, there were fish littered over the roof of the tool shed, and still more fish gasping in the pools of water at the amazed man's feet.

As the sky cleared, the astonished timber worker and his workmates began to gather the fish in some wooden baskets they had with them. Ten minutes later, there was another rain squall, and another shower of live fish. It wasn't a widespread spray from the overcast sky, but one solid line of fish, a 12-inch-wide stream of tiddlers emerging from one section of the clouds.

In local Welsh newspaper reports, Lewis described the bizarre shower of fish from the sky. He told how he felt the first of the falling objects glance off his head and slither down his neck. 'On putting my hand down my neck,' he said, 'I was surprised to find they were small fish. By this time I saw that the whole ground was covered with them. I took off my hat, the brim of which was full of them. They were jumping all about. The shed was covered with them. My mates and I might have gathered bucketfuls of them, scraping with our hands. There were two showers. It wasn't blowing very hard but it was uncommon wet. The fish came down in a body.'

To the Welsh workers the fall of fish from the sky was an isolated, mysterious wonder. However, great storms of live, and dead, fish from the sky are a worldwide phenomenon, which has been happening for thousands of years. Moreover, fish have not fallen from storm clouds whipped up by typhoons and whirlwinds; they have fallen from cloudless, sunny skies. In some falls, the fish have been 'quick-frozen' in blocks of ice; in others they have been dried and preserved.

Some of the earliest incidents are recorded by Greek historian Athenaeus in texts he gathered in the 2nd century AD from hundreds of writers living in the Greek islands. Athenaeus reported that his fellow writer Phoenias, '... in his second book, says that in the Chersonesus area it once rained fish uninterruptedly for three days, and Phylarchus in his fourth book says that the people had often seen it raining fish'.

There are also scores of reports of fishfalls from far more recent times. In February 1861, the island of Singapore was shaken by a violent earthquake, followed by six days of torrential rain. French naturalist François de Castlenau, who was on a research tour of the island, told the Academy of Sciences in Paris: 'The sun lifted, and from my window I saw a large number of Malays and Chinese filling baskets with fishes, which they picked up in the pools of water which covered the ground. On being asked where the fishes came from, they answered that they had fallen from the sky. Three days afterwards, when the pools had dried up, we found many dead fishes.'

American marine biologist Alan Bajikov witnessed a fall of fish in October 1947 while having breakfast with his wife in a café in Marksville, Louisiana. Sunfish, minnows and black bass came pelting from the sky shortly after a gentle shower of rain. Bajikov reported that although there had been rain showers, there were no whirlwinds or waterspouts (which could have swept up the fish from the nearest large stretch of water, the Gulf of Mexico, more than 80 miles away).

On two occasions in the 1830s, at Futtepoor and at Allahabad, in India, the fish that fell from the sky were not just dead, but neatly dried and preserved. In Essen, Germany, in 1896 when freshwater carp fell from the sky, they were encased in blocks of ice, as if they had been carried aloft in freezing clouds long enough to form into giant, scaly hailstones. And when a torrent of sand eels fell into the gardens of homes in Hendon, Sunderland, in 1918, the cascade lasted a full ten minutes, and landed only in one small, confined area.

There is no doubt that whirlwinds and tornadoes can scoop up light objects and small animals from the surface of the earth during a storm, scattering them over a wide area. However, in all the reported cases of fishfalls, fish have fallen from almost cloudless skies, unaccompanied by any other debris one would normally expect to be scooped up in a whirlwind. No one knows what the mysterious force is that can suck up fish from the depths of the oceans and lakes, directing them in one narrow funnel across a great arc, so high in the sky that they fall to earth over periods of days, long after any storms have passed.

Living Fossils

The engineers carving the great railway tunnel through the mountains between Saint Dizier and Nancy in north-eastern France in 1856 were experts with explosives. Confronted with a massive boulder of Jurassic limestone blocking their path, they set their charges, primed the detonators and retired to a safe distance to blast it in two. It took a few minutes for the dust to settle. Then, the labour squad moved back down the tunnel with their picks and shovels.

The boulder had been split neatly. But when they prised apart the stone with their picks to load it on to a rail truck to be dumped at the edge of the cutting, the workmen reeled back in horror. From the crack in the boulder, a hideous black bird was emerging. The bird was about the size of a goose, but it had a long savage beak lined with razor sharp teeth. Its four long legs ended in sharp talons, and spread between them was a thick leathery skin, glistening with a thick oil.

Slowly, the bird rattled and stretched its wings, its beak chattering as it choked desperately in the dusty air. It made a feeble attempt to flutter free down the tunnel, but only flapped for a few feet before it gasped and died.

The mystified workmen took the body of the dead bird to the nearby town of Gray, to a natural history museum, where an astounded expert immediately recognized it as a prehistoric pterodactyl.

The rock strata from which the living fossil had been freed is named after the Jura Mountains of the border of France and Switzerland. These are great soaring outcrops of limestone formed about 150 million years ago, in the

PREMIO £ 100 REWARD
RECOMPENSE

Examine este peixe com cuidado. Talvez lh e dê sorte. Repare nos dois rabos que possui e nas suas estranhas barbatanas. O único exemplar que a ciência en controu tinha, de comprimento, 160 centímetros. Mas já houve quem visse outros. Se tiver a sorte de apanhar ou encontrar algum NÃO O CORTE NEM O LIMPE DE QUALQUER MODO — conduza-o imediatamente, inteiro, a um frigorífico ou peça a pessoa competente que dele se ocupe. Solicite, ao mesmo tempo, a essa pessoa, que avise imediatamente, por meio de telgrama, o professor J. L. B. Smith, da Rhodes University, Grahamstown, União Sul-Africana.

Os dois primeiros especimes serão pagos à razão de 10.000$, cada, sendo o pagamento garantido pela Rhodes University e pelo South African Council f or Scientific and Industrial Research. Se conseguir obter mais de dois, conserve-os todos, visto terem grande valor, para fins científicos, e as suas canseiras serão bem recompensadas.

COELACANTH

Look carefully at this fish. It may bring you good fortune. Note the peculiar double tail, and the fins. The only one ever saved for science w as 5 ft (160 cm.) long. Others have been seen. If you have the good fortune to catch or find one DO NOT CUT OR CLEAN IT ANY WAY but get it whole at once to a cold storage or to some responsible official who can care for it, and ask him to notify Professor J. L. B. Smith of Rhodes University Grahamstown, U nion of S. A., immediately by telegraph. For the first 2 apecimens £ 100 (10.000 Esc.) each will be paid, gua ranteed by Rhodes University and by the South African Council for Scientific and Industrial Research. If you get more than 2, save them all, as every one is valuable for scientific purposes and you will be well p aid.

Veuillez remarquer avec attention ce poisson. Il pourra vous apporter bonne chance, peut être. Regardez les deux queux qu'il possède et ses étranges nageoires. Le seul exemplaire que la science a trouvé avait, de longueur, 160 centimètres. Cependant d'autres ont trouvés quelques exemplaires en plus.

Si jamais vous avez la chance d'en trou ver un NE LE DÉCOUPEZ PAS NI NE LE NETTOYEZ D'AUCUNE FAÇON, conduisez-le immediatement, tout entier, a un frigorifique ou glacière en demandat a une personne competante de s'en occuper. Simultanement veuillez prier a cette personne de faire part telegraphiquement à Mr. le Professeus J. L. B. Smith, de la Rho des University, Grahamstown, Union Sud-Africaine.

Les deux premiers exemplaires seront pay és à la raison de £ 100 chaque dont le payment est ga ranti par la Rhodes University et par le South African Council for Scientific and Industrial Research.

Si, jamais il vous est possible d'en obteni r plus de deux, nous vous serions très grés de les conserver vu qu'ils sont d'une très grande valeur pour fins scientifiques, et, neanmoins les fatigues pour obtantion seront bien recompensées.

Rewards were often offered for the finding of living fossils.

middle of the Mesozoic Era, early in the history of the Earth when dinosaurs roamed the planet and the reptilian pterodactyls, some with 50-foot wing-spans, soared over the oceans and primeval swamps.

According to reports in the *Illustrated London News*, the pterodactyl had been encased so snugly in the boulder that the limestone was left with a perfectly moulded imprint of its body, evidence that it may have become sucked into a thick muddy swamp which, in the course of millions of years, had solidified into rock.

But how had the air-breathing reptile survived for so long, encrusted inside the swamp mud without oxygen or food, under the enormous pressures which eventually turned the thick soil to rock?

The case of the French pterodactyl was the most spectacular find in a long catalogue of discoveries of living fossils and reptiles in states of suspended animation uncovered by quarrymen and stonemasons throughout the ages. *The Annual Register*, a scientific journal published in Paris, devoted most of its pages in 1761 to accounts of petrified creatures which had shown signs of life when freed from rocky chambers that had held their bodies long after their species had become extinct. The *Register* reported, quite casually, that the limestone blocks used as paving stones for the harbour at Toulon, on France's Mediterranean coast, were often split open by workmen who found they contained living shellfish with a wonderfully delicate flavour and taste. It also chronicled the notes of Ambroise Pare, who was principal surgeon to the 16th-century King Henry III of France. Pare had described how he was supervising workmen breaking up large stones in the garden of his home in Meudon, outside Paris when: 'in the middle of one we found a huge toad, full of life and without any visible aperture by which it could get there...'

A similar tale was told by the respected scientist Dr E D Clarke of Caius College, Cambridge, who described his own experience of an archeological expedition to locate fossils in an English chalk pit. At a depth of 45 fathoms (270 feet), Dr Clarke and his team had uncovered a layer of long-dead, fossilized sea urchins and the bodies of three tiny newts. Since the newts appeared to be perfectly preserved in the moist chalk, Dr Clarke carefully spread out their bodies in a sheet of paper to dry in the sunlight.

To his amazement, after a few minutes, they began to move. Two of them died a short time later, but the third 'skipped and twisted about as well as if it had never been torpid'. Curious to see how the newt reacted to water, Dr Clarke lowered it gently into a pond, where it slithered out of his grasp so quickly that it was never recovered.

He later gathered examples of all the species of newts in local ponds, in the hope of matching them with the scaly bodies of the two dead newts he still had as specimens; but all the amphibians appeared to be totally different to his living fossils. Amateur biologist the Reverend Richard Cobbold of Cambridge, who attended Dr Clarke's lectures and examined the fossil newts for himself, proudly confirmed: 'They are of an entirely extinct species, never before known.'

Before long, Victorian England was intrigued by reports of toads and frogs being discovered, locked deep inside rocks and boulders. In October 1862, local newspapers in Lincolnshire reported a live toad found encased in bedrock seven feet underground during the excavation of a cellar in a tavern in Spittlegate, Stamford. Three years later the *Leeds Mercury* ran a long, detailed account of a live toad found in a 200-million-year-old block of magnesium limestone 25 feet underground, unearthed by foreman James Yeal during the construction of the Hartlepool Waterworks. The toad, whose skin was the same yellow-white brilliance as the rock, had some difficulty breathing when its prehistoric tomb was cracked open, but it soon changed colour to a natural olive brown. Unfortunately, even though it appeared to have survived the millions of years underground, it 'croaked' after only two days in the modern world!

At the same time as wild claims were being made about living fossil toads being uncovered, experimenters were trying to recreate the conditions themselves. In 1825, Dr Frank Buckland, the Dean of Westminster, had tried burying a dozen luckless toads in his own home-made fossil tombs. Buckland carved small cavities in two blocks of sandstone and limestone and sealed the toads under glass before burying them three feet down in his garden. A year later, he exhumed his stone blocks. The toads buried in sandstone were all dead. However, those trapped under a sheet of glass in limestone chambers were not only alive, at least two of them had grown plump and fat.

However, it turned out that Buckland's experimental methods had been faulty. The glass covers had cracked, and it was possible that small insects had crawled into the chamber and provided nourishment for the fatted toads. In fact, when Buckland repeated the experiment and sealed the toads securely, they all died.

Buckland's failure only served to spark off more ghoulish attempts to bury toads alive to see if they could survive. According to *The Times* of 23 September 1862, one French experimenter who had encased 20 toads in suffocating moulds of plaster of Paris and buried them deep underground, was rewarded by finding four of them alive and healthy when he dug them up some 12 years later.

Even though toads and frogs can quite naturally spend six months alive buried in deep mud as part of their normal winter hibernation, the rash of cruel tests eventually proved too much for Victorian moralists. The attempts to recreate living fossils were abandoned after Dr Buckland's son wrote a stern letter to *The Times*, lambasting the directors of the Great Exhibition of 1851 who were intending to display yet another example, a toad allegedly found alive inside a lump of coal in a Welsh mine.

The whole of this era is commemorated in the legacy of the meal of greasy sausage meat hermetically sealed in a skin of thick, suffocating batter, which the Victorian children immediately dubbed 'toad in the hole'.

The records of the French pterodactyl fossil still leave the intriguing question: what if there is a giant rock somewhere out there, containing a prehistoric reptile or a dinosaur in a state of suspended animation? And what if that rock is already lying in the path of a 20th-century construction project, where the blasting crews and the bulldozers are preparing to move in?

Chapter Three

MYTH OR FACT?

While many of us shrug off the possibilities of voodoo witchery, the 'living dead' or the baying banshee, there are countless people who live in mortal fear of them. And while we may scoff at the likelihood of there being fairies at the bottom of our gardens, millions of ordinary, perfectly sane people rush to the horoscope page of their daily newspaper to see what life holds in store. Then there are the mysterious legends, such as the puzzle of the buried corpses at Glastonbury Abbey. Fact, or fiction? Sometimes it's not so easy to tell . . .

The Stars

When Ronald Reagan and Mikhail Gorbachev met at the summit conference at 1.30 p.m. on 8 December 1987 to sign the historic treaty eliminating intermediate range nuclear missiles, both world leaders were supported by their top military tacticians acting as their consultants. However, behind the scenes, the Soviet Chairman and the American President both had the hidden backing of their most secret advisors – the analysts of the Soviet secret service, the KGB, and a Californian astrologer! Remarkably, during Reagan's eight-year term in the White House, where much of his schedule and most of his top level meetings were organized by his wife Nancy, Ronald Reagan's presidency was firmly controlled by astrological predictions.

The belief that the power of astrology could shape policy and direct the President's life – and the destiny of the most powerful nation on earth – caused a storm of protest when it was revealed by his former White House Chief of Staff Donald Regan in May 1988. Embarrassed White House officials rushed to claim that Nancy Reagan's faith in the forecasts of the stars were never relied on actually to guide the President in any major political decisions. But their denials were brushed aside by earlier evidence of the President's own admissions that he and his wife consulted their horoscopes every day for advice on how to run their lives.

The Reagans are not alone in believing that the alignments of the Sun, the Moon and the planets in the sky determine not only the fate of everyone on the planet, but the destinies of cities, nations and the day-to-day running of business enterprises. In the United States there are 5,000 full-time professional astrologers, earning between them around $35 million each year from believers who are anxious to learn what fate has in store for them. In the US, Europe and throughout most of the world, more than nine out of ten popular newspapers carry daily horoscope columns, which are often the most avidly read feature for countless millions of readers.

Astrologers are consulted by business tycoons in control of vast industrial empires, by royals, by heads of government, by architects who want to ensure good fortune for building projects, by sportsmen and women who want to enhance their chances of success in sporting competitions, by famous celebrities in the world of entertainment who want to boost their careers, and by ordinary men and women who want to ensure a happy marriage.

American astrologer Joan Quigley, 'advisor' to the Reagans.

Which one of us does not know the name of the astrological sign we were born under? Which of us has not been cheered and encouraged, or depressed and dejected by reading a horoscope during a period of personal crisis? So why do powerful and important people squirm in discomfort if it is revealed they pay secret lip service to the most enduring, mysterious myth in the history of the human race? Can the movements of the Sun and planets in the heavens control events on Earth? If so, how do they do it, and how can we accurately interpret the signs in the heavens?

Astrology is the belief that the movements of the planets can affect us in our daily lives. It is not to be confused with astronomy, which is objective, scientific study of the heavens. Despite the fact that astrology has been debunked time and time again by scientists, and especially astronomers, its influence has been more widespread and has persisted longer than any other creed, religion or supernatural belief.

The history of astrology can be traced back to ancient Babylonia, now the site of modern Iraq, in 600 BC, when court astrologers began to draw up their first detailed maps of the movements of the planets and to relate their positions to periods of floods and disasters on earth. The first detailed handbook on astrology came from the Greek astronomer Ptolemy, in the 2nd century AD, when constellations of fixed stars were grouped into 'houses' and each given a specific aspect of earthly fortunes, such as riches, health, and disaster. Depending on the groupings of the Sun and the planets in these 'houses' at the time of somebody's birth, their future positions at any given time would determine the fortunes of those born under these signs. In addition, great cosmic events, such as comets, were held to foretell terrible disasters on earth.

Ptolemy was the greatest astronomical and geographic genius of his time. His detailed astronomical studies and astrological predictions were revered for 1,400 years as a faultless factual guide to the heavens and the fates of men. In European history, one cosmic incident alone, in 1066, reinforced the teachings of Ptolemy to the point where they were accepted beyond question. A great comet flared across the sky, and the astrological descendants of Ptolemy predicted with certainty that a king would die and the history of the world would change. It certainly did. A few months later Harold, King of Saxon England, was killed in the Battle of Hastings, and England became ruled by the Normans. The great founder of astrology, it seemed, had got the whole thing exactly right.

Ptolemy, however, had, in fact, got it wrong – just about as wrong as you could possibly get. His whole theory had been founded on one gigantic mistake, a cosmic blunder made by every astronomer and astrologer until Polish astronomer Nicolaus Copernicus published his great work, *The Orbits of Celestial Bodies*, in the year of his death, 1543. Ptolemy had stated categorically that the Sun and planets brought their influence to bear on mankind because they revolved around the Earth, the centre of the Universe. Copernicus, on the other hand, proved that the entire work of astronomy and astrology had been based on a totally wrong assumption. In reality, all the planets revolved around the Sun; the Earth was just another one of these planets.

Copernicus's discovery should have sounded the death knell of astrology. Not a bit of it. One hundred and forty years later, the English Astronomer Royal, Edmund Halley, proved by scientific observation that the 1066 comet which preceded the death of King Harold orbited the Sun and came around every 75 years like clockwork, regardless of any trivial events taking place here on Earth.

This should have been another nail in the coffin of astrology, but ironically, it was the work of Halley's great friend and contemporary, Isaac Newton, that gave a boost of bogus feasibility to astrology. Newton's research outlined, for the first time, the laws of gravitational motion. It explained about the forces that gravity exerts on the Sun, the Earth and the planets, and demonstrated how the pull of the Sun and Moon causes the tidal ebbs and flows of oceans.

Astrologers insisted that if far-flung planets could exert gravitational influences on the distant Earth, surely they could affect the personalities of the people of Earth?

But, in actual fact, it has been demonstrated time and time again that the gravity of the planets is so small as to be immeasurable.

With all the scientific evidence serving to debunk astrology, it is difficult to understand why it has persisted with such a dominant, all-pervading grip on the minds of men. Britain's wartime leader, Winston Churchill, was shrewd enough to employ an astrologer to advise him what effects the star signs were having on Adolf Hitler, an avid believer in astrology. Churchill, himself a sceptic about the ancient myth, believed that the study of astrology could give him a valuable insight into the mind of a vulnerable, superstitious enemy such as the German Dictator.

In the Middle Ages, every king, count, and Holy Roman Emperor had their own court astrologer, and Queen Elizabeth I used her astrologer, John Dee, as a personal adviser, military tactician and her first secret service agent, to spy on her enemies. William Lilley, the 17th-century astrologer who predicted the Fire of London and the Great Plague, became astral adviser to both Charles I and the Puritan religious zealot, Oliver Cromwell. In more modern times, few political leaders have been willing to admit that they have sought astrological guidance. However, President 'Teddy' Roosevelt never made any secret of his belief. He even kept a copy of his personal chart on the wall of his White House office and consulted it regularly. And British political leader David Steel admits to having had a personal chart drawn up when he was 17 which, he says 'has since proved uncannily accurate'.

Hollywood millionaire astrologer Carroll Righter, who died in 1988, was a major influence on the lives and careers of powerful and important people in American showbusiness and politics. For example, as an unknown struggling actor, film star Robert Mitchum worked as an assistant to Righter, helping him to cast horoscopes and predictions for many of the influential clients at Righter's astrological consultancy. Mitchum's own career took off shortly after his association with the astrologer. Whether this was through Righter's guidance or simply through meeting important film executives at the astrologer's home, Mitchum has never revealed.

The new breed of astrologers do not need to spend hours poring over charts of astronomical data as their predecessors did, plotting the exact position of the planets in the heavens at the moment of the births of their subjects. Now, armed with expensive computers, they can perform the most intricate calculations in fractions of a second, producing detailed print-outs of astrological predictions.

It is not just in the quest for heavenly guidance in personal relationships that astrologers are consulted. More and more business concerns are seeking the advice of astrologers when it comes to choosing key personnel for important jobs. For example, London employment agency executive Anita Higginson admitted: 'I look at people's star signs to discover certain characteristics, but I've never heard of people being recruited simply because they were born under the right star sign. We find that many of our front-line sales people are either Aries or Sagittarius because they are high profile communicators and leaders, although they can be impulsive.'

Insurance broker Trevor Thwaite offered the top jobs in his Nottingham-based organization to applicants who were born under the star signs he considers most effective. He explained: 'I have made a serious study of birth signs to judge the best zodiac indicators of people who make the best sales staff.' Thwaite's choices were: Gemini: those born under this sign are reckoned to be smooth-tongued and can often talk reluctant customers into signing business contracts; Leo: also good talkers with excellent powers of persuasion; Sagittarius: hard-working and dedicated, they make determined salespeople who won't take no for an answer.

In a survey of Wall Street financial advisers, in testimony presented to a Washington Senate investigation, it was revealed that nearly half of the financial directors in the investment world regularly consult astrologers before they make any decisions.

But it is in the delicate area of global politics and diplomacy that the revelations of contacts with astrology have led to an outcry. Winston Churchill was not the only astute politician to exploit the reliance of many world leaders on astrology. In the '50s and '60s, American CIA spy chiefs, always anxious to penetrate the policy-making sessions of potentially vulnerable governments, compiled their own list of world political leaders who took astrological advice. Through bribes and blackmail, they planted their own 'tame' astrologers in many political circles, including the governments of Mr Mehmet Shehu, Prime Minister of Albania, President Sukarno of Indonesia and Kwame Nkrumah, President of Ghana. One former CIA official admitted that they were able to steer the policies of these governments by inventing astrological guidance that was passed on by their own fortune tellers to unsuspecting presidents and prime ministers. Agents credit fake astrological predictions with avoiding a bloody civil war in Ghana, when President Nkrumah's astrologer was persuaded to advise him to pay a state visit to China. A bloodless coup was carried out in his absence.

However, the CIA have been powerless to prevent their own presidents consulting the stars. Ronald Reagan was one of the most superstitious US presidents of all time, never carrying less than five lucky charms in his pockets when he went to important policy meetings or disarmament negotiations. In his own autobiography, published in 1965 before he became Governor of California, Mr Reagan revealed the reliance he and his wife placed on astral predictions. Paying tribute to Hollywood astrologer Carroll Righter, he wrote: 'Every morning Nancy and I turn to see what he has to say.'

Although his own official biographies give his date of birth as 6 February 1911, the former President always refused pointblank to reveal the exact time, to prevent his rivals casting a precise horoscope and gaining an advantage on him. On his election as Governor, he came in for bitter criticism from state officials when, after taking advice from an astrologer, he decided his official inauguration ceremony should take place at precisely 10 minutes past midnight on 2 January 1967.

But the predictions of Carroll Righter failed to notify the Reagans of the assassination attempt on the President in 1981. After this, Mrs Reagan switched her allegiance to San Francisco astrologer Mrs Joan Quigley, whose White House horoscopes ruled the schedule of President Reagan for the rest of his term.

News of the Reagans' dependence on astrology came from former White House official Donald Regan. The ex-Chief of Staff in Washington had to liaise with Mrs Nancy Reagan to prepare the President's diary, and he claims the schedule was constantly altered and rearranged while Mrs Reagan consulted Mrs Quigley by telephone 3,000 miles away in San Francisco. After the news of Regan's revelations broke, Mrs Quigley explained: 'I'm a serious scientific professional. Mrs Reagan wanted to know if certain actions could be carried out at a safe time and I certainly advised her on that. Astrology is a complicated process, which the layman would have difficulty understanding. I always consult my astrological tables in my book, *The Ephemeris*, to allow me to find the correct relationships of the planets, the Sun and the Moon.'

Mrs Quigly said of the revelations: 'I resent the circus atmosphere surrounding this whole thing. I feel awful. I have never divulged the names of my clients or talked about my business. But I can assure you that a horoscope can tell you more about yourself than hours on a psychiatrist's couch.' Meanwhile, White House official Donald Regan complained: 'At one point I kept a colour-coded diary on my desk, with numerals highlighted in different inks, to remind myself when it was propitious to move the President of the United States from one place to another, or schedule him to speak in public, or commence negotiations with a foreign power.'

The news of Mrs Reagan's consultation with the astrologer caused an immediate alarm within the upper echelons of the CIA, who knew from their own experience how fake astrological advice can sway the policies of the leaders of nations. Their main concern was that Mrs Reagan's calls to San Francisco, made on open telephone lines from the White House and the Presidential retreat at Camp David, had been intercepted by KGB agents and then passed on to Russian leader Mikhail Gorbachev and his military advisers. With Mrs Reagan confiding over the telephone the President's exact schedule while she sought cosmic guidance for him, the Russians could eavesdrop on the most intimate details of his appointments system. They could hear the President's wife reveal all his moods and plans and, armed with the knowledge of the kind of stellar predictions being passed on to the White House, the KGB would know how to exploit the President's weaknesses and indecisions for their own purposes.

When the Intelligence chiefs asked FBI agents to visit Mrs Quigley's apartment in San Francisco on 5 May 1988 for an interview about the secrets she had discussed with Mrs Reagan, the astrologer could not be located. She had already fled from California to the safety of France, after her astrological charts had shown that a line-up of planets would exert such severe gravitational pull on the Earth that San Francisco and large parts of California would be destroyed by earthquakes, as she believed had been predicted by the prophet and mystic Nostradamus. Mrs Quigley returned some time later to find California still intact, but President Reagan's reputation as a careful, reasoning political leader was in tatters.

Despite scepticism about the value of astrology, very little scientific research has gone into answering one of our oldest mysteries: can the stars control our personalities and foretell our future? One meticulous independent study was conducted in the 1970s by French psychologist and statistician Michel Gauquelin, who made a survey of the birth signs of prominent members in different professions. In straightforward, statistical analysis, Gauquelin found that links between people's professional abilities, in business, politics, sport or the arts, and their zodiac birth signs were mathematically far greater than they would be according to chance. Convinced that he had established a clear scientific case for the powers of astrology, he expanded his area of research by offering free, detailed personal horoscopes to the first 1,000 applicants who fitted a random cross-section of the population.

As an experiment, Gauquelin sent each one of his unsuspecting applicants exactly the same personal horoscope, regardless of their zodiac signs. Ninety per cent of them replied, saying they had recognized their personal characteristics immediately, and assuring him that his astrological observations were pinpoint accurate. Eighty five per cent of their spouses also wrote to confirm that the horoscope had exactly captured the personality of their partner.

Dismayed, Gauquelin went back to the drawing board. For he had sent his delighted applicants the same personal zodiac profile – that of a convicted mass murderer!

The Banshee

The noise often begins as a low, wailing sound, a sad, mournful, sobbing cry. Then it rises to a wild, agonized shriek, a piercing, blood-curdling scream. Finally it dies away, fading into a soft, stifled lament. Sometimes, it can be the faint sound of muffled drums, beating out a sombre rhythm, often accompanied by a melancholy dirge on a pipe or flute. It is the sound of the banshee, the spirit which proclaims approaching death. The banshee is a ghostly figure, common in both Scottish and Irish myth, signalling that the end is near.

The word itself is derived from Gaelic 'bean shidhe', and means literally the woman of the fairies. But her purpose is far from the innocent enchantment of fairy myth. In Irish legend, the banshee usually takes the form of the spectre of a woman, brushing her hair and singing her song of mourning outside the family home of those about to die. But the song of death is never heard by the doomed person whose time has come. In Scottish myth, the banshee may appear as an old washerwoman, a solitary 'red fisherman', a headless horseman or simply the sound of an unseen drummer and piper playing a funeral march.

In Irish legend the banshee normally remains unseen and unheard as a form of guardian angel, watching over the members of great aristocratic families, guiding them away from danger and performing the last rites of 'keening' for them as death approaches. According to folklore, only the most privileged of families are protected by being haunted by a banshee. The spirit cannot express itself during a lifetime of guarding a favoured mortal, but can sound a wail of grief when its task is over, just before the moment of death, when its mortal charge is about to be taken from it.

One of the best authenticated instances of the wail of the banshee is the ghostly sound that echoed around the tiny village of Sam's Cross in the south-west of Ireland on 22 August 1922. The villagers had been aware of the comings and goings of fast convoys of cars carrying armed men. One of these men was Michael Collins, head of the Irish Government and Irish Army, who was touring military outposts besieged by rebel forces during Ireland's bloody civil war. Fearful of becoming embroiled in the conflict, the villagers stayed indoors until Collins and his bodyguard had passed through their tiny hamlet, heading back towards the town of Cork. As the sounds of car engines died away, the villagers heard another noise drifting on the wind. It was the wailing scream of the banshee. Then the noise died away. In the chill silence of the late summer evening, few of them could even discern the sound of gunfire on a quiet country road on the outskirts of the village. But they didn't need to listen to the noise of battle to know that the death of an important figure was about to take place.

Next morning, the villagers heard the news, which came as no surprise to them. Michael Collins had been killed by a bullet to the head in an ambush, only a few minutes after they had heard the wail of the banshee.

Psychic researcher Frank Smyth, who has carried out his own study of the myth, reports that the folklore of the banshee has even crossed the Atlantic in the wake of the millions of Irish emigrants who settled in the United States. The descendant of one Irish family, Boston businessman James O'Barry, described to Smyth how he first heard the banshee in Massachusetts as a small boy in the 1930s.

'I was lying in bed one morning,' said O'Barry, 'when I heard a weird noise, like a demented woman crying. It was spring and outside the window

The banshee's mournful wail is a sign that the end is near.

the birds were singing, the sun was shining and the sky was blue. I thought for a moment or two that a wind had sprung up, but a glance at the barely stirring trees told me this was not so. I went down to breakfast and there was my father sitting at the kitchen table with tears in his eyes. I had never seen him weep before. My mother told me that they had just heard by telephone that my grandfather had died in New York. Although he was an old man he was as fit as a fiddle and his death was unexpected.'

It was only some years later that O'Barry was told the legend of the banshee and it was then that he recalled quite clearly hearing the noise on the death of his grandfather.

In 1946 while serving as an officer in the United States Army Air Force in the Far East, O'Barry was awakened by the low howl of the banshee once more. He recalled: 'It was 6 a.m. and this time I was instantly aware of what it was. I sat bolt upright in bed and the hair on the back of my neck prickled. The noise got louder, rising and falling like an air-raid siren. Then it died away and I realized that I was terribly depressed. I knew my father was dead. A few days later I got notification that this was so.'

On one more occasion O'Barry heard the wail of the banshee, as he sat up in bed reading newspapers in his hotel room in Toronto during a business trip. He feared it signalled the death of his wife or his young son or his brothers, but he was strangely reassured that it was none of them. Only later that day, 22 November 1963, did he hear about the assassination in Dallas, Texas, of a close family friend – President John F Kennedy.

In Scottish legend the messenger of death takes on different forms. Folklore on the Isle of Mull claims that, during a family feud, the 16th-century chieftain Ewan was preparing to fight against his father-in-law, the MacLaine of Moy Castle, and was greeted on the eve of battle by an old woman washing a bundle of bloodstained shirts in a cold island stream. He knew she was a messenger of death, and next day he galloped into battle aware that he was going to die. Ewan was killed with one blow from an axe, severing his head from his body. The present clan chieftains maintain that the sight of a headless rider galloping across the hills of Mull is now the new messenger of death, taking over from the ghostly washerwoman.

In the north-east of Scotland, on Tayside, death in the Airlie clan is heralded by the sound of a drummer, whose eerie beat was heard three times in the last century foretelling the death of three members of the family in the next 40 years. In the 1840s the drummer sounded his warning in the home of the Ogilvie family, the chieftains of Airlie, at Cortachy castle, to warn of the death of the Countess. After her death, the Earl remarried and, in 1848, he threw a dinner party which included Miss Margaret Dalrymple as a guest. At the dinner table Miss Dalrymple remarked on the sounds of drums and a fife she had heard from the courtyard while she had dressed. The Earl and the new Countess paled.

The following morning Miss Dalrymple's maid, Ann Day, was clearing her mistress's bedroom wardrobe when she heard the sounds of the drummer in the courtyard below. When she realized the yard was empty, she became quite hysterical.

A day later Miss Dalrymple heard the drummer again and cut short her visit to Cortachy Castle. A few weeks later Lady Airlie died in Brighton, on the south coast of England, leaving behind a despondent note saying she believed the drums had been an omen of her impending death.

Several of the estate workers at Cortachy reported hearing the drums again, in 1853, shortly before the death of the heartbroken Earl. And in 1881, two relatives staying at the Castle heard the drums sound once more. They waited for a sudden and certain death, but the next few days passed uneventfully. It took more than a week for the news to reach them of the death of David Ogilvy, the 10th earl of Airlie, 4,000 miles away in America.

For the Celtic people of Ireland, Scotland and Wales, the legend of the messenger of death is not some remote historic figment of the imagination. In October 1966, when a towering coal-tip in the Welsh valleys became waterlogged and slipped, burying a primary school at Aberfan and killing 116 children and 28 adults, it was preceded by a strange howling noise. The headmaster, Mr Kenneth Davies, described it as a sound 'like a jet plane screaming low over the school in the fog'.

In 1988, in the modern world of high technology, a low screech began to wail out across the North Sea, rising to a deafening scream shortly before the deaths of more than 160 workers aboard the oil rig platform Piper Alpha. Less than a minute later, the platform erupted into a deadly fireball. Experienced engineers who examined the wreckage later came to the conclusion that the noise was caused by high pressure gas escaping from a relief valve as the disaster was about to strike the crew of the oil rig. However, one of the survivors had his own description of the awesome scream, which sounded shortly before his mates died in the icy waters of the North Sea. Rig fitter Derek Ellington, 45, from Aberdeen, explained simply: 'It sounded like the wail of the banshee.'

Voodoo

The shuffling group of nine farm labourers who presented themselves for work in the fields of the plantations of HASCO, the Haitian-American Sugar Corporation, were a sorry sight. They wore ragged clothes, worse than the tattered clothing of most other poor Haitian peasants, and they stood around in sullen silence while orders for gathering in the crops were issued to all the other labour gangs. But that year, 1918, there was a record harvest of sugar cane in the Caribbean republic of Haiti, and the HASCO manager needed all the hands he could find to work in the plantation.

The manager listened patiently to the explanation of village headman Ti Joseph and his wife Constance, who told him the labourers were from a remote part of the mountain area near Haiti's border with the Dominican Republic, and they were shy and nervous because they only spoke their own obscure dialect. The men couldn't understand French or the local Creole language, said Joseph, but if they were kept away from other workers, as a group on their own, they would prove to be tireless and efficient labourers.

Ti Joseph, like most other contract labour negotiators, agreed a rate of pay, to be handed over to him and shared with his team of labourers. The HASCO foreman agreed to give this morose group of villagers an opportunity to prove they were worth their wages. By the end of the day Ti Joseph's group had harvested the biggest quota of sugar cane, stopping only at sunset for a simple meal of unsalted millet porridge. For the rest of the week, the gang of labourers worked uncomplainingly in the sweltering heat and humidity, toiling in the fields, having only one plain meal in the evening, and earning valuable bonuses for their village headman.

On Sunday they rested as work stopped for the day, and the headman left them in the care of his wife, while he travelled to the capital of Port au Prince to spend some of the money he had made from the sweat of the labourers. His wife Constance took pity on the harvesters and escorted them to a local village for a small break from their toils, watching the spectacle of a church festival. But the workers stood around awkwardly and silently, showing no signs of joining in the festivity. Finally, Constance bought them all a treat, a packet of sweet biscuits made of brown sugar and salted nuts. The effect on the workers was dramatic. Chewing on the salted biscuits, they began to cry and wail. Then they staggered off into the mountains and headed back towards their village.

There they were greeted by relatives and friends who reeled back in horror. The sugar plantation labour gang were local men who had been buried in the village graveyard over the past few months. They were, in fact, zombies!

The tale of the zombie workers was published by American writer and explorer William Seabrook who settled in Haiti in the 1920s. His amazing report served only to confirm other ghastly tales of the gruesome occult practices on Haiti, the birthplace of the voodoo black magic cult and the graveyard of the zombies, the living dead. The mysterious practice of voodoo, which had, ironically, helped the black slaves of Haiti win their independence, turned against them to become a haunting oppression. And the zombie warriors, who fought tirelessly to defeat their colonial masters, had become pathetic ghouls trapped in a twilight world between life and death.

Until 1844, the territory of Haiti had occupied the entire mountainous mass of the sprawling island of Hispaniola, the first landing place of Christopher Columbus in his pioneering voyage of discovery to the New World. Originally inhabited by Arawak and then Carib Indians, the history of Hispaniola was first written in blood when the new European explorers embarked on a campaign of slaughter and massacre for the first 50 years after the arrival of Columbus. Hispaniola became a Spanish colony, and almost a

A Haitian woman said to be a genuine zombie.

desert island, after the extermination of the Indians, until it was repopulated by African slaves shipped from across the Atlantic. The unfortunate Africans, wrenched from their homes to work as slave labourers in the fields, brought with them only a few relics of their own culture. But they also brought an unquenchable belief in the African rituals of magic and the occult, which was to grow to become Haiti's own voodoo religion.

In the power struggles which followed, the island of Haiti was eventually ceded to the French, who built up their own repressive, but thriving, economy based on African slave labour and the crops of sugar, coffee and cotton. By the time of the French Revolution in 1789, there were 40,000 Frenchmen in Haiti, controlling a middle class of 30,000 mulattos of mixed race, and more than half a million slaves living in bondage and poverty. The new Emperor, Napoleon Bonaparte, had high hopes of using Haiti as a launching pad for a great naval fleet to recapture France's lost territories in North America. But for the black slaves, who had caught a glimpse of the freedom the French had won for themselves in the overthrow of their own royal masters back in France, their goal was independence from France.

In their bid to break free from oppression, the slaves were led by a mysterious priest and witch doctor, Boukman, who initiated rebellious slaves into voodoo rituals in the deep forests and sent them into battle against the French. Inspired by voodoo ritual and 'magic potions' which robbed them of the fear of pain or death, the black 'zombie' warriors staged a series of uprisings, in which they repaid the brutality of their French rulers with even more appalling savagery of their own. Eventually, under the leadership of General Toussaint l'Ouverture, they triumphed and declared an independent republic, although General l'Ouverture himself was to die in exile and captivity in France.

The new republic struggled into the 20th century, still beset by civil war and instability, with intervention by the French and the British until finally, from 1915 to 1934, it came under rule by the United States. During the 1940s and 1950s there were a series of *coups d'état* until a wily physician, Dr Francois Duvalier, seized power in 1957.

For Duvalier, known throughout Haiti as 'Papa Doc', the ancient religion of voodoo provided a powerful tool for unifying the people of Haiti in the belief that they all shared a unique, cultural bond unknown anywhere else in the world. When his rule degenerated into a cruel dictatorship in 1964, and he declared himself President for Life, voodoo and the mysterious myth of the zombie were enlisted as weapons to cow his people into a life of ignorance and supersition.

Duvalier gave himself the trappings of a high priest of voodoo and surrounded himself with a band of secret policemen, the Tonton Macoutes, meaning 'bogeymen'. The Tonton Macoutes revelled in their fearsome image as part state police and part witch doctors. Papa Doc encouraged voodoo worship, and terrifying tales were spread of the demonic powers of him and his henchmen, saying that anyone who opposed them would be turned into mindless zombies.

Soon the life of the country was completely governed by voodoo and black magic. Haitian peasants concoted bizarre rituals to prevent their dead loved ones from being raised from the grave as zombies. They insisted that their own families should take the same precautions for them on their death to ensure that they were not resurrected as living dead. The terror of villagers was heightened by documented examples of dead relatives, discovered years after their burial, alive but mentally deranged. Even the poorest peasants borrowed money to buy heavy ornate stones to place over the graves of dead relatives, in order to prevent voodoo doctors from digging them up and regenerating them as living ghosts. Bereaved families would take it in turns to watch over fresh graves for several weeks, until they were sure that the body inside was sufficiently decomposed as to be useless to voodoo witch doctors. In other cases, corpses were injected with deadly poisons, mutilated with knives and axes, and riddled with bullets to make sure they stayed dead.

These gruesome practices were actively promoted and encouraged by Duvalier, who needed a pervading atmosphere of fear and witchcraft to keep his grip on the population. But it soon provoked a reaction of disgust from abroad. In 1962, President Kennedy threatened to cut off any more foreign aid from the US to Haiti unless Duvalier introduced democratic measures. Papa Doc reacted angrily by declaring he had put a voodoo curse on the President. In fact, when President Kennedy was assassinated the following year, Duvalier claimed perverted 'credit' for his death and reinforced his power over the people of Haiti still further.

But even witch doctors who practise voodoo are not immortal. In 1971, Francois Duvalier died and his nervous people waited several weeks to make sure he would not rise again as a zombie. Then his son, Jean-Claude, just 19 years old, was installed as President and immediately nicknamed 'Baby Doc'. Western leaders watched closely to see if Haiti, virtually closed to outsiders for three decades, would become a modern democratic society. Their hopes were dashed as 'government by magic' continued under the regime of Baby Doc Duvalier.

In the meantime, another American President had grown impatient with the cruel injustices of the Haitian dictatorship. President Jimmy Carter, ignoring the voodoo curse which was apparently laid on Kennedy, announced that he, too, would retract aid to Haiti if the Duvalier family did not make moves towards granting Haitians basic human rights. In February 1978

Carter himself became the subject of a voodoo curse. The widow of Papa Doc, 'Mama Doc' Duvalier, summoned the Tonton Macoutes and a voodoo priest to a gory ritual in the capital, Port au Prince, where a pit was dug and a live bull was buried, together with a portrait of President Carter. The following year Iranian fanatics stormed the US embassy in Tehran, and when President Carter mounted a rescue effort, US special forces were bogged down in sudden sandstorms in the Iranian desert and many died in collisions involving their own aircraft. Carter was defeated in his attempt to win another term in the White House and left office a bitter and broken man.

Only two years later, a Harvard scientist, Dr E Wade Davis, who had managed to penetrate the veil of secrecy surrounding the voodoo practices in Haiti, announced: 'Zombie-ism actually exists. There are Haitians who have been raised from their graves and returned to life.'

Dr Davis had been recruited specially to study zombies by Dr Lamarque Douyon, the Canadian-trained head of the Port au Prince Psychiatric Centre. The two doctors carried out physical and mental examinations of 'recovered zombie' Clairvius Narcisse, who was declared dead at the Albert Schweizer Hospital in Port au Prince in 1962 but who reappeared alive in his home village two years later.

Narcisse was able to point to the scar on his cheek made by one of the nails driven into his coffin, and had astonished villagers by leading them to his own grave and digging it up to show them the empty coffin. According to Narcisse, he was 'killed' by his brothers for refusing to go along with their plan to sell off part of their family land. He could not recall how long he had been buried, but he was eventually unearthed by a witch doctor who cast a spell on him, which brought him back to life.

Another zombie studied by the doctors, a woman named Ti Femme, had been poisoned by her parents for refusing to marry the husband they had chosen for her and for bearing another man's child.

Dr Davis decided that both Narcisse and Ti Femme had been victims of a rare form of suspended animation, induced by the poison of a voodoo priest. The poison, he explained, is not fatal if administered in precisely the correct dose, but it can give all the convincing symptoms of death. He reported: 'Zombies are a Haitian phenomenon which can be explained logically. The active ingredients in the poison are extracts from the skin of the toad *Bufo marinus* and one or more species of puffer fish. The skin of the toad is a natural chemical factory which produces hallucinogens, powerful anaesthetics and chemicals that affect the heart and nervous system. The puffer fish contains a deadly nerve poison called tetrodotoxin.'

Dr Davis had compared the clinical reports of Haitian zombies with cases in Japan where people had suffered acute poisoning as a result of eating puffer fish from which the tetrodotoxin had not been completely removed. The Japanese case histories, he found, '...read like classic accounts of Haitian zombification'. In at least two cases Japanese victims had been declared dead, but had recovered before their funerals were held.

'A witch doctor in Haiti is very skilled in administering just the right dose of poison,' Dr David explained. 'Too much poison will kill the victim completely and resuscitation will not be possible. Too little and the victim will not be a convincing corpse.'

With the mystery of voodoo and zombies apparently solved, Baby Doc Duvalier's power over the people of Haiti dissolved virtually overnight. In 1986, he fled from his palace at Port au Prince to political asylum in France. Just to make sure that the junior dictator never returns to Haiti, a committee of witch doctors met in the capital and declared a curse on him. Regardless of the scientific evidence of Dr Davis, the witch doctors have warned that if Baby Doc sets foot in Haiti again, he will be turned into a zombie.

The curse seems to have worked so far.

King Arthur

The legend of King Arthur and his Knights of the Round Table is one of the most enduring myths in British folklore. The tales of Arthur's great victory to save his Celtic people from the invading Saxons, of his benevolent rule from his court at Camelot, and of his noble religious piety enthralled and inspired medieval England. He was called the 'once and future' King, and the myth was embellished with the promise that Arthur would return from his resting place on the Island of Avalon to protect Britain if she was ever again threatened by foreign invasion.

European folklore is peppered with mythical promises of sleeping monarchs who will be revived to save nations in time of peril, from Charlemagne, the King of the Franks, to Barbarossa, Frederick I of Germany, and the greatest of Irish heroes, Fionn McCumhaill. But of all the 'slumber kings', the tale of Arthur is so vivid that many historians believe it may actually have some historical authenticity.

There seems little doubt that there was, around the 5th century, a great chieftain, possibly a Romanized Briton, who turned the tide against the onslaught of the Saxon occupiers who were plundering the British countryside. Medieval scholars believe the character of King Arthur may be based on the real-life figure of a professional soldier, Ambrosius Aurelianus, who fought bravely against the invasion.

Certainly the battle-weary peasants of Britain were sorely in need of a national hero when the retreat of the Roman legions left them vulnerable and leaderless after centuries of colonial government. By AD 410 Britain, at least south of the Scottish border and the protective ramparts of Hadrian's Wall, had enjoyed 400 years of relative peace, prosperity and the protection of the Roman Army. A network of perfectly engineered roads had provided a sound infrastructure for trade and commerce, as well as allowing Roman legions to move quickly between their encampments and major cities. A well-oiled system of firm central government was another of the benefits imposed on backward Britain by its Roman masters. But when Rome itself was threatened by strife and plundering hordes of barbarians, Emperor Honorius had to pull his troops back to Italy and leave the Britons to fend for themselves. No sooner had the Romans left than Britain was plunged into civil war, prey to rival armies of warlords who saw rich pickings left behind by the enforced retreat of the former colonial masters.

The tyrant Vortigern managed to grab the most widespread power by reinforcing his own band of crude soldiers with two ruthless men imported from the European continent: the Anglo-Saxon mercenaries, Hengist and Horsa. Not content with being only lieutenants in Vortigern's dictatorship, Hengist and Horsa soon turned on their former allies, and Vortigern's regime collapsed in a bloody wave of rioting and looting.

Soon, other marauding bands of Anglo-Saxon private armies crossed the Channel to carve out their own share of the spoils, and the original inhabitants of Britain began to long for the return of the Roman conquerors.

But salvation was at hand in the form of a little known British general, Ambrosius Aurelianus. Pushed further and further west, towards Wales, the British armies, led by Ambrosius, eventually stood their ground on the battlefield of Mount Badon, around the year 518, and defeated the Saxons. The military mastermind credited with the victory is known only as Arthur. His triumph was said to have been so overwhelming that peace was restored for another 50 years.

Early Welsh scribes quickly made Arthur a 'king of wonders and marvels', and his deeds soon became known throughout Britain.

The *Annales Cambriae*, the Welsh annals written by monks, describe how Arthur fought for three days and nights before achieving victory. Intriguingly, they added the pious detail that Arthur carried 'The Cross of Our Lord Jesus' as a symbol on his battle shield. Another entry in the annals laments the battle of Camlann, in which 'Arthur and Mordred perished and a plague fell upon Britain and Ireland'.

Within the next few centuries, based on a few fragments of historical record, the legend of Arthur took on a life of its own, and grew in depth until it was woven into a rich tapestry of unproveable fact and undeniable fiction. Each retelling of the myth tailored the story to fit neatly into the unique national character of ancient Britons, blending a belief in the powers of magic and wizards with a conflicting faith in Christianity.

Arthur's birth was shrouded in magic and intrigue. His father, Uther Pendragon, King of England, had fallen deeply in love with Ygraine, the wife of his most loyal supporter, Gorlois, Duke of Cornwall. Overcome with lust, Uther persuaded his personal wizard Merlin to give him a potion which transformed him into the double of Gorlois, and he had the Duke killed while he entered Ygraine's bed-chamber in Tintagel Castle, posing as her husband.

The result of Uther's passion was the boy Arthur. The wizard Merlin claimed the infant and sent the baby off to be raised by a knight called Ector until he was 15 years old. On Uther's death there was a great gathering of all the nobility of England in London, and under the watchful eye of Merlin, the dukes and earls were invited to pit themselves against a magical stone, holding an anvil in which a sword, named Excalibur, was embedded

Engraved on the stone were the words. 'Whosoever pulls this sword from the stone and anvil is the rightful King of England'.

The lords and knights puffed and panted as they tried to pull the sword free, but as soon as young Arthur, ignorant of his royal parentage, grasped the sword firmly, it slipped easily into his grasp.

Arthur was proclaimed King, but it took many years of bitter fighting before his authority was accepted. One of the rebel nobles, Loth of Lothian, grudgingly offered his own beautiful wife, Morgause, to Arthur and the couple conceived a child. Arthur was unaware that Morgause was his own half-sister, a daughter of Gorlois and Ygraine, and Merlin prophesied that the boy who was born of their incest, Mordred, would eventually lead to the downfall of his kingdom.

In later years Arthur remarried, and he and his second wife, Guinevere, established their kingdom in Camelot. Embellishments of the legend spoke of the fabled Round Table, given as a wedding present to Guinevere, where all the Knights of Camelot were seated in a circle without any single person being given a privileged position higher or lower in authority than any other. Only one seat was left vacant, reserved for the brave knight who would one day succeed in the spiritual challenge to locate the Holy Grail, the most

Arthur, Guinevere and Merlin have their roots in real history.

revered relic in Christendom, the chalice used by Jesus Christ to sip wine at the Last Supper.

The Grail was believed to have been brought to England by Joseph of Arimathea, who fled from the Holy Land to escape the persecution of Jews angered by the fact that Jesus's body had been taken to Joseph's tomb after his crucifixion. Ancient legend, probably fuelled by devout religious wishful thinking, also claimed that Jesus himself had spent his early years in England learning the trade of a tinsmith in the West Country, hence the Bible's total lack of reference to the Saviour's early life in Palestine.

Although the adventures of the Knights of the Round table were tales of thrilling bravery, honour and dedication to the highest principles of gallantry, Arthur's own life was shattered by betrayal and dishonour. He lost his beloved wife, Guinevere, to his bravest knight, Sir Lancelot, which broke his heart. Eventually, forced by his ambitious son, Mordred, to publicly accuse the couple of adultery and treason, Arthur watched the break-up of his idyllic Kingdom of Camelot.

Lancelot and Guinevere, accompanied by a band of renegade knights, fled to France and were pursued by Arthur who forced a bloody showdown. Back home in Camelot, Sir Mordred exploited the situation to his own advantage, and when Arthur returned he found his throne had been usurped. Arthur and his loyal knights met Mordred and the rebel forces on the battlefield at Camlann. Amid the carnage and deaths of valiant knights, Arthur struck a mortal blow at his son; and Mordred, with his dying breath, plunged his own sword into Arthur.

The wounded king was taken away to the shores of an enchanted lake and carried off to die in a little chapel built by Joseph of Arimathea on the mystical island of Avalon.

The legend of Arthur had all the ingredients of a best-seller. It satisfied the Britons' hatred and distrust of foreigners by extolling Arthur's victories over invading Saxons. And while it was steeped in magic and sorcery, it also paid devout homage to Christianity. It had passionate romance, adultery, treachery, double-dealing, honour and gallantry in equal measures. And it had an optimistically happy ending, with the tragic but noble figure of the wounded King Arthur being borne to the mystical island of Avalon, promising to return to rescue his beloved people once more in their darkest hour of need.

All in all, the legend of King Arthur was a ripping yarn, and more glorious detail and embellishment was added with each retelling. In AD 1135 a Benedictine monk, Geoffrey of Monmouth, devoted a large part of his massive tome, *The History of the Kings of England*, to King Arthur, presenting his version of events not as legend and myth but as historical fact. Even the Norman rulers of conquered Britain were captivated by the fabulous picture of Arthur portrayed in the book. They saw Arthur as a home-grown hero who was a worthy rival to their own legendary King Charlemagne. And since the Norman invaders had fought and defeated the Saxon rulers of England in their own conquest, they felt this victory over the common enemy of King Arthur gave them some kind of kinship with their new British subjects.

The legends of Arthur were already well known in France at this time, having been carried there by the blood relatives of West Country Britons who settled in the province of Brittany in northern France. At Bayeux, also in France, the cleric Robert Wace rewrote large parts of Geoffrey of Monmouth's *History* with even more poetic licence and embellishment, adding flourishes of detail to the romantic code of chivalry of the Knights of the Round Table. Another Frenchman, Chrétien de Troyes, helped to popularize the tales of Arthur even further with several long epic poems in praise of the honour of Arthur's knights.

The story of King Arthur might have remained no more than a romantic legend but for the discovery of a startling record in the chronicles of Glastonbury Abbey. The Abbey's reputed association with Joseph of Arimathea made it the most logical location for the site of Camelot and the island of Avalon. In Arthurian times the area was surrounded by marshy swamps and streams, effectively making it an island. The Welsh called it Ynys Avallon, meaning the island of apples, and its description dovetailed neatly with the tales of the island where Arthur and his unfaithful Queen Guinevere were eventually buried.

Writing in the 10-year period between 1129 and 1139, historian William Malmesbury described how Arthur's grave was found standing between two stone pyramids in the ancient cemetery of the Lady Chapel of the Abbey. According to Malmesbury, the grave was marked with a cross inscribed with the words: '*Hic jacet sepultus inclitus Rex Arthurus cum Wenneveria uxore sua secona in Insula Avallonis.*' Translated from the Latin, it reads simply: 'Here lies the famous King Arthur with Guinevere, his second wife, buried in the Island of Avalon.'

Malmesbury's reports fit exactly with the Abbey's own records: that Bishop Dunstan raised the level of the cemetery in the 10th century and enclosed it with a wall. It is possible that the grave was discovered then. Abbot Henry of Sully is also reputed to have exhumed the coffin from its burial place 16 feet under the earth in 1190 and transferred it to the Treasury of the Abbey.

Eighty-five years later, King Edward and Queen Eleanor, having heard the tales of Arthur's grave from Welsh bards, journeyed to Glastonbury to celebrate the consecration of the Abbey's High Altar. On the arrival of the monarchs, King Arthur's coffin was broken open to reveal two separate chests, decorated with portraits of Arthur and Guinevere and their heraldic arms. The Queen was shown fully crowned, but Arthur wore a battle-damaged crown. His left ear was cut off and there were marks of his wounds from the battle with Mordred at Camlann. When the caskets were opened the King's bones were found to be those of a tall and powerful man, while those of Guinevere were of a delicate woman.

The following day King Edward and Queen Eleanor reverently wrapped the remains in fresh shrouds, keeping out the bones of King Arthur's skull, and his knees, to display to pious worshippers. The remains were encased in a mausoleum before the High Altar. King Edward then presided over a public ceremony to emphasize that he was the worthy and legitimate successor to King Arthur and rightfully the monarch of all Britain.

In 1960, archaeologists excavated the area where Arthur's tomb was reputed to have been. They found only evidence that a pit had existed there, and there were also the imprints of a stone memorial which had since been removed. The pit had been emptied and refilled at the time of King Edward's visit. It seems that the monks of Glastonbury had exhumed a grave and tried to cover up their traces.

Was it the grave of King Arthur and his Queen? Did the mythical King actually live and fight and love in the days of Camelot? And is his final resting place still undiscovered and undisturbed somewhere in the west of England, in a secret place once known to his Knights as the Island of Avalon?

Glastonbury Abbey

When architect Frederick Bond was given the task of excavating and exploring the ruins of Glastonbury Abbey in Somerset, western England, he faced a seemingly impossible task. Many of its ancient buildings had disappeared completely in the terrible destruction of the Abbey by the soldiers of Henry VIII, and the ravages of time and weather had helped to reduce the few remaining arches and columns of its two main chapels to rubble.

The Abbey had been founded in the 5th century by Saint Patrick before he left England on his mission to convert Ireland to Christianity, and the site had long been associated with the legend of King Arthur. As a popular place of pilgrimage, it had grown in power, wealth and influence under a series of monks and abbots who had enlarged the Abbey grounds and extended the splendour of its architecture. This had made Glastonbury a prime target for revenge by King Henry, who had broken with the Catholic Church over the controversy of his many wives and divorces. Henry ordered the Abbey razed to the ground so thoroughly that when the Church of England finally paid £36,000 for the ruins in 1907, there were few clues left to the exact layout of the ancient place of worship, and there was precious little money to pay for the extensive digging and research needed to piece together the elaborate medieval jigsaw.

The eerie ruins of St Joseph's Chapel, Glastonbury Abbey.

Bond, a leading expert of Gothic architecture and the restoration of old churches, realized that uncovering the remains of the ruined Abbey in the little time and money made available to him would need incredible luck and inspiration. Or divine guidance. The 43-year-old scholarly authority on ancient buildings had one untried gamble he hoped would pay off. But he didn't dare reveal it to the Church dignitaries. He decided, instead, to go 'straight to the horse's mouth' for the information he needed – by contacting the spirits of the long-dead monks and abbots.

Bond was a secret student of the occult, and one of his closest friends was psychic medium John Bartlett, who specialized in receiving messages from the spirit world in the form of 'automatic writing' transmitted to him while in a trance. In a seance at Bond's office in Bristol in November 1907, Bartlett made contact with a disembodied spirit, who guided his pen through a series of notes and drawings tracing detailed plans of the hidden foundations of the ruined abbey.

The messages, which seemed to flow effortlessly from Bartlett's pen, purported to come from a 16th-century monk, John Bryant, who spoke on behalf of the ghostly keepers of the Abbey whom he described as 'The

Company of Avalon'. The information given in these seances contradicted Bond's lifetime of experience of the layout of medieval monasteries, but when he was finally allocated his meagre budget two years later, he decided to direct his workmen to dig in the area where the ghostly writing said they would discover the underground foundations of old chapels and the stonework of ancient walls.

On the first few weeks of digging, Bond's team, working to the master plan of the dead monk, found walls and towers, doorways and fragments of stained glass windows. Bond's reputation soared as discovery after discovery began to piece together the shattered remains of Glastonbury Abbey. Fearful of the ridicule of fellow professionals and his clerical paymasters, Bond modestly took the credit himself and put his amazing finds down to a piece of inspired guesswork.

Ten years after the excavations had begun, Bond decided to reveal the source of his success, confident that the work he had already done would justify the unorthodox methods he had used. In a dramatic book, *The Gate of Remembrance*, he confessed to the mystic seances that had taken place, and admitted to the messages from the spirit world which had guided the shovels of his archaeological team.

After the publication of *The Gate of Remembrance*, Bond's reputation was left in tatters. A co-director was immediately appointed by the Church authorities to supervise Bond and to edge him out of control of any more excavation work. Within a year, the budget for any further digging under Bond's direction had been slashed, and he was reduced to a salary of only £10 a month.

In 1922, when the dust had settled, the Church society for the exploration and restoration of Glastonbury Abbey was quietly dissolved and Bond was banned from setting foot on the Abbey grounds ever again. He left for America, where he lived for the next 20 years, lonely and embittered. He never got over the deep hurt that Church leaders and fellow archaeologists could not accept his claim that the dead monk of Glastonbury had communicated with his colleague Bartlett's subconscious mind and had drawn mental images for him of the original plans of the Abbey.

Alchemy

There are many incentives that spur on scientists, researchers and philosophers to devote their lives to the quest for wisdom and truth. There is the desire for knowledge for its own sake; there are the honourable motives of gaining the ability to advance mankind, to pass on some greater understanding of the mysteries of Life, to enrich society and suceeding generations; and then there's greed, lust for power and the fear of dying.

There is no doubt that the alchemists who sweated over their crucibles and cauldrons made a modest contribution to the progress and understanding of the fledgling sciences of chemistry and metallurgy. But even this was unintentional. The objective of any alchemist who made a worthwhile chemical discovery was to keep the find a secret, to note the formulae and processes in uncrackable codes and ciphers, and to make sure the discovery could be of no benefit to anyone else.

Alchemy only had one purpose: to make its practitioners fabulously rich. There was also the possibility of an added bonus – immortality!

A corruption of the true scientific course of chemistry, the aim of alchemy was to turn base, mundane metals, such as iron, lead and mercury, into gold and silver. To Egyptian priests and chemists in 5,000 BC the idea of turning crude metal ores into the precious commodities must have seemed almost within their grasp. They had already conquered many of the mysteries of metallurgy. They could recognize the distinctive streaks of seams of metal in rocks and earth. They knew how to grind up soil and stone, how to heat the ore in furnaces and skim off bright shiny metals like copper and tin. But it was much more difficult to locate and mine the rare rocks which contained tiny glistening seams of gold, or to find twinkling specks of pure gold nuggets in the beds of rivers and streams.

Gold was not just rare, it was precious. It was soft enough to be moulded and shaped into ornaments of great delicacy and beauty. It seemed like a gift from the gods, and kings counted their power and wealth in the amounts of gold they possessed in their treasury. It could be stamped into coinage, bearing the imprint of a ruler's face, spreading his power and influence far and wide. It never tarnished or rusted, like ordinary metals. It had the aura of immortality and coin-makers thought, maybe, some of that would rub off on a king whose head was stamped into gold.

The Pharaohs, who faced an eternity of death in their pyramid tombs, became more and more frantic to be surrounded with gold as the symbols of their wealth and power. How much easier and richer life would be for all if a plentiful metal like lead or tin could be turned into gold.

The ancient Egyptians knew that something as common as sand mixed with wood ash would be miraculously transformed into tough, translucent sparkling glass, precious and expensive, almost like man-made jewels or diamonds. The secret of changing metals into gold obviously lay in understanding the inner workings of the kind of chemistry that turned sand into glass. So the quest began to find the key to the mystery. Blind to everything except the quest for man-made gold, the alchemists set off on a race without a winning post, a frantic, futile scramble around a chemical treadmill.

The history of alchemy is marked by cheats and charlatans, honest chemists and brilliant scientists, gullible monarchs like Queen Elizabeth I, who squandered a fortune on crack-brained alchemy schemes, and dictators like Adolf Hitler, who partly financed his rise to power with an alchemy swindle.

Generations of the most skilful Egyptian chemists had already seen their best efforts come to nothing by the time conquering warriors swept northward out of the Arabian peninsula in the 7th century AD and occupied the country, introducing Islamic rule. In the great library of Alexandria, the new Arab masters and scholars found a wealth of manuscripts, including the writings of Aristotle, who had lived a thousand years earlier.

According to Aristotle, every compound in the world was made up of only four elements – earth, air, water and fire. And it was only necessary to change the proportions of these components to form any substance. Aristotle's teachings were transcribed into Arabic and carried back across the Mediterranean by Moslem invaders who conquered Spain and established great universities at Toledo and Cordova.

In 1144 an Englishman, Robert of Chester, made the first Latin translation of Aristotle's theories, and Aristotle's faulty chemical formulae became the foundation of a pseudo-science which turned the lives of countless alchemists of the Middle Ages into a fruitless quest for the non-existent answer to the mystery of the transmutation of metals.

In addition to being able to turn base metal into gold, the philosopher Aristotle also held out a promise of the Secret of Eternal Youth. Any alchemist who successfully reduced a metal to its basic components, would find himself with an 'Elixir', possibly a powder or a liquid, which possessed magical properties. This 'Philosopher's Stone' could be taken in a drink, curing all illnesses and bringing the gift of immortality.

From then until the present day, scientists have laboured to convert one element to another, with varying degrees of success. For hundreds of years, in

101

castles and dungeons, alchemists muttered magic words and chemical formulae over bubbling cauldrons, trying unlikely combinations of lead, mercury, sulphur and arsenic to produce gold.

The brilliant 13th-century English scholar Roger Bacon, who, long before Columbus, had reached the scientifically accurate conclusion that the Earth was round, and who constructed early magnifying glasses, was a firm believer in alchemy. He had faith that the mystery would be solved sooner or later by thorough and detailed experimentation. He died frustrated and bitterly disappointed that alchemy had not been proved practical during his own lifetime.

Impatient with the slow progress of her officially approved buccaneers who plundered Spanish galleons sailing back from America, where they themselves had already looted Inca gold, Elizabeth I employed her own alchemist in a specially constructed laboratory in Somerset House, London. The alchemist laboured day and night to conquer the mysteries of making gold. Elizabeth dreamt of untold wealth, and of extending her reign indefinitely by sipping of the Elixir of Life. She lived to the ripe old age of 70, and the unsuccessful chemist lived out the rest of his days imprisoned in the Tower of London.

Ferdinand III, the 17th-century Emperor of Austria, was confident that alchemy would finance his victory in the Thirty Years' War against the Germans, Dutch and Swedes, when his Royal Alchemist produced brilliant nuggets of gold from a glowing furnace he had fed with lead and sulphur. Ferdinand was eventually forced to sue for peace when his empire was bankrupted. There is no record of the fate of the alchemist, but he was undoubtedly one of the many rogues and charlatans who saw rich rewards in alchemy, not by manufacturing gold, but by combining a blend of chemistry, magic and occultism to cheat his royal patron.

Clever conjuring tricks were used to fool the gullible. Apparently empty metal cauldrons were secretly lined with a layer of wax, concealing tiny nuggets of gold which were released into the boiling mixtures when they were poured over them, melting the wax. Hollow wands containing gold dust were used to stir the cauldrons and sprinkle flecks of real gold into bubbling broths of cheap metals.

The disillusioned Swiss physician and alchemist Paracelsus, who died in 1541, had tried to put a stop to the practice of alchemy, claiming that it was consuming too much of the talent and limited research facilities of early chemists. Celebrating his appointment as physician to the city of Basle, he burned the written works of earlier alchemists in a bonfire in the city square and urged scientists to abandon their search for manufactured gold and to concentrate on improving their research into medicines.

Frenzied alchemists at work, as depicted by Pieter Brueghel.

Modern scientific methods and knowledge should have finally finished off the ancient myth of alchemy when nuclear physics began to unravel the mysteries of the atom. Instead, they gave alchemy an unexpected boost when, in 1919, British physicist Ernest Rutherford shook the scientific world with the announcement that he had successfully changed one element into another. He had changed nitrogen into oxygen and hydrogen. He had not used any secret chemical processes or added any 'elixir' to the nitrogen gas sample in his laboratory, but had simply bombarded the nitrogen with radiation from the nuclei of helium particles. This transformed it to fluorine, as an intermediate element, before its final conversion into oxygen and hydrogen.

Rutherford's pioneering work was as uneconomic as it was radical. It had taken massive amounts of energy to produce only a few atoms of oxygen, but it had proved a fundamental scientific principle. It had finally shown that elements could be changed, even if it was not through the magical, mystical processes of alchemy.

Five years after Rutherford's breakthrough, a 36-year-old chemical worker in Munich, Franz Tausend, claimed that he had achieved the same atomic transformation, not by turning nitrogen into oxygen, but by turning iron oxide and quartz into gold. Tausend published a pamphlet, asserting that atomic nuclei were held together by vibrating harmonies, and that the frequency of vibration could be altered to produce different elements.

Tausend was greeted with wary cynicism by German scientific authorities, but he was a godsend to the newly formed Nazi Party. In 1924, Adolf Hitler had been sent to jail for plotting an armed uprising against the Government. He left his loyal supporter General Erich Ludendorff in charge of fundraising for the Party. Ludendorff had heard about the claims of Tausend and he gathered together a group of industrialists and investors to give him enough backing to demonstrate that his research really could produce massive profits. At a meeting in a Berlin hotel, one of the business investors was appointed to independently supervise Tausend's exhibition of his alchemic success.

The investor himself bought the supplies of iron and oxide specified by Tausend. The metals were melted together and locked in the impartial referee's hotel room overnight, away from any attempt at interference by the alchemist. The next morning, the solidified mass was reheated by Tausend, under the watchful eyes of his potential backers, and the alchemist added a small quantity of white powder to the molten mixture. When the crucible had cooled down, it was broken open and Tausend produced a gold nugget weighing a quarter of an ounce.

Overnight, investment money began to pour into the coffers of a new company formed as a partnership between Tausend and the officials of the Nazi Party. However, not all the money went to financing Tausend's new laboratory and workshop. Ludendorff managed to divert almost 500,000 marks into the bank accounts of Party funds, and when he resigned from the joint company two years later, he left Tausend to fend off the creditors.

Tausend, without any money for production, struggled for another two years to keep the debt collectors at bay, and on 16 June 1928 he staved off bankruptcy by finally producing an ingot of nearly 26 ounces of gold in one single night.

Faith had been restored in Tausend's methods and the investors who had been howling for his blood rushed to snap up share certificates in his new company. Sadly for trusting investors, that was the last pot of gold produced by the alchemist. In 1931 he was arrested, found guilty of fraud and jailed for four years.

But the future rise to power of the Nazis was secured by the profits of alchemy, and the income from Tausend's bubbling crucible was enough to set them on the road to seizing power in Germany and plunging the world into war only a few years later. And it was the violent course of that war which was to destroy the secret papers of one man who may have unlocked the mystery of alchemy.

London osteopath Archibald Cockren was no crackpot inventor of a secret, magic process for making gold, nor was he seeking to get rich quick by cashing in on alchemy. As part of his respected medical practice, Cockren used small quantities of gold to make medical solutions for the treatment of arthritis. Gold was an increasingly rare commodity during the stringencies of war, so Cockren began to experiment himself in finding a gold substitute – or making the real thing – in his tiny laboratory at home.

Cockren tested the reactions of different metals, including antimony, iron and copper, to which he added a secret catalyst powder capable of sparking off chemical reactions. In 1940 he noted in the brief diary he kept in his office: 'I entered upon a new course of experiment with a metal with which I had no previous experience. This metal, after being reduced to its salts and undergoing special preparation and distillation, delivered up the Mercury of the Philosophers, the Water of Paradise. The first intimation I had of this triumph was a violent hissing, jets of vapour pouring from the retort, like sharp bursts from a machine gun, and then a violent explosion, whilst a very potent and subtle odour filled the laboratory and its surroundings.'

That night he went home to repeat the experiment, and to submit his notes to the War Office. Outside, the air raid wardens were checking the blackout curtains along the street of terraced houses, and then the warning sirens began to wail. It was one of the worst Blitz raids on London, carried out by the bombers of the Nazi regime which, ironically, had been founded on the proceeds of Tausend's dubious experiments.

By the time the all clear signal had sounded, Cockren's house lay in ruins, the osteopath was dead and his research was shattered and burned to ashes.

Alchemy had helped to build up the war machine that destroyed the work of a dedicated researcher, who might actually have solved its mysteries.

Fairies

There can be few people who would not accept that Sir Arthur Conan Doyle, the doyen of detective thriller writers, had a brilliantly sharp, analytical mind. He showed the depth of his talent for unemotional, logical, detached reasoning in the creation of the most enduring character in the history of crime fiction, the formidable Sherlock Holmes. It probably follows, then, that when it came to finding the answer to a mystery or solving a perplexing riddle, Sir Arthur Conan Doyle was as clear-headed and rational as his brainchild, the supersleuth of Baker Street. Like Sherlock Holmes, Sir Arthur was nobody's fool.

Or was he? Did Sir Arthur have the wool pulled over his eyes by two little girls barely into their teens? Was he fooled by a simple trick into believing that the high-spirited, giggling girls had actually photographed fairies at the bottom of their garden?

The photographs, taken by 15-year-old Elsie Wright and her 11-year-old cousin Frances Griffiths, were, apparently, only meant for a family album or as souvenir snapshots to send to friends. In fact, the first print of the photographs which were to become the centre of a furious occult controversy was posted casually to a penfriend along with a chatty letter which only made passing reference to the astonishing picture.

Frances Griffiths, who was living with cousin Elsie while her father fought on the French battlefront in the First World War, had written to a friend in South Africa, where she had spent most of her young life. She told her: 'I am learning French, Geometry, Cookery and Algebra at school now. Dad came home from France the other week after being there ten months and we all think the war will be over in a few days. I am sending two photographs, both of me, one of me in a bathing-costume in our back yard, Uncle Jack took that, while the other is me with some fairies. Elsie took that one. Rosebud is as fat as ever and I have made her some new clothes. How are Teddy and Dolly?'

Frances had scrawled across the back of the photograph: 'Elsie and I are very friendly with the fairies. It is funny I never used to see them in Africa. It must be too hot for them there.'

The photograph showed Frances, nestled on a grassy bank near a beck, a small stream, at the bottom of the garden of the Wright's home in Cottingley, near Bradford, Yorkshire. She had her chin nestled in her cupped

Frances Griffiths with fairies, photographed by Elsie Wright.

hand. In front of her, dancing among the leaves and twigs, was a group of fairies, dressed in gossamer gowns, with wings fluttering. A fairy in the foreground played a set of pipes.

The photograph had been taken more than a year before in July 1917, when Elsie Wright had pestered her father Arthur to borrow his camera for a snapshot of Frances beside the beck that bordered their long, secluded garden. When she returned later that afternoon, her doting father began to develop the photographic plate in his darkroom. As the image appeared, he was annoyed to see what he thought were scraps of litter and old sandwich wrappings on the grass in front of the figure of Frances. Elsie blithely insisted that the white images on the photograph were fairies, and then skipped back outdoors to play.

A few weeks later, the two girls asked again to borrow the camera. They ran off to a clump of trees at the foot of the garden and took another snapshot. This time, when it was developed, Arthur Wright was amazed to see an image of his daughter, seated on the grass, being presented with a tiny flower-bud – by a gnome wearing a doublet, hose and a fancy shirt with a frilled collar. Arthur accused the girls of playing tricks with his precious camera – and he refused to let them borrow it any more. Intrigued by the images, he studied the photographic plates closely, but he could see no signs of hidden strings and wires propping up the fairy figures in front of the lens. He and his wife, Polly, even searched the girls' bedroom, looking for waste paper or scraps of pictures or cutouts which the girls might have used to fake the photographs. They found nothing.

Unsure if he was the victim of a lighthearted prank, or if he had unique, concrete evidence of the fabled creatures of folk myth, Arthur Wright made a few prints to show his neighbours for their novelty value, and thought no more about it.

It wasn't until 1919 that the story of the fairy photographs reached a wider audience. Polly Wright, who had an interest in spiritualism, attended a meeting of the Theosophical Society in Bradford and revealed the existence of the photographs taken by her daughter and her niece. The following year prints of the slightly overexposed photographs were collected by Edward Gardner, a leading member of the Theosophical Society, a society dedicated to exploring psychic phenomena and spreading the message of Spiritualism.

Gardener was fascinated. He ordered photographic expert Fred Barlow to make new copy negatives from the prints, correcting the errors of exposure – but without any touching up or improvements of the actual images. The result was a set of greatly enhanced prints, which showed the girls, the fairies and the gnome with startling clarity.

Even then, the photographs might have remained a curiosity, studied solely by followers of the Theosophist cult. Then: Enter Sherlock Holmes, in the form of Sir Arthur Conan Doyle.

The famous author had been commissioned by *Strand Magazine* in London to write an article on fairies for their Christmas issue. He asked to borrow the prints from Gardner, and showed them to Sir Oliver Lodge, a psychical researcher. Lodge immediately dismissed them as fakes and suggested, bizarrely, that the fairies in the prints might have been a troupe of dancers in disguise, reduced in size by a trick of photographic perspective.

But Sir Arthur, apparently keen to seek a second opinion, gave more credence to a report by a technical expert employed by Edward Gardner, who insisted that his own analysis showed that the fairy figures were not lifeless cardboard cutouts, but actually showed signs of movement captured by the camera's slow shutter speed.

Casting Edward Gardner in the role of 'Watson', Sir Arthur despatched him to Cottingley to conduct his own interviews with the Wright family and their niece. Gardner reported back that the Wrights were honest, reliable people who were plainly telling the truth. That was enough for Sir Arthur; he gave the Cottingley fairy photographs the backing of his considerable reputation and promoted them in his article in *Strand Magazine*.

Sir Arthur seems to have been swayed by the philosophy he himself invented for Sherlock Holmes when berating Dr Watson in the novel *A Study in Scarlet*: 'How often have I said to you, that when you have eliminated the impossible, whatever remains, however improbable, must be the truth.'

But the author had also put different sentiments into the mouth of his sleuth in an earlier novel, when the redoubtable Sherlock Holmes had proclaimed: 'Detection is, or ought to be, an exact science, and should be treated in the same cold and unemotional manner.'

So Sir Arthur hedged his bets.

As the Christmas edition of *Strand Magazine* sold out within days, Sir Arthur asked Gardner to go back to Cottingley, taking with him his own camera and a supply of photographic plates, secretly marked, without the knowledge of Elsie or Frances. He thought that if a new set of fairy photographs could be made, under controlled circumstances, he might have the definitive proof he was looking for. Sir Arthur then promptly departed for a lecture tour of Australia, while a storm of controversy broke out over the report in *Strand*: 'Fairies Photographed, an Epoch Making Event.'

The popular press had a field day. Sir Arthur, who had written under a pseudonym for the magazine article in order to protect the true identities of Frances and Elsie, was lampooned and laughed at. The *South Wales Argus* gave the Cottingley fairies as much credibility as Santa Claus. In London, the *City News* mocked: 'It seems at this point that we must either believe in the almost incredible mystery of the fairy or in the almost incredible wonders of faked photographs.'

The *Westminster Gazette*, however, adopted tactics more worthy of Sherlock Holmes. By following every clue and hint, they cracked the protective aliases used by Sir Arthur, and correctly identified Elsie and Frances. Their staff reporter travelled to Cottingley and conducted a first-hand investigation on the spot. He found no flaws in the story and, grudgingly perhaps, his own report to his paper classified the Cottingley Fairies as 'an unexplained mystery'.

In the meantime, the luckless Edward Gardner had been unsuccesful in his efforts to witness the apparitions of the fairies for himself. It rained in Cottingley for days on end, and the weather was obviously not conducive to fairy dancing and prancing. He therefore left his equipment behind with Elsie and Frances, with instructions to use the camera themselves.

The following month, back in London, he received a letter from Polly Wright, together with five photographic plates that had already been developed. Gardner was gratified to see the secret marks he had already made

Elsie Wright plays with a 'gnome' at Cottingley in 1917.

on the plates, showing that his own material had been used without substitution or tampering. The girls had succeeded in taking three more fairy snapshots. Although no adults had witnessed the event, the unsupervised girls had followed Gardner's instructions about focusing and exposure, and the plates were remarkably clear. One showed a close-up of Elsie being offered a tiny harebell flower by a fairy – who displayed a suspiciously fashionable '20s bobbed hairstyle and flapper dress. A second snapshot showed a prancing fairy in more realistic gossamer dress, flying in the air a few feet from the smiling face of Frances. And a third plate had captured the blurred image of two tiny figures in a 'fairy bower' of blossoms and twigs, shyly adjusting their dresses in the morning dew.

Gardner's unswerving belief was reinforced. He cabled the good news to Sir Arthur in Australia, who replied joyfully: 'My heart was gladdened when I had your note and the three wonderful pictures which are confirmatory of our published results. When fairies are admitted, other psychic phenomena will find a more ready acceptance. We have had continued messages at seances for some time that a visible sign was coming through.'

However, the new photographs failed to convince the sceptics. They even failed to impress Elsie's father, Arthur Wright, a bluff, down-to-earth Yorkshireman. Wright, who believed only in the benefits of education and reasoning, was baffled. He told friends he didn't see how an intellectual like Sir Arthur could be taken in 'by our Elsie, and her at the bottom of her class'.

The hubbub over the Cottingley Fairies soon died away. Decades later, in adulthood, Elsie and Frances still refused to be drawn into any debate about the authenticity of the photographs. The most telling, and ambiguous, verdict on the case was the perhaps the summing up of the newspaper *Truth*, in 1921. It deduced, sarcastically: 'For the true explanation of these fairy photographs what is wanted is not a knowledge of occult phenomena, but a knowledge of children.'

Sir Arthur died in 1930, still clinging to the belief that the folk legend of fairies had been verified as a concrete reality by the apparitions in Cottingley.

There may be some real scientific evidence for the timeless legends of fairies, gnomes and trolls, which are common in many northern European myths. Archeologist A McLean May made an amazing discovery in 1959 when excavating a gravel pit in Ireland – the country which, more than most, had folk myth rich in tales of fairies and leprechauns. Deep under the layers of gravel and clay he found the remains of three distinct civilizations, dating as far back as 7,000 BC He uncovered traces of ovens and cooking fires in tunnels so small they could only have been used by midgets. His research supported the theory that the early inhabitants of the tiny tunnels may have arrived in Ireland soon after the Ice Age, and possibly to other parts of the recently frozen North. The last survivors of the miniature people, now extinct, may have taken to the woods and other hiding places, and glimpses of them by later settlers could have given rise to the legends of the wee folk, the leprechauns of Ireland, the fairies of England and the trolls of Scandinavia.

Whatever the truth, fairy folklore is still strong in Ireland and other parts of the British Isles, including the Isle of Man where the islanders would never dare to pass over the Fairy Bridge of Balla-g-Lonney without bidding a greeting to the fairies and elves. When the cynical servicemen of the RAF station at nearby Jurby ignored the custom, they were warned by the locals: 'The little people will get their own back.' Fliers know all about mysterious 'gremlins', unexplained instances of failure and foul-ups which can plague machinery and aircraft without any apparent cause. But their base was afflicted by a whole series of minor mishaps – cash shipments to pay their wages never arrived on time and military vehicles started seizing up for no apparent reason – whenever they tried to drive over the Fairy Bridge. The problems ceased when the airmen adopted the custom of raising their hats, or saluting smartly, and paying homage to the Fairies of Balla-g-Lonney.

So who says fairies don't exist? The last word should to to Sir Arthur Conan Doyle, or at least his alter ego, the sage of Baker Street, Sherlock Holmes, who said reprovingly to his detractors in *The Memoirs of Sherlock Holmes*: 'You see, but you do not observe.'

Chapter Four

MYSTERIES OF THE MIND

Psychologists, psychiatrists and neurologists have been able to understand much of the workings of the mind. Yet it is still a mystery why some children are born outstanding geniuses, and why people can suddenly regain their memory after years of total amnesia. The work of hypnotists has shown that it is possible to do remarkable things to the mind, and others have given undeniable evidence of out-of-body experiences. Locked inside the human mind is a powerful, and perhaps inpenetrable, web of mystery . . .

Child Prodigies

In the 4th century BC the Greek philosopher Plato first tried to identify and channel the potential genius of child prodigies. 'They are the Children of Gold,' he proclaimed. He tried to predict whether they were most likely to have scholarly parents. Plato thought that, detected early enough and encouraged in the study of philosophy and metaphysics, prodigies could change the world in just one generation.

However, there is no predicting where a child prodigy will spring from. He or she may be the son or daughter of aspiring intellectual parents or of poor peasants who lead simple lives. All that the Golden Children have in common is awesome, unexplained mental powers.

In infancy, child prodigies usually display an astonishing command of language, literature, music or mathematics while children of a similar age are still struggling to speak their first words.

What we do not know is whether baby genius comes from inherited brain power, from a chance development in the womb, or an environmental factor at birth. One answer stems from an American experiment to try to produce Golden Children by genetic selection. The Nobel Sperm Bank in Escondido, California, was formed in 1980 by an elderly, eccentric millionaire, Robert Graham. It was to provide intelligent women who wanted to be mothers of superior babies with the male sperm of Nobel Prize-winning geniuses.

The aim of the sperm bank was, and still is, to increase dramatically the number of highly intelligent or gifted children in future generations. The first deliberately-conceived baby genius was born in 1982 to a 41-year-old unmarried psychologist, Afton Blake, in Los Angeles. She chose her baby's father from a portfolio, listing attributes which included good physical appearance and a high level of intelligence. The anonymous donor, identified by the sperm bank only as Number 28, is a brilliant computer scientist at a European university and an accomplished musician and athlete. His son, born in August 1982, was named Doron, an anagram of donor. By the time Doron was four months old, psychologists testing him at the University of California's Child Development Center declared that the baby had an IQ (Intelligence Quotient) of 200. The average rating is 100. At two years old, Doron was developing faster than children of the same age.

However, other child geniuses have astonished the world by their difference to their parents. One of the greatest geniuses and exceptional scientists of all time, Albert Einstein, was born the son of a bankrupt businessman in Ulm, West Germany, whose engineering workshop was barely profitable enough to support the family. The young Einstein spent much of his childhood visiting Bavarian taverns with his parents. His mother, although fond of music and literature, had no outstanding talents to pass on to her son.

By the time he was 14 years old, Albert Einstein had taught himself complex geometry and mathematics and was on his way to winning a place at the University of Zurich. In his mid-twenties he announced the first part of the Theory of Relativity and began to unlock the secrets of the Universe. Ten years later he had a scientific work published which explained the inner workings of the atom – and eventually led to the development of nuclear bombs and atomic power. Yet there had never been a hint of genius in the ordinary characteristics of his parents, Hermann and Pauline.

It was perhaps understandable that Wolfgang Amadeus Mozart, born in 1756, might show some musical ability. His father, Leopold, was himself a tolerable violinist. But the toddler outshone his father almost as soon as he could walk. At the age of three he taught himself to pick out chords on the keyboard of a harpsichord. At the age of five the child began to compose music while his father struggled to write down the score for him.

Soon Mozart mastered the technique of writing down musical notations for himself, and a year later performed before the Austrian Emperor in Vienna. At seven years old his first compositions were published. He gave recitals in Paris and Brussels, having taught himself to play the violin. The following year he played to George III in London, accompanied Queen Charlotte in an aria, wrote two symphonies and presented the score for one of his compositions to the British Museum.

His first opera, *La Finta Semplice,* was written at the age of 12. In the same year he wrote an operetta, two symphonies and a Mass. At 14 he was knighted by the Pope. Despite his dozens of symphonies and operas, Mozart finally died in poverty at the age of only 35, an enigmatic musical mystery and prodigy.

In the world of literature, the German poet and dramatist, Johann Goethe, and the British philosopher-economist, John Stuart Mill, were both able to read Greek by the age of three. Thomas Babington Macaulay, the 19th-century poet-historian, astonished and frightened his parents when, at only one year old, he looked out of the window of his nursery and asked profoundly, 'Is the smoke of that chimney coming from Hell?'

Conversely, the greatest playwright in the English language, William Shakespeare, was not a child prodigy. Nor was his genius passed on from his father, John. John Shakespeare was a prosperous businessman who overspent and in order to pay off his debts forced his son to leave school and seek

Ruth Lawrence received an Oxford University degree at 13.

employment. There is some evidence that Shakespeare was a teenage hooligan and thief, who was forced to flee from his home in Stratford after being caught deer poaching on the land of a local nobleman, Sir Thomas Lucy. Only in his late twenties did Shakespeare's timeless literary talent emerge and flourish.

In the 20th century, computer records have revealed a number of child prodigies in education. Wider access to university education has resulted in younger university entrants. The youngest entrant on record is Liu Xiaobin, the son of two teachers. Born in Hefei, China, in 1981, he passed his university exams at the age of five. At the age of two, Liu could read 3,600 complex Chinese characters.

Boy genius Andragone DeMello, born in 1977, became the youngest person to graduate from an American university when, at the age of 11, he gained a degree in mathematics from the University of California at Santa Cruz. Andragone first astounded his parents by saying 'Hello', when he was only seven weeks old. At two-and-a-half years old he was playing chess and working on geometry problems. At the age of three he calculated the volume of his bathwater and at four he was learning Greek, physics and philosophy. He was studying geology and geophysics at six years old and by the age of eight he had written complex computer programs.

His father, flamenco guitar player Augustine DeMello, admitted, 'I don't know where this amazing talent and genius comes from. He certainly hasn't inherited it from me. It sometimes frightens me being the parent of a child prodigy.'

In Britain, the youngest child prodigy to enter university is Ruth Lawrence. She gained a first class degree in mathematics at Oxford when she was only 13 and immediately began studying for a doctorate, hoping to beat the 18th-century record of Scottish prodigy Colin MacLaurin. (MacLaurin became Professor of Mathematics at Marischal College, Aberdeen, in 1717 when he was only 19 years old.)

From an early age, when she first showed signs of unusual intelligence, Ruth was coached intensively by her father: Harry Lawrence gave up his job as a computer consultant to become his daughter's full-time tutor. Many educational specialists who acknowledge Ruth's brilliant talent also claim that the relentless energy and instruction of her scientifically bright father has been a major factor in encouraging her success.

However, no one can account for the mysterious talents of baby Anthony McQuone of Weybridge, Surrey, who could speak Latin and quote Shakespeare at the age of two. His father, Anthony, claimed, 'I have no special talents and I have never had the ability to give Anthony any special coaching. He often corrects my grammar when I talk to him and he can produce such extraordinary facts from out of the blue that I have to buy an encyclopedia just to check what my baby son is telling me is correct.'

Anthony, who amuses himself by identifying and repeating the trademark symbols of 200 different models of motor car, has his own strange explanation for the source of his literary and linguistic knowledge. Interviewed by journalists in 1984, the two-year-old insisted that all the information was passed to him by a mysterious invisible friend, Adam. The toddler insisted that Adam was a grown-up with black hair, brown eyes, wearing a toga and *caliga* (latin for sandals). He added as an afterthought, 'Adam has a Van Dyke beard, too.'

Not only through intellectual achievement do child geniuses astonish the grown-up world. They can show the mature judgement and physical skill of experienced adults, or even beat them at their own games.

The youngest British international athlete was ten-year-old diver Beverly Williams, who competed against the USA in 1967. In 1988, 11-year-old Tom Gregory made sporting history by swimming the English Channel. The youngest ever boxing world title holder was Wilfred Benitz, who became light welter-weight champion in 1976 at 17 years old. The youngest international football player, Norman Whiteside, was the same age when he played for Northern Ireland in 1982. Five-year-old Coby Orr of Texas holds the record for the youngest golf player to score a hole in one, but the youngest to win the Open Golf Championship was 16-year-old Tom Morris, in 1868. Boris Becker was just a year older when he won the Men's Singles championship at Wimbledon in 1985, though Lottie Dod was only 15 when she won the Ladies Singles in 1887.

The mysterious world of child prodigies can bring wonder and delight to their parents, but it can also lead to misery and agony for little geniuses who feel alienated from children of their own age.

The brilliance of 12-year-old Ukrainian Seriozha Grishin gave him and his mother, Tamara, five years of bureaucratic torture from the Soviet education officials. He had been able to talk at the age of four months, walk at eight months and read and play the piano when he was little more than a year old.

The problems for Seriozha began when he was seven and his mother tried to enrol him in a local school in the town of Krivoy Rog, in the Ukraine. She wanted her gifted son to study along with children much older than him, but the school principal decided he would have to attend classes with other seven-year-olds. His teachers dismissed his talents, and his classmates called him an idiot, because his intellectual conversations were beyond them. They made him an outcast and used to lie in wait for him outside class to bully him and beat him up. His tormented mother, separated from her husband, eventually took him out of school and gave up her job as a music teacher to tutor him at home. The local authorities investigated the case, and committed Tamara Grishin to a mental hospital. They wrote on their official case file: 'Abnormal mother who does not work herself and refuses to let her son attend school. She is guilty of sheer disorder and failing to look after her child.'

Fortunately, within a few weeks friends and relatives had managed to get her released from the hospital. Then Tamara took her prodigious son to higher educational and medical specialists in Moscow and Kiev.

In 1987, the boy's genius was finally recognized when he was allowed to sit the entrance exam to the country's most prestigious seat of learning, Moscow State University, where he was promptly accepted into the Faculty of Physics with students ten years older than himself.

It is still a mystery whether babies can be developed into prodigies by ambitious parents who exploit their infant's abilities.

Perhaps Golden Children can simply be born to any parents, regardless of inherited intelligence.

Do child prodigies really have a mysterious gift that cannot be explained? Literary genius George Bernard Shaw was in no doubt about the futility of genetic selection as a way of producing child geniuses. The grizzled, bearded playwright was once approached by a gorgeous young actress who suggested that, with his brains and her beauty, they could produce a Golden Child to astound the world. He wrote to her, politely: 'But, alas, what if the child inherits MY looks and YOUR brains?'!

Hypnotism

I ts critics decry it as one of the most dangerous of the Black Arts, its supporters praise it as a safe and sound way of unlocking the full potential of the human brain. The baffling mystery, which has caused centuries of impassioned argument between scientists, psychiatrists and psychologists, is the awesome power of hypnosis.

Is it a force for good or evil, or just a harmless delusion and an entertaining trick of stage performers? The scientific experts of the British Medical

Association have condemned stage hynotism as dangerous. Performers usually know little about the mental and emotional backgrounds of the volunteers whom they call upon, for the delight of their audiences, to perform bizarre tricks and actions under hypnosis. But other medical authorities claim that hypnotism, and especially self-hypnosis, is a powerful psychological tool which can help patients lead fuller, healthier and more confident lives.

Tales of altered human behaviour during trance-like rituals were common in the histories of priests of Ancient Greek temples and African witch doctors, but it was not until the 18th century that the possible power of hypnotic suggestion began to be studied in any depth by doctors and psychologists in modern Europe.

In the 1700s, Austrian doctor Franz Mesmer, a devoted astrologist, concluded that distant stars affected human behaviour through their weak sources of magnetism. If that was the case, he reasoned, then bringing his patients into actual contact with more powerful sources, by stroking magnets over their heads, should produce even more profound results.

He began to experiment with patients in his consulting rooms in Vienna, reporting that cases of hysteria, madness and nervous disorders were being cured after his patients had entered a semi-conscious dream state. Soon, Mesmer realized that he didn't even need to apply magnetic iron rods to his patients: simply by using his fingertips, lowering the lights in the room and talking soothingly to his subjects, he could produce the same results. This was not the power of magnetism, Mesmer decided, but some unexplained force flowing between him and his patient. He called it 'animal magnetism'.

The hundreds of patients who flocked to see Dr Mesmer soon coined a new definition – 'Mesmerism'. But the Viennese police who infiltrated the mysterious goings-on in his consulting rooms decided he was conducting spiritualist seances instead of medical sessions, and his practice was banned.

In 1770, Mesmer moved to Paris and his revolutionary techniques took the French capital by storm. By 1784, so many of his followers had begun the practice of Mesmerism that the French Academies of Sciences and Medicine began their own investigation at the request of King Louis XVI, who had become worried that the new techniques were swamping the study of conventional medical practice.

At the same time, Professor Chastenet de Puysegur, a former President of the Medical Society of Lyons, who was conducting his own experiments, observed a new phenomenon. Once he had his subjects in a trance, he could actually control their actions by the merest suggestion. He appeared to have total control over their own will. De Puysegur's conclusions, together with the Academy report, was enough to convince King Louis and his medical

Franz Anton Mesmer developed the doctrine of 'animal magnetism'.

authorities that Mesmerism was a dangerous cult of evil mind-benders who would corrupt and dominate French citizens.

Mesmer was discredited, and in 1789 he moved to Switzerland where he died in obscurity 36 years later, still convinced that he had tapped the power of the human mind, and embittered that he had been rejected by the leading researchers of orthodox medicine.

However, Mesmer's techniques lived on, not as a serious tool of medical research, but mostly as a form of public entertainment for stage shows and parlour games.

There was no further serious research until 1842, when hard-headed Scottish psychologist James Braid undertook his own experiments. Braid found he could induce a trance just by asking his patients to concentrate their vision on a bright light held before their eyes. The reactions of his patients he defined as 'somnambulism', literally sleep-walking, and he coined a new phrase for his work – hypnotism.

His work sparked off a revival of medical experiments, which included surgery being performed on willing patients who experienced no pain while doctors carried out major operations. However, most of the eminent surgeons of the day, like London specialist Sir Benjamin Brodie, who had watched a hypnotized patient having his leg amputated, dismissed the technique as little more than 'a debasing superstition'; and once again hypnotism became the entertaining tool of stage performers.

Even eminent medical men who still believed that hypnotism had some scientific value could not resist the temptation to demonstrate the demeaning qualities of their powers. There was, for instance, a celebrated 19th-century surgeon, Rudolf Heidenhain, who liked to conclude his lectures on hypnotism by putting some of his eminent colleagues in a trance and making them crawl on all fours on the floor, barking like dogs, or purring like cats and lapping up milk from imaginary saucers.

The Victorian obsession with hypnotism in the music halls of England further debased the technique. Audiences howled with laughter as willing volunteers clambered on stage and went through degrading acts like stripping off their clothes and trying to play music on imaginary instruments.

Later still, in the 20th century, even the sober and respectable directors of the BBC were humiliated and baffled when they decided to try to combine the entertainment value of a stage hypnotism act with a serious study of the phenomenon. It was in the early days of television, in 1946, when the BBC men conducted their own experiment. During a rehearsal in their broadcast studios at Alexandra Palace in north London, members of the production crew sat in a studio as a stage hypnotist put them in a trance. When the producer asked his cameramen and studio technicians to move to the next sequence in his script, he got no response: the entire production team at their camera viewfinders and in front of the monitor screens in the control room were all in a deep trance. The director eventually had to ask the hypnotist to free his staff from the mind-numbing effects of the trance and to snap them out of their frozen state.

After this event, the BBC decided they would never again attempt to broadcast any live display of hypnotism, for fear of sending the viewers of their fledgling broadcast service into hypnotic trances in front of their TV sets at home. And since then, the BBC have maintained a strict ban on broadcasting examples of hypnotists at work, although viewers are allowed to see subjects who are already in a trance, provided they cannot witness the actual act of hypnotism itself.

Six years later, in 1952, live demonstrations of hypnotism suffered another severe blow. A stage volunteer, Grace Rains-Bath, who had agreed to be hypnotised during a performance at a London theatre, sued hypnotist Ralph Slater who had 'regressed' her on stage until she behaved and acted like a young child. Mrs Rains-Bath claimed in court that she had suffered depression and anxiety and had cried like an infant for months afterwards. She was awarded damages against the stage performer.

Later that year, Parliament passed the Hypnosis Act, which gave local authorities the power to ban stage hypnotism shows. That ban throughout the whole of London remained in force until 1988.

Hypnosis has still been practised elsewhere with varying degrees of public acceptance or scepticism. One particular field where it has had a mixed reaction is in police work, where it has been used mainly to attempt to extract vital pieces of half-remembered evidence from victims and witnesses to crimes. In the United States, the Boston Police Department has a specialist Hypnosis Unit, which reports that in about 75 per cent of the cases in which they are asked to give assistance, enough new information has been provided by witnesses in a trance to give investigators new leads. Their senior investigator, Inspector Patrick Brady, explained: 'A person who has seen a violent crime committed or been the victim of a violent experience has an automatic tendency to blot that out of their mind. It is a fundamental self-protection mechanism to save that person from emotional trauma and psychological disturbance. Our job is to unblock that mental barrier through hypnosis and get our witness to recall details which their mind would sooner forget. We find that interviews under hypnosis are just as valuable in providing proof of innocence as proof of guilt.

'Someone falsely arrested and charged with committing a crime may come up with vital proof under hypnosis, perhaps remembering a key witness who will attest to his or her innocence. Hypnosis on a victim of a violent attack who wants only to forget their experience can help us construct an accurate identikit picture of their attacker. Other details which have been suppressed by the mind, like a car licence number, can also spill out of a subject in a trance and help us to solve vicious crimes.'

Although the evidence of hypnotised witnesses is often enough for police to pursue a fresh lead, it is only very rarely allowed to be presented in American courts. Sergeant Charles Diggett, a veteran New York cop who used investigative hypnosis in more than 400 cases during his career, added: 'Interviews under hypnosis must be videotaped and kept on file until the case is closed. In order for the tape to be accepted in court, the hypnotist has to be seen to be neutral throughout the session. They must keep silent whenever possible and let the witness do the talking. If an investigator prompts his subject or makes any suggestions, the information produced cannot be accepted as evidence.

'Even allowing for subconscious prompting, I firmly believe it is impossible for a hypnotist to manipulate his subject's mind. It is impossible to make someone say or do something against their will. Experiments have proved this time and time again. Hypnosis isn't mind control, it is only a trigger that can release what's already there by refreshing the memory.

'A person can tell lies under hypnosis, just as they might when giving a normal statement, or else, in rare cases, they can fantasize, but further investigation will eventually reveal the truth.'

But despite the American experience, in 1988 the British police forces were strongly advised against using hypnosis to obtain evidence. In a confidential notice to Britain's 43 police forces, Home Secretary Douglas Hurd warned that hypnotic evidence would be ruled as inadmissible in courts and that witnesses would not be cross-examined about anything they had recalled while in a trance.

Outside the fields of forensic and medical research, hypnosis has been hailed as a revived psychological tool by a new wave of practitioners. These people prefer to define their techniques as 'auto-suggestion', where their subjects are shown how to hypnotise themselves in order to increase positive aspects of their own personalities and mental powers.

Driving instructor Doug Beattie of Dundee was threatened with blacklisting by the Driving Instructors' Association after he revealed that he calmed his students' nerves by hypnotising them before their driving tests. He admitted: 'I make two visits to their homes in the two weeks before their test and hypnotise them. On the day of their test I take them to a side-street near the test centre and hypnotise them again to keep them calm, cool and collected during their driving exam. It seems to work. Eight out of ten pupils pass their test first time.'

Several leading celebrities also claim to have benefited from lessons in 'self-hypnosis'. Comedy actress and writer Lily Tomlin, who was struggling to complete a film script, claims she used self-hypnosis to speed up her writing and produce a box-office hit. Actor Sylvester Stallone used hypnosis to overcome shyness and lack of self-confidence – and to write the script of his enormously successful Rambo movies.

Nervous schoolchildren have been encouraged to pass exams, and sportsmen and women have equally been spurred on to greater achievements by hypnosis. Boxing champ Muhammad Ali, for example, used self-induced hypnosis as a 'psyching' process before his professional bouts.

Although London's Westminster Council lifted its 36-year ban on public performances of hypnotism in 1988, there were still adverse reports from around the world of innocent people suffering at the hands of stage hypnotists. In Italy, police had to scour Rome to trace stage hypnotist Giucas Casella after he had given a hypnosis demonstration on the national television network. Casella was found in a Rome hospital, recovering from a wound in his neck. He had inserted a metal skewer to demonstrate to his TV viewers that his mind could ignore pain while he was under a trance. The Rome police had gone in search of Casella after an urgent call from medical authorities in Palermo, where eight-year-old Giusto Durante had spent three hours in a trance after watching the television performance. The boy was unconscious, with his hands so tightly clasped together that his fingers had become swollen and black. Even powerful sedative drugs injected by doctors failed to relax his muscles. Young Giusto unclasped his blackened fingers only after the hypnotist shouted to him down the telephone: 'One, two, three, your hands are free!'

On another occasion, Scottish psychiatrist Dr Prem Misra warned that he was still giving treatment to 16 patients who had suffered after-effects from stage hypnosis performances. One was a man who still stripped off all his clothes every time he heard a hand-clap. Another was an elderly woman who had been 'regressed' to her youth, which had been spent in a Nazi death camp. She was now reliving the horrors anew, long after the mental scars had healed. A third was a young wife who had become schizophrenic after a stage hypnotist had convinced her, playfully, that her husband had been unfaithful to her.

Dr Misra explained: 'There are powerful mental forces at work in hypnotism which can be potentially very, very dangerous.'

Amnesia

Memory can be the fond recollection of a joyful past event, or the recapture of a painful moment which has caused grief and sadness. Whatever the emotion, the powers of recall hidden inside the human brain are a living record of our past experiences. Sometimes they can be recalled with startling clarity, at other times they are no more than a hazy recollection of fleeting moments in our own personal history.

Memory is also the function of our stored wisdom, a living record of our acquired learning, which gives us the ability and skill to tackle present-day tasks, from the performance of complex jobs to recognition of familiar, everyday objects, places and people.

But what happens deep inside the memory banks of the brain when a person is stricken by amnesia? Amnesia is not simply a period of forgetfulness. It is a profound mental helplessness which prevents victims from remembering any past events, trivial or crucial.

The memory cells, situated towards the rear of the brain, just above the portion which controls sight, are well protected inside the bony armour of the skull. Linked to other centres which command the mastery of thought, feeling, movement and recognition, the memory is capable of storing billions of bits of information in the form of electro-chemical signals. Neurological specialists have mapped the distinctly different areas of the brain accurately, but they are still unable to fully understand the unexplained mysteries of its inner workings.

Powers of mental storage and recall vary from individual to individual. Many so-called memory experts claim that memory resembles a muscle which can be strengthened and improved with constant exercise. Science knows of rare cases of 'eidetic' or 'photographic' memory – the ability to re-project remembered material just as if it is visually displayed and to be able to recall fine detail.

Photographic memory was the key factor in allowing a 28-year-old female bank clerk from Kenton, Middlesex, to give police an astonishingly accurate description of a man who broke into her flat and raped her. The attacker had assaulted her in the darkness of her bedroom, and had switched on a lamp for only a few seconds to steal some loose change from her purse. It was enough for the young woman to recall his features so precisely that the artist's impression she helped to draw for police was as accurate as a photograph. The rapist was arrested almost immediately and sentenced at the Old Bailey in 1986 to seven years imprisonment.

More usually, photographic memory is displayed as a curious mental oddity. The most prodigious memory man on record is Bhandanta Vicitsara, a Burmese monk who could recite from memory 16,000 pages of Bhuddist prayers. To give another example, engineer Dominic O'Brien of Guildford, Surrey, who suffered from dyslexia, was able to memorize the correct sequence of 312 playing cards displayed in front of him in a random sequence. Testers and umpires who shuffled six packs of cards spent 90 minutes showing him the cards, one at a time. One-and-a-half hours later, he was able to repeat the exact order of the cards, taking half an hour to recite them.

At the other end of the memory scale are the sufferers of amnesia who cannot recall key moments of their lives. Amnesia is usually the result of physical damage to the skull which actually injures the cells of the brain. Often, the brain recovers with only a gap in memory. Car crash victim Alan Woodward of Bristol, for example, spent a year in the twilight world of amnesia, unable to recognize his wife and two children, until his memory was jogged by a sports headline in a local newspaper. As soon as he saw it, he was able to reel off the 11 names of the players of his local football team. Afterwards the memory of his own personal life slowly began to return.

Another road accident victim, Nick Reading of Stockton, Warwickshire, had total amnesia at the age of 27 when he suffered head injuries. He could recall nothing of his childhood, his marriage or the birth of his first child. Even when he had recovered fully from the physical effects of his injuries, he remained unemployed, unable to remember the skills he had learned as an experienced and highly-paid bricklayer.

Physical injury is not the only cause of total amnesia. Traumatic terror can produce such a mental shock that a victim blots out the memory of it so effectively that they are unable to recall the event years later, regardless of how hard they try. One such event may have been the cause of the bout of amnesia that Hungarian-born Maria Tandi had, when she lost nearly all memory of the first 28 years of her life. By 1988, when she was 78, hospital officials in Claybury, Essex, where she had been a patient for half a century, had still not been able to piece together the origins of the severe fit of depression which had caused her loss of memory.

Maria, a former domestic servant in Wales, was first admitted to hospital when she lost the ability, or the will, to speak. Even 50 years later, she was still only able to mutter a few simple words and phrases. Maria was able to recall only fragments of her childhood. She remembered a garden with cherry trees and flowers in a remote corner of Eastern Hungary. Her next memory was of events nearly 20 years later, when she worked as a maid in an apartment in Dob-Utca, a smart residential district of Budapest. She could also recount the names of her six sisters, but could not describe them. Her mind remained blank, until she remembered a train journey across Europe and a short sea crossing to Dover, where she joined other refugee girls hoping to start a new life in England.

Shortly after Maria arrived in England, she received a letter from home, telling her of the death of her mother. Psychiatrists believe that the shock may have been so great that not only did Maria's memory close down, but she even forgot how to speak. Fifty years later, she was still living quite contentedly in her silent world, totally unaware of anything that had happened to her since 1938, including the cataclysm of World War II.

An equally tragic and mysterious case of amnesia struck BBC radio producer and medieval music historian Clive Wearing. In 1984, he suffered a brain inflammation when the virus, *Herpes simplex*, which normally causes blisters such as cold sores, suddenly flared up in his brain tissues. From then on, he lived in the terrifying world of a man locked into the present, with no memory of anything that had happened around him any longer than a few seconds before. He would often break down in tears and rush to his wife, Deborah, when he noticed her at the other end of the room (thinking he was having a long-awaited reunion with her) even though he had been talking to her only a few minutes before. The disastrous brain inflammation which almost cost the musician his life in a fevered coma that lasted for a month left him with irreversible amnesia.

It is a rare condition. Although about 50 people a year in Britain fall victim to the same illness, most of them make a full recovery. In an attempt to cope with the simple tasks of day-to-day living, Wearing kept a continuous diary of everything around him. His ability to read and write were unaffected, but he had difficulty reading his diary entries because, no matter how often he looked at the pages of the book, he could not remember his own handwriting. Within a minute of studiously poring over a diary entry, he would totally forget what he had read.

Mealtimes were a constant agony for him, as he frequently ate until he was sick, thinking he had only just sat down to dinner and forgetting that he had already been at the table for half-an-hour and consumed several courses. He was aware only of the food which was then in front of him, and did not realize he had eaten his fill.

Surprisingly, his awareness only of a small segment of the present did not rob him of his musical talents. As part of a documentary research film, Clive Wearing was taken back to Cambridge University, where he had first graduated with a degree in music, and was asked to play the organ in King's

College. It was an experience he had enjoyed countless times before as a student and a graduate, but when he saw the chapel organ he told the film crew and his wife: 'I've never seen this before. What am I supposed to do?'

However, once seated on the organ stool, Wearing played the instrument perfectly, to his own amazement. Seconds after he completed the organ recital, he turned round. Seeing his wife, he grasped her emotionally, not remembering that she had sat behind him during the entire performance. Turning round again, he saw the organ and was convinced, yet again, that he was seeing it for the first time. Then he asked to be introduced to the members of the documentary film crew, who had been his constant companions for days.

Later, when Wearing saw the film footage of his performance at the college organ, he watched in bewilderment, not able to remember the occasion and hardly daring to believe that he was witnessing himself playing the music. By the time he had finished watching the film, he could not even remember the opening sequence of the documentary or the scene where he had played the King's College organ.

For the largest group of amnesia sufferers – elderly people striken by senile dementia – there is some hope on the horizon. More than half a million people in Britain are victims of the brain disorder Alzheimer's disease, which relentlessly robs them of their memory and their chance of a fulfilling, independent life. Researchers and scientists have now discovered synthetic hormones which can alter the workings of the human mind.

One of Britain's most distinguished scientists, Nobel Prize winner Professor Archer Martin, had to abandon his pioneering studies in 1984 when, at the age of 74, he contracted Alzheimer's disease and began to lose his memory. Although the disease was in a relatively early stage, Professor Martin found he could no longer remember the details of notes he had just studied, and specialist doctors at Addenbrooke's Hospital, in Cambridge, warned him that nothing could be done to halt the decline of his brilliant mind. Within a few years, they told him, he would be 'a human vegetable'.

By 1988, after Professor Martin had volunteered to become a guinea pig in trials of a new experimental memory drug THA at London's Institute of Psychiatry, his astonishing mental powers began to show dramatic signs of recovery. As he prepared to renew his own research career he found that, for the first time in years, he was able to analyse and remember complicated articles in the science journal *Nature*. He said: 'My own life had begun to fall apart around me. I even missed presentations and awards ceremonies because, after I set out to attend them, I would forget where I was going and I would board the wrong train or plane. Now my brain has been restored to useful work, I can enjoy reading research papers once more, although I had to renew my subscriptions to scientific journals. I had completely forgotten that my wife had cancelled them because they were useless to me when I had no real memory to benefit from them.'

Even though researchers still do not understand the workings of the human memory or the emotions milling around inside our highly developed brains, they expect the 1990s will produce a spectacular breakthrough in 'brain pills' that may make amnesia only a memory. Moreover, scientists predict a new range of synthetic hormones that will totally alter human mental abilities and emotions. At Utrecht in Holland, university research Professor David De Wied prophesied that the discovery of a new 'memory drug', the hormone DGAVP, will wipe out the scourge of amnesia and may even be used on healthy patients to dramatically increase their memory power. Also in Utrecht, the 'contentment pill', based on the hormone ACTH 4–9, has been shown to produce feelings of wellbeing and confidence in depressed elderly people who have almost given up the will to live. This drug has also been found to increase concentration and motivation in healthy young people.

In Canada the 'forget drug', the hormone oxytocin, which is released naturally in women to ease them through the pain of childbirth, has been tested on disturbed psychiatric patients to wipe out the memories of traumatically disturbing experiences that have left victims deeply emotionally scarred. Dr De Wied predicts confidently; 'We will be able in the future to affect all the processes of the brain. And if, as it seems likely, the ageing process of the brain is caused by the deficiency of hormones, we will be able to replace them and perhaps even reverse the ageing process itself.'

Out-of-Body Experiences

It is an accepted scientific fact that no two bodies can occupy the same space at the same time. But there is one mystery which has puzzled philosophers and researchers for centuries: Can one body occupy two distant spaces at the same time? Or, is it possible to be in two different locations in the same instant?

Many recent studies of 'out-of-body experiences' claim that it is perfectly possible for a person's own psyche to drift out of their body and move to another location, while their physical being stays in its original position, undisturbed.

Some personal testimonies to such experiences, or 'astral projections', as they are defined by mystics and psychics, may just be the result of delusions and imagination. Most of the first-hand accounts come from patients who have undergone surgery. Usually, their experiences can be accounted for by the anaesthetics they have been administered, which have been known to produce wild fluctuations of brain behaviour in unconscious patients. But other, more positively credible reports, have been compiled by research into hospital patients who have actually been declared clinically dead and who have been resuscitated after a period of time – sometimes many minutes. Having returned to consciousness, they have given similar accounts of experiencing their souls parting from their bodies and travelling in an unknown dimension.

In many primitive cultures, the belief that the soul can leave the body and travel to another place runs deep. Ancient Indian religious teachings detail how supernatural powers can be achieved through meditation, including the ability to leave the physical body and fly through the sky. Even more recent folklore says it is unwise to wake a sleepwalker, because it may prevent the soul being able to re-enter the body, which is in a physical, but soulless, state.

Independent eye-witness evidence of a person being physically, or spiritually, in two places at the same time is virtually unknown; but the evidence seems to exist in the case of the Catholic friar St Anthony of Padua. St Anthony lived from 1195 to 1231 and travelled as a preacher in northern Italy and southern and central France. He was an honoured visitor to many

131

churches and was in great demand as a guest preacher throughout his far-flung parish. According to meticulous medieval church records, he preached two memorable sermons – in two different places at the same time.

While preaching a sermon in a church in Limoges in France in 1226, during which all the congregation watched their guest friar with careful attention, St Anthony very abruptly stopped in the middle of his prayers. He pulled the cowl of his robes over his head and knelt silently for several minutes. The congregation waited, restlessly, until the preacher finally rose to his feet again and continued his address to the churchgoers. Only later that day did the townsfolk of Limoges realize that the Saint's brief interruption to his devotions was not an opportunity for solitary meditation. To their amazement and delight they found that while the figure of the friar had been kneeling in full sight of the entire congregation, he had appeared at the same time before the congregation of another church several kilometres away and read the lesson during the service. Then he had disappeared from the pulpit just as mysteriously as he had arrived.

Although St Anthony himself never left any written record of his apparent out-of-body experiences, the same phenomenon has been described many times by figures as diverse as eminent scientists and tortured prisoners. Dr Auckland Geddes, later Lord Geddes, described his own experiences in clinical detail in a paper presented to the Royal Medical Society of Edinburgh in 1937. Lord Geddes recounted to his fellow members of the respected Society how he had been in bed at home, stricken with acute food poisoning, when he suddenly became gravely ill. 'I wanted to ring for assistance, but found I could not, so I gave up the attempt,' he said.

'I realised I was very ill but at no time did my consciousness appear to be dimmed, but I suddenly realized that my consciousness was separating from another consciousness which was also "me".

'Gradually, I realized that I could see not only my body and the bed in which it was, but everything in the whole house and garden, and then I realized that I was seeing not only things at home, but in London as well, in fact wherever my attention was directed. I was free in a time dimension of space.'

Geddes recalled how his spirit re-entered his body, in terms amazingly similar to the accounts of others who have experienced the same detached feelings of hovering between life and death. He told the meeting that he saw his maid enter his bedroom. 'I realized she got a terrible shock,' he said. 'I saw her hurry to the telephone. I saw my doctor leave his own patients at his surgery and hurry over to my house and I heard him say, "He is nearly gone." I heard him quite clearly speaking to me on the bed, but I was not in touch with my own body and I could not answer him.

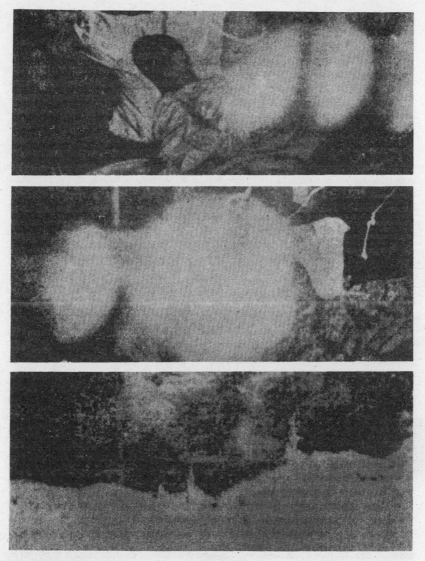

These photographs show the spirit leaving a patient's body.

'I was really cross when he took a syringe and rapidly injected my body. As my heart began to beat more strongly, I was drawn back and I was intensely annoyed because I was so interested and I was just beginning to understand where I was and what I was seeing.

'I came back into my body, really angry at being pulled back, and once back, all the clarity of vision of everything and anything disappeared and I was just possessed of a glimmer of consciousness which was suffused with pain.

'I think the whole thing simply means that, but for medical treatment, I was dead to the three dimensional world.'

The experience of being able to roam freely through space and time is consistent with the account of a violent prisoner, Ed Morrell, who was held in Arizona State Penitentiary in 1910. While in prison, Morrell frequently had to be restrained by warders and put into a straitjacket. Morrell claimed that his torture was added to when the bindings were soaked in water and slowly shrunk, squeezing him so tightly that he lapsed into unconsciousness. During these agonized blackouts, he felt his spirit float free and he was able to travel at will, even examining the perimeter area around the prison in accurate detail, in readiness for an escape plan. Morrell also claimed that he could direct his spirit freely across the United States and that in one of his out-of-body travels he met the woman he was later to track down and marry after his release from the penitentiary.

Morrell told the story of his experiences later in San Francisco to writer Jack London, who used them as the basis for his book *The Star Rover*.

A large amount of detailed research into out-of-body experiences was gathered by American psychiatrist Dr Elisabeth Khubler-Ross, who spent over 20 years counselling terminally ill patients, young and old. Khubler-Ross's records of the graphic accounts she received from her patients hovering on the brink of death tally almost exactly with the reported experiences of Lord Geddes made some 40 years before.

The patients told the psychiatrist about their sensations of floating free, feeling at peace and spiritually powerful, before being summoned back, usually reluctantly, to their pain-racked bodies. She documented her findings in her book *On Death and Dying*, published in 1970, and added her own personal endorsement later: 'Before I started working with dying patients, I did not believe in life after death. I now believe in it beyond a shadow of a doubt.'

Dr Khubler-Ross reported that many of her patients who had come to accept the inevitable outcome of their terminal diseases were convinced that their spirits left their bodies for prolonged periods, during which they were surrounded with a powerful, peaceful force, and that they often encountered dead friends and relatives who had come to prepare them for a new existence after death. The patients felt great joy and happiness, and few of them felt any desire to return to their physical bodies. Many of them who had suffered short periods of clinical death with no detectable heartbeat or pulse were drawn back to their bodies only out of a sense of responsibility to those they would leave behind, or by the reassurance of a vision of a heavenly presence who explained that it was not yet time for them to die. Dr Khubler-Ross was convinced that many of her patients who had floated free of their bodies before being medically revived had no fear of finally dying.

The writer, novelist and war correspondent Ernest Hemingway had his own visions of death when he was wounded by a burst of shrapnel while acting as a volunteer ambulanceman in Italy during World War I. He did not exactly undergo any great spiritual surges as he lay seriously injured and semi-conscious, waiting for the battlefield first aid which saved his life. In his own terse style, Hemingway reported it as: '...my soul, or something, coming right out of my body, like you'd pull a silk handkerchief out of a pocket by one corner. It flew around and then came back and went in again, and I wasn't dead any more.'

Hemingway, who, in 1961, in a fit of depression, committed suicide by shooting himself, never explained if the experience gave him any confidence, or doubts, in the prospect of life after death.

Out-of-body experiences are not solely confined to seriously ill patients, or those under sedation or close to death American researcher Dr Charles Tart, of the University of California, undertook a series of experiments to see if healthy volunteers who claimed they underwent frequent out-of-body experiences could produce any evidence under carefully controlled laboratory conditions. He put his volunteers on a bed in a darkened room, with electrical contacts wired to their head to record their brain wave patterns. Also in the room, hidden on a shelf out of sight of the volunteer, was a slip of paper with a number written on it. If the volunteer attempted to get up out of bed to try to cheat, by clambering up high to read the hidden number, the electrical contacts would break and the deception would be detected immediately. As an added precaution to prevent cheating by collusion with any of his own staff, Dr Tart used a random number generator to compute the figure 25132, which he wrote on the slip of paper himself without anyone else knowing the chosen number.

Dr Tart's most convincing volunteer was a young woman who claimed that she had enjoyed out-of-body experiences since her childhood and could induce them almost any time she wished. On her first night in the experimental 'bedroom' nothing out of the ordinary happened and the electrical brainwave patterns showed that she had a normal night's sleep. On

135

the second night, she claimed she had floated free of her body and she had seen a clock on the wall, even though the clock was hidden from her view as she lay on the bed. She reported that she had seen the clock clearly and read the time on it as 3.15 a.m. The printout of her brainwave patterns was checked against a time recorder and the researchers discovered that her sleep had become erratic and disturbed at exactly that time.

On the third night, the volunteer again reported a vision of the hidden clock in the early hours of the morning, and the time of her experience co-incided exactly with the same brainwave disturbances shown on the recorder. On the fourth night, concentrating deeply before she retired to bed, the volunteer awoke in the morning to repeat, with complete accuracy, the digits on the slip of paper lying on the shelf above her. She also said she had glanced at the clock as she read the number, and gave the time at around 6.00 a.m. The researchers later confirmed that her sleeping brainwave patterns had jumped wildly at 5.57 a.m., around the time she described her spirit as floating free of her body.

But do these crude experiments, or the personal recollections of eminent doctors, writers and hospital patients, really prove that men and women can travel away from their bodies and project their spiritual beings to other places on earth and into different dimensions? Since the publication of Dr Khubler-Ross's research, thousands of people have come forward to testify to similar experiences. Could all these just be delusions and illusions, nightmares and fits of troubled sleep?

The respected, pragmatic scientist Dr Carl Sagan of NASA's space experimental programme has his own theory, which would mean that almost anyone is capable of such an experience, and would regard it as a vivid, genuine memory of a truly spiritual event. He explains: 'Every human being has already had an experience like that of travellers who return from the land of death; the sensation of flight and emergence from darkness into light; an experience in which the heroic figure may be dimly perceived, bathed in radiance and glory. There is only one comon experience that matches this description.

'It is called birth.'

Chapter Five

BEYOND THE REALMS OF SCIENCE

Can we really believe that the powers of high-technology have reached such sophistication that we are on the brink of being able to make radio contact with aliens in outer space? You may laugh, but a number of extremely eminent scientists think we can. However, no matter how we marvel at 20th-century scientists and inventors for their brilliance, foresight and ingenuity, it seems that primitive civilizations, such as the Nazca Indians or the Dogon tribesmen, or the ancient practitioners of acupuncture could have told them more than a thing or two . . .

Alien Contact

E ver since primitive man first drew himself upright and stared up at the heavens, he has pondered the eternal question: Is there life out there? For thousands of years we have been enthralled by the awesome prospect of creatures, or beings, existing out there in other galaxies, living in civilizations far more technologically advanced than our own. The terrible bug-eyed monsters of science fiction may only have been the product of writers' imaginations, but to millions of readers such creatures are real glimpses into the future.

In our galaxy alone, there are more than 100,000 million stars, and according to eminent astronomer Professor Archibald Roy, of Glasgow University, at least one-fifth are stable and cool, like our own Sun. About half of those, some 10,000 million stars, also have planets – the most important single requirement for developing life. Astronomers hope that many of these planets will be surrounded by organic 'fog' containing vital DNA-like molecules which could be the key to life itself.

In the late 50s, the Chinese-born astrophysicist Su-Shu Huang of North-western University, Illinois, described the types of conditions in which life could exist beyond our galaxy. It should be neither too hot, so that water would evaporate, nor too cold, so that it would be permanently frozen. With a combination like this, there is no logical reason why extraterrestrial life should not take root and flourish.

The dream of sending or receiving messages from aliens in outer space is as old as man himself. Before the discovery of radio waves, we had few reliable means of sending messages over even short distances. In ancient civilizations, beacons of burning wood on hilltops were a simple, effective signalling system; but these could only spell out the most simple of messages, usually a sign of alarm. The invention of the electric telegraph by Samuel Morse in 1836 was, therefore, a great scientific leap forward. With a distinct code of short or long bursts of electricity, the whole alphabet could be used to send elaborate and clearly understood messages.

Morse Code was not restricted only to pulses transmitted down a telegraph wire. The code could work equally well by using flashes of light beamed out by a lantern, or by rays of sunlight reflected off a mirror. It was this that gave the French inventor Charles Cros the idea of constructing a giant mirror. He would use it to flash bursts of reflected sunlight from Earth to Mars, in the hope of making contact with Martians. The mirror would be tilted back and forth in a such a way that beams of light could be flashed on and off.

There were, however, problems with Cros's idea. A mirror large enough to be able to send light as far as outer space would have to be so big, it would have been impossible to tilt it. Also, there was no guarantee that the Martians, if indeed there were any, would recognize it as a message at all: it might be just light reflecting off a giant terrestrial lake. Besides, how would they recognize a message in Morse Code if they saw one? And how would they signal back to Earth? Needless to say, when Cros died in Paris in 1888, the idea died with him.

Later, engineers working for the American inventor Thomas Edison came up with a more practical idea. They proposed building a giant floating raft on Lake Michigan, USA, with arms ten miles long, strung with the newly patented electric light bulbs Edison had invented. These would be switched on for ten minutes, then off for ten minutes, giving a clear indication to any watchers in space that an intelligent civilization on Earth was trying to make contact. However, inventive and curious though he was, Thomas Edison was also a hard-headed businessman. He decided that the tens of thousands of light bulbs needed for the experiment would be better used for the more down-to-earth purposes of illuminating the homes and streets of New York and swelling his fortune, as well as for providing finance for more mundane experiments he had in mind. So this idea did not get far, either.

In the 19th century, the thought of contact with alien life sent a thrill of expectation through many curious minds, and feelings of horror in others. In 1898, the science fiction writer H G Wells gripped their imagination with his sci-fi horror story, *War of the Worlds*, in which Earth is invaded by Martians in deadly war machines. But any real attempts to contact other planets were viewed by many Victorians as an invitation to trouble: civilizations in outer space might see Earth as an easy target and come down to invade it.

Nevertheless, one Paris newspaper publisher of the time was bold enough to offer a prize of 100,000 francs for anyone who could make contact with alien life in our own galaxy, or even further out in space. As a concession to thousands of fearful readers, who warned him not to encourage their fellow countrymen to dabble in the unknown, he made one exception to the rules of the competition: there would be no prize for anyone raising an answer from Mars. The publisher explained that since everyone was pretty certain there was probably intelligent life on Mars anyway, communicating with Martians would be too easy, and it wasn't worth him risking his money! In the event, no one claimed the prize, and many Europeans, still badly rattled by the graphic fiction of H G Wells, heaved a sigh of relief that reckless scientists weren't going to advertise their presence to potentially hostile aliens after all.

But whether we like it or not, we on Earth have been beaming signals into outer space since we began radio broadcasting during the early decades of this century. Radio and television programmes broadcast around the world 'leak' out into space, and although their signals grow weaker and weaker over the vast distances, it is possible they may be intercepted in some remote galaxy.

Many scientists have already tried to unscramble incoming radio signals from the endless crackle of natural cosmic radio waves that swamp the universe. But which radio frequency they should choose to listen into, or which ones they should transmit their own messages from, is anybody's guess. Here on Earth, our radio stations all select their own individual frequencies and wavelengths to avoid their signals interfering with each other; so the job of sorting out the millions of radio frequencies and identifying alien broadcasters seems an almost impossible task.

In 1943, Dutch astronomer Hendrick Christoffel van den Hulst came up with the most logical answer so far in identifying frequencies from outer space. He calculated that if hydrogen atoms changed their energy state through cosmic influences, they would emit a tiny burst of radio energy in the 21-centimetre radio wavelength. Since hydrogen is the most abundant element in the universe, any advanced civilization with a knowledge of atomic physics and radio waves would almost certainly have discovered it. Thus, broadcasting and receiving on the 21-centimetre waveband would provide a common, intergalactic radio network.

The first official, methodically planned attempt at contacting alien life via radio waves was made in 1960, when American radio astronomer Dr Frank Drake turned the 85-foot-diameter dish antenna of the National Radio Observatory at Green Bank, West Virginia, towards the stars Tau Ceti and Epsilon Eridani. He was particularly interested in these two stars, because they appear to be of the same breed as our own Sun, and also because, on the cosmic scale, both are relatively close to us, just 11 light years away. (A light year is the distance light, and a radio signal, travels in one year, about six million, million miles.) Within 12 light years of our home planet there are 18 star systems with 26 stars and probably hundreds of unseen planets. Dr Drake's experimental radio probe, therefore, pointed at a potentially fertile part of the galaxy. The experiment was codenamed Project OZMA, after Frank L Baum's mythical Land of Oz. The project was conducted in strict secrecy, because the scientists involved feared public ridicule or criticism for wasting valuable research time and equipment. Dr Drake listened continuously, and unsuccessfully, for three months before admitting that intelligent life so close to Earth would really be too much to hope for. 'It would be a case of celestial overpopulation,' he told colleagues.

Just in case there is a possibility that alien civilizations have evolved, but have no knowledge of radio waves, Dr Drake has employed another method of letting the rest of the universe know that there is intelligent life on Earth. One of the leading scientific advisers on the 1972 Pioneer probe project, he was involved in developing the cosmic 'message in a bottle', which was thrown out into the oceans of space. The space probe, designed to explore the far-flung planet Jupiter, was launched on a special path to let it spin into deep space after it had completed its survey mission. Attached to the side of the spacecraft is a plaque, engraved with a coded message, showing the location of the planet Earth and a diagram of a woman and a man raising his hand in a greeting. Also included is a plain hint for the finder to try calling Earth on the 21-centimetre radio wavelength.

In 1976, four years after the Pioneer project began, the radio search for messages from outer space resumed again. By this time it was thought there was a slim chance that a patrolling alien spacecraft might have spotted and captured the drifting Pioneer probe as it continued its endless journey through space. American astronomers Benjamin Zuckerman and Patrick Palmer, also at Green Bank Observatory, tuned into the radio wavelength shown on the Pioneer probe. For four long years their research staff took it in turns to listen in for broadcasts, but they heard nothing but silence. Pioneer is probably still lost in the wandering debris of space, and it looks as though no one out there has yet read its message.

According to scientific author Ian Ridpath, it is just as well; for Ridpath believes the figure of a man with an upraised arm may be considered a threatening character by alien life forms. He experimented using the same gesture towards a cageful of rhesus monkeys, who form part of the same evolutionary scale as man. The monkeys thought he was about to attack, and they launched themselves towards the bars of their cage in angry defiance.

A far more colourful and welcoming message was blasted off into space in 1977. This was aboard the twin Voyager space capsules that flew to the planet Mars, the fictional home of the threatening aliens in *War of the Worlds*. The spacecraft carries two video discs that electronically portray life on 20th-century Earth. The sounds of nature are represented by the songs of birds and other animals, and peaceful greetings from the varied races and peoples on Earth are recorded in 55 different languages. Scientists admit that the chances of the Pioneer or Voyager probes being detected and recovered by alien life forms are so remote as to be beyond calculation. Travelling at only a few thousand miles a minute, the spacecraft will take hundreds of years to leave our own planetary system and reach distant galaxies.

The main hopes of opening a line of communication between us and the stars still lie in radio waves, travelling at the speed of light, and most research efforts are being concentrated in that direction.

Although Project OZMA lapsed, it was not forgotten, and it became the forerunner of dozens of schemes for eavesdropping on space. For instance, in America there is an organization called the Search for Extraterrestrial Intelligence. Known as SETI, it is backed by agencies like NASA. Film director Steven Spielberg, who made millions of dollars out of his science fiction hit film *E.T.*, is one of the many sponsors who has provided funding for their Project META, an 84-foot radio telescope hunting for unusual microwave frequencies in 'hot' areas of space. The sensitive piece of listening equipment is tucked away in the apple and peach orchards of Harvard University in Massachusetts, and the project was devised by scientist, writer and broadcaster Carl Sagan. SETI is now planning a major seven-year search, scheduled to begin on Columbus Day, 12 October 1992. This will be a coordinated world-wide effort, using newly-developed equipment capable of monitoring up to 70,000 radio channels. With the addition of new computer technology, it should soon be able to listen in on 10 million frequencies. Another phase of the project will include beaming messages to every single one of the detectable stars in the universe, in the hopes of getting a reply.

So, the race is well and truly on to find out if there is anyone out there; but it will be a long one. Even at the speed of light, a radio message may take 20 or 30 years to reach the nearest alien civilization. And it will take equally long for any aliens to send a reply back to Earth. The whole process will be rather like a very expensive, interplanetary telephone conversation, where the callers on each end of the line can only exchange brief phrases every few decades!

In the meantime, the babble of radio and television waves that have erupted from Earth since the turn of the century have a long headstart on the more recent messages of encouragement sent out by the dedicated scientists. If an alien civilization could actually decode and understand those early broadcasts, they could have already listened to radio reports of world wars, famines and disasters, and seen television broadcasts of soap operas, game shows and Presidential elections.

They may have decided that, judging by what they have heard and seen so far, they just don't want to return our calls.

The Dogon

For the 2 million members of the primitive Dogon tribe, scratching out an existence in the African republic of Mali on the edge of the Sahara Desert, life has changed little over the centuries. The tribes-people live in scattered villages, in dwellings made of mud and straw. They tend their flocks of scrawny goats, plant and reap meagre harvests of grain, and gather firewood on the sparse cliffs of the Bandiagara Plateau, 300 miles south of Timbuktu, where their ancestors settled some 500 years ago. And they worship their gods in the sky, lavishing particular reverence on the brilliant twinkling lights of the star system of Sirius, the brightest star in the night sky.

Many other tribes pay homage to the bright beacon of Sirius, beaming across space from 8.7 light years away, one of the closest stars to Earth. It is quite understandable that the attention of the early civilizations of the Northern hemisphere should be attracted to Sirius, because of its overwhelming prominence over all the other stars. The ancient Egyptians based their annual calendar on the rising of Sirius at certain times of the year, which they knew heralded the annual flooding of the Nile River.

But the belief and faith of the Dogon tribe is unique. For five centuries they have worshipped not just the vivid light of Sirius, but also its white dwarf companion star, Sirius B, invisible to the naked eye. What is so amazing is that the ancestors of the Dogon tribe had known, with certainty, of the position of Sirius B without the use of any powerful telescopes or precise astronomical instruments.

It was not until the middle of the 19th century that astronomers in Europe and America began to suspect the existence of another star close to Sirius. Laborious detailed observations and calculations of the irregularities of its orbit led them to conclude that the gravitational force of its hidden companion was exerting enormous force on Sirius. Then, in 1862, while testing a new telescope, American astronomer Alvan Graham Clark caught the first glimpse of the dense white dwarf companion. He named it Sirius B.

It was not until 60 years later that English scientist Sir Arthur Eddington first explained why the tiny Sirius B could cause such wild wobbling in the orbit of its much bigger adjacent star. He published his findings in 1928, explaining for the first time how Sirius B was a white dwarf, a giant star, which had collapsed under the power of its own mass to a fraction of its original size, but still exerted a powerful gravitational pull on neighbouring star Sirius.

Eventually in 1970, after the advent of the space age, sophisticated telescope lenses and highly sensitive cameras finally captured the first images of Sirius B. It was a major triumph for the precise calculations of the modern scientific astronomers.

To the Dogon tribe, however, all this was old news. It only confirmed what they had known all along. They had known for centuries that Sirius B was out there in space. They even had their own name for it – Po Tolo. They knew it was composed of super-dense cosmic material and they knew it orbited round Sirius in an elliptical path every 50 years.

They knew all this and they had known it from the beginning of their unwritten history, they explained. And they knew it because they were originally taught the secrets of the stars and planets and given the basic elements of their civilization by alien visitors from the Sirius star system!

How could these African tribespeople have discovered the precise scientific secrets of distant galaxies and planets so far ahead of sophisticated scientists armed with the benefits of modern technology? Their explanation of visitors from outer space is patently absurd and incredible. But the only alternative answer is just as unbelievable.

In 1931, two of France's most eminent anthropologists, Marcel Griaule and Germaine Dieterlen, arrived on the Bandiagara Plateau to make a study of the Dogon tribe. They had decided to devote several years of extended research into the origins and culture of the tribe. Drawn deeper and deeper into Dogon civilization, they virtually lived with the tribe for the next 21 years.

When Griaule and Dieterlen arrived, they found a tribe already steeped in the knowledge of the secrets of Sirius. Their religious rituals revolved around homage to Sirius, its hidden companion Sirius B, and a third, as yet undiscovered star. The symbols of the star system were woven into the patterns of their blankets, in designs which seemed to be hundreds of years old. They were depicted on their pottery, their wooden carvings and on the clay walls of their shrines.

Sir Arthur Eddington's discovery of Sirius B in 1928 was only known to a handful of astronomical students in England. The arrival of the two anthropologists on the Bandiagara Plateau was only three years later. Is it possible that in that brief space of time an entire semi-literate population could have pirated Sir Arthur's scholarly work and incorporated it into a fake tribal history, complete with fraudulent artefacts of cloth and pottery, just to impress and fool two French researchers?

It's doubtful that the anthropologists knew enough about recent astronomical discoveries to be much impressed by such an elaborate confidence trick. It took 15 years before Marcel Griaule was trusted sufficiently by the elders of the tribe. Then, he was indoctrinated into their occult ceremonies and was initiated into the creed of the alien visitor from Sirius, whom the Dogon called 'The Nommo'. According to the elders, the Nommo was a weird, amphibious creature from space, who had come to spread civilization on Earth and who had given the Dogon the beginnings of their unique culture.

After 20 years' experience of the history of the Dogon, the anthropologists published their historic research in the prestigious *Journal of the Society of African Research*. The paper, entitled *A Sudanese Sirius System*, explained in great detail the Dogon's mysterious advanced knowledge of planetary and stellar systems. It concluded, with cautious understatement: 'The problem of knowing how, with no instruments at their disposal, men could know of the movements and certain characteristics of virtually invisible stars has not been settled.'

For Marcel Griaule it was the culmination of his life's work. When he died in 1956, a quarter of a million Dogon tribespeople gathered at his funeral in Mali to pay their respects.

Griaule's long-time partner in research, Germaine Dieterlen, left Africa and returned to Paris to take up the post of Secretary General of the Society for African Studies at the Museum of Mankind. It was there that the additional joint research she published in 1965 for the French National Institute of Ethnology caught the imagination of American scholar Robert Temple. Temple, an authority on Sanskrit and Oriental studies, travelled to Paris for lengthy interviews with Dieterlen and journeyed to Mali, determined to get to the bottom of the mystery of the Dogon's mythology about visitors from outer space. Afterwards, he admitted: 'In the beginning I was just investigating. I was sceptical. I was looking for hoaxes, thinking it couldn't be true. But then I began to discover more and more pieces which fitted.'

The primitive tribespeople patiently explained to Temple how The Nommo, whom they described as 'the monitor of the Universe, guardian of its spiritual principles, dispenser of rain and master of water', had landed in a spaceship 'ark' in the north-east of their country early in the tribe's history.

Temple reported in his 1976 book, *The Sirius Mystery*: 'The Dogon describe the sound of the landing of the ark. They say the word of Nommo was cast down by Him in the four directions as He descended, and it sounded like the echoing of four large stone blocks being struck with stones by children according to special rhythms in a very small cave.

Presumably a thunderous vibrating sound is what the Dogon are trying to convey. One can imagine standing in a cave and holding one's ears at the noise. The descent of the ark must have sounded like a jet aircraft landing on a runway at close range.'

Dogon priests described how the ark from Sirius raised a whirlwind of dust as it finally settled on the dry dusty earth. Then, they told Temple what they knew about the solar system, how the surface of the Moon was 'dry and dead like dry, dead blood'. In crude drawings in the sand they retraced ancient outlines showing Saturn with a ring around it, the movements of the planets around the Sun, the spinning of the Earth on its axis and the orbit of Venus. They scratched out a sand drawing of the planet Jupiter showing the four major moons circling round it, and they claimed the diagram dated back centuries before Galileo had first seen those moons on his telescope.

To demonstrate their knowledge of the close-packed material of Sirius B, the compacted white dwarf, a Dogon priest produced a single grain of their cereal crop. The stellar matter of Po Tolo, he explained, was so dense that even a grain was so massive 'that all earthly beings combined cannot lift it'. It was a stunningly accurate description of the mass of a dwarf star, and one that could hardly be bettered by any precise scientific definition.

The priest also described a second, unseen red dwarf star orbiting Sirius. This star, he said, was not as dense as Sirius B, or Po Tolo, but was four times lighter in mass. The Nommo visitor came from a planet which circled this undiscovered star.

For Temple and other researchers, the mystery of the advanced astrological knowledge of the Dogon is still unsolved. It is possible that members of the tribe learned basic astronomical sciences from colonial French academies which had been established in their area as recently as the beginning of the 20th century, or even from the Moslem University which flourished in the provincial capital of Timbuktu in the 16th century. Further back in history it seems certain that the Dogon tribe, who originated from the northern coast of Africa, along the shores of Algeria, Libya and Egypt, might well have been in contact with advanced Mediterranean cultures.

Indeed, Mediterranean myth is rich in legends of strange amphibious creatures. Such legends brought a civilizing influence to the barbaric, primitive peoples of Earth. Ancient Greek legend records the mysterious Telchines, scaly creatures, half man, half fish, who inhabited the island of Rhodes, and they were described by Greek historian Diodorus Siculus as 'the discoverers of certain arts and introducers of other things which are useful for the life of Mankind'. The Telchines are portrayed as submarine visitors from the depths of the oceans, with the heads of dogs and the scales of fish over their bodies.

Babylonian myth records the arrival of Annedoti, the Repulsive Ones, who were also fish-men. Their leader was Oannes, who hatched from a giant egg and who instructed the Babylonians 'in everything which would tend to soften manners and humanize mankind'.

These Greek and Babylonian descriptions all tally with the pictures painted by the Dogon tribe. Even eminent evolution experts agree that back in the mists of the dawn of time, all human life evolved from amphibious creatures who first crawled on to dry land out of the primeval oceans. But only the Dogon insist that the fish creatures who gave them their mysterious scientific knowledge came from outer space. And only the Dogon pinpoint the precise location of the origin of their visitors, an unknown planet orbiting an unknown red dwarf star in the cluster around Sirius.

Is it just fanciful legend? Or is there another hidden star circling silently round Sirius? Could powerful orbiting space telescopes trained on the Sirius cluster discover this hidden star and its unknown planet within the next few years? And what would be the reaction of sceptical scientists to the primitive Dogon tribespeople, who would simply shrug and say: 'We told you so'?

Acupuncture

Carrying out complex surgery is one of the most daunting challenges facing modern medical science. Surgeons must be knowledgeable about the innermost workings of the human frame, and skilled with the tools which allow them to explore and repair the organs of the body, cutting and stitching, amputating or transplanting.

In the team of experts who must all use their skills to carry out a successful operation, the anaesthetists are key members. Their job is to hold the patient in a dangerous limbo between consciousness and death, keeping them sedated only to the level where the patient's own vital body responses do not collapse completely, while preventing the patient from becoming alert enough to experience the pain and anguish which could result in fatal shock. Even with the most skilful techniques, a prolonged operation can lead to serious physical damage, and anaesthetists must employ every resource at their command, including powerful drugs and numbing gases.

Or must they?

Thousands of doctors find no need to keep their patients deeply unconscious, even during the most serious and lengthy periods of surgery. On the

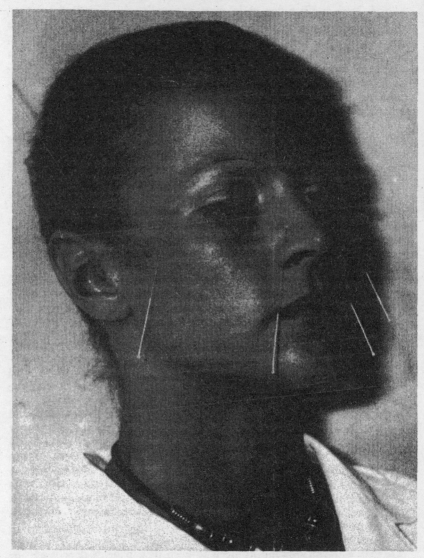

An addicted smoker undergoes acupuncture treatment.

contrary, they prefer their patients alert and able to respond to requests and give directions to the doctors – even while their bodies are in the middle of delicate and bloody operations. These doctors are the practitioners of acupuncture, an ancient and mysterious medical art where simple treatment with needles, barely pushed into the skin, seems able to effect astonishing recoveries. Acupuncture has been known to cure serious illnesses and harmful drug addictions, and can even induce a harmless state of painlessness where surgery can be performed on a patient who is wide awake without them feeling any discomfort.

For doctors who are trained to accept that illnesses usually have organic causes, acupuncture is a baffling enigma. But to ancient and modern Chinese healers, acupuncture is a simple matter of manipulating and balancing vital life forces inside the body. The technique, known to the Orient as chen-ts'u, or 'needle stab', has been practised for about 5,000 years. Before the days of refined metals, doctors were forced to use the simple tools of needles of flint, bone and bamboo. According to ancient legend, Chinese doctors stumbled accidentally on the secrets of acupuncture when they noticed that soldiers superficially wounded with bamboo arrows sometimes recovered later from serious illnesses located in other parts of their body, far removed from the site of the arrow injury. By studying case histories they slowly began to map out 'channels' under the skin where they believed vital forces controlling the health of the body flowed through key points. Translating this work into a great written medical reference book took nearly 1,500 years, finally producing the comprehensive *Yellow Emperor's Book of Internal Medicine*, carefully transcribed in 1,000 BC.

The book consists of 34 volumes of a lengthy dialogue between the Emperor Huangti and his chief physician Ch'i Pai, summing up their knowledge of the causes and treatment of diseases. The treatise gave rise to an entire tradition of medical practise based on the belief that good health manifests itself in the life spirit, 'Chi'. Chi pervades the whole Universe as a balance of opposite and complementary forces of 'Yin and Yang'.

The Yin force is said to be a soft, shadowy, watery female power inside the body, offset by the Yang force of dry, masculine toughness. Illness, according to the Chinese health philosophy, is simply a result of imbalance in these forces. The life spirit Chi flows through humans in 12 pairs of parallel channels, or meridians, down each side of the body, with each meridian linked to a vital organ – the heart, small intestine, bladder, kidney, gall bladder, liver, lungs, colon, stomach, spleen and two 'organs', unknown to Western medicine, which control the blood circulation and temperature.

On each meridian are a number of sensitive acupuncture pressure points, or gates, which control the flow of Chi. Stimulation with a needle can increase the current of Yin or Yang until the forces are balanced and good health is restored. Continuous research by acupuncturists, who originally believed there were 365 pressure points corresponding to the number of days in the year, has now identified almost 2,000 of them.

The existence of these pressure points in the body, totally unrelated to the locations of illness or disease, is denied by most of traditional Western medical teaching. Chinese charts and tiny pottery models show a complex network of meridians running in illogical lines through the nervous and muscular systems of the body. For kidney disease the diagrams show that the insertion of a needle in the sole of the foot can produce healing effects on the kidney, the vital organ located in the small of the back.

There are more than a dozen hidden pressure points on the heart meridian, which runs from the chest to the finger tips, each one a 'spirit gate' which can cure heart disorders with a needle forced gently into the correct point. Heart Point number 7, for instance, is one of the cluster of points near the pulses of the wrist, and treatment there, according to the specialists, can cure an irregular heart beat and even overcome fearful apprehension, ranging from stage fright to whimpering cowardice.

Sometimes, where simple needle treatment is not enough, a more progressive form of acupuncture is used where the ends of the needles furthest from the puncture entry in the skin are tipped with tiny blobs of burning herbs. These, it is claimed, transmit additional healing force into the meridian. An even more modern technique links the needles to power generators to shoot small pulses of low voltage electricity into the meridians.

Conventional medical authorities have tried hard to dismiss acupuncture as a quack pseudo-science which only produces beneficial results on gullible patients who are cured simply due to a strong psychological belief that the treatment is of some benefit. However, this ignores the fact that veterinary surgeons who have practised acupuncture on unbiased animal patients have produced astonishing cures. These range from racehorses afflicted with ripped muscles and tendons to pet dogs suffering from paralysis and bone disease.

The ancient textbooks of acupuncture techniques do not confine themselves solely to treating human patients. Early acupuncture journals showed details of acupuncture points for the treatment of elephants, and were eagerly sought after by Oriental merchants who valued their jumbos as important assets in countries where they were used as beasts of burden.

Although the technique was widespread throughout the East for thousands of years, when it was introduced into Europe by French Jesuit missionaries just 300 years ago, it almost totally failed to gain any following. Then, in 1939, French diplomat and Oriental scholar Georges Soulie de Morant produced a five-volume reference work of acupuncture methods. This led to a revival of interest which has now produced in France a network of some 1,500 registered medical practitioners and ten fully-equipped public and private hospitals with their own acupuncture departments.

In its own traditional home of China, the fortunes of acupuncture have fluctuated between accepted medical practice and condemnation as an outdated primitive medicine. In 1822, the Imperial Court of the Ching Dynasty declared acupuncture as barbaric and inferior to the new science of herbal medicine, and its practice was forbidden. However, it still flourished in remote country regions and gradually gained back its popularity. But it was outlawed again in 1922, when it proved futile against the plagues of typhus and dysentery which swept through Manchuria. The plagues claimed the lives of hundreds of thousands of victims and, denouncing acupuncturists as charlatans, the Chinese leader Chiang Kai-shek banned acupuncture altogether. He then launched a programme of building western-style hospitals and doctors' surgeries, stocked with drugs and chemical medicines.

The Communist government which succeeded Chiang Kai-shek drove acupuncture even further underground, vowing they would eliminate archaic superstitious medicine practised by 'witch doctors'. Fortunately, however, the traditionalists found their fortunes revived by Chairman Mao Tse Tung, himself the son of a peasant villager, who tolerantly rehabilitated the techniques and allowed acupuncturists to practise alongside their new colleagues trained in western clinical medicine and surgery.

A breakthrough in renewed research in acupuncture proved to be the catalyst for the ancient art to gain acceptance in the eyes of many previously sceptical western specialists.

In 1959, Chinese doctors announced that they had found important new meridians. By inserting just two needles in carefully selected spots under the skin, they could provide almost total analgesia for some patients undergoing major surgery. Now, acupuncturists could take their place in modern operating theatres working alongside recognized specialists.

Although the analgesic effects were successfully produced in only ten per cent of patients, the results were formidable. There were no weakening, potentially fatal aftereffects like those produced in anaesthesia. No longer were patients drugged into the twilight world of unconsciousness. Even patients undergoing open heart surgery were able to remain fully conscious, wholly aware of their surroundings and fully able to feel scalpels and forceps entering their body, but without any experience of pain. Other patients were able to sip water and eat small amounts of food, without any discomfort, while surgeons performed operations on them.

The technique was even successful in caesarian section childbirth cases, where joyful mothers were able to see their babies from the moment of birth.

And Chinese dentists reported that they could produce total relief from pain just by the pressure of a finger on a vital meridian spot.

Between 15 and 20 per cent of all operations in China that require more than a local anaesthetic are now carried out using general acupuncture analgesia techniques. A fully equipped anaesthetist stands by, in case of emergency and so that the acupuncturist has access to modern electronic tools, such as electro-cardiograms and resuscitation machines. The techniques have more than a 75 per cent success rate, and more than 100 different types of surgical procedure have now been successfully carried out using acupuncture as a pain-killer.

Just as important is the discovery that acupuncture can make a mysterious contribution as a cure for emotional and psychiatric problems. When acupuncture is used for treatment of a physical illness, patients who enjoy clinical cures also report that they feel an improved sense of emotional well-being. Now the treatment is being prescribed as a therapy for a wide range of psychiatric troubles.

Since the heart point meridians may have success in helping a patient to overcome fear and anxiety, experiments with different pressure points appear to have the effects of altering other symptoms of harmful and stressful human behaviour. For example, acupuncture 'maps' show that the ear is a junction of pressure points governing a wide range of emotions. One French researcher, who studied ancient Egyptian treatment of sciatica by inserting needles in the ear, found he could cure cravings for drugs such as nicotine and heroin by using the same method.

The treatment has been refined even further by a Russian scientist who modified a simple office stapling machine to insert a sterilized metal pin inside the patient's ear, where it is left permanently. The staple looks like a tiny metal ornament in the ear lobe. When the addict feels overcome by desire for a forbidden drug, he can apply immediate acupuncture to himself by reaching up and waggling the staple.

The latest analytical data of modern medicine may have come up with one possible explanation for the effects of acupuncture. Research in Europe had discovered the existence of endomorphins, the natural pain-relieving drugs produced inside the brain. Endomorphins are released in response to pain signals which are transmitted through the nervous system. They have been defined as 'the brain's natural opium', producing relief from pain and a soothing emotional effect on tortured bodies.

As for the actual details of the mechanisms that produce endomorphins, we do not yet have all the facts. But perhaps, when the Emperor Huangti and his doctor Ch'i Pai first drew their own maps of the meridians of the body, they stumbled on the secret trigger points which let our bodies heal themselves.

The Nazca Indians

To the early road builders of South America, the barren plateau of Nazca, on the west coast of Peru, was something of an obstacle on the route of the plans for a highway stretching down the length of their continent. With theodolites and tripods, surveyors' maps and tape measures, they slowly forged across the featureless Nazca desert, pausing only to admire the previous efforts of ancient Inca Indians, who had seemingly attempted to plot their own way through the dusty wilderness.

Occasionally they cut across the lines of an old Incan 'path', a shallow furrow in the desert floor stretching arrow-straight into the distance, or a broken line of boulders dotted across the landscape towards the horizon. At other times they found their own route running parallel to the ancient lines. They admired their astonishing geometric regularity and the undeviating accuracy of some lines which ran straight for more than 20 miles. To the builders, the lines, etched by a civilization 2,000 years old, were plainly tracks which marked the shortest distances between long-forgotten temples and villages. Where the lines crossed the path of the Pan American Highway, being built for 20th-century traffic, the route planners filled the furrows and bulldozed away the boulders without a second thought.

By 1927, after the first thin line of a single-carriage highway had already been laid between Lima in the north and Nazca, and was stretching south towards the border of Chile and Bolivia, the Peruvian Government had acquired the machines which would dramatically cut down the laborious, time-consuming survey techniques for planning the next link in the highway. They had imported three second-hand biplanes and an aerial survey team took off to fly the length of the plateau between the Pacific Ocean and the spine of the Andes Mountains to map out the rest of the route.

Cruising at 3,000 feet above sea level, surveyor Toribio Xesspe looked down with pride on the black ribbon of tarmac as it cut across the 200 square mile plateau of Nazca. He saw quite clearly the ancient lines of Nazca, the furrows and rows of boulders, where they intersected the completed section of road. Slowly, as the landscape unfolded beneath him, he began to realize that the lines were not simply random tracks across the desert: they formed recognizable patterns.

Xesspe instructed his pilot to interrupt their journey south and ordered him, instead, to put the aircraft into a steep climbing turn over the desert.

When they levelled out at 6,000 feet, both men gasped in astonishment at the sight below them. In every direction, as far as the eye could see, the lines had taken on the shapes of a vast drawing board, covered with elaborate portraits of gigantic animals. There was the stark outline of a humming-bird with a wingspan of more than 200 feet, there were graphic drawings, in boulders and trenches in the dust, of a killer whale, fish and animals, insects and birds, ferocious warriors wearing crowns, and more than 100 spirals, triangles and over 13,000 perfectly straight lines. All on an unbelievably huge scale.

Until Xesspe's historic flight, the mysterious patterns of the Nazca desert had been invisible from ground level, identifiable only as ditches and cairns of rocks. Now they were clearly displayed as a giant art gallery, whose exhibits were meant to be seen only by witnesses who could hover high in the skies, thousands of feet above the desert.

The ancient Inca civilization, which had drawn the lines in the desert, had flourished in 200 BC, about the same time as the Roman Empire had been spreading its power and domination by building military roads to carry its centurions and cavalry throughout Europe. But the lines of Nazca, when viewed from the air, were obviously not tracks or roads or trade routes. The great curving sweeps of stones served only to form part of the feathered wings of enormous birds; straight lines which ran for miles across natural ditches and cracks in the desert floor suddenly ended abruptly; others, of equal length, crossed each other at carefully fixed angles, pointing to different parts of the compass.

To Xesspe and his pilot, they looked uncannily like the neatly engineered runways of the modern airport they used for their landings and take-offs. But who would have built broad runways and landing sites for aircraft on a desert in Peru in the days before the American continent had even been introduced to the wheel? And why?

The first scientist to try to unravel the mysteries of the lines of Nazca was the late Professor Paul Kosok of Long Island University, New York, who began a study of the desert patterns 12 years after their discovery. His first task, guided by aerial survey photographs, was to walk along the lines and curves with his research teams, brushing away the centuries of sand that obscured many of the designs. Then he would be able to take sharper, more accurate photographs and construct more detailed plans and diagrams.

In the roasting desert temperatures, it was a job best carried out in the cool of the early morning air. And it was after a year's toil, having only restored a few dozen clear outlines, that Kosok thought he had answered the riddle. Sweeping the blur of sand away from one of the giant 'runways' at dawn on 22 June 1940, Kosok saw the sun rise above the Andes Mountains, precisely at the far end of the line which stretched straight across the desert. It was the morning of the winter solstice in the Southern Hemisphere, when the sun, which had retreated far to the north, began the apparent journey south again to bring its warming rays sweeping back over the tropical areas of Peru.

To Kosok the answer was obvious. The lines on the desert were part of a giant astronomical calendar used by ancient Inca farmers to fix the best times each year to plant and harvest their crops.

However, Kosok was still mystified about the reason for the colossal drawings of beasts and men-like figures. Throughout the next two decades, until his death in 1959, he devoted his life to trying to understand the enigma of the lines in the Nazca desert.

For most of his research work he was joined by German-born archeology and astronomy expert Maria Reiche, who had lived and worked as a school governess in Cuzco, Peru's ancient Inca capital, since before the Second World War. Working together they plotted the paths of hundreds of the straight lines in the desert and proved, to their own satisfaction, that the individual paths catalogued not just positions of the sun during the different seasons of the year, but also the locations of stars, and even entire constellations.

Maria Reiche also solved the puzzle of how Incan peasant draughtsmen could have directed a work force of labourers over hundreds of square miles of featureless desert to dig the furrows and place the lines of boulders, whose designs could only be comprehensible from thousands of feet above. Over scores of interviews with old Indians living on the edges of the Nazca desert, she discovered that the Indians themselves had found countless examples of withered wooden pegs rammed into the dry, caked earth, left there by previous generations. Within living memory, there had been evidence of the crumpled remains of stakes which had been driven into the desert floor along the straight lines and strategic points in the curves of the animal designs. Reiche was able to prove that the ancient designers in fact worked with small scale models and enlarged them into gigantic proportions section by section in the desert. Each fragment of the model would be marked out with pegs.

While Reiche agreed with Professor Kosok that the straight lines were diagrams of the sun, moon, stars and planets, the pictures of animals and the other artistic designs, she claimed, were simply there for adornment.

Indeed, Inca culture had produced countless beautiful objects of little practical value that still survive today.

Archeologists have unearthed exquisite Incan gold jugs for carrying water, where simple clay pots could have done the job just as well, and amazing cloths woven with intricate, beautiful designs, where coarsely spun wool would have kept out the desert cold just as effectively. For the Incas believed in art and beauty for its own sake. Thus, while the straight lines were practical scientific calculating tools, the exotic designs surrounding them were to soften the sharp geometric outlines with drawings of grace and beauty.

The conclusions of Professor Kosok and Maria Reiche satisfied most of the modest intellectual curiosity about the lines of Nazca. However, there was a far more vivid and imaginative theory about their origins put forward in the 1970s by writer Erich Von Daniken, the author who intrigued millions of readers around the world with his book *Chariot of the Gods*.

Von Daniken claimed there was archeological and cultural evidence that alien astronauts, in the form of gods from outer space, had visited Earth in centuries past and left their impression on the civilizations of many races. Von Daniken himself paid a visit to Nazca and announced that the straight lines on the desert in fact formed a gigantic landing strip for space travellers to set down their spacecraft. The ancient inhabitants of Nazca may have once witnessed the landing of a space ship, he claimed, and had decided to etch out their message of welcome in the hope that the space travellers would return. The lines on the desert, only meaningful from a great altitude, had the clear invitation: 'Land here – everything is prepared for you.'

Some people took Von Daniken's theory seriously, and at least one pilot brought his light aircraft in, landing safely and taking off again from one of the 'runways'. However, more serious-minded people questioned why space voyagers, presumably travelling in high-tech space craft while crossing the cosmos, should need anything as mundane as a rough desert airstrip in order to touch down on Earth.

Later still, Jim Woodman, an American aviation consultant and business-man, came up with an intriguing, and far more credible, answer to the riddle of the Nazca desert. When he visited the site, he found a number of stone pits situated at the ends of some of the lines, which seemed to him to have been the remains of some sort of ovens. Then, on fragments of pottery, he discerned some strange drawings, which appeared to depict a globe and a type of straw canoe. It looked like an ancient Incan version of a hot-air balloon. He then found samples of cloth in Incan graves, more than 1,500 years old.

Analysis of the cloth showed that the fabric had been tightly woven, enough perhaps to hold large volumes of hot air. Piecing all the evidence together, Woodman concluded that the oven pits he had found could have been 'burning pits', which would have funnelled hot air into the cloth, forming hot-air flying craft. Woodman was convinced that the Incans had, in fact, mastered the art of hot-air ballooning, and that they had been able to soar high above the desert to admire their handiwork.

Together with members of the Miami-based International Explorers Society and an English balloon expert, Julian Nott, Woodman set out to prove his theory. Using fabric spun by local Indians and a basket woven from reeds, he and Julian Nott took off in their hot-air ballon in November 1975. Clinging precariously to the reed gondola, with Nott piloting the frail craft, their balloon, *Condor 1*, soared high over the Nazca desert. The jubilant explorers in their 'ancient Incan' flying machine were able to see, in glorious detail, the great panorama of the desert designs beneath them.

It may well have been that Jim Woodman had found the answer to the mystery of the lines of the Nazca desert.

Who knows?

Perhaps the draughtsmen and architects of the desert drawings had taken favoured guests on pleasure flights high into the atmosphere to admire from the air the astonishing designs which were a meaningless jumble of patterns to earthbound mortals.

Maybe, however, the answer to the mystery is a complex mixture of all the varying theories. The straight lines on the desert floor may have been an ingenious astronomical calendar, built under the watchful eye of surveyors who floated thousands of feet up in the air to check the progress of the work against their detailed drawings. Perhaps the geometric lines were built for Incan farmers, to be used from the practical vantage point of ground level as an agricultural diary. And, just in case they were mistaken for any kind of landing site, they were overlaid with the enormous designs of killer whales, spiders and huge fierce warriors as a warning: 'This is the work of giants, stay away! Land here at your peril!'

One day, we may know the answer for sure.

Nikola Tesla

For the young Yugoslavian inventor Nikola Tesla, America was to be the land of opportunity. When he first arrived in New York in 1884, clutching only four cents in coins as his entire assets and a few technical papers, the 28-year-old did not have to wait for long to find his first job. He was quickly snapped up by the Edison company, for whom he designed and developed the power generators for the Niagara Falls hydro-electric power plant. He also invented 24 different types of dynamos, demonstrated long range radio transmissions systems and spurned a nomination for the Nobel Prize for Physics. While his work made billions of dollars for producers and suppliers of electrical equipment based on his inventions, Tesla, once described by Lord Kelvin, President of the Royal Society, as 'a pure genius', died alone and barely financially solvent in his cheap room at the New Yorker Hotel in Manhattan in 1943. Before Tesla's body was removed to a funeral parlour, an unusual thing occurred. FBI agents ransacked his room and seized all his documents on the grounds of 'national security'.

The mysterious, moody scientist who turned his back on the chance of fame and fortune is believed to have invented an atomic beam weapon, which is only now being developed as the awesome destructive power behind the Star Wars defence system. Four years before the Wright Brothers had even struggled into the air in their first powered flying machine, Nikola Tesla had actually devised a means of destroying ballistic missiles – even though ballistic missiles were not invented for another 70 years!

Within three years the temperamental, petulant Tesla had abandoned the security of his well-paid job with Edison to set up his own rival electrics company Twelve months later he had been granted more than 30 patents.

It was the income from these inventions which allowed him to retreat to the Rocky Mountains of Colorado Springs in 1899 to carry out his most important secret experiments. Tesla had set himself the task of surrounding the entire planet with one all-encompassing energy field, using the Earth itself as a gigantic booster for his own powerful generators. He envisaged this pulsating radiation of energy carrying radio messages around the world, as well as providing a form of wireless electrical energy.

His generating station in the Rockies was built around a central laboratory which was dominated by a 200-foot metal mast, topped by a copper ball three feet in diameter. Inside the laboratory was a circular electrical coil, which carried the low voltage energy for his transmitter. A secondary coil was wrapped around the mast, which protruded into the sky. Tesla planned to tap the colossal energy reserves of the Earth itself, to increase the power from his own 10 million-volt generator.

In his initial experiments, Tesla's coils radiated so much energy that they were able to light up an array of 200 incandescent lamps at a distance of 25 miles away, simply through the force of the electrical power.

Next, he turned his attention to harnessing the power potential of the Earth. As Tesla's mast sent a pulse of high frequency radio waves bouncing of the upper atmosphere, the signals were tuned to match the frequency of the returning 'echo'. With every echo acting as an amplifier in the mast, drawing energy from the Earth, the power output grew and grew. With each pulse the

Nikola Tesla – why did the FBI seize his papers?

growing energy became more and more forceful until the copper ball erupted with fingers of fire shooting hundreds of feet into the air from the glowing mast. The sheets of electricity were accompanied by deafening crashes of noise. Tesla had succeeded in generating man-made storms of lightning.

But his research ceased abruptly. Even though he was financed from the almost bottomless coffers of the railroad magnate J P Morgan, Tesla began to withdraw again into his own secret world, working on profitless theoretical research. Hoarding his laboratory notes to himself, it was three decades before Nikola Tesla gave any hint of the astonishing new project that consumed the rest of his working life. In 1934 he described a new piece of apparatus he had developed which embodied all the principles of the Laser Light – a device which was not, in fact, to be successfully developed until 1960.

It was exactly the same scientific basis as the laser, only Tesla was talking of shooting an atomic stream an infinite distance, capable of destroying anything in its path if he chose to adapt it as a weapon of destruction.

Although Tesla never explained any details of his invention, the secrets were carefully noted in his research journals seized by the government agents in his hotel room when he died.

The spectre of Nikola Tesla was raised again in 1977, when Canadian authorities reported mysterious electrical storms and radio blackouts occurring high in the atmosphere above the Arctic regions. Experts from the Central Intelligence Agency in Washington were enlisted to try to discover the source of the energy which was causing the chaos in the skies over Canada. They reported back that they believed a Soviet military rocket base at Semipalatinsk was responsible for ripping apart the fabric of the upper atmosphere – testing an atomic beam weapon based on the research carried out by Nikola Tesla 40 years before.

If Tesla's research work had actually borne fruit, he may have developed a ray gun which could have destroyed nuclear missiles as they curved over the Earth in low orbits on their way to their targets. The trajectory for American missiles aimed at the Soviet Union would take them above the Arctic Circle.

The powerful beams which were punching holes in the radiation layers around the Earth may also be capable of causing unpredictable disturbances in weather patterns. Canadian scientist Andrew Michrowski warned: 'It is quite clear to me that the Russians are doing experiments based on Tesla's ideas and in doing so have changed the world's weather.'

Watson W Scott, Director of Operations at the Canadian Department of Communications in Ottawa, revealed bluntly: 'I have been told this could be an attempt to pinpoint the exact frequencies used by Tesla in his work. Are these experiments connected with the great drought of 1976 in Britain, or the warm weather in Greenland melting the glaciers, or the snow in Miami?'

THE WORLD'S GREATEST
UFO ENCOUNTERS

Photograph Acknowledgements

Fortean Picture Library 8, 9, 54, 55, 59, 60, 62, 69, 72, 92, 93, 97, 102, 104 ttop, 104 bottom, 109 top, 109 bottom, 110 bottom, 111 top, 111 bottom, 112 top, 112 centre, 112 bottom, 122, 127 bottom, 145, 149/Janet & Colin Bord 127 top/Michael Buhler 20/Werner Burger 119/Rod Dickinson 134/Stephen C. Pratt 108/William M. Rebsamen 138/August C. Roberts 94, 110 top/Dezs Sternoczky 117

Contents

1 Dangerous Liaisons

Protect Yourself

There should be a warning on the side of every UFO that reads: alien encounters can harm your health. And this is not simple paranoia. There are plenty of reports of people being harmed by extraterrestrials. Sometimes they suffer through exposure to the energy fields associated with UFOs. Then there are the more life-threatening episodes that occur during alien abductions – intrusive examinations, unwanted surgery and the embedding of 'implants' in the body. And sometimes there is outright hostile intent.

Even an innocent UFO sighting can result in psychological problems, including anxiety, mania, depression and post-traumatic stress disorder. In other cases, severe physical effects – burns, eyesight damage, radiation sickness and even cancer – have been reported. One consistent feature of reports of UFO sightings and alien encounters from across the globe is that they cast the human witness as a victim. Usually, there is little doubt that those involved in such episodes have experienced ill effects; the medical evidence is there for all to see.

Alien Aggression

The first hostile alien encounter took place two months after Kenneth Arnold had first reported seeing flying saucers over the Cascades. In August 1947, geologist Rapuzzi Johannis was climbing the Italian Alps above the village of Villa Santina when he saw a group of aliens. Johannes raised his geologist's pick in greeting,

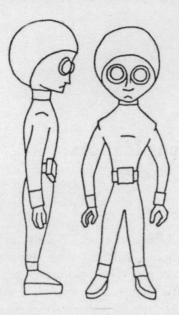

Drawings of two entities seen by Rapuzzi Johannis, August 1947, at Raveo near Villa Santina, Italy.

but his gesture misinterpreted. The aliens immediately fired a beam of light at him that knocked him down the mountainside. Fortunately, his fall was halted by some loose rubble. But the fall left him semi-paralysed and he faced a painful crawl home.

Another unprovoked attack occurred in France on 1 July 1965, when farmer Maurice Masse encountered a similar group of aliens near Valensole. The aliens pointed a 'stick' at him. Although he did not see what happened next, he found himself being flung to the ground. His muscles were paralysed, but he remained conscious.

Too Close for Comfort

On 20 May 1967, a UFO encounter left fifty-two-year-old Canadian engineer Stephen Michalak injured. Michalak's hobby was geology and he was out hunting for minerals near Falcon Lake, eighty miles east of Winnipeg. He heard the sound of geese cackling and looked upwards. He saw two disc-shaped craft hovering overhead. One flew away, but the other landed not far away. Michalak noticed that the object was changing colour as if cooling. He felt waves of heat coming off it. They carried with them a vile, sulphurous odour.

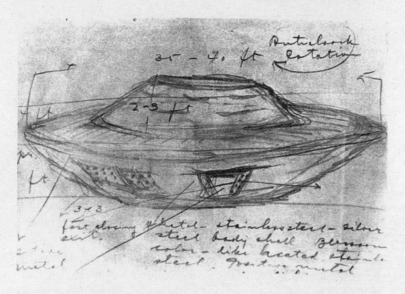

Steve Michalak's sketch of the UFO he saw close-up when it landed near Falcon Lake, Manitoba, Canada, on 20 May 1967.

As Michalak approached the craft, a doorway opened in its side and a brilliant violet light spilled out. The doorway closed again as he got closer. In a foolhardy move, Michalak reached out his hand to touch the surface of the ship. It was hot and he immediately drew his hand back, but his glove had already melted. At that moment, the disc tilted and a blast of light from an 'exhaust panel' in the side hit Michalak in the chest, setting fire to his shirt. He tore off his burning shirt as the spaceship disappeared out of sight.

The two-mile trek back to the highway was agonising and Michalak vomited countless times. When he returned to Winnipeg he was treated for first-degree burns and released. Two days later he returned to the doctor suffering from a mysterious malady. The doctor prescribed pain-killers and sea-sickness tablets, which were of little help. For several days after the incident he was unable to keep his food down and he lost twenty-two pounds in weight. His blood lymphocyte count was down from twenty-five per cent to sixteen per cent. Medical reports also showed that he had skin infections and rashes. He suffered from nausea, diarrhoea, generalised urticaria and blackouts, and generally felt weak and dizzy. He also experienced numbness and chronic swelling of the joints. Then, in August 1968 – fifteen months after the encounter – a geometric pattern of burns appeared on his chest.

Over eighteen months, Michalak was examined by a total of twenty-seven doctors, at a cost of thousands of dollars, but none explained the cause of his symptoms. The case was also investigated by a number of government departments.

The Canadian Department of National Defense examined the encounter site. They found higher than normal background radiation, along with silver fragments that had been exposed to great heat. The full results of their investigations were never made public. A file itself was eventually released, but it was incomplete and contained so many deletions that it was not much use. However, a number of independent researchers have pointed out that Michalak's symptoms are reminiscent of radiation exposure. If this was the case, Michalak is far from alone in experiencing these symptoms after an encounter with a UFO.

Blinded by the Light

On the evening of 7 January 1970, two unfortunate skiers were out on the wooded slopes near the village of Imjarvi, Finland. The temperature was far below freezing that night and Esko Viljo and Aarno Heinonen had stopped briefly at the base of a slope to try and warm themselves when, suddenly, the air was filled with a strange buzzing sound. Then they saw a glowing light surrounded by mist, spiralling downwards into a clearing. The fog began to spread out through the woods and the sound increased in pitch. Then, through the mist, a strange figure appeared. The encounter was cut short by a silent but dazzling explosion of light. It blasted the mist apart, leaving Viljo and Heinonen shrouded in darkness.

The shock was too much for Heinonen, who had been closer to the explosion. He stumbled forward and collapsed. One side of his body was completely paralysed. Viljo helped him to his feet and, together, they began to trudge back to the village.

It was an arduous journey in their enfeebled state. On the way, Heinonen's condition worsened, and the two men were forced to abandon their skis. By the time they reached the village, Heinonen was seriously ill. He was vomiting frequently. His head was pounding and he found that his urine was discoloured. One doctor who examined Heinonen noted that he exhibited the symptoms of radiation sickness, but could find no obvious cause, and, eventually, the symptoms disappeared.

Although Viljo had been further away, he had not escaped unscathed. There were problems with his eyes and he suffered excessive tiredness. The both men suffered post-traumatic stress, which badly affected their memories. But gradually, some recollection of the small, wax-coloured alien they had seen inside the glowing mist came back to them. This, they were sure, was the cause of the medical problems.

One theory was that they had encountered some entirely natural phenomenon that, as well as causing their physical injuries, had triggered a vivid hallucination. Professor Stig Lundquist of the University of Uppsala in Sweden considered that option in the Heinonen and Viljo case. The incident occurred up in the region of the Northern Lights and he investigated local atmospheric conditions, but he concluded that these were unlikely to be the cause of the incident:

'I do not think that I can explain the phenomenon as being naturally occurring,' he said.

Cornish Contretemps

On 17 September 1977, Caroline Bond and Peter Boulter suffered a similar encounter. The young couple were doing some work on an old post-office in the village of Newmill in Cornwall. Caroline was astride her moped, about to ride off, when she felt her skin tingle. She looked around to see a strange green mist drifting towards her, a few inches off the ground.

She leapt off her moped and ran back inside the building, screaming that she had just seen a ghost. Peter could hardly take this seriously, but he could see her terror was very real. When he went outside to take look, he saw a strange light soaring away into the sky. It was travelling relatively slowly and took a long time to disappear. So he went back inside and watched it from an upstairs window. It was then he noted that the light was no longer alone. It now seemed to have smaller red lights alongside it.

Meanwhile, Caroline, who had recovered her composure, leapt back on her moped and set off in pursuit. On the way, she came across several other villagers who had also seen the strange light, though none of them had had her ringside seat.

Soon after the encounter, Peter and Caroline became seriously ill. They suffering aching muscles, pounding headaches, vomiting and other symptoms that had been reported in the Finnish case. Peter went though a series of exhaustive tests, but nothing could be found. Eventually the mystery illness cleared up without treatment. Caroline, who had been closer, was more seriously affected. The possibility of appendicitis was considered. She was operated on and her appendix removed although, on examination, it seemed perfectly healthy. After some weeks, she began to recover. Nevertheless, the trauma of the encounter remained with the two of them for many years even though they had not seen any aliens or even anything that they could identify as a spacecraft.

Attack in the Forest

Scottish forester Bob Taylor was another victim. While working in the woodlands outside Livingston in West Lothian on 9 November 1979, Taylor came upon a strange egg-shaped object about twenty feet across in a clearing. It 'faded in and out of reality', he said, as he watched. Then two dark objects around a foot in diameter with six legs, like old-fashioned sea mines, sped towards him. They were round with spikes. He was knocked to the ground and remembered feeling a strange pulling sensation on his legs. When he came to, Taylor was alone, but he found himself in a terrible state. His trousers were torn. His head was pounding and his legs felt like jelly. Partially paralysed, he had to drag himself home painfully along the ground.

The police were called in. A major inquiry followed and the site of the encounter was cordoned off like a crime scene while the forensic team went over it. They found mysterious triangular indentations in the ground. Taylor's trousers were sent away for forensic analysis. However, the police eventually reported that they could find no evidence of an alien force, even though the credibility of the witness and the physical effects that he suffered were undoubted. Like the previous victims, he eventually recovered.

Burning Ring of Fire

On 13 March 1980, a sub-contractor was driving home from Worcester to Stratford-upon-Avon. When he passed near the village of Haselor, he had a close encounter. A cigar-shaped white craft surrounded by a red glow flashed passed his car. It was so big it filled the windscreen. As it passed by, the steering wheel suddenly became unbearably hot – a burning ring of fire. He let go and the car swerved. His hands suffered serious burns.

Scientists have explained that fluctuating magnetic fields produced by the UFO induced electrical eddy currents inside the metal steering wheel, heating it up. Such an intense field could have caused all sorts of other health problems if the UFO had hung around longer.

The ABC of After-Effects

The after-effects of alien abductions can have serious long-term effects. American UFOlogist Jerome Clark divides them into three stages. The initial stage, which Clark calls 'immediate after-effects', usually involves physical problems, such as nausea, irritated eyes, an unusual thirst, scoop-like cuts in the legs and nose-bleeds that can last days or weeks.

The second stage, 'intermediate after-effects', usually start a few weeks or even months after the abduction. It is then that the psychological difficulties begin. These include recurring nightmares, flashbacks, panic attacks and an irrational anxiety when returning to the area of the abduction – even though the victim may have no conscious memory of the event itself. Even so, this stage is often marked by the obsessive need to return to the site of the abduction, as if the victim is willing it to happen again.

The final stage in Clark's outline are the 'long-term effects'. These can occur years after the abduction and often involve changes in the personality and outlook of the abductee. Often these changes can be for the better. Some abductees have discovered hidden artistic talents or a previously unacknowledged spiritual side to their nature.

Stage One and Two

UFOlogist Leonard Stringfield encountered stage-one after-effects after Mona Stafford, Elaine Thomas and Louise Smith had been abducted by a UFO while driving down Route 78 in Kentucky on 6 January 1976. They wanted to keep their story a secret but information was leaked to the local press. Stringfield picked up on the story and persuaded them to meet him on 29 February.

'The effects of the close encounter were still painfully apparent,' said Stringfield. 'They looked drained and tense.' All three women had experienced severe weight loss, and Smith had what Stringfield described as 'a round, pinkish-grey blotch' on her body.

Smith also suffered second-stage effects, which lured her back to the site of the encounter, where she seems to have been abducted again. On 28 January she was in bed asleep when she was woken by strange voices. They urged her to get dressed and drive back to Route 78. Once she arrived at the site of the encounter, she stood there not knowing what to do. A feeling of terror came over her and she felt a pulling at her hands. Then she fled back to her car and drove off. She later noticed that three rings were missing from her hand – rings that normally required lubricating with soap before they could be removed.

Stafford, too, suffered second-stage effects. Disturbing mental images came and went. For a while she moved back in with her parents but, when she returned to her trailer, she was woken one night by 'mental voices'. A bright light came flooding in through the doorway and she saw a small being standing there.

Epilepsy

MUFON's Robert J. Durrant has suggested that encounters or abductions may cause temporal lobe epilepsy. Unlike normal epileptic attacks, when the victim suffers fits, convulsions and unconsciousness, TLE often produces hallucinatory effects. This is because the temporal lobe is not connected to any muscles that can convulse. Instead, it controls higher functions of the brain, such as memory and learning. Durrant has studied Whitley Strieber's auto-biographical accounts of his abduction experiences, *Transformation* and *Majestic*, and says that all the symptoms of temporal lobe epilepsy are present in Strieber's writings. These include floating sensations, paranormal experiences, anomalous smells, enhanced imagination and episodes that seem to have intense personal meaning. However, Strieber has undergone two series of tests for TLE. Both of them proved negative. This has led to the suggestion that aliens communicate telepathically with their abductees through the temporal lobe, hence the similarities between TLE and abduction experiences.

Implants

One of the most obvious after-effects of abductions is the discovery of an alien object implanted in the body of the abductee. Chief of Abduction Investigations for the Houston UFO Network, Derrel Sims has spent twenty-five years investigating abductions, and has himself been abducted. Implants are his field. In 1995 he called in Dr Roger Leir to remove two objects from an abductee known as Mrs Connely. Although her abduction had occurred twenty-five years before, in 1970, until the implants showed up on an X-ray, she had no idea of their existence. The T-shaped objects were found in her toe. They were about a fifth of an inch in height and made from an ultra-hard, unidentifiable metal, which was highly magnetic. The implants were sheathed in a dense, dark grey membrane that could not be cut with a sharp scalpel. Mysteriously, they were attached to nerve endings in a part of the body where no nerves are known to exist. Mrs Connely's case might help to explain why scoop-like scars are frequently found on the lower leg area ofabductees.

Unexplained Pregnancies

Perhaps the most disturbing of the after-effects of alien abductions are unexplained pregnancies. The evidence indicates that our extra-terrestrial intruders are running a programme to create a human–alien hybrid. There are numerous reports of aliens abducting women, impregnating them, returning them home, then abducting them again a few months later to take the foetus. This has a devastating affect on the women involved.

One such is Indiana housewife Kathie Davis. One evening in 1977, at around 9:30 p.m., she saw a light about the size of a baseball floating around her backyard. She went outside to look for it. She spent no more than ten minutes looking for it then, finding nothing, went to a friend's house for a moonlight swim. But when she arrived it was already 11 p.m. More than hour of her life was missing. Later, when she returned home from the swim, she felt an inexplicable chill and a fogging of the vision. Later she recalled an abduction experience. Neighbours confirmed this. They had seen a flash of light and felt their house vibrate as if there had been an earth tremor.

Kathie recalled being given a gynaecological examination by aliens. Abduction expert Budd Hopkins believes that she was impregnated by the aliens. A few months, she was abducted again. This time, during a second examination, she reported feeling a terrible pressure inside her. Then, under hypnosis, she became disturbed and cried out: 'It's not fair. It's mine.'

Later, she began having disturbing dreams. In them, she gave birth to a weird-looking, super-intelligent hybrid. Other abductees also reported dreaming of giving birth to so-called wise babies. Later Kathie recalled having a phantom pregnancy when she was teenager. When she was abducted years later she was introduced to a half-alien half-human hybrid that she recognised was her daughter.

In November 1983 she was abducted once again. This time the aliens removed some of her ova. During an abduction in April 1986, she was shown two elf-like infants. She was told that these were her children, too. The aliens told her they had nine of her offspring altogether. Although none of Kathie's extraterrestrial pregnancies was confirmed medically, she was left with a series of unexplainable scars that had resulted from the experience.

Lethal Encounter

At around 11:30 p.m. on 17 March 1978, service engineer Ken Edwards left the M62 motorway at the turn off to Risley. He was on his way home from a trade union meeting in Cheshire. His route took him through a deserted industrial area, much of which was derelict. As he passed the vast Atomic Energy Authority complex, his headlights picked out a weird figure, standing alone at the top of an embankment. Edwards stopped his van to investigate.

The creature was over seven feet tall and did not look human. Its arms came out of the top of its shoulders. Its body was silver, but its head was black and shaped like a goldfish bowl. It held its arms out ahead like a sleepwalker, then start walking down the embankment. The odd thing was that it walked at right angles to the steep slope, but did not topple forward.

When it reached the road, Edwards noticed that it had no knee joints. Its legs articulated from the hips, making its movement rather stiff. Then the creature stopped. It turned its head towards Edwards. Two pencil-thin beams of light shot out its eye socket. The beams came straight through the windscreen and hit Edwards full on. The effect was immediate.

'My head was swimming with strange thoughts,' he said. 'There were hundreds of them, all racing through my mind at once. I also felt very odd. It was a sensation like two enormous hands pressing down on me from above. The pressure was tremendous. It seemed to paralyse me. I could only move my eyes. The rest of me was rigid.'

The creature then carried on across the road. It walked straight through a ten-foot-high security fence as if it was not there, and vanished into the trees beyond. At this point, Edwards' mind went blank.

The next thing he recalled was arriving home at around half-past midnight. He had no idea how he had got there. He walked into the house, where his wife Barbara was waiting for him. She was anxious and could have been angry, but she noticed the state he was in. When he saw his wife, he blurted out: 'I've seen a silver man.' This sounded crazy and his 'missing time' story sounded a bit thin. But when they noticed that his watch had stopped at exactly 11:45 p.m., she took it seriously.

The couple went to the local police station. The duty officer thought the story was crazy too, but Edwards' obvious sincerity impressed him. The police contacted the atomic plant and Edwards reluctantly agreed to go back to the scene of the encounter with them. They were met by a team of twenty-five AEA security guards who carried batons. When Edwards related his incredible story, not one of them so much as smirked. Then they made a cursory search of the area, but they refused to go into the trees where Edwards had seen the creature disappear.

It turned out that the AEA complex was a UFO hotspot. Eight sightings had been reported in the area around that time. And four local youths had seen a cigar-shaped craft flying over the plant on the day of Edwards' encounter. Two police constables, Rob Thompson and Roy Kirckpatrick, followed up several leads. They checked out nearby Warrington College in case the students there had pulled some stunt, but they were not holding a rag week at the time and no link was established. Edwards was not impressed by this line of investigation.

'I wish they could tell me how they did it,' he said. 'How they blew up my radio and walked through a fence, some stunt.'

The police also wondered whether Edwards had seen a fireman clad in a silver radiation suit. They took him to the AEA complex and, without warning, had a member of staff in a silver fireman's suit walk out in front of the car. Edwards was unfazed.

'It was nothing like it,' he said.

Unable to shed any further light the matter, the police closed the case.

But the case was far from closed for Edwards. The 'missing' forty-five minutes between his watch stopping and the time he arrived home troubled him. He worried that he might have been abducted. But he could not simply put the matter out of his mind. He had physical proof that something had happened. The beams from the creature's eyes had damaged both him and his vehicle.

Where he had gripped the steering wheel, Edwards's fingers were bright red, as if badly sunburned. After the encounter he found that the van's two-way radio did not work. When an electrician examined it, he discovered that the circuit board was burned out. The probable cause of this, he speculated, was an enormous power surge through the aerial.

Then, less than a year after his strange encounter, Edwards fell ill. He lost all energy and began to suffer from stomach cramps. When he went to hospital, the doctors diagnosed cancer of the kidneys. In 1980, Edwards underwent major surgery. All seemed well but, after a couple of months, cancer cells appeared in his throat. The disease seemed unstoppable. Four years after the encounter with the silver-suited alien, Edwards was dead.

UFO investigators Peter Hough and Jenny Randles later discovered that unusual experiments were being carried out in a building near the AEA complex. But no one will say whether an experiment was underway that night.

Death Ray

The Edwards' case is reminiscent of another encounter when a victim was zapped in Brazil. On 13 August 1967, forty-one-year-old Ignacio de Souza and his young wife Louisa were returning to their ranch at Pilar de Goias, Brazil. The ranch had its own landing strip, but the couple were astounded to see that what had landed on it in their absence was no ordinary aircraft. What they saw was a spacecraft that looked like 'an upturned wash basin' on the runway. Near to it, were three alien entities wearing yellow ski suits.

De Souza loosed off a shot at one of them with the .44 carbine he was carrying. The UFO fired back and he was hit by a green beam that came from the craft. Realising that their reception was far from friendly, the aliens then climbed into the spaceship and it took off. Until the encounter de Souza had been good health. But afterwards, he suffered from nausea and uncontrollable shaking.

He was flown to hospital in nearby Goiana for tests. He had leukaemia and died two months later.

Grievous Bodily Harm

Probably the best-known UFO encounter that caused harm to humans involved restaurant owner Betty Cash, her friend Vickie Landrum and her grandson, Colby. The case received enormous media coverage worldwide because the victims sued the US government for $20 million.

The deadly encounter took place on the chilly night of 29 December 1980, when Betty, Vickie and Colby were driving down an isolated section of Highway 1485, which took them though a pine and oak forest near Huffman, Texas, some fifteen miles outside Houston. The two middle-aged women and the young boy had had their evening meal at a roadside restaurant in nearby New Caney and were now heading towards home in Dayton. At around 9 p.m., they had just rounded a bend in the highway,

Interpretation of UFO event by artist Michael Buhler: Huffman, Texas.

when ten-year-old Colby pointed out a blazing light in the sky. A huge diamond-shaped vessel loomed in front of them. It descended to tree-top level, straddling the road. They found their way blocked by a jet of fire that looked like the exhaust of a space rocket.

Cash, who was driving, stopped the car less than sixty yards from the mysterious object, which glowed so brightly that, in the surrounding forest, it could have been day. The three of them got out of the car to investigate, only to be met by a wave of tremendous heat. Colby became distressed and Vickie Landrum got back into the car with him. But Betty Cash continued to gaze mesmerised at the dazzling object, even though the intense heat was burning her skin and the bright light was damaging her eyes. It was only when the object began to move that Cash heard Landrum's pleas and returned to the car. But as Cash touched the handle of the car door, she found it was red hot and burned her hand. Her wedding ring also burned into her finger.

The craft then made a loud roaring noise. As it took off into night sky, some two dozen unmarked black helicopters swept into view. The three witnesses later identified them as CH-47 Chinook twin-blades, and they were either pursuing or escorting the mysterious craft. Cash set off in pursuit of the unidentified aircraft and the fleet of dark helicopters. After a mile or so they had to turn onto a larger highway. One of the helicopters turned back and buzzed the car, deafening the passengers with the roar of its engines. They got the message, turned off the highway and headed home.

All three of them were stunned and bewildered by the encounter. At first they thought it must have been a hallucination, but then they learned that, in the outskirts of Houston, residents had also seen bright lights and helicopters in the sky that night. Then there were the injuries that they had sustained from the strange encounter.

Cash's eyes were so swollen that she unable to see for a week. She suffered from vomiting and diarrhoea, various aches and pains, blistering of the scalp and temporary hair loss. Three days after the encounter, her condition deteriorated to the point that she checked into the emergency room of a nearby hospital. Betty did not tell the-hospital doctors about her UFO encounter – they treated her as a classic burns victim, until Colby revealed what had happened. Vickie Landrum and Colby also exhibited burns, although to a lesser extent. Both had swollen eyes and suffered vomiting and diarrhoea, and Vickie had some hair loss. When the three of them were examined, it was discovered that their symptoms were consistent with exposure to ultra-violet, microwave and X-ray radiation. Later Betty suffered cataracts and developed breast cancer and had to have a mastectomy.

A few months later, Cash and Landrum sued the US government for $20 million in medical compensation for the injuries they had suffered, with the help of Peter Gersten, a lawyer who specialises in UFO cases. The lawsuit proved to be a long and drawn-out one. Although it was ultimately a futile exercise, officers from every branch of the services were dragged into court. They insisted that the US military was neither involved in or responsible for what had happened. Finally, in 1986, a judge dismissed the case on the grounds that Cash and Landrum could not prove the 'UFO' that had caused them injury was the property of the US government. However, this ignored the presence of the Chinooks.

While the US government is in full-scale denial of the facts, the UFO community has broken into four factions when it comes to the Cash–Landrum case. One faction believes that they saw a top-secret nuclear-powered US military aircraft with extraterrestrial connections. Another faction believes that they witnessed the test-flight of a US military spacecraft back-engineered by US scientists from their examination of alien wreckage. An anonymous US intelligence office apparently confessed: 'The craft was an alien craft piloted by military aircraft pilots.'

A third faction believes that what they saw was a UFO intruder being shepherded out of US airspace by the military, while a fourth say what the Texas trio saw was one of the many manoeuvres conducted by the ultra-top-secret alliance between the US government and an alien force. All four agree that the helicopters were there to seal off the area in the event that the mysterious craft was somehow forced to land.

Houston-based Boeing aerospace engineer John Schuessler, a thirty-five-year veteran of many UFO investigations, studied the case and concluded that what Cash and Landrum had seen was a UFO, which may or may not have been in difficulty. The US military had deployed a fleet of helicopters to follow it and Cash, Landrum and Colby suffered injuries as a direct result of their encounter.

He discovered the helicopters came from Fort Hood, in Waco, Texas, and from an aircraft carrier anchored in the Gulf of Mexico – a vessel he cannot name. Schuessler says that the military helicopters were on a monitoring mission. The aliens are now here in such force that, although the US government is in communication with them, it can do nothing to prevent their frequent sorties. Schuessler discounts the idea that the aliens are here to create a new hybrid species using the terrestrial gene pool. Nor does he believe that the aliens are out to destroy us, although they are exploiting our resources in a number of mysterious ways. But the US government can do little more than keep tabs on their foraging expeditions – one of which was witnessed by Cash, Landrum and Colby.

Schuessler interviewed Air Force generals and congressmen, who gave him a lot of answers – but many of them turned out to be contradictory or downright lies. This convinced him that there was something to the story, or why would senior figures go to such great lengths to deny it? He pursued the matter through covert sources, who confirmed the story. But none of them would make any on-the-record admission. Nor could the government admit its impotence in court. However, a helicopter pilot came forward to give details of what had happened that night, but subsequently recanted. 'Obviously, his superiors shut him up,' Schuessler said.

Reviewing the witnesses' injuries, Schuessler said: 'Betty Cash's after-effects were the most drastic because she was out the car for the longest period of time and was exposed directly to the UFO. Within twenty-four hours, she had swelling, blisters on the face and sunburn. She was vomiting for weeks and, after three

weeks, a large amount of her hair fell out. In the years that followed, she suffered twenty-five to thirty hospitalisations, many of
them in intensive care. She developed cancer and a low red blood
cell count, she had bone marrow problems and then, eventually, she
had a stroke.'

He believes that her illnesses were cause by exposure to some
kind of radiation.

'I am not saying it was ionising radiation,' he said. 'The electromagnetic spectrum has a wide range of radiation that one can be
exposed to. At first, the doctors were totally baffled and the initial
doctor she went to in emergency care actually consulted other doctors who understood UFOs. Her long-term doctor, who was an
expert in the field of radiation sickness, felt that she had been
exposed to ionising radiation because her skin had the texture and
the feel of it. She couldn't have skin grafts on the burns because of
the texture of her skin.'

He could not get any more out of the doctors, for fear of breaching patient confidentiality, but they believed that the injuries were
genuine and not self-inflicted.

With no federal money to compensate them, Betty Cash, Vickie
Landrum and Colby tried to rebuild their lives. After years of drifting, Cash returned to live with her family in seclusion in Alabama.
Throughout this unsettled time, she was dogged by ill-health. She
contracted cancer, which she was certain was induced her UFO
encounter and also suffered a near-fatal heart attack. She said these
illnesses, together with intrusion by the press and assaults by the
government on her credibility in the years following her encounter,
virtually destroyed her life. She died on 29 December 1998, eighteen years to the day after her UFO encounter.

Vickie Landrum has also suffered health problems since the
encounter. Like Cash, she too drifted from place to place for years,
before disappearing into a very private life.

Only Colby appears to have come through unscathed. He suffered no long-term ill effects from the encounter and held down a
good job in Houston, Texas. However, he refuses to talk about his
experience.

'Many people have been injured emotionally as well as physically by their encounters with UFOs and have had their lives devastated,' says Sue Pitts, Alabama assistant state director for the Mutual
UFO Network. She tells the story of Falkville police chief Jeff
Greenhaw who photographed and chased an alien in 1973.

'Folks thought Jeff was hoaxed or was himself lying,' says Pitts.
'He lost his job. His wife divorced him. For years he's lived in seclusion in Alabama, refusing interviews.'

The sad case of Betty Cash, Vickie Landrum and Colby is far
from an isolated one. In the 1994 book *Taken*, author Karla Turner
describes symptoms similar to those exhibited by Betty Cash that
were suffered by a number of women abductees. Four of them
reported waking up with badly irritated eyes. Two of them suffered
inexplicable 'sunburn' and sudden hair losses. One, 'Beth', woke up
the morning after her abduction with a pounding headache, aching
muscles and dizziness. She felt extreme nausea and suffered from
diarrhoea and repeated vomiting. He eyes were so badly swollen
that she could not see. The parallels to Cash's symptoms are so close
that some have suggested that Cash, Landrum and Colby were
abducted.

Curiously, another of Turner's abductees, 'Amelia', reported
lying in bed surrounded by light – she was not alone and this was
witnessed by friends. The ceiling then opened. She looked up to see
a helicopter with two aliens inside. She could describe the helicopter and the aliens, but her friends were dazzled by the light and saw
nothing more.

Silver Linings

The effects of a UFO encounter, or an alien abduction, are not necessarily harmful. In some cases victims have reported that the experience has changed their life for the better. They have discovered
hitherto unknown artistic talents, the development of psychic skills,
a new awareness of environmental issues and profound lifestyle
changes. Some UFOlogists argue that these beneficial transforma-
tions may actually hold the key to a true understanding of UFO phenomena as a whole.

One such transformation was experienced by Peter Holding. As a teenager, he had a number of UFO encounters including an abduction-like experience. In the middle of the night, Holding woke suddenly and experienced an overwhelming compulsion to go to the window. When he opened the curtains, he noticed that there was no glass in the window. In its place was a mesmerising bright light with colours swirling around it. The next thing he knew the image had disappeared and the window had glass in it again. Soon after, Holding developed a previously undetected artistic talent for painting and photography. His works often incorporate the swirling image he saw during the encounter. He found that he could sell his paintings. His photographs have been published and he won a bursary to study art. It became his career, though he had no thought of becoming an artist until after the encounter.

Betty Andreason developed a talent for drawing after her abduction. A similar transformation was experienced by another witness known in the literature only as Bryan. He had had a lifelong history of UFO encounters and, during his adolescence, had a number of night-time visits from extraterrestrial entities. These encounters heralded a sudden explosion of artistic talent. He excelled at art school and went on to make his living by painting.

Psychic Powers

Many abductees have also shown a marked increase in their psychic awareness and abilities after their encounter. Dr John E. Mack, Professor of Psychiatry at Harvard Medical School, has come across several cases in his extensive work with abductees. One of his subjects was a woman named Eva. She had several UFO encounters. After an abduction, she developed telepathic contact with the alien entities. This has opened a gateway to a wide range of paranormal phenomena. She began to see ghosts and, during a near-death experience, she saw a doorway into another dimension.

One famous psychic who now attributes his astonishing powers to a UFO encounter is world-famous spoon-bender Uri Geller. One day when he was four or five years old and was living in Tel Aviv, Israel, he went into the overgrown garden across the road from the apartment block where he lived. He heard kittens crying and walked towards the sound. Then, suddenly, he felt something hovering above him. When he looked up, he saw a ball of light, not the sun, but a pulsating sphere of light in the air. Years later he could still remember this vividly.

'I remember all the sounds stopped, as if time itself had stopped,' he says. 'I looked at this thing for about ten seconds when, suddenly, a beam shot out of it and hit my forehead and knocked me back. It didn't hurt, it just pushed me back on to the ground.'

He suffered no physical after-effects, but soon afterwards, spoons started to bend in his hands. Geller is convinced that his experience was responsible. And he has a number of theories.

'My most bizarre theory is that the energy is coming from a higher intelligence, maybe extraterrestrial in form,' he says. 'Maybe a baby extraterrestrial that ran away from its parents is playing havoc with me and my life.'

Brazilian psychic Thomaz Green Morton, who is one of the world's most gifted paranormal practitioners, also believes that he got his prodigious powers from an extraterrestrial source. He was struck by a beam of light from a strange cloud while out fishing. Since then he has been able to perform psychokinesis and materialisation, and he has been investigated by numerous scientists, including NASA astronaut Dr Brian O'Leary.

Like Uri Geller, he can bend metal objects just by holding them. He can also transform a dollar bill into a bill made up of numerous other world currencies fused together. His favourite trick is to manifest perfume, which pours from his skin. In front of a camera and under the strictest scientific conditions, he can take a regular egg and materialise a chick inside it, which then breaks out of the shell.

Healing Powers

Other abductees have developed mediumship, dowsing abilities and healing powers after their encounters. In one case in 1978 Elsie Oakensen encountered a dumb-bell-shaped UFO while driving on a motorway in Northamptonshire. She was struck by the light of the object as it hovered above her car. Then quite spontaneously it disappeared. At the time, she thought it was just a brief encounter, but later she discovered that it had lasted a couple of hours. Within days, she developed spectacular healing abilities. She even cured her granddaughter, who was deaf, after doctors had suggested that no cure was likely. Oakensen was sure she had no such ability before.

Sometimes a UFO encounter has a more direct beneficial effect. Witnesses have reported miracle cures simply from seeing a UFO. In one striking case, an American law enforcement officer was pursing a UFO, when he was zapped by an energy beam at close quarters. Shortly before, a pet alligator had inflicted a painful bite on his hand. After the encounter, the bite mark was gone. The wound had spontaneous healed. It is thought that the intense energy fields that UFOs generate could be harnessed in the same way that radiotherapy is now used.

Much the same thing happened to a famous French biochemist. He told the story of his miracle cure to French UFOlogist Aimé Michel, who was allowed to publish an account of the abduction, only provided that he did not use his name and identified him as 'Dr X'.

In 1968, Dr X was thirty-eight and was living with his wife and fourteen-month-old son in a house overlooking a valley in southeast France. On the night of 2 November 1968, he awoke to hear the cries of his son. There was a thunderstorm going on outside. His wife was sound asleep, so Dr X got up to attend to the child. He did so with some difficulty. A couple of days before he had been chopping wood and had slipped. The axe had struck his left leg, bursting an artery and causing extensive internal bleeding. The wound had been treated by a doctor, who had examined it again the previous afternoon.

He already had problems with his right leg. During the Algerian war, a mine had exploded, fracturing his skull. This damaged the left hemisphere of his brain, paralysing the right side of his body. The paralysis passed after a couple of months, but left the muscles of his right side permanently wasted. This cost him a career as a musician and he could not stand on his right leg alone. Even so, he managed to totter to his son's room.

The boy was standing up in his crib, shouting, 'Rho, rho'.

This was the word the child used for a fire in the hearth or any bright light. He was pointing to the window. Dr X assumed he was indicating the lightning flashes that were visible through the cracks in the shutters. He got the boy some water and settled him down again. He could hear a shutter blowing back and forth in the breeze. It was in an upstairs room. He went up and closed it, noticing, in his half-asleep state, that the room was bathed in a pulsating light.

After closing the shutter, he felt thirsty and went downstairs to get a drink of water. Still puzzled by the pulsating light, he went out onto the terrace to investigate. It was 3:55 a.m. by the kitchen clock, he noted. Outside, he immediately saw the source of the flashing light. It was being emitted by two disc-shaped silver UFOs that hovered over the valley. They had long antennae sprouting from them. These seemed to be collecting electricity from the storm clouds. A glow would start at the furthest end of the antenna, build up along its length, then discharge suddenly as a lightning bolt to the ground. The build up happened rhythmically and the discharge bathed the whole valley with a pulsating light.

The two craft merged into one and the pulsating ceased. The united object then moved up the valley towards him. Dr X saw the underside was covered with rotating dark bands, causing patterns that defied the laws of science and logic. When the craft got within five hundred yards of Dr X, he began to feel that it had noticed him. It turned a bright beam of light on him, which bathed the whole house in an intense glow. He raised his hands to protect his eyes. Then there was a loud bang and the craft shot skywards so fast that it appeared to be a single streak of light.

When Dr X went back inside it was 4:05 am. He did not think that he had been outside for one minute, let alone ten. He went back upstairs and woke his wife. He told her what he had seen. As he talked excitedly to her, he paced up and down, stopping every so often to make notes and draw sketches of what he had seen. Suddenly, his wife noticed that he was walking normally. He pulled up his pyjama leg. The axe wound had healed completely. This was impossible in such a short time. What is more, his withered right leg was functioning perfectly too.

However, the encounter seemed to have disturbed him psychologically and he experienced some form of amnesia. After Dr X went back to bed, his wife noticed that he was talking in his sleep. She noted down what it was saying. One of the things he repeated was: 'Contact will be re-established by falling downstairs on 2 November.'

She did not tell him about this. When he awoke at 2 p.m. the next day, she suggested that he should write to the UFOlogist Aimé Michel, who was a friend. Why should he do that, he asked. His wife then discovered that he had lost all recollection of the UFO sighting the previous night. When she showed him the notes and sketches he had made, he grew alarmed.

Later that afternoon, Dr X tripped and fell down the stairs. It was as if something had grabbed his leg, he said. He hit his head and suddenly total recall of his experiences the previous night flooded back into his head.

However, there were other worrying effects from a subsequent encounter. Twelve days later, he dreamed about seeing another UFO. It was not like the ones he had seen. It was bright, luminous and triangular. Three days after that, he felt an itching sensation on his stomach. The following day a red triangle appeared around his navel. The dermatologist was baffled and wanted to write a scientific paper about it. Dr X prevented him.

Dr X contacted his friend Aimé Michel, who discovered that there had been a rash of UFO sightings around the area the night Dr X had seen his flying saucers. He suggested that the red triangle might be psychosomatic in origin. Dr X agreed, only to find that a similar red mark had appeared on his son's stomach the next day.

The experience left Dr X depressed and confused. The triangle disappeared, but reappeared every so often. Gradually Dr X began to take an interest in ecology. Other injuries he suffered healed up miraculously. However he has become sensitive to poltergeists and ghosts in the house. Aliens also pay visits and take him on journeys over impossible distances.

Spiritual Fulfilment

Sometimes the after-effects are more subtle, such as an urge to find greater spiritual fulfilment. One of Dr Mack's subjects, named Lee, found that a classical, intrusive abduction spiritually transformed her life. She told Dr Mack that the encounter was 'a priceless opportunity for spiritual growth and sensitivity to all sentient beings, ranging from insects to those of other dimensions and planetary systems'.

Another of Mack's subjects, Catherine, said that her abduction had boosted her intuition and given her a 'greater sensitivity to other people's auras'. In his assessment of the case, Dr Mack said: 'The acceptance of the actuality of her experiences, whatever their source may ultimately prove to be, has permitted Catherine to deal more effectively with the powerful effects and bodily feelings that accompany them and to reach a higher, or more creative, level of consciousness.'

Debbie Jordan had a spiritual awakening of a more religious nature. She had suffered multiple abductions, beginning in childhood, and was once artificially inseminated by an alien. Even so, she has drawn spiritual nourishment from it.

'The experiences changed from being physical in nature to being more mental, psychological, psychic and spiritual,' she said in an interview in 1996. 'I have since become aware of being taught Hinduism and Eastern religions I didn't have any previous knowledge of at all.' Now she has no terror of further abductions. 'It's like going to school. It opens my mind. It's changing everything about me inside – the way I look at life and God and myself and my fellow man.'

Another abductee reported more practical results of this alien education. During her abduction she was interrogated by the aliens. If she answered their questions, the extraterrestrials said, they would answer some of hers.

'We went on like this for quite a while,' she said. 'Because I left school at fourteen, I never learned anything. Anything I did learn, I learned through these experiences. In fact, without these experiences, I would be illiterate. I wouldn't have any interest in maths or history or anything like that.'

Positive lifestyle changes are also reported. Abductees frequently convert to vegetarianism or give up smoking; others change their attitude to the work they do and change career as a result. This happened to Elaine and John Avis after they and their three children were abducted in 1974. Driving on the outskirts of London, the family saw a light in the sky. Their car was then engulfed in a green mist. Again, although they thought this was a momentary experience, they discovered later that it had lasted two hours. Regressional hypnosis revealed an abduction, during which the family members underwent a thorough medical examination at the hands of the alien. But instead of being traumatised, the family members acquired a new-found self confidence. New, different avenues opened up for each of them. John became intensely creative and began to write poetry, while the son, Kevin, who had previously experienced learning difficulties at school, became an A-grade student. John and Elaine gave up smoking and drinking after the encounter, and the whole family gave up eating meat and developed strong feelings on the subject of the environment.

Abductees frequently report that the aliens are here to warn us that humankind is about to destroy the planet with nuclear weapons or our assault on the environment. Such things have been reported by contactees.since the 1950s.

In all these cases the after-effects were real, but no one knows why they happen. Some suggest that the alien presence has had a direct effect on the brain or consciousness of the victim. Others point out that similar changes in people had been observed in the aftermath of harrowing wartime experiences.

Frying Tonight

UFO encounters are best avoided, according to French UFOlogist, Jaques Vallee. He points out that the phenomenon dictates that a large amount of energy must confined in a restricted space. Just how dangerous this could be to human beings was calculated by American physicist Professor Galloway, who saw a UFO while driving along a highway in Louisiana one night. As he grew closer, the light from the UFO became as powerful as a car's headlights. Knowing the energy emitted by headlights and estimating the distance to the UFO, he was able to work out that the light energy it was emitting was equivalent to the output of a small nuclear reactor.

Dr Edward Condon, who conducted the University of Colorado's UFO investigation for the USAF, checked the figures and confirmed his conclusion.

Duck and Cover

Aliens have also taken a more direct approach in helping humankind to save itself from itself by turning their attentions on nuclear weapons facilities. In the 1950s, when extraterrestrials first contacted humankind, they warned us about nuclear weapons. We took no notice. Since then, they have decided to take the matter into their own hands.

One attack came at the height of the Cold War. On 27 October 1975, the air-raid sirens sounded at Loring Air Force Base in Maine. An unidentified flying object had penetrated the secure air space above the Intercontinental Ballistic Missile (ICBM) installation – one of over two thousand across America that were maintained in a state of constant readiness in case of a Soviet sneak attack. Even though the radar contact had not identified the incoming object as a Soviet missile, the military personnel on the base ran to their emergency stations, ready for the attack that they had spent so long preparing for.

A jet fighter was scrambled to check out the situation. But the pilot, Flight Sergeant Steven Eichner, found that the incoming object was not a Soviet missile. It was something far more exotic. Eichner saw an object that he described as 'a stretched-out football about the length of four trucks, hovering motionless in the air'. It was like nothing he had ever seen before.

It circled around the base for forty minutes then left as quickly as it had arrived. But it returned again the following day. This time it hovered over the base at a height of 160 feet, then landed between two ICBM silos. The military police took charge. They sent vehicles rushing at it in a suicide attack. But instead of retaliating, the UFO shot up into the air and disappeared. The emergency was over, but what no one knew was that this was the beginning of what was to become a sustained campaign of alien intervention at ICBM sites across America.

Sabotage

Just a few weeks after the Loring intrusion, the massive Malmstrom ICBM complex near Lewiston, Montana, played host to a similar but far more baffling UFO encounter. On 7 November, the security alarm sounded, indicating someone had intruded on to the base. The system showed that the problem was in the area of missile silo K-7. A Sabotage Alert Team was despatched. When they reached K-7, they saw a huge disc that was as large as a football field and glowing orange, hovering over the area. As they watched, the UFO sent a beam of light, as brilliant as daylight, down into the silo.

The SAT team was ordered to go in closer but refused. They were armed with machine guns, but none of the team opened fire. Air Force jets went in, but as they neared the object, it vanished. Then when the planes had passed, it suddenly reappeared. Eventually, it shot vertically into the sky until it disappeared from the radar.

A team of technicians was sent down into K-7 to check that everything was okay. They found that the launch and target codes for each of the missiles had been altered. These are the seven-digit codes that prevent the missiles being launched except by direct order from the President. They also fix each missile's target destinations. The codes are the ones that are kept in a black briefcase handcuffed to an officer who always accompanies the Commander in Chief wherever he goes. How these codes came to be altered remains a mystery.

Documents released by Colonel Terence C. James of the North

American Defense Command (NORAD) reveal that, during this period, twenty-four UFO sightings were reported over six different missile silos at Malmstrom. Michael Hesemann investigated the incident in his book *UFOs: The Secret History* and concluded: 'If at that moment an atomic war had broken out, the US would have been helpless. Not one rocket could have been started.'

Defenceless

Such incidents were not confined to Loring AFB and Malmstrom. From 27 October to 19 November 1975, there was a wave of incidents during which UFOs targeted a number of America's ICBM facilities. But it does not seem to have ended there.

On 18 January 1978, several witnesses saw a UFO hovering over McGuire AFB in New Jersey. An MP working for Air Force Security gave chase and found the UFO hovering over his car. Shortly after, the MP saw a three-foot-tall alien, which he said was 'greyish-brown, with a fat head, long arms and a slender body'. He panicked and loosed off five rounds at the alien and one at the UFO hovering above him. The UFO soared vertically and was joined by eleven other craft in the sky.

Afterwards, the body of the alien was found by a runway by a security patrol. A 'bad stench… like ammonia' was coming from it. Later that day, a team from Wright–Patterson came and sprayed the body with chemicals. They then crated it up, loaded it onto a C-141 transport place and left.

Dakota Shoot Out

On 16 November 1977 a UFO encounter took place at Ellsworth Air Force Base in South Dakota, about seven miles south-west of Nisland. A Freedom of Information Act request unearthed the following account:

'At 2059hrs., 16 Nov. 1977, Airmen 1C Phillips, Lt. A. Lims Security Control, telephone WSC. and reported an O2 alarm activation at L-9 and that Lims SAT #1, A-1C Jenkins & A-1C Raeke were dispatched, (Trip #62, ETA 2135hrs.)

'At 2147hrs., A-1C Phillips telephones WSC and reported that the situation at L-9 had been upgraded to a COVERED WAGON PER REQUEST OF Capt. Stokes, Larry D., FSO.

'Security Option 11 was initiated by WSC and Base CSC. BAF (Backup Security Force) #1&&2, were formed. At 2340hrs., 16 Nov. 77, the following information was learned: Upon arrival (2132hrs.) at Site #L-9. LSAT. Jenkins & Raeke, dismounted the SAT vehicle to make a check of the site fence line.

'At this time Raeke observed a bright light shinning vertically upwards from the rear of the fence line of L-9. (There is a small hill approximately 50 yards behind L-9.)

'Jenkins stayed with the SAT vehicle and Raeke proceeded to the source of the light to investigate. As Raeke approached the crest of the hill, he observed an individual dressed in a glowing green metallic uniform and wearing a helmet with visor.

'Raeke immediately challenged the individual, however the individual refused to stop and kept walking towards the rear fence line of L-9. Raeke aimed his M-16 rifle at the intruder and ordered him to stop.

'The intruder turned towards Raeke and aimed an object at Raeke which emitted a bright flash of intense light. The flash of light struck Raeke's M-16 rifle, disintegrating the weapon and causing second and third degree burns to Raeke's hands.

'Raeke immediately took cover and concealment and radioed the situation to Jenkins, who in turn radioed a 10-13 distress to Line Control. Jenkins responded to Raeke's position and carried Raeke back to the SAT vehicle. Jenkins then returned to the rear fence line to stand guard.

'Jenkins observed two intruders dressed in the same uniforms, walk through the rear fence line of L-9. Jenkins challenged the two individuals but they refused to stop. Jenkins aimed and fired two rounds from his M16 rifle.

'One bullet struck one intruder in the back and one bullet struck one intruder in the helmet. Both intruders fell to the ground, however, approximately fifteen seconds later Jenkins had to take cover from a bolt of light that missed him narrowly.

'The two intruders returned to the east side of the hill and disappeared. Jenkins followed the two and observed them go inside a saucer shaped object approximately 20ft in diameter and 20ft thick. The object emitted a glowing greenish light

'Once the intruders were inside, the object climbed vertically upwards and disappeared over the Eastern horizon. BAF> #1 arrived at the site at 2230hrs., and set up a security perimeter. Site Survey Team arrived at the site (0120hrs.) and took radiation readings, which measured from 1.7 to 2.9 roentgens.

'Missile Maintenance examined the missiles and warheads and found the nuclear components missing from the warhead. Col. Speaker, Wing Cmdr. arrived at the site and set up an investigation. A completed follow-up report of this incident will be submitted by order of Col. Speaker.

'Raeke was later treated at the base hospital for second and third degree radiation burns to each hand. Raeke's M-16 rifle could not be located at the site.'

The Soviet Threat

At first the strange alien craft attacking American air bases were thought to be part of the Soviet threat. But the flight characteristics and eyewitness reports from highly trained Air Force observers led the brass to conclude that these were no terrestrial intruders. It was only years later, after the collapse of the Soviet Union, that they discovered that Soviet missile sites also had their hands full with alien intruders: 124 KGB UFO files were released, revealing that Russian nuclear facilities were receiving similar UFO attention.

On 28 June 1988, a UFO was seen by four witnesses flying back and forth over a military base near the nuclear test site of Kapustin Yar in the lowland of the Caspians for two hours. The KGB report said that the UFO flew over the weapons storage area and beamed a shaft of light down into the missile silo. The report fails to mention whether the missiles in the depot were nuclear.

In March 1993, Colonel Boris Sokolov of the Soviet Ministry of Defence told US TV journalist George Knapp that he had been flown to an ICBM base in the Ukraine. On the way, he had been given a top-secret report describing an incident that took place there in October 1983. The report said that a UFO had come close to triggering World War III after it had penetrated Soviet air space and had hovered over the nuclear missile silos. Attempts to shoot the alien craft down had failed when the automatic mechanism for firing the defensive missiles packed up. This was thought to be due to the influence of the UFO. Again the launch codes for the ICBMs had been scrambled, putting that part of the Soviet nuclear arsenal out of action.

Benign Intent

The Russians are now convinced of the aliens' benign intentions. In February 1997, Italian UFO researcher Giorgio Bongiovanni went to the Russian town of Tever to meet a delegation from the Russian military, headed by General Gennadi Reschetnikov of the Air Force Academy. He said: 'The main attention of UFOs is on all of humanity. But above all it has been the US and Russia, since they have the most powerful nuclear reserves in the world. I think this is the reason the aliens are worried.

Reschetnikov is the highest ranking member of the Russian military to confirm the existence of UFOs and he believes that the aliens are particularly interested in the spiritual condition of humankind. He thinks the aliens are curious about human behaviour and, although they influence us for the good, they expect something in return. That something could be the destruction of nuclear weapons.

Balance of Terror

UFO intrusions at nuclear bases on the continental United States and in the former Soviet Union may explain the aliens' evident interest in USAF airbases in the United Kingdom. One of the security policeman at RAF Woodbridge in Suffolk in 1980 says that he was told by Lieutenant Colonel Charles Halt that a UFO had sent down beams of light over the weapons depot that affected a cache of nuclear weapons that were illegally stored there. The Ministry of Defence was highly concerned when tiny holes were discovered, burned through the walls of the depot.

It is interesting that in none of these cases was the UFO misidentified as incoming ICBMs by either the American or Soviet war rooms, prompting a nuclear response that could have resulted in global annihilation. This is because UFO activity had already forced the two sides in the Cold War to improve their communications, according to UFO researcher Colonel Robert O. Dean.

Between 1963 and 1967 Dean was stationed at NATO's Supreme Headquarters of Allied Powers Europe (SHAPE) in Paris. He was allowed access to the war room there, which was officially known as the Supreme Headquarters Operations Center (SHOC). He says that throughout the 1950s and 1960s NATO defence systems regularly tracked large, circular metallic objects flying in formation over Europe. They appeared to be coming from the Soviet bloc and misidentification of UFOs as Soviet missiles came close to triggering a nuclear exchange.

'On three occasions while I was stationed there,' he says, 'SHAPE went to full nuclear alert.'

Along with other senior military personnel, Colonel Robert O. Dean was shown a number of photographs and videotapes depicting aliens while working at SHAPE.

These brushes with nuclear holocaust prompted the commander of SHAPE, General Lemnitzer, to start a three-year, in-depth study of UFOs. He also established a hotline between SHOC and the Warsaw Pact commander. After the hotline was installed, the situation grew less tense. It led to a direct phone line being established between the White House and the Kremlin. So it was UFOs that led to the thawing of the Cold War and the beginning of *détente*.

Alien Activist

UFOs have intervened elsewhere. In 1986 a number of UFOs were seen hovering over a secret nuclear facility that had been built by the Brazilian government to produce weapons-grade plutonium, in violation of international agreements. Prominent UFO researcher Dr Jim Hurtak investigated the case and discovered that the appearance of the UFOs had attracted the attention of the media, which subsequently discovered the nuclear facility. Because it was built in defiance of treaty commitments, its construction was found unconstitutional and it was closed.

Hurtak believes that events like this show that aliens come with benevolent intentions. Michael Hesemann also believes it is reasonable to extrapolate that extraterrestrials would intervene if human belligerence reached a point where annihilation of the planet became inevitable.

But why are the aliens so interested in our well-being? Dr Hurtak thinks that extraterrestrials are linked with 'ultraterrestrials', or higher spiritual forces, who have intervened before at key moments in history. Indeed, human life on this planet may only be an experiment that aliens have a vested interest in seeing succeed.

Abduction researcher Dr John Mack often hears the aliens' views on human nuclear destructive capabilities from his abductees. He sees their motives for intervention in human affairs as far less altruistic. 'The survival of man figures large in the well-being of creatures we haven't yet met,' he says.

UFO researcher Michael Lindemann also believes that nuclear war on Earth might have untold consequences in other dimensions. Extraterrestrials normally adopt a hands-off approach that allows humans to learn by their own mistakes, he says. They only intrude when it is critically important, not necessarily for their own agenda, but for a larger reason, such as the balance of the cosmos as a whole.

However, much of the information about UFO interest in nuclear installations in the West and in the former Soviet Union is still withheld from the public. It may be some time before we can fully assess its impact.

Target Brazil

Alien attentions are not always so benign. Sometimes they attack for no apparent reason. In the late 1970s, they brought their malevolent attentions to bear on the northern Brazilian states of Maranhao and Para, which together cover an area larger than the state of California. Throughout the decade, there had been a huge wave of UFO reports from this area. But these soon turned out to be no ordinary sighting reports, where the witness sees lights in the sky that perform extraordinary aerobatics before disappearing at an incredible speed. In northern Brazil the UFO fleet had come with hostile intent. Hundreds of thousands of people reported that UFOs fired on them with beams of light. Some people were chased by balls of light that knocked them unconscious and left them with bizarre wounds.

The epicentre of the alien attack was the remote area around the cities of Belem, Sao Luis and Teresina. Manoel Laiva, the mayor of the small town of Pinheiro, estimated that, in just one year, as many as 50,000 people in the area reported UFO sightings. French UFOlogist Jacques Vallee says that UFOs were being seen every night at the peak of the wave in late 1977. Some were seen descending from the sky to hover over houses and probe the interiors with beams of light. Others were seen emerging from the sea, leading to speculation that the aliens had established an underwater base off the coast.

The alien assault was so widespread that it plainly caused the authorities some concern. When amateur UFOlogists turned up to investigate, they found a crack team from the Brazilian Air Force already on the ground. At the time, the Brazilian government would not confirm or deny the attacks, but in July 1987 all was revealed when Brazil's top UFOlogist A.J. Gevaerd interviewed the head of the Air Force team.

Colonel Uyrange Hollanda, who by then had retired, told Gevaerd that the Air Force's top-secret mission to investigate the alien attacks was called 'Operation Saucer'. The investigation began in September 1977 and ran for three months. It had been instigated at the request of the state authorities of Maranhao and Para. They had already begun to investigate hundreds of reports of attacks but soon found they had something on their hands that they were ill equipped to cope with. The civil authorities had sent medical teams out to the remote areas where the reports were coming from. The doctors examined the victims, took statements and sent back their findings. When the civil authorities back in the state capitals read these, they found them so disturbing that they insisted the

Air Force take some sort of action.

Stationed at the headquarters of the 1st Regional Air Command at Belem, Colonel Hollanda was ordered to lead a team into the jungle to investigate. At the time, the frequency of the attacks was at an all-time high. Hollanda's team comprised forty specialists. They were a mixture of civilian and military scientists – doctors, biologists, chemist, physicists and engineers. The team's official mission was to collect eyewitness reports from villagers, ascertain the source of the attacks, and monitor all alien activity using special photographic equipment. Hollanda also had secret orders to attempt to make contact with the aliens to find out what they wanted.

Operation Saucer's primary objective was the island of Colares, just to the north of Belem. The UFO reports were at their peak there. When the UFO team reached the area, they discovered that most of the inhabitants of Colares had fled in panic. Even the schoolteachers, the dentist and the sheriff had turned tail. And they had every reason to flee.

Dr Wellaide Cecin, who was working on the island during the attacks, had treated thirty patients injured by the aliens. Victims had been struck by beams of light that left them with blackened skin, anaemia, loss of hair, inexplicable red patches on the skin, numbness, uncontrollable shaking and puncture wounds. The aliens often attacked after the victims had gone to bed at night. When the beam hit them, they found themselves immobilised and unable to scream. The beam pressed down on their chest like a huge weight and burned them like a cigarette end. Scientists on the Air Force team suggested that the alien energy beam could have been a complex combination of ionising and non-ionising radiation. If such a beam contained pulsed microwaves, it would disrupt the central nervous system, paralysing the victim, cause hallucinations and even affect long-term behaviour.

Aerial observers were deployed each night to film UFO activity. During the first few weeks, they spotted UFOs every other night. They saw balls of light as well as large, structured craft fly directly over their heads. The alien craft did not attack them, but they gradually started moving in closer, as if they were observing the team sent to observe them.

During their investigations, Hollanda's team also encountered large, disc-shaped craft and cylindrical UFOs, as well as much smaller vehicles. Another strange UFO often seen was box shaped. Dubbed the 'flying refrigerator', it made a humming sound that remained at the same pitch despite changes in speed and acceleration.

The balls of light also came in a variety of sizes. When some of these moved close to the Air Force observers, the intensity of their brilliance diminished and the observers were then able to make out the shape of a vehicle inside. They were tear shaped with a transparent canopy, similar to that of a helicopter. Under the canopy a number of alien figures could be seen. The aliens were generally of the classic Grey type, about four feet tall, with big black eyes. Other types were also seen. Hollanda's team took photographs of the craft they encountered, and made a series of sketches of the aliens.

Although the aliens showed no hostile intent towards the Air Force team, their attacks on local hunters and fishermen continued. A variety of craft were involved. Among of the most deadly were large, cylindrical UFOs the villagers called *camburoes*. These would hover over an area and send out powerful beams of light that would sweep back and forth across the ground. One witness, Joao de Brito, related what happened when a friend of his was attacked.

'He felt the light bearing down on his body,' de Brito said, 'and he felt his strength being sucked out of him. He was sure he was going to die. The flying thing was shaped like a cylinder, and he could hear voices coming from it in an unknown language. It left him powerless and he ended up in hospital.'

When the villagers tried to escape the bright beams of light and sheltered in their homes, they found that the alien beams could easily slice through roofs and walls. The local people's only experience of anything similar was the menace of wild animals, so they lit huge fires down by the river and gathered around them. Strangely this seemed to deter the aliens – to begin with. But after a few weeks, they got used to the fires and the attacks resumed.

About seven weeks into Operation Saucer, the UFO activity began to increase dramatically and the aliens appeared more hostile. Each time Hollanda moved his team to a new area of operation, a UFO would already be hovering over their destination when they arrived. This left Hollanda feeling that the aliens were able to read his thoughts and anticipate his every move. He became increasingly aware that his team had become the object of intense scrutiny. In one extraordinary incident, Hollanda and one of his men set off up one of the Amazon tributaries in a small boat. They were about seventy-five miles from Belem when Hollanda decided to return to camp. A sudden storm meant that the rivers in the area were flooding rapidly, making navigation difficult. As they turned a bend in the river, they saw a huge oval-shaped UFO, around three hundred foot tall, hovering over the bank. As they watched, a door slid open at the top of the craft and a figure emerged. It began to float gently towards them. Without his full force around him, Hollanda decided it was time to make a strategic withdrawal, gunned the out-board motor and made a rapid escape.

Although the Air Force team itself had not been attacked, Holland believed that all of them had been abducted. Hollanda believed that he had undergone multiple abductions himself and all the team members reported experiencing periods of 'missing time'. Hollanda himself had a series of strange dreams. These are common in abductees and are often unconscious memories of the abduction experience.

During his interview, Hollanda told Gevaerd that he had been physically and psychologically examined by the aliens. He said this was for some sort of preparation, but he did not know what for. Hollanda even gave Gevaerd a drawing of one of extraterrestrials holding a pistol-shaped device used in the examination.

It was clear that abduction was part of a long-term alien agenda, as abductions from the area had been going on for quite some time. Sixteen-year-old Antonio Alves Ferreira had been first taken on 4 January 1975. He had heard a buzzing sound in the back yard of his parent's house in the Indigo district of Sao Luis. When he went outside to find out what it was, he saw a small disc hovering over the house. He was not alone. Around five hundred other witnesses reported seeing the same UFO. Since the first encounter Ferreira has been abducted eleven times. Three humanoid aliens are responsible. They told him they were from the planet 'Protu'. They made a clone of him to use and left it as a double on Earth, while he was on their craft. He learned their language and, on one occasion, recorded their conversation. This is the only known recording of on alien speech.

Then on 10 July 1977, a chicken farmer from Pinheiro named Jose Benedito Bogea was on his way on foot to Sao Luis when he was pursued by a bright, bluish-green light.

'I raised my arms,' he said, 'and I saw a bright flash of light. It knocked me to the ground. I felt like I'd had an electric shock. Then I passed out.'

When he came too he found himself in a strange alien city with avenues and gardens. Later he was transported back to Earth and dropped off some seventy-five miles from where he had been abducted. He had been missing for twenty-four hours.

Ninety days after Hollanda's team began their investigation, Operation Saucer was suddenly stopped. Hollanda was ordered to close down the operation and forget about it. This was easier said than done as Hollanda continued to feel the effects years after the operation ended. He said he could feel the presence of the aliens in his home. Sometimes he could see them and sometimes he could just feel they were there.

After Operation Saucer, Hollanda also found that he had acquired paranormal abilities. He was able to read people's thoughts. Later he found he could predict the future. He would know in advance that people were about to turn up at his house and he could tell what was going to happen at work.

Despite these fringe benefits, the abduction experience had a profound and disturbing impact on Hollanda. During the interview with Gevaerd he would often break down and cry. His wife became so concerned that she tried to stop the interview. In an effort to help Hollanda come to terms with the experience, Gevaerd arranged regressional hypnosis for Hollanda. But two days before the first session, Hollanda committed suicide. Gevaerd believes that he was the victim of the profound psychological trauma that can be incurred by exposure to extraterrestrials.

Before Hollanda died, he gave Gevaerd copies of a number of documents that had been included in the detailed report he had submitted to the Armed Forces Headquarters in Brasilia. He also gave Gevaerd copies of some of the five hundred photographs the team had taken in the area. After Hollanda submitted his report, he got no response from the authorities and the outcome of Operation Saucer is unknown.

By the early 1980s, the frequency of UFO sightings and alien attacks in the area had dropped significantly, but they have never stopped completely. Gevaerd believes that aliens have selected remote areas in Brazil where they can go about their activities with impunity. The principal agenda behind the attacks, he says, is some form of biological experimentation. Other investigators have come to the same conclusion.

Fighting Back

Human beings are a resilient species. Even in the face of alien aggression we are not going to give up without a fight. Since 1980 and the beginnings of America's 'Stars Wars' programme, weapons have been under development that can shoot alien craft from the skies.

They had one of their first successes on 28 September 1989, when a mysterious object was shot down over Long Island, New York. According to UFO researchers Brian Levin and John Ford of the Long Island UFO Network, the craft was destroyed using a 'Doppler radar system' built by the III Electronics company in conjunction with the Brookhaven National Laboratories, as part of the Strategic Defense Initiative.

Some three years later, on 24 November 1992, a second UFO was downed in the same area. Around 7 p.m., eyewitness Walter Knowles saw what he described as 'a tubular, dark metallic object with blue lights on each end' moving slowly over South Haven Park. Then he saw a blinding flash of light and the spacecraft

makes the STS 48 video so controversial is that it also
the craft made off at these astonishing speeds because the
fired on by some exotic weapons system. Careful analysis of
video shows that a double flash of energy was aimed at one of the
craft. Its response is immediate. It changes direction and acceler-
ates away at incredible speed.

Kasher was employed to work on the Star Wars programme
until 1996. He points out that, despite the huge amounts of money
spent, no anti-ICBM umbrella was ever built. Meanwhile, $35 bil-
lion is spent every year in a 'black budget' to develop all sorts of
covert technologies.

'It is entirely conceivable that what appears to be a weapon firing at the objects in the STS 48 video may, indeed, be the result of
some covert black budget,' he says.

What's more, it backs former Pentagon alien technology expert
Colonel Philip Corso's thesis that the US have been secretly fight-
a covert war against the aliens for 50 years. He too believes that
was developed not only to protect against Soviet ICBM

crashed into the park. John Ford later obtained a video, shot by Brookhaven Fire Fighters, that shows the charred wreckage of the alien ship.

Over recent years, the number of reports of hostile exchanges between the military and UFOs has risen dramatically. It also appears that military attacks on UFOs have been carried out using exotic technology. Many investigators now believe that much of today's military technology, particularly weapons developed in the Strategic Defense Initiative and now the National Missile Defense programme, has been created with the express purpose of repulsing an alien invasion.

Even more remarkable evidence that this is the case comes from a video shot by one of the TV cameras aboard NASA's Space Shuttle *Discovery* on 15 September 1991. It shows number of strange glowing objects entering the picture. They are seen to respond to a series of flashes from Earth, make a ninety-degree turn – something impossible for a terrestrial craft – then accelerate. The video comes from the US cable TV channel N

NASA

of NASA missions.

enormous controver-

. NASA maintains that

an ice crystals or space

of the Shuttle's altitude

discredited by Dr Jack

Nebraska, Omaha.

stals. We proved that was

ice crystals couldn't change

d.'

s that the objects were at the

He also calculated that they

SDI was to be used not only to attack but
also to defend agains

US government po
1967, the National Sec
secret intelligence ser
Hypothesis and Survival
adequate defense measure
Michael Michaud, Deputy
Office of International Sec
solar systems are a potentia
threat to them. Even if an a
within its own ranks, it wou
take the measures it felt w

It was President Reagan who instigated the Star Wars programme.

Under Attack

The modern military's gung-ho attitude could well be because the armed forces themselves have been under attack since flying saucers first appeared in our skies.

One of the earliest hostile encounters occurred over Kentucky on 7 January 1948. Captain Thomas F. Mantell was flying an F-51 Mustang when he was asked to check out reports of a strange flying object. At 2:40 p.m. he made visual contact at 15,000 feet:

'It appears to be metallic, of tremendous size,' he radioed back. 'I'm trying to close for a better look.'

He followed it up to 30,000 feet where, though he was a very experienced pilot, he lost consciousness due to lack of oxygen and crashed. Richard T. Miller was in the operations room at Godman Air Force Base and heard Mantell's last words.

'My God, I see people in this thing,' he said.

It appears he got too close. Witnesses saw the plane being enveloped in white light. It 'belly flopped' onto the ground, but came off remarkably unscathed – seeing that it had just fallen from 30,000 feet. And Miller said that it had crashed more than an hour after its fuel was supposed to have run out.

An eerily similar encounter took place between a military helicopter and a UFO over Ohio in 1973. On 18 October, Captain Lawrence Coyne and his three crew members were approaching Cleveland Hopkins military airport, when they saw a red light approaching them at high speed on a collision course. Coyne took evasive action and tried to put an emergency call through to the control tower, but it was blocked by interference from the alien craft. Then they saw a cigar-shaped UFO, around sixty-five feet in length. It had a domed top with portholes. It sent out a green beam of energy, which enveloped the helicopter.

Coyne shouted: 'My God, what's happening?'

The beam pulled the helicopter upwards, towards the alien craft. Together they ascended at a rate of around 1,500 feet a minute until they reached 5,000 feet. Then the energy beam flicked out, releasing the helicopter, and the UFO took off at tremendous speed. Numerous eyewitnesses saw the encounter. People stopped their cars on the nearby highway to watch. They described how the green light illuminated the entire area.

Another encounter occurred over pre-revolutionary Iran. When the Shah was still in power, Iran was one of the US's staunchest allies and the Iranian Air Force was equipped with the latest American attack aircraft. At around 1 a.m. on 19 September 1976, Iranian military radar operators detected an unidentified object flying at an altitude of six thousand feet over the Merkabah Tower in Tehran. An F-4 Phantom jet was scrambled from Shahrokin Air Force Base to intercept the mysterious craft. As the interceptor jet sped to within twenty-two miles of the object, the aircraft's instrumentation panel suddenly went dead. The pilot tried to report the malfunction, but the communications equipment was also out. He turned, breaking off the intercept and heading back to base. Then, when it presented no further threat to the UFO, the Phantom's systems came back to life.

In the mean time, a second Phantom had been despatched to intercept the UFO. This time, when the jet got within striking distance, the UFO sped off. The Phantom gave chase, but suddenly the pilot saw 'flashing strobe lights arranged in a rectangular pattern' pulsing in front of his face. Even so, the pilot made another attempt to close in on the UFO. This time a brightly-lit object emerged from the UFO and began moving at high speed towards the jet. This was plainly a hostile act. The pilot automatically retaliated with a Sidewinder. But as he tried to activate it, his weapons system went dead and he lost all communications.

The Phantom was now in imminent danger. The pilot jinked and janked, and banked his jet into a steep dive. Looking around to see if he had shaken the bright object that had been fired at him, he saw it circle around and rejoin the UFO. Almost immediately, the pilot's weapons system was reactivated and his communications returned.

The pilot then saw the UFO fire another missile. This one

descended rapidly towards the ground. It made a controlled land-ing, then cast a brilliant luminescence over an area that the pilot estimated to be around two miles in diameter. While the pilot was watching it, the UFO disappeared.

A fatal encounter took place between the US military and an alien craft above Puerto Rico on 28 December 1988. At 7:45 a.m. hundreds of eyewitnesses saw a huge, metallic-grey, triangular craft, the size of a football field, hovering over Saman Lake in the Cabo Rojo area, which is one of the island's UFO hotspots. 'It was enormous, with many flashing coloured lights,' said eyewitness Wilson Sosa.

Two US Navy F-14 'Tomcats' were scrambled from Roosevelt Road Naval Base to intercept it. When they caught up with it, the alien craft took evasive action. In an attempt to shake them, it spi-ralled downwards in tight circles. One F-14 nearly collided with the alien craft, but the UFO jinked out of the way. Despite its size, the alien craft was much more manoeuvrable than the Tomcats.

'The jets tried to intercept it three times,' Wilson Sosa said, 'and that's when the UFO slowed down and almost stopped in mid-air.'

Then, in a seemingly suicidal attack, one of the F-14s flew directly at it. The witnesses braced themselves for a collision. Instead, they saw the aircraft disappear as if it had been drawn into the bigger craft. The other F-14 then approached the rear of the craft. It too was swallowed up. Afterwards the huge craft gave out a blinding flash, and split into two smaller triangular ships, which sped away in opposite directions.

Retribution

The aliens may only have been getting their own back. Puerto Rican Professor of Chemistry Calixto Perez said that he examined a dead humanoid being in 1980. It had been killed by Jose Luis 'Chino' Zayas, a Puerto Rican teenage who, with a bunch of friends, had come across a group of small humanoids while exploring the caves at Tetas de Cayey. One of them turned on Zayas and he battered it to death with a stick, stoving its head in. They kept the corpse as a trophy. It was preserved in formaldehyde by a local undertaker.

Later it was seized by officers who said they were attached to NASA, and photographed, before being 'lost' by US officials.

Rules of Engagement

The official policy of the Soviet Air Force was to actively intercept all UFOs and the Russian military established what became the biggest organised effort ever to track and catalogue UFO encounters. Soviet pilots were ordered to get as close to UFOs as possible in an attempt to identify them. However, there were encounters that really scared the authorities. This led to a reversal of policy. Standing orders were issued that pilots should avoid all contact.

Meanwhile, South Africa maintained a 'search and destroy' policy and, in 1990, two South African Mirage FIIG jets, armed with experimental Thor-2 laser cannons, hit a UFO and downed it in the Kalahari desert.

Tony Dodd of Quest was contacted by Captain James Van Greunen, a special investigations intelligence officer with the South African Air Force, who provided Dodd with a small dossier on the case. This contained a report that showed the UFO had been clocked by radar travelling over six thousand miles an hour when it was hit. A special team was sent to the crash site where they found a large silvery disc embedded in the ground. High radiation readings were reported and the craft was carefully shipped back to Valhalla air base.

Once the craft was inside a hangar, a hatchway opened up and out stepped two creatures. They were four feet tall, with grey skin, no body hair, over-large heads and huge slanting eyes. The aliens were taken to a medical unit where they were examined. Passed as fit, they were shipped to Wright–Patterson AFB.

Soon after Van Greunen met Dodd in England, he was ordered home by the South African government. He later fled to Germany where he published his story.

2 Evidence

Photographic Evidence

In the face of official denials, many people refuse to believe in the reality of UFOs and, since the beginning of extraterrestrial visitations, UFOlogists have known that witness reports – no matter how unimpeachable the eyewitness – were not enough. So they have struggled to get convincing evidence on film. The problem is that, in these days of science fiction blockbusters and hi-tech wizardry, almost anything can be faked. The most amazing effects can be produced by even the humblest camera.

'The adage that the camera cannot lie was disproved as soon as it was invented,' says UFO researcher Nick Pope.

The footage showing the alien autopsy and the alien interview were worth hundreds of thousands of pounds. Even a good still picture of a UFO can be worth a lot of money. So no photograph can be taken at face value. It has to be thoroughly investigated by skilled researchers. And even then it might be impossible to prove that the picture is genuine.

In the early days of the UFO sightings, anything went. UFOlogists assumed that if an image looked like a UFO, then it was a UFO. Many photographs of alien 'spaceships' were published in the 1940s and 1950s, fuelling the burgeoning UFO fever. To modern eyes many of these snapshots are obvious, crude fakes made by hanging models from trees or tossing hubcaps in the air. But no one looked too closely. Even fairly dubious pictures were considered good publicity. This naive approach was courting disaster.

The Camera Does Lie

UFOlogy's nemesis came in the form of Alex Birch, a teenage boy from Sheffield. In February 1962, Alex and some friends saw a formation of flying saucers above their garden. Alex succeeded in taking a photograph of the extraterrestrial fleet. Even though no one else in Sheffield had seen the craft, the photograph was taken at face value. Birch and his father were treated like heroes. They were invited to London to file their sighting report in person with officials of the British Air Ministry. And Alex addressed a packed audience at the inaugural meeting of the British UFO Research Association.

Among UFO enthusiasts it was one of the most talked about photographs in years. The problem was that the UFO lobby were so eager to believe that it was genuine that nobody carried out any meaningful investigation. All the picture showed was a smattering of dark blobs on a grainy picture of the sky. Nevertheless, the case entered UFO folklore as an unsolved mystery.

Ten years later, Alex Birch had grown up and he decided to confess. The photograph was a trick. He had painted a few crude flying saucers on to a sheet of glass, propped it up in his back garden

A fake UFO photograph, made in the early 1990s in the former Soviet Union

and photographed it against some blurred tree branches and the sky. To the uncritical eyes, the result vaguely resembled UFOs hovering in mid-air. Cleverly he had avoided including in the shot any reference point, such as a building, which would give the viewer some idea of the size of the objects and their distance from the camera.

Two photographs were taken of a UFO in his garden by Ralph Ditter at Zanesville, Ohio, USA, on 13 November 1966. He later admitted a hoax.

Birch's confession caused a sensation. The general view was that he had set the cause of UFOlogy back years. In fact, in the long run, he probably did it a great service. After his schoolboy hoax, UFO enthusiasts would never be as gullible again. UFO bodies set up guidelines that were to be used when investigating photographic cases. Over the years, these have been constantly refined and improved. These guidelines were used to review old UFO photographs and obvious fakes were thrown up. They also allowed UFOlogists to guard against new hoaxes and helped them weed out what were termed 'accidental fakes'.

Authentication

Just as the human eye can easily be deceived, the camera is open to being fooled. If an eyewitness is willing to believe that a perfectly ordinary light shining through a mist-filled sky is a UFO, a camera will not tell them it's not. In fact, a camera can be a liability when UFO spotting. You experience what you see very differently through the limited frame of a viewfinder than with the naked eye.

Because a camera freezes an instant in a single shot, things that looked quite normal in motion can appear as anomalous in a photograph. A common example of an 'accidental fake' can occur when a bird flies through the scene. For just a fraction of a second that the shutter is open, the bird's wings will be caught in a configuration that would not normally be seen by the human eye. And when that is rendered in the two dimensions of a photographic print, instead of the three dimensions of real life, it might look deceptively like a flying saucer – even if the photographer had no intention of producing a fake.

Calling in a photographic expert is now an automatic first step. They can pick out things like lens flare and other aberrations. In all, around five thousand photographic cases have been investigated around the world and a very small number – perhaps only fifty – really seem to be unexplained. Most are a mixture of accidental fakes, common confusion and out-and-out trickery. Even when visual evidence appears irrefutable, few experts would stake their reputation on a picture being genuine.

'Photographs are poor evidence because there are so many things we can do to technically produce images,' says retired USAF colonel and prominent UFOlogist Wendelle Stevens.

Stevens himself goes to great lengths to authenticate the photographs that are sent to him. He interviews the photographer, visits the place where the pictures were taken and takes his own shots from the same spot to use as a reference. By comparing his picture with the original he can usually work out how big the object is and how far it is from the lens. This eliminates the photographs that have been faked using models.

Another technique Steven employs is an evaluation of the 'blur factor'. The amount of blurring on the object, relative to that of other objects in the picture, helps determine whether the object is moving, and if so, how fast. The approximate speed and direction of flight can also be gauged from the 'edge definition'. This exploits the Doppler effect, where light waves from the leading edge are compressed, while those from the trailing edge are stretched.

The distance of an object from the lens can also be judged by 'atmospheric attenuation'. This is caused by moisture in the atmosphere that cuts down the amount of light reaching the lens. Computer analysis also picks up the 'chroma factor'. As red light is more readily absorbed by the atmosphere than blue, the image should contain a greater component of blue the further it is from the camera.

UFO Down

Winnowing out the accidental fake is never easy. One seemingly cast-iron photograph was only discredited after twenty-three years. In November 1966, a famous scientist was driving across the Williamette Pass in Oregon. He had a camera with him and was planning to take photographs of the snow-decked peaks. But as he was driving, he saw out of the corner of his eye a strange object zipping skywards. Reacting instinctively, he fired off a shot.

When the photograph was developed it showed a flat-bottomed disc climbing from the trees, sucking a plume of snow in its wake. More remarkable still was the fact that three separate images of the UFO were on the one print. It was as if the craft had dematerialised and rematerialised several times during the few hundredths of a second that the camera shutter was open. The cameraman was not certain of what he had seen and wished to remain anonymous. He was a big-name biochemist with a PhD and a reputation to lose, certainly not your average hoaxer. Besides, the photograph seemed to speak for itself.

The impeccable credentials of the photographer did play a part in how seriously the case was taken. *Photographic Magazine* conducted an investigation and gave the picture a clean bill of health. The optical and physical characteristics of the camera and image were even used to deduce the approximate shape, size and speed of the mysterious object.

Then in 1993, researcher Irwin Weider announced that the photo was a fake. Everyone was shocked. For years Weider had believed the photograph really did show a UFO. *Photographic Magazine*'s investigation seemed conclusive. But then Weider had taken a trip through the area where the picture had been taken and thought he saw a UFO himself. He drove up and down the road the same stretch of road and found that the 'UFO' only appeared under very specific conditions. This aroused his suspicion. He began conducting experiments, taking pictures from his moving car and using different shutter speeds. He eventually discovered that the UFO was actually a road sign, which appeared to be a flying saucer due to the interaction of the car and camera. He could even reproduce the triple image at the right speeds.

The world of UFOlogy was stunned by this news, but it just goes to show how carefully photographic evidence must be evaluated. However, Weider's tenacious methods do not always bear fruit.

The Genuine Article

There are some UFO photographs that cannot be dismissed. One such picture was taken by farmer Paul Trent, who snapped a flying saucer over his ranch near McMinnville, Oregon on 11 May 1950. The photograph's background and foreground were both clear, allowing the UFO's size and distance to be estimated. Subsequent computer enhancement has revealed that the disc is solid, between sixty and a hundred feet in diameter, and made from a highly reflective material.

Then on 16 January 1958, when the Brazilian naval vessel *Almirante Saldanha* was carrying a team of scientists to a weather station on Trindade Island – an uninhabited rock in the South Atlantic – a UFO appeared low above the ocean and flew past the ship. It circled the island and headed away. More than a dozen people on the ship saw it. One of them was the expedition photographer. He had his camera to hand and took a sequence of shots clearly showing the object.

When the Brazilian captain got back to port, he had the film processed and the resulting pictures were handed over to the military. The Brazilian military's top photo reconnaissance experts examined them and could find no fault. After some deliberation, the Brazilian government released the film and admitted that they were unable to account for what the pictures showed. As the technology has developed, the Brazilian photographs have been regularly reassessed. Even computer enhancement of the photographs has failed to prove them fakes. Even so, sceptics continue to denounce the photographs as a mirage.

Other convincing pictures have come to light more recently. UFOlogist are surprised that, with the growth of camera ownership, they are not inundated with hoaxing and accidental fakes. However, everyone is now so alert to the possibilities that only the genuine cases get left behind.

In 1983 police officer Tony Dodd photographed a UFO near Addingham in Yorkshire. He sent his negatives and prints to Ground Saucer Watch, a UFO research group. They used computer enhancement and a process called 'density slicing' to analyse the pictures and found that the UFO was above the horizon and air-

A UFO photographed at Trindade Island, South Atlantic Ocean, 16 January 1958.

borne. The grain of the film was analysed using a technique called 'edge enhancement', which confirmed that there was nothing supporting the flying object. GSW identified vapour come from the craft. This vapour trail blended with the atmosphere, convincing investigators that an image of a UFO could not simply have been matted into a picture of the sky. 'Colour contouring' was used to confirm that the UFO was spherical. GSW concluded: 'The UFO appears structured and thirty feet in diameter. This represents Britain's first confirmed UFO photograph.' Sceptics still doubt the evidence of their eyes.

A UFO photographed at Trindade Island, South Atlantic Ocean, 16 January 1958.

Even though it seems to be impossible to find that one piece of clinching photographic evidence, that does not mean that UFO photographs as a whole do not tell their own tale. Dr Bruce Maccabee, an optical physicist for the Surface Weapons division of the US Navy, has been called in to investigate numerous cases. He has seen more UFO photographs than most and he has come to some very clear conclusions.

'I believe that UFOs are real and that they are alien in origin,' he says. 'I have established this through my own research and the study of many years of evidence. Photographic cases are often inconclusive and frustrating for the investigator. That final piece of evidence simply may not be available. However, there are suffi-cient numbers of impressive cases where it can be established with reasonable conviction that some kind of extraordinary craft was photographed. Such evidence provides a case that demands to be answered by the scientific community.'

The Test of Time

Among the UFO photographs that have stood the test of time are those taken by Paul Villa in New Mexico in the 1960s. They were widely published at the time and UFOlogists believe that they are some of the best ever taken. Even so, there are some puzzling aspects to Villa's story that have caused some sceptics to doubt the evidence of their own eyes.

Villa's story began ten years before he photographed his first series of saucers in 1963. While working for the Department of Water and Power in Los Angeles, he had been contacted by extra-terrestrials. One day in 1953, he was in the Long Beach area when he was overcome with an urge to go down to the beach. There, he met a strange man nearly seven tall. This spooked Villa. He felt afraid and wanted to run away, but then the strange man addressed him by his name and told him many personal things about himself that only the closest of friends would have known. And he could mind-read. At first Villa was puzzled. Then he realised that the being he was talking to was a very superior intelligence – not just a more than averagely intelligent human being but a super-intelligent extraterrestrial.

'He knew everything I had in my mind and told me many things that had taken place in my life,' Villa recalled. 'He then told me to look out beyond the reef. I saw a metallic-looking, disc-shaped object that seemed to be floating on the water. Then the spaceman asked if I would like to go aboard the craft and look around, and I went with him.'

It was too good an opportunity to miss. Once on board the saucer, Villa met other extraterrestrial beings that were human-like in appearance, though 'more refined in face and body'. They had an advanced knowledge of science and explained to him many things that baffled scientists. They told Villa that the galaxy where the Earth resides was just one among an unfathomable number of galaxies that were inhabited across the entire universe – it was a single grain of sand on a vast beach – and that a superior intelligence governed the universe and everything in it. The aliens had bases on the Moon, but their main base was Phobos, one of the two satellites of Mars. Phobos was actually hollow and had been constructed by the aliens. The alien technology was so advanced that their spaceships could penetrate the Earth's airspace without being detected by radar, unless they wanted to call attention to their presence. Alien craft were regularly visiting Earth and the aliens said that more and more sightings were going to take place to increase public awareness of their existence. They then reassured Villa that they had come to Earth on a friendly mission to help humankind.

Born Apolinar Alberto Villa Jr. in 1916, Villa was of mixed Spanish, Native America, Scottish and German descent. He later came to believe that he had been in telepathic communication with aliens since he was five. Although his formal education did not take him beyond tenth grade, he had a mastery of mathematics, physics, electrical engineering and mechanics. He served as an engineer in

A UFO photographed by Paul Villa near Albuquerque, New Mexico, USA, on 16 June 1963, the US Air Force and made his living as a mechanic in civilian life.

Ten years after the Long Beach encounter, on 16 June 1963, Villa was contacted telepathically by aliens. He was told to go to a place near the town of Peralta, New Mexico, about fifteen miles south of Albuquerque. He drove there alone, as instructed, arriving at 2 p.m. Soon after, a flying saucer appeared. It was between 150 and 160 feet in diameter. The ship hovered low in the sky and seemed to pose at various distances so that Villa could get good shots of it. He took a series of photographs. In some of them the craft is framed by the trees, and some show his truck in the foreground. This reference is exactly what photographic experts need if they are going to prove a picture genuine.

When the spacecraft first appeared between the trees, the bottom was glowing amber-red, as if it was red hot. The colours changed to shiny chrome, then to dull aluminium grey, then back to amber. At one point it became so bright it was painful to look at it. When it passed over his head, he could feel the heat it gave off and it gave him a tingling sensation all over his body.

The upper half of the craft was domed and could turn independently from the lower half, though during flight it remained stationary while the lower part rotated. When it did this it gave off a whirring sound like a giant electric motor or a generator. At other times the craft buzzed, or pulsed, or was completely silent. It could do complex aerobatics like flipping onto one edge with its bottom half rotating. The aliens later told him that they did this to demonstrate how they had created an artificial gravity-field within the craft. In such manoeuvres, they remained perfectly comfortable inside.

When the spacecraft hovered over his truck, some three hundred feet up, it caused the truck to rise slowly into the air and float about three feet from the ground for a few minutes. When the craft was about 450 yards away, a flexible probe emerged. It bent into different angles and shapes as it probed the trees and the ground. At the same time, a small, shiny orb came flying out of the spacecraft and disappeared behind trees. It suddenly reappeared, this time glowing red in colour, then shot off at incredible speed. Thoughout the whole display Villa took pictures.

After half an hour, the alien craft landed, settling down on three telescopic legs. Then, through a previously invisible door, five men and four women emerged. They were between seven and ten feet tall and beautiful to look at. They were well proportioned, immaculately groomed and wore tight-fitting, one-piece uniforms. The aliens told Villa that they came from 'the constellation of Coma Berenices, many light years distant'. This did not exactly pinpoint their home. Constellations are only patterns of stars in the sky, as seen from Earth, and Coma Berenices is noted for the large number of galaxies it contains.

Although the aliens were perfectly able to communicate with Villa telepathically, they could also speak many Earth languages. During their conversation, which lasted an hour and a half, they spoke to Villa in both English and Spanish, which was Villa's native tongue. Villa noted that when they talked among themselves they spoke in their own tongue which, to his ears, sounded like 'something akin to Hebrew and Indian'.

They told Villa that the spacecraft they travelled on operated as a mothership for nine remotely controlled monitoring discs. Manoeuvred from instrument panels inside the mothership, they picked up pictures and sound and relayed them back to the television monitor panels. This remote-viewing system was remarkably like the one first seen by George Adamski.

Villa returned to New Mexico in April 1965 to take a second series of photographs. This time the aliens appeared to him in several locations. The best photographs were taken at a place about twenty miles south of Albuquerque on 18 April. Again, when the photographic session was over, the ship settled on its tripod landing gear and the crewmen got out for a chat. This time there were only three of them. They had tanned skin and light brown hair, but they were shorter than the ones he had seen before, only about five feet five inches tall. They talked to Villa nearly two hours, discussing both general topics and personal matters.

A third set of photographs was taken on 19 June 1996. These showed some of the mothership's remotely controlled discs and spheres. The discs were from three to six feet in diameter and were photographed both on the ground and in the air. Often they were surrounded by smaller spheres. Larger discs were also launched from the mothership. Villa estimated that these were some forty feet in diameter. Some of them had flexible, probing antennas, which Villa said resembled the antennae of certain insects – though these are not visible in the photos. But in all his meetings with the aliens, although they would let him photograph their ships, they would not allow him to photograph them.

Villa has other photographs showing one of these remotely controlled discs that he made himself – to the exact specifications given by the aliens. It was about three feet across and was photographed during a test flight being monitored by one of the alien spheres. The disc crashed during the test, due a to slight error that Villa had made. However, the problem was soon rectified.

As it is impossible to distinguish the disc made by Villa from the real alien McCoy, this has been taken as proof that Villa made all of them. However, in none of the photographs is there any hint that the objects are suspended or have been superimposed. Atmospheric 'thickening' – the effect that makes distant objects less well defined than those close to – shows that the objects are not models. William Sherwood, formerly an optical physicist for Eastman-Kodak, studied all the Villa photographs and said they are genuine.

Because his pictures were so widely published in the 1960s, Villa was accused of making a fortune from them. He did not. In fact, he spent his own money sending out free copies. He also spent much of his free time writing to world leaders about what the aliens meant to mankind. In 1967, Ben Blaza of UFO International asked Villa's permission to copyright the photographs. Villa granted it, but made very little money himself.

Nor was Villa an attention seeker. His shunned publicity and rarely granted interviews to the media. He has also been threatened. Helicopters seem to follow him and he has been shot at.

British UFOlogist Timothy Good followed up on the Paul Villa case. In correspondence, Good pointed out the inaccuracies in certain prophecies the aliens had made. The aliens had said that seventeen nations would have the atomic bomb by 1966 – there were probably no more than ten by the year 2000. They said that Ronald Reagan would be elected president in 1976, though he did not make it to the White House until four years later. Worse, they said that there were 'canals' and 'pumping stations' on Mars, and that 'cacti and other plants' grew in certain locations on the red planet.

When asked whether the aliens had lied to him, Villa said no, they just did not tell the whole truth. 'Why should they? People would just make money from that info. Besides, how can humanity appreciate anything if it is beyond their capacity to understand?' he said.

Villa told Good that Walt Disney Studios and the US Air Force had both studied his negatives and found no fault in them. According to Villa, Dr Edward Condon, who headed the University of Colorado's USAF-sponsored investigation team that studied UFOs from 1966 to 1968, said they were the best pictures he had ever seen. But Good could find no mention of Villa or his photographs in Dr Condon's book *Scientific Study of Unidentified Flying Objects*.

In 1976, Villa drove Good around the locations near Albuquerque where he had photographed the alien craft and met their crews. At one of them, Good asked Villa what the other crew members were doing while he was talking to the alien he assumed was the pilot. 'Oh, they were just bathing their feet in the river,' he replied without batting an eyelid.

Like William Sherwood and other researchers who met Villa, Good was impressed and concluded that there was something to his story. Paul Villa died of cancer in 1981.

Scientist's Sightings

Strange lights were seen in the sky over Lubbock, Texas, on the night of 25 August 1951. They were witnessed by an Atomic Energy Commission executive and his wife from their back yard and simultaneously observed by four respected Texas scientists from their vantage point in another part of town.

Approximately three dozen bluish lights were seen. They had

the appearance of a giant flying wing, which moved back and forth across the night skies. Several hundred people in the area witnessed the same phenomenon over the next several days.

On 31 August, Carl Hart Jr. photographed the lights, but photo analysis could not prove Hart's pictures were genuine.

Single Exposure

On 24 May 1964, Jim Templeton, a fireman from Carlisle in the North of England, took his young daughter out to the marches overlooking the Solway Firth to take some photographs. Nothing untoward happened, although both he and his wife noticed an unusual aura in the atmosphere. There was a kind of electric charge in the air, though no storm came. Even nearby cows seemed upset by it.

Some days later, Mr Templeton got his photographs processed by the chemist, who said that it was a pity that the man who had walked past had spoilt the best shot of Elizabeth holding a bunch of flowers. Jim was puzzled. There had been nobody else on the marshes nearby at the time. But sure enough, on the picture in question there was a figure in a silvery white space suit projecting at an odd angle into the air behind the girl's back, as if an unwanted snooper had wrecked the shot.

The case was reported to the police and taken up by Kodak, the film manufacturers, who offered free film for life to anyone who could solve the mystery when their experts failed. It was not, as the police at first guessed, a simple double exposure with one negative accidentally printed on top of another during processing. It was, as Chief Superintendent Oldcorn quickly concluded, just 'one of those things... a freak picture'.

A few weeks later Jim Templeton received two mysterious visitors. He had never heard of 'Men in Black' – they were almost unknown in Britain at that time. But the two men who came to his house in a large Jaguar car wore dark suits and otherwise looked normal. The weird thing about them was their behaviour. They only referred to one another by numbers and asked the most unusual questions as they drove Jim out to the marshes. They wanted to know in minute detail about the weather on the day of the photograph, the activities of local bird life and odd asides like that. Then they tried to make him admit that he had just photographed an ordinary man walking past. Jim responded politely, but rejected this suggestion. At this point, they became angry, got back into the car and drove off leaving him there. He then had to walk five miles across country to get home.

Polaroids

Another alien contactee who could back his story with photographic evidence was sign painter Howard Menger, whose alien encounters began in 1932. His alien contacts came from Venus and demonstrated super-human abilities. At 1 a.m. on 2 August 1956, he snapped a series of Polaroids showing a spacecraft landing and a 'Venusian' getting out. The creature had broad shoulders, a slim waist, long, straight legs and long, blonde hair that blew in the soft warm summer breeze. However, Polaroid photography was in its infancy and the photographs are vague and indistinct. Menger only managed to catch the creature in silhouette against the glowing spacecraft. However, Menger explained that the blurring effect around the figure was caused by the electromagnetic flux surrounding the craft.

Menger later found himself employed by the extraterrestrials to help them learn human ways. He had to cut their hair into Earthly styles and introduce the aliens to Earth food. In return, they took him on trips to the Moon. Unfortunately, his photographs of the Moon came out no better than his portraits of the aliens.

Carroll Wayne Watts, a cotton farmer in Loco, Texas, managed to get some Polaroids of the aliens who abducted him in April 1967. As usual, Watts was stripped naked and examined. Just as he was getting dressed, he tried to steal an alien paperweight. He was alone in the room when he pocketed the two-inch-long piece of metal. Nevertheless, one of his captors came marching in, reached into his pocket and removed the paperweight. Watts was then knocked unconscious.

Polaroid shots of aliens served Police Chief Jeff Greenhaw little better. At 10 p.m. on the night of 17 October 1973, Greenhaw received a call from a woman reporting that a flying saucer had landed in a field near Falkville, Alabama. There, Greenhaw encountered a seven-foot-tall metallic humanoid. He tried to communicate with it, but got no response. But he did manage to snap a series of Polaroids before the alien fled – its huge steps allowed it to easily outplace Greenhaw's patrol car.

'He was running faster than anything I ever saw,' said Greenhaw.

The pictures clearly show the outline of a metallic creature. With his position as chief of police on the line, Greenhaw had no reason to fake the photographs, so his evidence had to be taken seriously. His pictures certainly bought him no money and no fame. Within two weeks of the encounter, an arson attack on his house destroyed the original prints, he began receiving threatening phone calls, his car blew up mysteriously and his wife walked out on him. The pictures brought him unwanted publicity. It was said that he had been

Photograph taken by UFO contactee Howard Menger some time during 1957-8: shows alleged spacewomen walking towards Menger.

duped by a prankster wrapped in silver foil and he was forced to resign as police chief. This was hardly the action of a hoaxer.

Polaroids were also unlucky for twenty-three-year-old Filiberto Caponi. Over a couple of months beginning in May 1993, he had taken a series of photos of an extraterrestrial creature in his home town of Ascoli Piceno. He had found it in a sack, but in subsequent shots the sack was gone and the creature seems to have undergone some type of physical development or growth. At first Caponi thought he had stumbled onto some form of bizarre genetic experiment.

In November 1993, his Polaroids were broadcast on the Italian TV station RAI-DUE. Soon after, the Italian police took Caponi in for questioning. He was charged with 'creating panic'. The police confiscated the photographs and he was forced to sign a confession saying he had faked the whole thing.

Big-Nosed Greys

Former US Navy petty officer Milton had access to the famous Grudge/Blue Book Special Report 13 on UFOs, which the US government claims never existed. He also saw a file belonging to Majestic-12, President Truman's secret commission set up to investigate UFOs, while he was a quartermaster under the Commander in Chief of the Pacific Fleet. In the files, Cooper saw a series of photographs of 'big-nosed Greys'. These creatures had struck a deal with the US government. They came from a dying planet that orbited Betelgeuse. Led by His Omnipotent Highness Krill, they had chosen Earth as their new home. The deal was that, in exchange for alien technological secrets, they would be allowed to share the planet and abduct humans occasionally for experimentation. Unfortunately, the deal soon broke down and the aliens went on an abduction spree. But the treaty was patched up and remains in operation to this day.

Undisputed Evidence

On the night of 2 August 1965 fourteen-year-old Alan Smith saw a UFO from his back garden. It changed colour from white to red then to green. The quick-thinking teenager got a camera and photographed the object. He sent the image to the USAF investigation team, who were known as Project Blue Book. They passed it on to the USAF Photo Analysis Division. The analysts concluded that the object was a mile from the camera and thirty feet in diameter. However, in an attempt to debunk the sighting, the report on the photograph concluded that it could have been made by photographing 'a multi-colored revolving filter flood-light'. Twenty-one years later the America UFO group Ground Saucer Watch subjected it to computer analysis which confirmed that it showed 'an extraordinary flying craft of large dimensions'.

Moving Pictures

While it is relatively easy to fake photographs – or produce fakes by accident – it is much harder to falsify moving pictures. Although fifty years ago home movie cameras were comparatively rare, with the advent of video, there has been huge increase in home movie making. These days video cameras are often on hand during UFO sightings and video footage has provided some of the best evidence that UFOs are actually structured flying vehicles, produced by an extremely advanced and non-terrestrial technology.

Despite the abundance of excellent footage in the UFO archives, a film or video fails to carry any real weight unless it has been subjected to a rigorous series of tests. The most exacting professional analysis is extremely expensive though, so it is only possible to submit a small proportion of movie material for specialist examination.

Over the years new technology had provided ways of testing photographs undreamed of when early UFO images were made. NASA has developed powerful computer programs that can rebuild images sent back bit by bit from cameras deep in space. The pictures are scanned electronically then sent to Earth as radio waves. On the way they get mixed up with other electromagnetic radiation. Atmospheric interference further degrades the signal, but when the incoming data stream is picked up on Earth, NASA's computer programmes can rebuilt the original and enhance and sharpen the image. When this technology is applied to ordinary photographs, film and video, it can reveal the most sophisticated trickery. As researchers have become vigilant, the number of UFO photos and video submitted for scrutiny has tumbled.

One of the world's leading experts in UFO film and video analysis is Jim Dilettoso. He has been doing this kind of work since 1977, when he was approached by UFO researcher retired USAF Colonel Wendell Stevens who asked him to look at footage from the controversial Meier case. Stevens chose Dilettoso because he had a background in optical special effects and the latest image processing techniques. With these skills at his command, he pioneered many of the analytical tools that are currently in use to scrutinise UFO footage.

Dilettoso's company – Village Labs of Phoenix, Arizona – is packed with sophisticated equipment. It owns a number of Cray supercomputers along with the most powerful graphics-generating system ever constructed. As well as analysing UFO films, Village Labs uses this equipment to carry out image analysis work for NASA and make the latest specials for Hollywood.

Technology and the procedures Dilettoso has developed over some twenty-five years in the business aside, some footage still passes muster. One video that got the Dilettoso seal of approval

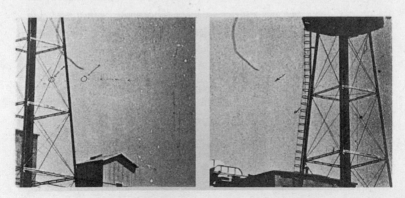

Two frames from a film of UFOs, made on 15 August 1950 at Great Falls, Montana, USA, by Nicholas Mariana.

was shot by Tim Edwards in August 1995. Edwards was out in the back yard of his home in Selida, Colorado, with his daughter when he saw a large cylindrical UFO hovering in the sky. He got his Hi-8 video camera and filmed it continuously until it disappeared, shooting six minutes in all.

The footage eventually found its way to Dilettoso, who started the laborious process of analysis. When reviewing video or film footage, the job of the analysts is to look for evidence of fakery. There are two principal ways a hoax can be perpetrated these days. It can be done in the old-fashioned way using models, or, these days, an image can be produced digitally by computer.

Discovering if an image has been generated by computer is relatively easy. The first thing Dilettoso does is examine the 'vertical interval' – the black bar that divides one video frame from the next. This acts like a fingerprint, with each video machine producing a vertical interval with slightly different characteristics. Obviously if the footage has been shot on one camera in a continuous sequence, all the vertical intervals will be the same. But if the image has been created digitally or edited by a computer the vertical interval will be altered in the process. If this shows that the footage has been interfered with, Dilettoso looks for evidence that an image has been 'gen-locked'. This is a movie technique whereby one image is superimposed on top of another.

Discovering if a model has been used is far more difficult. The only way to do this is to try and calculate the object's size and distance from the camera. Dilettoso then makes an estimate of its direction of flight and its speed. Taking all these things together should tell you whether the object is small enough to be a model. If possible, Dilettoso likes to go to the location where the footage was shot. Then he shoots a tape on the same camera to use as reference.

In the case of the Edwards' tape, it was easily enough to fly up to Colorado and visit Edwards' backyard. Dilettoso was able to shoot from the same position as Edwards, using Edwards' Hi-8. The process of analysis was made easier because Edwards was standing under the eaves of his house when he shot the video. The camera was pointing upwards so the guttering appeared in the foreground. This was key to Dilettoso's analysis.

'When we survey the unknown, we need to know what the characteristics of the known are,' he says.

Dilettoso could measure the dimensions of the gutter and the distance of the camera from it. He could also establish the brightness of the sun reflecting off other surfaces nearby. Dilettoso then used a computer to create a database from the original footage. He located the darkest object in the shot and the brightest. Then he created a scale showing the relative shades of luminosity of those in between. It was then possible to calculate the approximate distance to the UFO, using the intensity of the reflected light as reference. The quality of reflected light from a large object high in the sky is very different from that reflected from a model a few feet from the lens. This provides a basic test to decide if UFO footage is a fake.

When it has been established that an object is large and some distance from the camera it is then necessary to establish whether it is under intelligent control and not a cloud or some other windborne phenomenon. To do this, Dilettoso examines the 'motion blur' of the image. By examining the small differences in the clarity of different parts of an image, it is possible to tell which way the craft is moving and how fast. This must match the speed and direction worked out from the footage as a whole. The motion blur also helps an expert tell whether it is the object that is moving or the camera.

The Edwards footage passed all these tests with flying colours. Dilettoso's conclusion was that the object shown in the video was not a model and was not computer generated. But the really startling result was Dilettoso's estimate of its size. He reckoned that Edwards' UFO was between half-a-mile and a mile in length.

In such convincing cases, UFO researchers ask for a second opinion. In the Edwards' case, the tape was sent to Dr Bruce Maccabee. He agreed that it was not a model but estimated that the object was only between four hundred and eight hundred feet long. 'This was close enough to our estimate to say we were in general agreement,' said Dilettoso.

Case Unsolved

In Britain other footage has withstood the most rigorous examination. On 13 March 1993 Stephen Woolhouse saw a bright light in the sky that drifted silently over farmland behind his house in Bispham, Lancashire. He had a video camera to hand. It was loaded with tape and ready to roll. He filmed the glowing object before it was swallowed up by the darkening skies. The tape was examined by experts from the Northern Anomalies Research Organisation, which confirmed that it showed a flying object. It was neither an airship nor a helicopter according to local air-traffic control. It had no flashing navigation lights and Woolhouse's house was sixteen miles from the nearest airfield. The case remains unsolved.

But in 1996 a spectacular video was released that shows a ball of light creating a crop circle in Wiltshire. A year later evidence was found that indicated that the video was not genuine, merely a sophisticated piece of computerised trickery. But uncovering the hoax took a great deal of time and skill.

Birds on the Wing

At 11:10 a.m. on 2 July 1950 Warrant Officer Delbert C. Newhouse, a veteran Navy photographer, shot about thirty feet of film of ten or twelve strange, silvery objects in the sky near Trementon, Utah. As the objects flew in a westerly direction, one of them veered off from the main group and reversed its course.

After a thousand hours of investigation of the Newhouse film, the Navy Photographic Interpretation laboratory concluded that the objects filmed were not aircraft, birds, balloons or reflections, but were in fact 'self-luminous'.

The 'Robertson Panel' – five distinguished non-military scientists convened by the CIA in 1952 to discredit UFO sightings – concluded otherwise. They decided the objects were a formation of birds reflecting the strong sunlight.

Just Jets

At 11:25 a.m. on 5 August 1950, in Great Falls, Montana, Nicholas Mariana shot nearly twenty seconds of film of two disc-shaped objects as they moved across the sky.

On some of the 250 frames, the objects are seen passing behind the girders of a water tower, which gave film analysts an opportunity to measure the objects' approximate altitude, speed, azimuth, distance and size. It was also a sequence that would have been very difficult to have faked.

Mariana admitted that he had seen two jet fighters on their final approach to a nearby Air Force base just prior to his sighting of the objects, but insisted he knew the difference between the jets and the objects.

The Robertson Panel decided that Mariana did not know the difference – that he had filmed the jets.

The Norfolk Footage

Some of the best UFO footage ever taken was shot in 1997 when Norfolk became a centre of UFO activity. Weird flashing lights were seen in the night sky. Huge cylindrical motherships were floating aloft. And during the day, even when it was clear and sunny, menacing black triangular craft performed seemingly impossible, high-G manoeuvres silently above the broads. Similar sightings had been reported around the world in the 1990s, but what made the Norfolk sightings significant was that they were filmed.

While being open-minded on the subject, David Spoor, a long-time resident of Aulton Broad near Lowestoft in Norfolk, had no interest in UFOs. Then on 19 August 1997, when he was pottering in his back garden, he spotted a cigar-shaped object with a strange strobe light flashing around it in the sky.

'It was a white, self-illuminated cylindrical craft,' says Spoor, 'high in the sky and travelling silently west to east. It seemed to be ringed by bright strobe lights, which flashed randomly but weren't attached to the body of the craft.'

He reckoned that it was forty or fifty feet across, though it was hard to estimate because he could not tell accurately how far it was away. At first it was stationary, then it travelled across the sky at around forty to fifty miles an hour.

As luck would have it, Spoor had recently borrowed a video camera from a friend. He rushed inside to get it. Then, camera in hand, he filmed the UFO as it sailed silently across the sky. Unlike so much UFO footage, the resulting film was clear and unmistakable. But Spoor's coup did not end there. This was just the first of a series of films that would soon make him the Cecil B. De Mille of the UFO world.

In January 1998 he filmed blue beams of light coming at him across a field on the Suffolk border. He could not tell where they were coming from. On 2 February 1998 he shot a number of luminous orbs travelling slowly and silently across the sky. On other occasions he filmed other objects making high-speed manoeuvres that would have generated G-forces no human pilot could withstand. And he filmed numerous black triangles, flying in formation.

Like many people who have seen UFOs, Spoor found his life turned upside down. His house seemed to become the focus for strange forces. Keys bent and twisted in the locks. Lights switched themselves on and off without rhyme or reason. And, most sinisterly, at night, the family's bedrooms were lit up by bright lights which appeared to hover above their yard. Spoor's response was sanguine. He bought a video camera and made his own survey of the skies. Although at first he had questioned his own sanity, by the end of the year, he had shot nearly three hours of footage showing UFO activity over Norfolk. These were backed by his own accounts of the sightings.

Naturally he wanted to find out whether others had witnessed the same thing. A quick check of the local papers told him that others were reporting the odd UFO sighting, but nothing on the scale he had witnessed. However, he made discreet enquiries and found that he was not alone. Another man in the vicinity had also noticed the intense aerial activity. His name was Peter Wrigglesworth. He, too, had filmed the UFOs and had taken his footage to well-known Norfolk UFOlogist David Dane.

Dane was impressed with Wrigglesworth's film and, making enquiries of his own, Dane discovered Spoor and introduced him to Wrigglesworth. This was to become the one of the most productive partnerships in British UFOlogy.

The hours of footage that Wrigglesworth and Spoor had shot was viewed by numerous experts in the field. A number of movie and TV companies in America approached them. At a UFO conference in Laughlin, Nevada, the editor of *UFO* magazine Graham Birdsall offered to authenticate their film for them. He was impressed.

'The object certainly does not conform to any known aerial craft, largely because of the strobe-like features around it,' said Birdsall.

America's leading UFO investigation organisation Quest International had the computer analyst Russell Callahan look at the footage, but he made little progress with Spoor's original film because, apart from the UFO, there was nothing else in the shot to use as a point of reference. For Birdsall this was not a problem.

'All the computer analysis in the world won't tell us where it's from,' he said.

As the UFOlogist most closely involved in the case, Dane, too, believes that the craft are of extraterrestrial origin.

'In all my thirty years' experience of UFOlogy,' he said, 'I've never come across anything quite like this. I still have difficulty taking it in. It is without doubt the best UFO footage I've ever seen.'

Other UFOlogists who have seen the videos are equally enthusiastic, though researcher George Wingfield urges scepticism.

'Something pretty strange is definitely going on above Norfolk,' he said. 'But what it is is another matter. The two men seem genuine and sincere, but that doesn't necessarily mean they're filming what they think they're filming.'

Some have even suggested that the object Spoor filmed on 7 December 1997 was in fact Venus. The planet was visible that night, but it was on the other side of the sky. Others say that Wrigglesworth and Spoor may have filmed aircraft – perhaps experimental ones. The RAF bases at Wattisham, Coltishall, Honington and Marham are nearby. While it is possible that the Jaguars, Tornadoes, air-sea rescue helicopters and conventional military aircraft stationed there may explain some of the sightings in the area, experts say they do not account for all of the objects filmed by Wrigglesworth and Spoor.

In an effort to get to the bottom of the mystery, Dane showed some of the footage to Paul Beaver, a pilot and aeronautical expert who writes for the top military aircraft magazine Jane's *International Defence Review*. At first, he was sceptical.

'My first thoughts were that some of the footage was of kites, or models,' he said, 'but in one sequence, where two black wedge-shape craft are carrying out incredible manoeuvres, I felt that they were more likely RPVs [remotely piloted vehicles] or UAVs [unmanned aerial vehicles] – largely because of their size and the G-forces involved. I wouldn't put it past the military in these areas to be involved in UAV research.'

The RAF said that none of the bases in the vicinity were testing UAVs, but a spokesman at RAF Coltishall explained that, even if they were testing top-secret aircraft, they would obviously refuse to tell anyone. He said that the military carried out very little night flying in the Norfolk area, though, and would offer no opinion on what the craft Wrigglesworth and Spoor had filmed were. But the MoD were adamant.

'No UFOs have penetrated UK airspace, and nothing has been picked up by our detectors,' they said.

Although both Twentieth Century Fox and the BBC have expressed an interest in buying the footage, Wrigglesworth and Spoor have rejected their offers. They say they do not feel that this valuable footage should be exploited for financial gain and they fear that they would be become the centre of a media circus.

'This footage represents the ultimate media scoop, and a lot of people in a position to broadcast it will come away considerably richer for the privilege,' says Dane who is acting as agent for the film. 'Although none of us are "in it for the money", we do want credit to go where it's due. I am not prepared to let footage or individual stills fall into the wrong hands as I believe the whole episode would quickly degenerate into a circus.'

But this stance – however honourable – leaves Wrigglesworth and Spoor open to the charge that they are afraid to open themselves up to proper scrutiny.

Radar Contact

Although photograph and film can be faked, the evidence of trusted and experienced observers is hard to refute. So how can the evidence of highly trained air traffic controllers and military radar operators be dismissed when they see an unidentified blip flashing across their screens?

In the early hours of 21 December 1978 the crew of a Safe Air cargo plane en route from Blenheim to Dunedin, in New Zealand, were requested to search for some explanation for the unusual radar returns that were being tracked at Wellington Airport. Air traffic controller John Gordy said that the targets on his radar screen were unlike any he had ever seen before. As Captain Vern Powell flew his Argosy into the area over New Zealand's South Island, he saw several strange lights. They followed his aircraft for just over eleven miles along the coast before they disappeared. Captain John Randle, also flying an Argosy, on the same route, also diverted into the area and reported seeing UFOs. And at Wellington they were going crazy.

'At one stage our radar controllers had five very strong radar targets where nothing should have been,' said the head of Air Traffic Services at Wellington.

When the Australian TV Channel O from Melbourne heard of this sighting and others in the area, they contacted one of their reporters who happened to be on holiday nearby. The reporter's name was Quentin Fogarty and, when the TV company gave him the details of the sightings, Fogarty jumped at the assignment. He began his report by interviewing the UFO witnesses. Then he persuaded Safe Air to fly him along the same route to film background footage for the programme on the night of 30–31 December, this time in an Argosy flown by Captain Bill Startup.

Fogarty got lucky. Once again, radar picked up the strange returns. At 12:10 a.m., the crew were filming in the aircraft's loading bay when suddenly they saw a number of strange lights in the direction of Kaikoura on South Island.

They radioed Wellington control for information and were told: 'There are targets in your ten o'clock position at thirteen miles appearing and disappearing, not showing at present, but they were a minute ago.' For some time after that, Wellington radar detected a series of targets that came within five miles of the plane.

At 12:22 a.m., the crew were able to correlate both a visual sighting and a radar contact. A formation of six mysterious lights formed up alongside the plane. 'Let's hope they're friendly,' said Fogarty as he trained the TV camera on the UFOs. They seemed to be around a hundred feet in length and the bright lights seemed to be coming from their domed cabins.

Several seconds of film were shot of the UFOs. During the rest of the flight various other targets were seen and also confirmed by radar. On the return flight, more sightings were made, and more footage was shot of what Fogarty described as 'a sort of bell shape with a bright bottom and a less bright top'. As the flight continued, there were further sightings, again confirmed by radar.

Photographic expert Dr Bruce Maccabee flew out from Washington to New Zealand to study the footage. Maccabee was soon convinced that Fogarty had recorded something truly inexplicable and the Wellington case is widely regarded as one of the most convincing in UFO history.

Nevertheless the sightings have remained controversial, even though they were confirmed by radar. Sceptics have attempted to dismiss Fogarty's pictures as anything from the stars, Venus or Jupiter to the moonlight reflecting off a cabbage patch, and even, somewhat bizarrely, Japanese squid boats. But the air crew, who flew that route regularly, know they saw something extraordinary. Fogarty remains completely baffled by what he encountered that night. And the air traffic controllers are convinced that something strange was out there – something that deserved the official tag 'UFO'.

Bogeys over Washington

There can surely be no more famous case of radar-detected sightings than those that occurred over Washington, D.C. in 1952. The huge number of radar contacts caused consternation in military circles. Even the US government's own UFO investigation project feared an alien invasion.

The sightings took place over three consecutive weekends: 19–20 July, 26–27 July and 2–3 August. Around 11:40 p.m. on 19 July, Edward Nugent, an air traffic controller at Washington National Airport, spotted seven unidentified blips on his radar screen. They were around twenty-five miles south-west of the city and travelling at around a hundred miles an hour. Over the next few hours, two radar stations covering the airspace above Washington, D.C. detected eight UFOs in the restricted area around the Capitol building and the White House. For security reasons no civil or military planes are allowed to fly through that restricted zone without special orders. But the UFOs took no notice of that. They were moving so fast that their time within the restricted zone passed in the blinking of an eye. They could accelerate to astonishing speeds, stop dead and turn on a sixpence. These anomalous blips appeared on the capital's radar screens throughout the night and into the early hours of the morning and were confirmed by the sightings of pilots and ground observers.

At 3 a.m., two USAF F-94 Lock Starfire all-weather jet fighters were sent up from Newcastle Air Force Base in nearby Delaware. But when they got airborne, the UFOs simply disappeared, only to return again when the jets had landed. The last one left the capital's radar screens at 5:30 a.m.

The alien fleet turned up again the following weekend. They were first spotted by a National Airlines pilot who saw several of them flying high above his aircraft. He described them as looking like the 'glow of a cigarette'. Again, they were picked up on radar and seen by observers on the ground and in the air. At 11 p.m., two Starfires were scrambled from Newcastle AFB, but again the objects disappeared as the jets closed in and reappeared after they left. However, when a second wave of interceptors went in, the

UFOs remained where they were and the USAF pilots were able to make visual contact with four of them. One of the pilots, Lieutenant William Patterson, reported the UFOs closing on him rapidly. He was surrounded by blue lights, but they fled before he got permission to attack them.

Civil airline pilots also saw the UFOs. Captain S. Pierman of Capital Airlines was one of several who gave visual confirmation of the radar contacts. But the moment he reported his sighting by radio, the object shot away at an incredible speed.

'In all my years of flying I have seen a lot of falling or shooting stars – whatever you call them,' said Captain Pierman. 'But these were much faster than anything I have ever seen. They couldn't have been aircraft. They were moving too fast for that.'

Air traffic control had seen the UFO's extraordinary retreat too.

'It was almost as if whatever controlled it had heard us, or had seen Pierman head toward it,' said Harry Barnes, the senior air traffic controller that night.

Many people came forward with explanations. Some suggested that the radar contacts were simple radar errors or temperature inversions, where pockets of increased temperature in the lower levels of the atmosphere can cause anomalous radar reflections. To explain the pilots' visual corroboration, it was said that the excitement of the radar flap led them to mistake normal lights for UFOs. But these explanations ignore the fact that the pilots' sightings corresponded exactly to the behaviour of the radar contacts.

Leading UFO researcher Don Ecker has led the investigation into the Washington flap and remains convinced that it presents some of the most important evidence in UFO history. Ecker had discovered that it was not only both civil and military pilots who visually confirmed the radar contacts.

'They were witnessed by some of the radar operators that literally left their scopes and went outside and looked physically into the sky,' he says.

He has also dismissed the idea that the contacts could have come from temperature inversions.

'The radar operators were skilled personnel,' he says. 'They were responsible, literally, for bringing in, and having go out, tens of thousands of air travellers every day. The military radar experts were depended upon to keep our skies safe from enemy intrusions, and these guys had, beyond any shadow of a doubt, dealt with things like temperature inversions.'

Ecker also discovered a cover-up. Edward J. Ruppelt was head of Project Blue Book, the US Air Force's official UFO investigation and as such was the man charged with investigating the flap. But when he looked into the case, he found the authorities less than forthcoming. Ruppelt discovered that the authorities 'were going to great extremes and lengths to get this swept under the rug as soon as possible,' says Ecker.

As the Air Force refused to give information to its own UFO investigator, Ruppelt had to turn to the press. He was bitter about being sidelined and, when asked what the Air Force was doing about UFOs entering restricted airspace, he commented: 'I have no idea what the Air Force is doing; in all probability it's doing nothing.'

Major Donald Keyhoe, who would later become a founder member of the National Investigations Committee on Aerial Phenomena (NICAP), was also involved in the investigation. *True* magazine published his analysis of the sightings in 1953, under the title 'What Radar Tells Us About Flying Saucers'.

In the article, Keyhoe shows just how seriously the Pentagon took the sightings by citing remarks made by Director of Operations Major General Roger S. Ramey at the time.

'The Air Force, in compliance with its mission of air defence of the United States, must assume responsibility for the investigation of any object or phenomena in the air over the United States,' Ramey said. 'Fighter units have been instructed to investigate any object observed or established as existing by radar tracks, and to intercept any airborne object identified as hostile or showing hostile interest. This should not be interpreted to mean that air-defence pilots have been instructed to fire haphazardly on anything that flies.'

Ramey's remarks demonstrate that the Air Force believed that the radar contacts were very real. Again Keyhoe pointed out that the radar operators would have been very familiar with false returns, such as temperature inversions. Nevertheless they felt that the blips required further investigation to show they were real. In the same issue, *True* magazine quoted an anonymous USAF spokesman who said: 'We don't know what these things were and there's no use pretending we do.'

While the USAF and its investigators were stumped, the US government knew just what to do. Within months of the Washington sightings, the CIA convened the Robertson Panel, which recommended using all means available to allay any public interest in the UFO phenomenon – and the cover-up and the debunking started.

The cover-up continues to this day and it involves not just the US military, but also the military authorities of America's European allies. In the summer of 1998, a four-day workshop reviewed all the physical evidence associated with UFO sightings across Europe that had been accumulated by seven top UFO researchers. They paid particular attention to radar contacts. This presented difficulties, as the workshop's report states: 'The panel concludes from these presentations that the analysis of radar records is a very specialised activity that requires the services of radar experts. The panel also notes that information from military radar can be obtained only with the co-operation of military authorities, and that most military authorities do not offer this co-operation... further study of this phenomenon by means of radar-visual cases may not be feasible unless the relevant authorities recognise the mission of an official UFO research organisation.'

Pacific panic

In the months after the Japanese attack on Pearl Harbor, America was on tenterhooks. An attack on the mainland, perhaps a full-scale invasion, was expected at any time. On the evening of 25 February 1942, air observers reported aircraft approaching the Pacific coast near Los Angeles. At around 7:20 p.m., lights were seen in the sky near an important defence plant. At 2 a.m., radar reported unidentified contacts out over the sea. Air-raid sirens sounded. Los Angeles was plunged into darkness and anti-aircraft guns filled the skies with flack. A formation of UFOs flew over the city, high and very fast. The guns continued pounding for another hour. When they eventually fell silent, it was found that the city had not been attacked. No bombs had been dropped. No aircraft downed. The only damage done to the city was caused by anti-aircraft shells.

Canadian Contacts

In the later 1940s and early 1950s Goose Bay in Labrador became a UFO hotspot. On 29 October 1948 a UFO was tracked by radar as it streaked across the bay. The following night it returned. This time contact was maintained for four minutes and it was calculated that the object was travelling at over 625 miles an hour.

Two years later, a UFO was seen in the same area by Captain James Howard, a pilot with BOAC. On closer examination, he saw that it was actually a mothership accompanied by a gaggle of other flying objects. They fled when he approached. The sighting received huge press coverage and even prompted Air Chief Marshall Lord Dowding to say that he believed in flying saucers.

The UFO returned to Goose Bay on 19 June 1952, when a strange red light appeared in the sky over Goose Bay Air Base. It was also picked up by radar. Witnesses on the ground saw the light suddenly turn white and increase in brilliance. At the same time, the radar contact seemed to flare. Then it disappeared simultaneously from sight and the radar screen.

Visual Confirmation

On the night of 13 August 1956, multiple radar contacts were made over RAF Bentwaters in Suffolk. Six ground stations and one airborne station independently reported five contacts with objects flying at incredible speeds. Twenty radar personnel confirmed the contacts. Nine visual observers confirmed the contacts with sightings of brilliantly lit objects in the sky.

The first contact was made by Bentwaters Ground Control Approach Radar, which calculated that the object was travelling at speed of around 4,250 miles an hour. Other slower objects followed in its wake. Bentwaters asked for confirmation from the USAF base at RAF Lakenheath. When it was received, the RAF scrambled two fighters to investigate the intruders. One of them was vectored on an intercept course. It had both visual and radar contact. But suddenly the ground station saw the UFO double back and begin to chase the fighter. The pursuit continued for several minutes before the UFO disappeared. The pilot returned home safely, though shaken and puzzled.

The Guardian

UFOs returned to Canada in 1989. An object was tracked on radar before it fell towards the ground near West Carleton, to the west of Ottawa, on 4 November. The area was immediately sealed off and huge helicopters and military units, specially trained to deal with UFO retrievals, were flown in. The source of this story, who called himself the 'Guardian', also said that the aliens themselves were tracked on radar.

The Guardian said that the alien craft used a pulsing electromagnetic field to fly and was built from a matrixed-dielectric magnesium alloy. It also generated cold fusion radiation. He also said that the alien mission had a malevolent purpose. It was the start of an alien invasion.

MUFON's Bob Oeschler, a former NASA mission specialist, investigated. The Guardian sent him a package in February 1992. The package contained a video, several documents and maps of the area. The tape was thirty minutes long, with the first six minutes showing actual movement, the rest was just stills. The video showed strange lights, movements of 'aliens' around the craft and also a full-frontal shot of an alien's face.

The video was analysed and it had signs of editing, also the scenes of the craft were duplicated by researchers using toy remote controlled helicopters, some flashing lights and some flares. They were also able to purchase an alien mask from a costume shop identical to the one in the video. This case eventually caused Oeschler to resign from MUFON.

Physical Evidence

Not all UFO encounters depend for their credibility on the relia-
bilty of eyewitnesses, photographs that can be faked or radar contacts that can be withheld by the authorities. Sometimes alien craft
leave physical evidence.

One of these cases occurred in the small agricultural settlement
of Delphos, Texas. One November evening in 1971, sixteen-year-
old farm hand Ronnie Johnson was just finishing his day's work
when he suddenly looked up to see a large, mushroom-shaped
UFO, hovering just above the ground in front of him. Caught
unawares, he was paralysed with fear and the light from the craft
was so bright it temporarily blinded him. After a few moments, the
craft began to ascend and Ronnie came to his senses and ran off to
get his parents. He returned with them in time to see the UFO
shooting rapidly up into the sky. But had that been the end of the
story, it is unlikely that anyone would have believed them.

However, on the ground in front of them, in the very place the
object had been hovering, they saw a circle in the earth about eight
feet across that was glowing brightly. It did not appear to be hot and
Ronnie's mother bent down and touched the glowing ring. As she
did so, her fingers became frozen and numb. They remained that
way for several weeks after the encounter.

This case became one of the most thoroughly investigated in the
history UFOlogy. But it was far from unique. Thousands of UFO
encounters have left behind physical evidence. Investigators call
them 'physical trace cases', or encounters of the second kind. They
provide the most solid evidence alien spacecraft have visited Earth.

The world's leading expert on physical trace cases, Ted Phillips,
investigated the Delphos case. A civil engineer from Branson,
Missouri, Phillips has visited four hundred and fifty UFO sites and
investigated some six hundred encounters over the past thirty
years. From his studies, he says that around the world over five
thousand UFO trace cases have been reported.

Phillips first became interested in UFOs when his father told
him about a pilot who had been buzzed by a flying saucer. He
began to investigate sightings in his home state of Missouri in the

1960s. In 1966, he came across a case in Florida where contactee John Reeves had photographed the footprint of an alien after one had visited his home.

The first case that brought Phillips to prominence occurred the following year. Three men were out hunting when they saw a flying saucer descend into the valley where they had been camping. No only did the men manage to photograph the UFO, they also had physical evidence of it. It swooped so low that it had scorched a tree and damaged the men's camping equipment. Phillips documented the case and took his findings to established UFO researcher Dr J. Allen Hynek of North Western University. Hynek, who is often described as the 'father of UFOlogy', was so impressed that he asked Phillips to work out a methodology for the systematic investigation of physical trace cases. They worked together until Hynek's death in 1986.

According to Phillips' definition, a physical trace case is a UFO sighting where one or more people witness an object, on or near the ground, and once the object leaves the area a number of physical changes to the environment can be found. In the cases Phillips has investigated, these have included impressions left in the ground from landing gear, rings of crushed vegetation and burnt soil, and even alien footprints. He has also come across a number of hoaxes.

'They were very easy to spot,' he says. 'People pour petrol on the ground, ignite it and try to make a ring. Sometimes they simply dig indentations in the soil, but when you've seen hundreds of examples of real traces caused by a UFO, you realise that the effects are very specific and extremely difficult to replicate.'

When he arrives at the sight of a UFO encounter, the first thing Phillips does look for signs of a possible hoax. But at Delphos he was soon satisfied that the case is genuine and began taking soil samples with a cylindrical boring inside and outside the ring. Chemical analysis revealed that the soil from inside the ring had been completely dehydrated down to a depth of fourteen inches. The soil would not even rehydrate when placed in water. But when soil from outside the ring was put in water, it dissolved readily.

The soil in the ring remained affected for quite some time. Six months later, the area was covered by a heavy show fall. When Phillips cleared off the snow and threw a bucket of water on to the soil, the ring reappeared, as the soil there still refused to absorb water.

Phillips carries out most of his work without using professional laboratories. This cuts out the cost of expensive lab work, but Phillips is also suspicious of labs that are directly connected to the government. He believes that they could not be relied upon if his evidence was about to yield significant findings.

'Given the fact that the government is obviously covering up a great deal of information regarding the UFO phenomenon,' Phillips says, 'it would be overly optimistic to think they would help provide evidence for the existence of visiting UFOs.'

But Phillips made an exception in the Delphos case, because there was no other way to find out why soil was so determinedly dehydrated. Phillips called in the help of the leading UFOlogist Stanton Friedman. They had worked together on a number of UFO cases. Friedman found an independent lab called Agra-Science, which specialised in doing soil analysis for farmers. The lab tested Phillip's soil samples for thermo-luminescence to reveal whether the earth had been subjected to intense heat. According to Friedman, the results showed that the soil had been irradiated by some intense form of energy, possibly microwaves.

The soil samples were also sent to another independent laboratory at Oak Ridge. The scientists there examined them under an electron microscope and discovered that the soil had strange crystalline structures, unlike anything they had even seen before. The soil particles were coated in a mysterious substance, which explained why they could not absorb water.

Phillips tried growing seeds in the affected soil, using soil taken from outside the ring as a control. The seeds would not germinate in the affected soil, though they flourished in the control. Eventually, though, the soil recovered and plants began to grow in it again.

Categories of Evidence

The Delphos case is only one of hundreds of UFO cases where physical traces have been left that have been investigated by Ted Phillips. Phillips has assembled a huge amount of evidence. He has been able to divide physical trace cases into three broad categories. One involves the classic disc-shaped flying saucer, metallic in appearance and thirty to forty feet in diameter. When they land, witnesses often seen humanoid aliens in the area. These flying saucers leave a scorched ring of soil about thirty feet in diameter and indentations thought to be left by the landing gear.

Then there are small circular objects, eight to ten feet in diameter, which often glow brightly. They leave a smaller ring of singed or dehydrated soil. A scorched earth ring of this sort was found in Kofu City, Japan, in 1975, when Masato Kohno saw a UFO land.

Egg-shaped craft leave four indentations, again thought to be made by landing gear. From Phillips' tests of the soil compression in these marks, they would have to be made by an object weighing some twenty-five tonnes.

Phillips has also investigated so-called 'saucer nests'. These are circular areas of flattened crops that appear in fields. They show none of the intricate patterns of crop circles and often show genetic mutations in the plants not normally associated with crop circles. As Phillips' trace cases always involve sightings, he distinguishes 'saucer nest' cases from crop circles – which do not – and believes that they may be two separate phenomena. Similar 'saucer nests' appeared in France in 1990.

Footprints

Some 23 per cent of physical trace cases involve the sighting of the craft's alien occupants and sometimes Phillips is lucky enough to get a photograph or a plaster cast of an alien footprint.

'If we get word of the landing a week or a month after it happened, the chances are that the site would be so beaten down by the weather or local people that any footprints would have been destroyed,' he says. 'In cases where the information has reached us earlier, we have found either a partial footprint or a series of fresh ones.'

He frequently runs into footprints of Greys, who leave footprints like an impression from a moccasin, the size and depth of those left by a small child.

Phillips' work has been officially dismissed and derided. But Friedman maintains that the evidence he presents is indisputable.

'What we are looking at here is empirical evidence that just cannot be dismissed by the "noisy negativists",' he says. 'Hallucinations cannot dehydrate fourteen inches of soil. Nor consistently leave physical, testable and tangible evidence such as phosphorescent rings in the earth.'

Beach Bummer

A UFO crashed on the beach at Ubatuba, Brazil in September 1957. Ibrahim Sued, a journalist with leading Brazilian newspaper *O Globo*, received a letter about it on 13 September. The letter was signed and read:

'As a faithful reader of your column and your admirer, I wish to give you something of the highest interest to a newspaper man, about the flying discs. If you believe that they are real, of course. I didn't believe anything said or published about them. But just a few days ago I was forced to change my mind. I was fishing together with some friends, at a place close to the town of Ubatuba, Sao Paulo, when I sighted a flying disc. It approached the beach at an

Examining a presumed UFO landing site, near Richmond, Virginia, USA

Tully, Queensland, Australia, 1966: area of flattened reeds, possibly made by UFO.

unbelievable speed and an accident – a crash into the sea – seemed imminent. At the last moment, however, when it was almost striking the waters, it made a sharp turn upward and climbed rapidly on a fantastic impulse. We followed the spectacle with our eyes, startled, when we saw the disk explode in flames. It disintegrated into thousands of fiery fragments, which fell sparkling with magnificent brightness. They looked like fireworks, despite the time of the accident, which was noon. Most of these fragments, almost all, fell into the sea. But a number of small pieces fell close to the beach and we picked up a large amount of this material, which was as light as paper. I am enclosing a small sample of it. I don't know anyone that could be trusted to whom I might send it for analysis. I never read about a flying disc being found, or about fragments or parts of a saucer that had been picked up.'

Sued sent two of the three samples to the Aerial Phenomena Research Organisation, a UFO group in Tucson Arizona, while the third was retained by Brazilian UFOlogist Dr Olavo Fontes for further study.

The three samples looked like pieces of irregular and highly oxidised metal, coloured dull whitish grey. Dr Fontes' sample was

Martians' footprints in the sand, after a UFO landing at the home of John Reeves, Florida, USA. in December 1966.

tested at the mineral production labs in the Brazilian agricultural ministry. They applied chemical, spectrographic analysis and X-ray diffusion techniques on the metal. These tests indicated that the material was very pure magnesium. The chemist also noted that the normal trace elements expected in magnesium samples were all missing.

Fontes used up all of his sample in a series of further tests. Part of it went to a chemist who conducted an X-ray investigation at the labs of a geology unit. The geology lab determined that the magnesium was of a very high purity, with a reading of 1.87, compared with a normal reading of 1.74. Pieces were also sent to the Brazilian Army and Navy research departments, but both the Army and Navy kept their findings secret.

ARPO sent a sample to the USAF, but the sample they sent met with an 'accident' while they were testing it. The USAF asked for a further sample to be sent. APRO declined. They tried to conduct tests with remaining the sample but it soon became too small to be of any use. APRO still retains one small chunk in their vaults.

Alien Artefacts

Those who have had contact with aliens have often tried to bring back some sort of alien artefact with them as proof of their contact. Betty Hill asked the aliens who abducted her whether she could take one of their books. At first, they seemed to give their permission, then changed their mind. Maybe the aliens have got wary because evidence they have supplied before has been comprehensively derided.

Howard Menger, one of the first alien contactees in the 1950s, was taken to the Moon and brought back a lunar potato. It was sent to the analysts LaWall-Harrisson Consultants in Philadelphia. They found that potato was indistinguishable from the terrestrial variety, however the protein content was some five times higher than that of any Earth potato. At that time, the UFO community was still very trusting and no one suspected that the government was conducting a cover-up, secretly exploiting alien technology for their own ends, or that the military and intelligence agencies were colluding with the aliens. So Menger naively sent his extraterrestrial spud to the Central Intelligence Agency. The CIA jumped at the chance of analysing the specimen. Two weeks later, Menger and his wife visited the CIA laboratories and were allowed to watch the analysis in progress. They were shown pieces of potato under the microscope and other pieces soaking in various fluids in sample jars. Menger was impressed with the rigour of their approach. He never heard from them again.

Alien Implants

Since the Earth was first visited by flying saucers, there have been some people who have doubted the existence of our extraterrestrial visitors. These sceptics have found the idea of alien abduction even harder to swallow. But fortunately, many abductees can prove what they have been saying. They have physical proof in the form of alien implants.

Like many abductees, Pat Parrinello experienced strange phenomena from childhood. It began when he was just six; he was woken by a brilliant light in his bedroom and found himself paralysed. Since then he has had many such experiences. He has been monitored constantly by aliens and visited by the familiar, large-headed Greys.

Unlike most alien abductees, Parrinello has full conscious recall of his experiences and has not had to resort to regressional hypnosis. He clearly remembers every detail of the abduction, including the humiliating medical examinations that most people manage to blank out.

It was after one abduction that Parrinello was convinced that aliens implanted a small device in his hand. It showed up clearly on an X-ray. And in August 1995, he became one of the first abductees to undergo surgery to retrieve an alien implant. This was no simple matter. After Parrinello took the decision to have the implant removed, he suffered weeks of alien intervention designed to stop him. He suffered severe head pains and often found the abductors' UFO following him. Nevertheless he was determined to go ahead.

The operation was done by Dr Roger Leir in his offices in Ventura, California. Parrinello had been taken to Leir by UFOlogist Derrel Sims, who was investigating the case. At the same time Sims was also investigating the abduction case of a woman named Janet, who had an implant in her foot. Leir operated on her at the same time.

The operations had to be carried out under conditions of the strictest security. Dr Leir was afraid that he might risk losing his licence for performing such an unconventional procedure.

'People with credibility who put themselves forward in this field can wind up out of business,' said Leir

Nevertheless Leir risked having the entire procedure videoed. Although the tapes could have been used against him in any medical ethics hearing, he knew they would be vital in establishing the validity of what he was doing.

Leir began the operations with an experiment. With the patient under a strong local anaesthetic, which numbed all sensation in the area of the implant, Leir tapped the implant gently. Both Parrinello and Janet jerked violently in response. It was all Leir could do to prevent Janet leaping from the operating table. There was no doubt that the anaesthetic was working and Dr Leir had no explanation for their reactions.

Next Leir used a meter to detect any magnetic field given off by the implants. It showed a massive reaction. The needle practically went off the scale, indicating a powerful electromagnetic field. This made removing the implant difficult using surgical implements with metal blades. But when the implants were removed the field miraculously dissipated.

An object 4 mm by 2 mm was retrieved from Parrinello's hand. It was dark and covered in a membrane made of keratin and haemoglobin. These are both proteins found naturally in the body. This casing was the sort of covering that builds up around all foreign matter that enters the body and its genetic fingerprint showed a DNA match with Parrinello. But Leir was certain that it was not a cyst or anything else that grew naturally in the body. He had seen nothing like it before. It was so strong that it could not be cut open by a sharp surgical scalpel. It also contained numerous nerve endings. This may explained the Parrinello's response when it was tapped.

'If these objects were actually left in the body by alien beings, it would not be difficult for the aliens to adapt them by forming them along the lines of the body's own chemistry,' says abduction expert Professor Mack.

Leir had to make a deep incision to remove two objects from Janet's toe. They were of similar composition, were triangular in shape and measured 1.5 mm by 1.5 mm. Sims sent all three to the University of Houston for more detailed investigation. Scientists there discovered that,

Alleged alien implant found in roof of an abductee's mouth.

under the organic membrane, they were made of shiny, black metal strips. Chemical analysis indicated that the implants are metallic and consisted of eleven different elements, including boron, a met-alloid substance used to harden steel, which does not occur naturally in the body.

It was also discovered that the implants glowed green when subjected to ultra-violet light. Sims used this property to detect implants under the skin of other abductees. This led to the recovery of another thirteen alien implants from the bodies of abductees in 1996. Sims has collected more than thirty in all.

Despite this concrete evidence, some sceptics are still not convinced. Arch-debunker Philip Klass claims that there is no provable link between the alien implants and extraterrestrials. Although abductees believe that the implants are used by the aliens to monitor them, Klass says that the devices have no obvious purpose and claims that they are mundane growths that can exist inside the body for years without the host noticing because they cause no discomfort or pain. Klass points out that Parrinello had a swelling in the region of the hand where the implant was found as long ago as 1984. However, just because the implant has been in his body for a long time does not mean that it is terrestrial.

What exactly the implants are for, even Sims admits, no one knows. But they had been surgically implanted in people who had no record of surgery, so they must have some purpose, he reasons. Some researchers believe that they are tracking devices – like the transponders not much bigger than a grain of rice programmed with an electronic code that ostrich farmers implant in the neck of their birds to keep track of them. However, Sims does not believe they are tracking devices. He thinks that they are some sort of monitoring device, although they may also be used to control abductees.

Implant Programme

There is a discernible implant programme underway. The earliest reported abduction case occurred in late 1957. No implants were associated with abductions for nearly ten years. Then in 1966, scars began appearing on the bodies of abductees, though they were not recognised in any numbers until the mid-1970s. The vast majority of implant cases seem to have occurred in the US, critics say, pointing out that scars are rarer in abductees in other countries, even where abductions are numerous. However, this is probably because more of an effort is made to look for them in America.

But implants are not unknown in other countries. Social worker and UFOlogist Keith Basterfield investigated the case of 'Susan', a young abductee from Adelaide, South Australia. She had her first contact with aliens when she was ten years old in 1971. Two different species of aliens were involved in Susan's abduction. Tall humanoids were in command, while the small, large headed Greys did all the menial jobs.

A number of encounters ensued over the years. These involved periodical medical examinations to monitor her development. Then in 1991, during a routine visit to the dentist, an X-ray was taken. This showed a shadowy, unidentified object implanted in her mouth. To investigate this, a second X-ray was arranged for a few weeks later. But in the mean time, Susan was abducted again and the implant removed. The second X-ray showed no trace, and meanwhile the first set of X-rays had gone missing.

Surveys have suggested that as many as one in three people can find an unusual scar of unknown origin on their body, if they looked for one. This could mean that a third of the population has been abducted at one time or another. Abductees believed implants were first placed in their bodies in the late 1970s. Most said the devices were being implanted by forcing them up the nose. Abductees often wake from their abduction with a severe nose-bleed.

The number of implantation cases rose meteorically in the 1980s. By the end of the decade, about one in four abductees had implants. The aliens had broadened their scope and were implanting in the head, via the mouth and the ear as well as the nose. Then in the 1990s, implants were discovered in other parts of the body, such as the foot and the hand – as in the cases investigated by Sims and removed by Leir in 1995. But these cases are still uncommon.

Implant Investigation

The most extensive scientific examination of an alien implant was undertaken by Dr David Pritchard, a physicist from the Massachusetts Institute of Technology. He undertook a full study of an implant recovered from the genitals of a male host, who believes that he was first abducted from his home in New York in 1955. Despite examining the object under an electron microscope and subjecting it to the very latest techniques of mass spectroscopy, he was unable to identify it – although this does not actually prove that it was of alien origin.

'Analysis shows nothing "unterrestrial" about it, quite the opposite,' he says. 'It does not appear to be fabricated, but rather has the overall characteristics of something that grew. [But] it is possible that the aliens are so clever that they can make devices to serve their purposes yet [which] appear to have a prosaic origin as natural products of the human body.'

But American researcher Martin Cannon has a more sinister explanation. He believes that abductees are not being kidnapped by aliens at all, but by some covert arm of the US government, possibly the CIA. The implants are mind control devices that makes ordinary members of the public the unwilling and unconscious slave of the intelligence community. The abduction memories are planted deep in their minds by post-hypnotic suggestion – that's why they usually have to be retrieved by hypnotic regression. The memories of the alien abduction cloak any memory of what really happened. Even if the screen slips and the abductee remembers what really happened, they are easily discredited because they have already claimed that they were abducted by aliens and – in the public's eyes – are already seen as 'kinda flaky'.

Crop Circles

Early one morning in July 1991, Rita Goold got lucky. She and her fellow crop circle investigators were holding vigil near the tiny Wiltshire hamlet of Alton Barnes, where on previous occasions some of the most celebrated crop circles had made an appearance. Shortly after 3 a.m., as the dawn mist crept across the field, a luminous white tube descended from a cloud, slowly at first, pouring forth what the witnesses described as a fluid-like substance. Narrowly missing the field, it hit the ground on a nearby hill.

'As it came down', said Goold, 'it shot out two arms, covering the top of the hill – it must have been eight hundred feet across – and in each arm all this stuff was pouring in, finding rivulets, clouding and making formations, and as it was doing this, the tube was emptying. Then the tube collapsed and vanished.'

The event lasted eight seconds in all.

'It was like something out of a Steven Spielberg movie,' Goold said. Another colleague described it as 'biblical'.

The next day Goold and her friends could find no trace of any disturbance when they visited the hillside in daylight. However, news spread through the crop circle fraternity that Goold and her mates discovered the mechanism behind the crop circle phenomenon.

Dr Terence Meaden was particularly thrilled. He had spent years investigating the phenomenon. But while many insisted that crop circles were caused by flying saucers coming into land, Meaden had consistently argued that there must be a purely scientific explanation.

Meaden had studied tornadoes and put forward the hypothesis that a static vortex of ionised air – similar to a tornado – was responsible for even the most complex patterns. He called the mechanism responsible a 'plasma vortex'. It was, he maintained, a rare but entirely natural effect that occurred only in certain climatic and topographical conditions.

Although crop circles appeared to be a relatively a recent phenomenon, Meaden believed that crop circles had once provided the inspiration for prehistoric stone circles in the area. He also said that his plasma vortices might explain UFO sightings. Blasphemy indeed.

On the other side of the fence, there were those who said that, although the first crude crop circles were caused by UFOs landing, their alien occupants had discovered that they were a good way to announce their presence to humankind. After all, the complex

Crop circles at Westbury, Wiltshire, 1988.

patterns they were producing showed all the hallmarks of intelligent design. A third faction agreed that non-human intelligence was involved, but pointed the finger at Gaia – the notion that the Earth itself is an intelligent entity – or other paranormal entities or psychic energies. To Meaden and his supporters, these theories came from the crankier end of New Age beliefs. But certainly something extraordinary was going on. The pilot of a light aircraft saw an eighty to ninety foot circle formation in a field near Stonehenge, which must have been created in just 45 minutes. It followed the Fibonacci series, forming a highly complex pattern seen in fractal geometry. It had not been there when he flew over the same field three-quarters of an hour earlier.

'At every stage, the circles phenomenon stretches and tests our perception of reality,' said one researcher.

Snowflake patters, spider's webs and the double helix of DNA appeared, along with alien circuit diagrams and star maps, and geometric designs where the flattered crops were brushed in various directions, simulating texture.

'Whatever, or whoever, made them is an artist of genius,' said John McEwen, art critic of the *Sunday Times*. Others compared them to modern-day devotional art that uses mystical symbols and sacred geometry to communicate with the world beyond. Or perhaps it was the world beyond using mystical symbols and sacred geometry to communicate with us.

'This force may be powerful enough to act as a catalyst for the many physiological and psychological effects – both curative and malevolent – that are often attributed to circles,' said investigator Rob Irving.

The Men Who Fooled the World

As the design of the circles became more and more complex, Dr Meaden found it increasingly difficult to explain them using his plasma vortex theory and, privately, he began to suspect there was a simpler explanation. There was. Their names were Doug Bower and Dave Chorley. These two Southampton-based sexagenarians – known as Doug and Dave in the tabloids – claimed to be 'The Men Who Fooled the World'. For fifteen years they had been sneaking into the fields of Hampshire and south Wiltshire and creating complex crop circles with nothing more than a three-foot wooden board and some string. They had all winter to plan the next year's circles and, each summer, they were determined to outdo the previous year's designs. They both had a keen interest in art and sought out inspiration in galleries and libraries. The first design for one of their early efforts – two circles joined by an avenue and flanked by sets of short, parallel bars – was pinched from a book on Russian painting.

Although they were denied recognition, they enjoyed the fact that their creations were being hailed as the work of a higher intelligence. But they got a bit peeved when researchers began publishing books and making money out of their latest alien entity theory. So they decided to reveal all and went to the newspapers, only to discover that few committed researchers accepted their story.

Journalists soon unearthed other groups of covert circle makers. The artist Rod Dickenson also admitted that he had made circles.

Crop circles: 'pictogram' formation at Alton Barnes, Wiltshire, July 1990.

Crop circles, southern England, 1996: Windmill Hill, Avebury, Wiltshire.

They used tape measures, balls of string, garden rollers and specially constructed devices made out of pram wheels to flatten the crops. 'I make art for people who don't realise it's art,' he explained. 'What is really an art experience is interpreted as a paranormal experience.' Some journalists also admitted making circles during their investigations of hoaxing, further perpetuating phenomenon. *The Guardian* even sponsored a circle hoaxing competition in 1992, which was won by a team from Westland Helicopters who called themselves 'Masters of the Cereal Universe'.

Were the Hoaxers a Hoax?

While Dr Terence Meaden and his scientific colleagues were happy to cede the field, those who believed in an extraterrestrial author were not. Rumours spread that Doug and Dave – along with anyone else who supported the hoax theory – were merely pawns in a much deeper conspiracy to discredit the circles. And who was behind this conspiracy? Whitehall, the CIA and extreme factions of the church were blamed. Even such distinguished UFOlogists as Jacques Vallee talked of crop circles being caused by the testing of top-secret space-weapons, spun off from the 'Star Wars' programme. The human circle makers were simply being used to muddy the water for serious researchers.

Some more benign souls wondered what mysterious forces inspired Doug and Dave.

'Many human circle makers are, after all, reluctant to claim individual formations as their own work,' said the ever optimistic Rob Irving. 'Perhaps they are aware of a greater force at work, an inherently mysterious guiding hand which shapes and controls their nocturnal efforts.'

By the summer of 1993, the anti-hoax faction knew that they needed hard evidence to support their position. They began applying the strictest scientific methods to their work. They took soil samples and samples of the crops themselves and tested them for evidence of microwave radiation, or intense heat. Some researchers detected changes in the plants' crystalline structures. Others showed differences in the growth rates between seeds taken from the plants flattened in the circles and those taken from the standing crops around them. A wealthy American research team found, in one large formation, minute emissions from radioactive isotopes that do not occur naturally. However, the sceptics were happy to stick with Doug and Dave's story.

The litmus test was to find a way to tell a hoaxed circle from a genuine one. The man who applied his mind to this task was a Michigan-based biophysicist, Dr William C. Levengood. His analysis confirmed that samples displayed anomalous variations. They showed significant differences in their cellular structures when compared to control samples. Both abnormally high and low radiation levels were both found. Most significantly, he found that samples of wheat and the local chalk were covered in a rust-coloured, glaze-like substance he discovered to be meteoric dust. On the other hand, as a scientist, he did not entirely dismiss Terry Meade's work. His conclusion was that crop circles were made by intelligently controlled plasma vortices.

Scientific Encounters

Close Encounters Classified

Things used to be so easy. In olden days, when someone saw a strange phenomenon in the sky, it was an angel or a fiery chariot or a pillar of light or glowing crucifixes. But with the advent of the UFO in the second half of the twentieth century things got altogether more problematic.

For sceptics though, things are still easy. UFO reports fall into just two categories: the misidentifications of a mundane object or the result of some mental aberration. But the fledgling science of UFOlogy began to look for ways to classify real physical flying objects. To quantify and qualify accounts of UFO encounters and to give the subject the gloss of scientific empiricism, UFOlogists began to categorise reports based on the shape of the object, its movement and the witnesses' level of interaction with it. The idea was to find a way to analyse the UFO data statistically and work out whether there were any patterns underlying it.

To start with there was very little interaction between human witness and the craft they saw, but as UFO sighting reports and photographs flooded in, in the wake of Kenneth Arnold's saucer sighting of 1947, 'saucerology' concentrated its attention on what the flying craft looked like and it was discovered that they came in seven essential varieties:

1. **Disc-shaped** – These are the classic flying saucer, flat and round like an ice-hockey puck. Most have a domed upper section, making them more like a hub cap. Some are domed on both the upper and lower surfaces, and some have a broad rim. Disc-shaped UFOs include the flying saucers seen by Kenneth Arnold, the probe ships photographed by Paul Villa, the craft that took George Adamski to the Moon and the 'sports model' that Bob Lazar worked on in Area 51. The most famous photograph of a disc-shaped UFO was taken by Paul Trent over his farm in Oregon in 1950.

2. **Spheroid** – These are globe-shaped craft, although they also appear as elongated or flattened spheres, as ovoid or egg-shaped or as SLOs – Saturn-like objects that are spheroid with a band around the middle. These were particular common in Europe from medieval times and appear in woodcarvings – a fine example comes from Basel, Switzerland in 1566. Almira Baruana photographed an SLO over Trindad in 1958, and Robert Taylor had an encounter with an ovoid craft about twenty feet across in a forest clearing in Scotland in 1979. Two round objects with spikes knocked him to the ground. When he regained consciousness, all three were gone.

UFOs photographed over Conisbrough, South Yorkshire, by Stephen Pratt,

UFOs over Italy, 26
September 1960.

3. **Cylinder** – These cigar-shaped objects are almost as common
    as saucer-shaped craft and may explain the phantom airships
    that were seen at the end of the nineteenth century. One of the
    earliest sightings of this type of craft in modern times was
    made by Ella Fortune, a nurse from the Mescalero Indian
    Reservation in New Mexico, on 16 October 1957. She saw it

UFO ('luminous disc') photographed over Paris, France, 29 December 1953 by
engineer Paul Paulin. 2-minute exposure, during which the motionless UFO
jumped sideways and again remained motionless.

hovering over nearby Holloman Air Force Base. Like discs, these craft sometimes have domed protuberances, tapered or rounded ends, portholes or fins. They are not as common as they used to be. The most famous example is George Adamski's 'mothership', for which he provided detailed specifications.

Close-up of UFO photographed by George J. Stock at Passic, New Jersey,

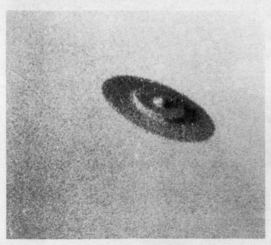

UFO at Barra da Tijuca, Brazil, 7 May 1952.

American military plane, S-47, saw dark red UFO at 400 metres over Utah, 1966, and pilot took this photograph

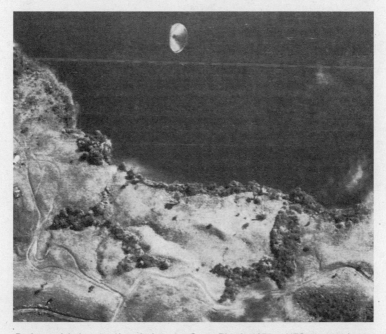

During aerial photography mission over Costa Rica in 1971, a UFO appeared on one frame of the film. Previous and following frames were clear - they were taken at 17-second intervals.

UFO photographed 12 March 1967 by New Mexico State University student west of Picacho Peak, New Mexico, USA.

UFO photographed by contactee Harold Trudel, in East Woonsocket, Rhode Island, USA, 10 June 1967.

UFO photographed 3 July 1960 between Cordoba and Yacanto, Argentina, by Captain Hugo Niotti of the Argentine Air Force (later Vice Commodore).

4. **Flying Triangles** – These triangular-shaped craft have become common since the late 1980s. There is some argument whether they are extraterrestrial craft at all. They are possibly man-made as part of black projects that back-engineer technology from downed alien craft. They are commonly seen at night and are identified by the triangular arrangement of the lights on the underside. They vary in size enormously, from relatively small craft to ones half-a-mile across. They vary in shape, too. Some are conical, like the one Ron and Paula Watson of Mount Vernon, Missouri, saw in 1983, when its occupants were mutilating one of their cows. David Spoor of Norfolk photographed some smaller, more agile triangles in 1998.

5. **Polygonal** – These are craft with more than three sides, such as the diamond-shaped craft that abducted Betty Cash and Vicki Landrum in December 1980 or the five-pointed star seen over Australia the same day in 1978 that Frederick Valentich disappeared. A pentagonal UFO hovered over Shiogama City in Japan in September 1986. It was seen by more than twenty people and photographed by Akira Maezuka.

6. **Balls of light** – These are among the most common UFOs sighted. They occur as a single point of light, but more often come in formations. The most famous example is the 'string of pearls' photographed by student Carl Hart over Lubbock, Texas in 1952. They are often dismissed as a natural phenomenon, such as bolides or 'earthlights' – coloured lights thought to be produced over areas of tectonic stress – and are often seen at Hessdalen, Norway, or over the Yakima Indian Reservation in Washington State. However, the witnesses often report that the unidentified lights are attached to or surround a solid craft.

7. **Exotic** – This is the category where sightings of UFOs that do not fit into any of the other categories end up. They are usually one-offs. In 1967 RAF Intelligence Officer J.B.W. 'Angus'

Brooks saw a huge flying object that took the form of a giant cross. In 1996, a number of witnesses saw a 150-foot high rotating octagonal pyramid over Pelatos, Brazil. One witness, Haroldo Westendorff, was flying his light aircraft when he encountered it. He said that he saw its peak open and a disc-shaped object fly out. The sighting was confirmed by local air traffic controllers. A seventy-one-year-old Polish farmer named Jan Wolski saw a barn-shaped flying object. A family who also saw it said it had multicoloured rotating corkscrews coming out of the corners. And hundreds of witnesses saw a huge boomerang-shape fly over the West Coast.

The first truly scientific attempt at classifying UFOs came from the most influential figure in early UFOlogy, Dr. Josef Allen Hynek. A professor of astronomy at Northwestern University, Hynek was employed in 1948 by the US Air Force to investigate UFO reports. He was consultant to the three major Air Force UFO studies – Projects Sign, Grudge and Blue Book. Although these programmes were largely designed to debunk UFO sightings, Hynek became convinced that there was a real mystery at the heart of the UFO phenomenon. So, after Blue Book was closed, he established the Center for UFO Studies (CUFOS), which remains one of the largest UFO groups in the world, to continue his research.

Hynek's most famous contribution to UFOlogy was his famous 'close encounter' classification system, which was brought to public attention by the Steven Spielberg movie *Close Encounters of the Third Kind* in 1977. Spielberg gave Hynek a walk-on part in the film in recognition of his contribution. Hynek's classification system lent some much-needed scientific weight to the otherwise outlandish UFO reports.

Hynek gave UFOlogy intellectual respectability by recognising that sighting reports were its principal source of data. Rather than dismissing reports because they seemed bizarre, Hynek insisted that witnesses should be listened to. Their reports were real evidence that required proper scientific evaluation. Hynek divided accounts into two types: those where the witness was more than five hundred feet from the object and those where the witness was less than five hundred feet from the object – so-called close encounters.

Within the first category, he identified three different types of report. These were:

1. **Nocturnal lights** – These are lights in the sky that cannot be accounted for by man-made craft, meteorological or astronomical phenomena.

2. **Daylight discs** – These are solid craft, not necessarily disc-shaped, that cannot be accounted for by man-made craft.

3. **Radar visual** – These are anomalous readings on an electronic device, not necessarily radar, that cannot be explained by any man-made phenomena.

The second category – the close encounters – was also subdivided into three types:

1. **Close encounters of the first kind (CEI)** – This is where the witness comes within five hundred feet of an anomalous object, but it has no interaction with the witness or the environment.

2. **Close encounters of the second kind (CEII)** – This is where the witness comes within five hundred feet of an anomalous object that leaves some damage or physical evidence in the environment.

3. **Close encounters of the third kind (CEIII)** – This is where alien beings are seen inside or close to the object, and who may or may not have some contact with the witness.

Since Hynek first devised this system, the relationship between humankind and aliens has moved on apace, and it has been necessary to add new categories. There are now close encounters of the fourth kind (CEIV). These occur when witnesses experience mental or physical changes due to direct interaction with alien beings. Close encounters of the fifth kind (CEV) involve witnesses who can initiate encounters by contacting aliens physically or mentally. Then there are close encounters of the sixth kind (CEVI), where the witness is 'possessed' by a non-physical alien entity.

Hynek did not include these last three categories in his system because he was sceptical about abduction accounts. He did not feel that there was enough solid evidence in abduction reports to evaluate them scientifically. However, since he died in 1986, a new generation of UFOlogists has made full use of these new classifications.

Although Hynek's system is still the most widely used system of classification, many UFOlogists feel that it is too crude to be useful in investigating modern encounters. Some have tried to devise other systems, but these attempts have usually come to grief. Either they are overly complicated or they rely too much on one or other of the theories of what is happening in UFO encounters. However, one other classification system has been making gains on Hynek's old categories. This is the Vallee Classification System (VCS), devised by the French UFOlogist Jacques Françis Vallee. A graduate of Hynek's astronomy course at Northwestern University, Vallee is one of the leaders of the European 'psychosocial' school of UFOlogy. However, Vallee devised a system that can be used by any of the competing factions within UFOlogy.

Vallee's system looks at three main aspects of UFO reports and classifies them under three categories: Fly-Bys (FB), Manoeuvres (MA) and Close Encounters (CE). Close Encounters is the 'highest' category while Fly-Bys is the 'lowest'. Each of these categories is subdivided into five subcategories:

Fly-bys (FB)

- FB1 – UFO is seen flying in a straight line.
- FB2 – UFO is flying in a straight line that leaves behind physical evidence.
- FB3 – Fly-by with alien beings seen on board.

UFOs: a close encounter of the second kind.

- FB4 – Fly-by with the witness experiencing a sense of altered reality.
- FB5 – Fly-by that results in injury or death.

Manoeuvres (MA)
- MA1 – UFO seen travelling in an erratic manner.
- MA2 – UFO manoeuvres causing physical effects.
- MA3 – UFO manoeuvring with alien beings seen on board.
- MA4 – UFO seen travelling in an erratic manner with the witness experiencing a sense of altered reality.
- MA5 – UFO manoeuvres that cause injury or death.

Close Encounters (CE)
- CE1 – UFO comes within five hundred feet of the witness, but they feel no effects.
- CE2 – UFO comes within five hundred feet of the witness and leaves traces of landing or injures the witness.
- CE3 – UFO comes within five hundred feet of the witness with alien beings visible.

- CE4 – The witness is abducted.
- CE5 – Abduction that results in permanent injury or death.

Within each of these subdivisions, cases are graded according to their intensity, the amount of detail given and their effects on the witness. Then each report is also given a credibility score based on three other criteria: the reliability of the source, the thoroughness of the investigation of the sighting, and possible explanations.

The Vallee system is much more complex that Hynek's classification, but this simply reflects the increasingly complicated nature of the UFO phenomenon. And it does have the advantage of retaining the old 'close encounters' category.

Natural Causes

Most UFO researchers agree that the majority of flying saucer sighting reports can be dismissed as misperception, misidentification of unusual aerial events, such as meteorological effects, and downright hoaxes. When those cases are set aside there are still a large number of events in the skies that cannot be accounted for by normal means. But there is now a growing body of UFOlogists, especially in Europe, who seek to explain many of these genuine sightings, not as alien spacecraft, but as the result of a hither-to-unidentified natural phenomenon. Their theory is that these genuinely unidentified objects are so-called 'earthlights', thought to be produced by fault lines in the earth's crust.

For many years, the idea that earthlights – sometimes called balls of light (BOLs) – lies at the heart of the UFO phenomenon has been shunned by mainstream UFOlogy, which concentrated almost exclusively on the idea that UFOs were alien spacecraft. However, the early explorer of the unexplained, Charles Fort (1874-1932), who gave his name to 'Fortean phenomena', was among the first to observe that strange 'meteors' appeared to coincide with earth tremors and earthquakes. Bu it was only in the 1960s, after the discovery of tectonic plates, that several UFOlogists took the next step and began to correlate UFO sightings and geological fault lines.

French researcher Ferdinand Lagarde found that at least forty per cent of low-level flying saucer sightings occurred over, or close to, fractures in the earth's crust. Veteran American UFOlogist John Keel also began to look at the association between the appearance of unusual lights and areas of faulting and anomalies in the earth's magnetic field.

In the 1970s, earth-mysteries researchers Paul Devereux and Andrew York mapped strange phenomena reported over the centuries in the English county of Leicestershire and found that both meteorological anomalies – such as 'strange lightning' – and UFO sightings occurred most often over the fault-line regions of the county.

In 1977 Dr Michael Persinger, a neuroscientist and geologist, then at Laurentian University in Canada, and researcher Gyslaine Lafreniere published a study of the United States that pointed to a correlation between high levels of UFO activity and the sites of earthquake epicentres. Persinger and Lafreniere theorised that UFOs were electromagnetic phenomena arising from magnetic fields in the atmosphere caused by the squeezing of rocks under pressure. This is related to the scientifically respectable piezoelectric effect, by which certain crystals give off electricity when squeezed or distorted. In the run-up to an earthquake, tremendous energy would be generated by tectonic stress distorting the mineral crystals found in the earth's crust.

Possible ball lightning photographedin the summer of 1978 by Werner Burger at Sankt Gallenkirch, Vorarlberg, Austria.

There could be other natural mechanisms at work here too. Light can be produced when enormous forces crush certain crystals. When the earth's tectonic plates move against each other the friction also generates an enormous amount of heat. Water in the surrounding rock would be vaporised. It would become ionised, collect around the fault and be expelled as luminous plumes of ionised plasma into the air above.

Normally these naturally occurring crustal forces would operate evenly over very large geographical regions and without having a visible effect. But at times of tectonic stress, these forces could become focused in a few small areas of particular geological resistance or instability – such as fault lines, mineral deposits, stubborn rock outcrops, hills and mountains – where the electromagnetic forces generated would produce strange airborne lights. This idea was tested experimentally in Boulder, Colorado, by the US Bureau of Mines, who filmed rocks with high crystalline content as they were placed under stress and allowed to fracture. Prior to this shattering, what looked like mini UFOs were created in the laboratory due to chemical and electrical charges emitted by the rock. This was the first demonstration of what has come to be known in UFOlogy as the Tectonic Strain Theory, or TST.

Devereux has pointed out that, if you scaled up the Boulder experiment to the size of mountains, it would produce enough earthlights to explain the UFO activity you see in 'window areas', which are invariably areas of tectonic stress. In 1982, he applied this theory to his study of sightings in the UK's most active UFO window in the Pennine Hills.

Dr Persinger continued his research and further explored and refined the TST theory. In 1986, he was joined geologist by John Derr in a study of a wave of lights seen over the Yakima Indian Reservation, Washington State. During the 1970s, firewardens on the reservation photographed huge orange balls of light hovering above rocks. They had also seen smaller ping-pong-sized balls of light dancing along ridges. The area had long been prone to unusual meteorological effects, such as glowing clouds.

Derr and Persinger discovered that the lights appeared most

often along the ridges that cut across the reservation. These were riddled with fault lines. They also appeared around Satus Peak. Here a fault line broke the surface at the site of one of the strongest earthquakes that occurred in the region in the thirteen years covered by their study. Another wave of sightings occurred in the seven months before a big earthquake that occurred while Derr and Persinger were at work.

The significance of the Yakima study is that the reservation is in the foothills of the Cascade Mountains where, in 1947, Kenneth Arnold saw the first flying saucers –nine glittering objects flying in formation over a mountain ridge. This made a strong tie between 'earthlights' and UFOs.

A second study that made that connection occurred in the remote valley of Hessdalen in Norway. Hessdalen is seventy miles southeast of the remote northern town of Trondheim. The region is rich in copper and other metals. In November 1981 the people in the isolated farms in the valley saw strange yellow and white lights. They appeared just below the summits and ridges of the surrounding mountains. Along with regular balls of light, they saw inverted Christmas trees and bullet-shaped lights with the pointed end downwards. The farmers also heard underground rumblings and saw flashes in the sky.

As the phenomena were clearly linked with UFOs, the Norwegian Defence Department was called in. In March 1982 two Royal Norwegian Air Force officers turned up in Hessdalen to study the situation. By the summer of 1983, sightings had become increasingly frequent. They became big news in Scandinavia, but the Norwegian Defence Department came up with no explanation. Suspecting another official cover-up, Norwegian and Swedish UFO groups pooled their resources and set up Project Hessdalen. From 21 January to 26 February 1984 activity in the valley was monitored twenty-four hours a day with a range of specialist instruments, including radar – even though temperatures dropped as low as minus 30 degrees Celsius. Nevertheless the team managed to capture numerous strange lights on film and pick them up on radar. This sometimes proved baffling. On one occasion, several members of the team noticed a strange undulating sensation in their chests when the lights appeared. In another case, a bright light was seen travelling across the sky. But although it appeared constant to the naked eye, it appeared on the radar screen only every second sweep.

More earthlights were seen in the US when local newspaper reporter John Bennett heard reports that crowds of people were going to watch displays of strange lights at a ranch outside the town of Ada, seventy miles south-east of Oklahoma City. Deciding to investigate for himself, Bennett drove out to the remote ranch that afternoon. He parked his car and waited. As dusk approached, he

saw an orange light appear in the middle of some trees. At first, he thought it was the lights of a house. But he changed his mind when the glowing orb started growing steadily larger until it was about three feet across. Then it began darting back and forth, changing colour as it did so. Suddenly a piece broke away and started bouncing across the field in front of him.

'It looked like a luminous basketball,' said Bennett.

Project Hessdalen researched mystery lights in Norway.

After some time, the light went out. Another witness told Bennett that he had seen another light earlier that had come right up to the fence where he was standing.

'I didn't move, and it was like it was looking right at me,' he said.

Light phenomena are frequently reported along the San Andreas Fault in California, and in 1973 a strange streak of light was photographed over the Pinnacles Mountain Monument nearby by physicist David Kubrin. As it moved it created shock waves. Then it stopped dead and began to spin before dissolving. What amazed

Kubrin was that it had exhibited signs of having mass – by producing shock waves – but somehow managed to stop without decelerating.

In 1989, geochemist Paul McCartney published his report of his investigation into the appearance of earthlights in north-west Wales in 1904 and 1905. Balls of red light were seen at various sites, but showed up most regularly over the field next to the chapel in Llanfair. He traced the sightings on a map and found that they ran down the course of the Mochras Fault that runs out into Tremadog Bay. Similar lights were seen in many parts of Wales during a wave of earthquake activity that lasted from 1892 to 1906. The area lies next to the Lleyn Peninsula which is one of the UK's most active earthquake areas. In July 1984, it was the epicentre of an earthquake measuring 5.5 on the Richter Scale. The lights reappeared briefly. The evening before the earthquake local people saw a brilliant white light, said to be the size of a small car, float in from the sea and land on the beach.

Then between 1 November 1988 and 21 January 1989 researchers from Quebec University made fifty-two sightings of strange light while on a seismic monitoring expedition to the Saguenay/Lake St John region of south-east Canada. Balls of light, both stationary and moving, were seen several hundred feet up in the air, some persisting as long as twelve minutes. And fireballs up to ten feet in diameter repeatedly popped out of the ground – sometimes only a few yards away from the observer. This research team, again, linked these UFO-type phenomena to rising tectonic strain in the ground that led up to an earthquake in the area.

The link between earthlights and UFOs has split the world of UFOlogy in two. The old-guard UFOlogists continue to advocate the extraterrestrial spacecraft theory and argue that small balls of lights can hardly explain solid-bodied craft that are seen in daylight – or, indeed, the sixty per cent of UFO sightings that do not occur near fault lines. On the other side of the fence are the new model earthlight researchers who point out that the phenomenon is not confined to small balls of light. With an appropriate build up of energy, earthlights can reach the size of a conventional flying-saucer. And they contend that, if earthlights are made from some kind of plasma – hot, electrically charged gas – they would also appear shiny and metallic in daylight, explaining the 'silvery discs' reported by Kenneth Arnold and many other witnesses.

To resolve the argument one way or the other, more data is required. A new Project Hessdalen has been set up in Norway and an expedition is planned to the Australian outback, where there has been persistent earthlight activity. Meanwhile, a research group headed by Paul Devereux has shown that geomagnetic anomalies and sightings of dancing lights around the increasingly active volcano, Popocatapetl, in Mexico have coincided with that country's recent prolonged UFO 'flap'.

'The fact is that the vast majority of UFOs are described as balls of light,' says Devereux. 'But it's only subjective interpretation that turns them into the lights of an alien craft.'

However, some consider this research, no matter how fascinating, as a diversion from the real business of UFOlogy – finding aliens.

More Windows

Paul Devereux's work on UFO window areas has opened the way to even more exotic theories. It has long been noted that window areas tend to feature not only UFOs but also other sorts of strange phenomena, including monster sightings and time anomalies. This has led John Keel to suggest that windows are portals between our reality and a supernatural dimension. He believes these represent points of weakness in the boundary between the two realities that allow strange phenomena to flow into our world – and possibly take us in the opposite direction. This would explain alien abduction and mysterious disappearances. If a window is the result of natural physical energies induced into the atmosphere by local geological factors, then they should remain relatively constant across time. So a window area would not only produce modern-day UFO sightings, but also reports of strange phenomena down the centuries. Deveraux's study of the historical records shows that the Pennine Hills is just such a window.

At the centre of the window on the Yorkshire–Lancashire border is the UK's most UFO-plagued town – Todmorden. It boasts dozens of sightings and six alien contact cases – out of just a hundred in the whole of the UK. In one case, a policeman from Todmorden was being abducted, but while he was being dragged into the UFO his boot caught on something and split.

Another case involved children's home worker Jenny, who was on her way home after horseback riding on the hills around Walsden. As she walked down the steep path from the moors to the town, she noticed that her dog was looking up into the sky. She look upwards to see what it was looking at and saw a lens-shaped object with coloured light under it floating silently at around roof-top height. As she stood and stared there was a telepathic exchange of information between her and the occupants of the UFO.

'It was like being plugged into a computer,' she said.

Contact ended when the UFO split into three separate glowing pieces and shot off in different directions.

UFOlogist Peter Hough has spent over twenty-five years studying the Pennine window and has come to the conclusion that we live in a multiverse, where other dimensions intersect with our own.

'Certain areas act as access points,' he says.

However, there may be a more prosaic explanation. Fiery balls of light appeared above the ancient church in the village of Linley, Shropshire. At the same time, the locals reported the presence of a poltergeist. Metal door latches opened themselves, crockery moved by itself and chairs were hurled across the room. Dr Michael Persinger says that earthlights might also be triggered by a localised increase in the Earth's magnetic field, which would explain these other bizarre happenings.

Abductions Experts

Although there have been numerous well-documented cases of alien abductions since the 1960s, many UFOlogists refuse to believe then. So in an attempt to discover whether they were really happening, in June 1992, the first Abduction Study Conference was held at the Massachusetts Institute of Technology. Three of the world's leading experts attended. They included Budd Hopkins, a pioneering investigator in this field, and Dr David Jacobs, associate professor of history at Temple University, who had been investigating UFOs for twenty-five years.

Chairing the conference was Dr John E. Mack, professor of Psychiatry at Harvard Medical School and a Pulitzer Prize winner. He was also a founder of the psychiatry teaching department and Cambridge Hospital, Harvard, and director of the Program for Extraordinary Experience Research at the Center for Psychology and Social Research.

The conference concluded that, although people from a whole cross-section of society had been abducted, their reports showed a remarkable consistency. The same type of aliens were involved in most cases. The abduction procedures were the same and abductees reported similar details of what they were subjected to. If alien abduction was some form of delusion, the accounts should differ wildly. Yet they showed consistent and repeated patterns. This was strong evidence that victims really were being abducted.

Greys were almost always responsible, though in some cases they are directed by taller humanoid aliens. Victims found themselves under the total control of the aliens. Inside the craft, they were forced to strip, made to lie on a table and subjected to intimate examinations and invasive surgery. Victims were then returned, though usually their memories had been wiped clean of the events, which could only be accessed through regressional hypnosis.

Added to that, Professor Mack pointed out, the victims often had hard physical evidence of their abduction. People returned with scars on their bodies that were fully healed though they were not been there before the abduction. Strange implants have been located on X-rays and CAT scans. Some have been removed and examined.

Chemical analysis of the implants has shown that they were usually made from elements found on Earth. But one of Professor Mack's colleagues, a nuclear biologist, ran tests on an implant taken from the nose of an abductee and discovered that the implant was not a naturally occurring biological structure. It was made

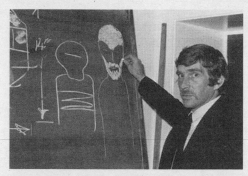

PC Alan Godfrey, who in November 1980 was allegedly adbucted into a UFO at Todmorden, West Yorkshire.

from manufactured fibre. Leir's work on isotope ratios had not been done at this time.

The leading sceptics also turned up at the conference. They dismissed the physical evidence provided by Professor Mack and others, and claimed that no reliable evidence for abduction exists outside the victim's imagination. The villain of the piece, according to the sceptics, was the use of regressional hypnosis techniques to recover hidden memories. The Society for Psychical Research's Kevin McClure claimed that the abduction researchers using hypnosis are not qualified psychologists. When they did use qualified ones, McClure said, they implanted memories. He alleged that, under hypnosis, victims were encouraged to recount details that support the abduction scenario by asking leading questions.

McClure also argued that False Memory Syndrome may also be to blame. This is a disorder where the subconscious creates a bogus memory to cover up some painful childhood trauma such as sexual abuse. Abductees may be subconsciously creating false memories of an alien abduction to protect themselves from the real memories of a more traumatic experience.

Professor Mack, a psychologist by training, dismissed this theory.

Painting by Dr Susan Blackmore of a hypnotising alien.

'There is not a single abduction case in my experience or that of other investigators that has turned out to have masked a history of sexual abuse or any other traumatic cause,' he said. 'In fact, the reverse has frequently occurred – that an abduction history has been revealed in cases investigated for sexual or other abuse.'

Psychologist Susan Blackmore of the University of the West of England had another theory. She claimed that an abduction experience could be induced artificially by stimulation of the temporal lobes – the part of the brain where memories are stored. A Canadian research team under Dr Michael Persinger from the University of Sudbury, Ontario, supported this thesis. They had designed a helmet that generated a magnetic field. Dr Persinger claimed that, when this field was applied to the back of the brain, it could produce an alien abduction experience in people who have never previously claimed to have had one. But when the device was tried out on Dr Susan Blackmore, she said she felt 'someone pulling my arms and legs' and 'sudden and uncontrollable emotions'. This is hardly an alien abduction experience.

The author of *Allergies and Aliens*, Albert Budden, also said that electromagnetic fields create memories of alien abductions. He was convinced that the wave of abduction reports over the last forty years is caused by electromagnetic pollution. Electromagnetic radiation in the atmosphere is strong enough to affect the temporal lobes of abductees' brains, he says, causing abduction-like experiences. All abductees are electrically hypersensitive, he believes, and their experiences are a symptom of their allergic reactions to electromagnetic fields in the environment.

But Hopkins, Jacobs and Mack pointed out that over-active imaginations, false memories and electromagnetic simulation of temporal lobes cannot explain physical scars on abductees' bodies or the implants taken from them.

Dr Sue Davidson, a psychotherapist, thinks all abductees are raving mad. 'I have not come across the phenomenon of abduction by aliens except as a delusional belief of someone suffering from schizophrenia,' he says. But how does that explain cases like that of Travis Walton, where there were other witnesses to the 'space-napping'? Are they all mad? If they are then it is an insanity that is widespread in society. In 1995, Robert Durant compiled the statistics on alien abductions. He discovered that some five million Americans had reported having been abducted over the previous fifty years. That works out at about 274 a day. Assuming that it takes six aliens to abduct a human – abductees rarely report that they have seen more than six – and that each six-alien team abducted twelve humans a day, you would need just 137 to cover the whole of America.

And UFOlogists have now tied the alien abductions to the mutilation of livestock as further evidence that aliens are conducting genetic experiments planet-wide. Again, bizarrely butchered carcasses are not caused by hallucinations, delusions or false memories.

Alien of the Soul

So how do the earthlight theorists explain the phenomenon of alien abduction? It might not be as hard as you think. Let's look at one of the most celebrated alien abduction cases in the whole of UFOlogy – that of Travis Walton, whose abduction formed the basis of the 1993 movie *Fire in the Sky*.

Walton was abducted one November evening in 1975, from a forest track near his home in Heber, Arizona. A lumberjack, he was travelling home with the rest of the wood-cutting crews in the truck, tired after a long day's work, when, in a clearing up ahead, they saw a strange, glowing ball of light. As the truck came closer, Walton jumped out and rushed towards the mysterious object, which cast a ring of light on the ground. It was about twenty feet across and floated in the air unsteadily, emitting strange beeping and rumbling sounds.

A blue-green bolt of light zapped out of the object. Walton heard a crackling sound and felt 'a numbing shock… like a high-voltage electrocution'. It lifted him up and flung him to the ground. The rest of the crew fled. By the time they returned to the scene, the mysterious ball of light was seen shooting skyward, and Walton had disappeared.

Five days later, Walton turned up naked in a phone box. He was seriously dehydrated, delirious, dazed, distraught and half-dead. He had been knocked out by the bolt of light. Later he recalled regaining consciousness in some sort of spacecraft, surrounded by 'foetus-like' aliens, with large dark eyes and marshmallowy skin.

It certainly seemed that something odd had happened in the woods the evening he went missing. But had Walton had an encounter with an earthlight rather than an alien spaceship? Certainly what Walton and his workmates saw was the right size and shape to be an earthlight. And reports from around the world of earthlights mention that they make strange sounds, just like the ones Walton and his workmates had heard.

As earthlights are an electromagnetic phemonemon, one could easily have zapped him with a bolt of electricity. If Walton had suffered a massive electric shock, he might have been left in a confused mental state. He could have wandered off into the forest and lost himself there for days. In that case, what were the strange aliens Walton recalled?

According to Canadian neuroscientist and earthlight proponent Dr Michael Persinger, an individual exposed to enormous electromagnetic fields is likely to experience a number of effects on his or her body, brain and mind. These effects could include impaired memory and vision. At its most extreme, an electromagnetic field might put a victim into a trance-like state where the boundaries between waking and dreaming become blurred and they might suffer intense hallucinations.

The area of the brain most sensitive to changes in magnetic and electrical fields is the area of the temporal cortex. Under the cortex proper lie the amygdala and hippocampus. Stimulation of the amygdala produces intense emotional feelings, while alterating the function of the hippocampus can modify memory and release dreams into the waking state.

In an effort to explain alien abductions, Michael Persinger has been running a series of experiments in which volunteers have the temporal cortex of their brains subjected to magnetic fields. Subjects sit in a darkened soundproof cubicle, wearing a helmet that creates magnetic 'vortices'. Computer-controlled electrodes directed these into various areas of the temporal cortex with great precision. During the course of the experiment, subjects see visions or feel some sort of presence. One even said the cubicle was haunted by the devil himself.

Persinger has found that when a subject has undergone several of these sessions, it takes little to trigger what he calls 'the mystical state of mind'. The magnetic helmet often induced vivid scenes from infancy and childhood.

Journalist Ian Cotton tried this out. He found himself sitting in a darkened cubicle with a magnetic helmet on. The first thing he was conscious of was a strange noise, then he went into a lucid dream state. He said that it was as clear as if his 'inner eye' was a video camera, and he saw vivid scenes from his childhood. He saw the pattern of the wallpaper in his bedroom and the red roses on the tablecloth in his childhood home, along with other long-forgotten details, with lifelike clarity.

In one particularly telling experiment, the subjects were asked concentrate on a single light in front of them. It was a normal sixty-watt electric light bulb, but many subjects described seeing slit-mouthed, grey-skinned aliens and horrific medical probes – images common to the typical UFO abduction scenario.

Medical researchers who have conducted experiments with psychedelic substances such as dimethyltryptamine (DMT) and LSD have had similar effects. Drugs induce vivid hallucinations and infantile regression with some people even claiming to have re-experienced their own birth trauma. As well as occurring in certain vegetables and seeds, DMT occurs naturally in the body. Native American tribes take it as a means of seeing spirits, contacting dead ancestors or communicating with the gods. Modern users of the drug find themselves in a deep mental state, where they see primitive creatures not dissimilar to Grey aliens. One research subject also reported being escorted by alien entities to a kind of landing platform at a space station. There he met android-like creatures that were 'a cross between crash dummies and the Empire troops from *Star Wars*'. Another said they saw a 'giant, complex control panel' and creatures that were 'bipedal and roughly human size'. These are all familiar images from abductions.

According to UFO researcher Alvin Lawson, the archetypal image of the Grey alien inhabits this very realm of our imagination. It is a kind of primal template of the mammal. Lawson says that the Grey, with it large eyes, tiny features and a small, wasted body, is essentially an elaborate image of the human foetus and as such is an archetype lodged deep within our minds. Certainly, the image of a baby is closely associated with the Greys, who are the most common abductors. Women regularly report that the aliens take their babies and, more commonly, their foetuses. Many abductees, men as well as women, report aliens probing their reproductive organs. And UFOlogist Dennis Stacy says that the Grey abduction motif is associated with the trauma surrounding abortion.

A number of researchers now believe that the alien abduction experience can be triggered by a variety of temporal lobe stimuli in those with sufficient sensitivity. This sensitivity can have been induced by trauma – either a physical trauma such as an electric shock or a psychological trauma such as an incident of child abuse. Such stimuli sensitise the temporal cortex. What's more, they are cumulative, each one leaving the subject more susceptible the next time.

British investigator Albert Budden has interviewed numerous abductees, and found that virtually all of them have suffered such trauma. Electrical sensitivity is common among them. When such people come within the influence of high-tension wires, for example, the electromagnetic field can precipitate hallucinations of such vividness that they think they really have encountered a UFO or aliens.

Abductees usually end up back in their own bed. Companions are not aware that they have been missing and abductees often feel that they have been abducted in some abstract or spiritual sense, while their body has been left behind in bed. Finnish abductee Rauni-Leena Luukkanen-Kilde said that during her abductions it was her 'astral' body that boarded the spaceship. The scars that manifested themselves on her physical body later appeared as a result of the trauma to her spiritual self, she thought.

Alien Races

The Grey alien became the best known species of extraterrestrial when alien abductee Whitley Strieber put the picture of one on the cover of his 1987 best-seller *Communion*. However, despite the enduring fame of the Grey, on the night he was first abducted, 26 December 1985, Strieber actually encountered three other types of creature.

One was the robot-like being that initially led him out of the bedroom of his country home in upstate New York. Then, in the forest outside, he encountered a large number of short, stocky beings in dark blue overalls. They had wide, blue faces, 'glittering, deep-set eyes', pug noses and broad, human-like mouths, he said. It was only later, when he found himself inside the circular room, that he encountered Grey-like beings – but their eyes, although black, were not almond shaped but 'as round as buttons'.

Strieber's case is by no means unique. While virtually every abduction case involves Greys, abductees regularly see a variety of aliens during their experiences. Dutch therapist Hilda Musch made a survey of abductees in the Netherlands and found that 85 per cent of them reported encounters with aliens other than Greys. Numerous different types have been reported since contact with extraterrestrials began. Sceptics say that there are as many types of alien as there are people who report them. But that is not entirely true. Contact reports do show some degree of consistency. In fact, all the aliens reported being seen over the past century can be categorised into one of four classes:

1. **Humanoid** – These are essentially human in shape, though witnesses have the strong sense that they are not human. This class includes Greys.

2. **Animalian** – These are animal-like creatures, including reptilian aliens and Chupacabras.

3. **Robotic** – These are entities that have a distinctly mechanical appearance.

4. **Exotic** – This is a catch-all category for those that do not fit into any of the categories above, and makes up just five per cent of the sightings.

Each class of alien can be further divided into types. The most recognisable type of Humanoid is called the Human. This is simply because it is nearly impossible to tell 'them' from 'us' – except they are usually better looking with blond hair and blemish-free complexions. These 'Nordic' types used to be very common visitors to Earth. They were the aliens who visited George Adamski first on 20 November 1952, landing somewhere between Desert Center, California and Parker, Arizona. They had long blond hair, high foreheads and seemed to radiate great love, warmth and understanding.

Then there are the familiar 'Short Greys', which are the main alien type seen on Earth. Before they were made famous by Whitley Strieber, they had made an appearance at the end of the movie *Close Encounters of the Third Kind*. This, UFO sceptics said, would spark a rash of copycat sightings. It did not happen. Short Greys had already appeared in movies in the 1940s and 1950s. They were the pilots of the flying saucers that crashed at Roswell in 1947. But in the literature they predated that, first

'Grey' alien entity, as portrayed by Rod Dickinson; oil canvas, 7ft x 7ft.

appearing on the cover of the magazine *Astounding Stories* in 1935.

Greys are often not very nice. But as astronomer Carl Sagan once remarked: 'I would love it if there were aliens here, even if they are a little short, sullen, grumpy and sexually preoccupied.'

Closely related are Short Non-Greys. They are like Greys but they are very hairy or have green skin and are common visitors to Latin America. It was a pair of the Green race that geologist Rapuzzi Johannis encountered when out studying rock formations in northern Italy on the night of 14 August 1947. They were about three feet tall and had green faces. When they came within six feet of him, Johannis noticed their hands. They had eight jointless, opposable fingers. Small green Short Non-Greys appeared in the movie *Invasion of the Saucermen* in 1957.

The Animalians also include some creatures that are not formally thought of as extraterrestrials – such as Yetis, swamp creatures and goblins. Bigfoots, for example, show all the characteristics of being alien. Some even have spaceships. Stephen Pulaski and two boys came across a dome-shaped craft that had landed near Greensburg, Pennsylvania, on 24 November 1973. Suddenly, two large, bear-like creatures appeared. They were eight feet tall with glowing, yellow-green eyes. Being a good American, Pulaski pulled a gun and shot at them. It had no effect. The boys then fled. Pulaski gave them covering fire, to no avail.

Abductee Betty Andreasson saw an entirely different type of Animalian. When she was abducted from her home in South Ashburnham, Massachusetts, on 25 January 1967, she was taken on a saucer-shaped craft to some other world where she saw three-feet high lemur-like creatures. They were headless and had eyes on the ends of prehensile stalks.

Robotic aliens come in just two types. The most common is the Metallic, which is mechanical and made totally out of metal. Lee Parish of Prospect, Kentucky, saw three machine-like beings on 27 January 1977. Under hypnosis, he said that two of the slab-like creatures were six foot tall. One of them was bulky and white, the other slim and red. The third towered above the others. It was around twenty feet tall and black. Scottish forester Bob Taylor is also thought to have encountered Robotic aliens in 1979 when he was attacked by two metal beach balls around a foot in diameter with six legs that emerged from a UFO. He smelt a pungent odour before passing out. There is also a rare type of Robotic alien that has parts made out of a substance that resembles flesh. They are called Fleshy Robots.

The Exotic category of aliens again has two main types. The Apparitional are at least partially transparent, while the Physical are completely solid. Hans Gustafsson and Stig Rydberg encountered a Physical Exotic while out driving near Domesten in Sweden on the night of 20 December 1958. They noticed a glow in the woods and stopped to investigate. In a clearing, they saw a spacecraft with four odd-shaped creatures jumping around the landing site. The amorphous, blue-green blobs were six feet tall and hostile. The two men barely escaped the suction force of the blobs' onslaught.

Aliens are a mixed bunch and several types often appear together. In May 1969 Brazilian soldier Jose Antonio was abducted by two short aliens in silver suits. On board their craft he met another alien who was about four feet tall with wavy, waist-length hair, large eyes, a mouth like a fish and deep-set greenish eyes. And in July 1983, Ron and Paula Watson encountered four aliens in Mount Vernon, Missouri – two silver-suited humanoids, a Bigfoot with shaggy hair all over its huge body and a 'lizard man'.

That there is an enormous variety of aliens is no real surprise. After all, there is a huge variety of life on earth. And alien visitors are hardly a rarity. Huge numbers of aliens have dropped in. An American survey found that some five million people have been abducted by aliens over the past fifty years – almost three hundred a day. It is estimated that the average abduction team comprised six aliens. From the length of time each abduction takes, it has been worked out that they can perform a maximum of twelve abductions per day. That means that 140 aliens have to be at work day and night to cope with the workload in the US alone.

Lizard Men

The lizard man Ron and Paula Watson saw was six foot tall, with green reptilian skin, webbed hands and feet, and glowing, cat-like eyes with vertical pupils. This was a sighting of a reptilian alien. Indeed these 'reptoids' are the most common species of alien after the Greys, and, for that reason, the most fascinating.

One was seen in Italy on 6 December 1978. Twenty-six-year-old night-watchman Fortunato Zanfretta saw four bright lights moving behind a house at Marzano in Genoa. He went to investigate and was confronted by a nine-feet-tall bipedal reptoid, which pushed him to the ground and then vanished. Zanfretta picked himself up and ran to his car. On the way, he felt a sudden heat, heard a loud whistling sound and saw a huge triangular craft soaring up into the sky. He radioed his colleagues for help and, when they arrived, he took them to where the craft had taken off. There, they found a depression the ground. It was twenty-five feet across and shaped like a giant horseshoe.

Under hypnosis, it was discovered that Zanfretta had been abducted by the reptoid and taken on board its craft for a time. He could not remember much about the spacecraft's interior, but he gave a vivid description of the alien. It had horn-like projections on its forehead above luminous-yellow, triangular eyes, pointed spines on either side of its head and a stocky body. Its skin was dark green and marked by a series of horizontal folds or ribbing.

Numerous UFOlogists have collected reports of similar sightings. 'When a so-called reptilian is repeatedly described as having the same scaly skin, claws for fingers, and extreme interest in sexuality, one must pay attention,' said Dan Wright at MUFON's 1995 symposium in Seattle.

In the autumn of 1938, near the town of Juminda in Estonia, two eyewitnesses saw a three-foot high creature with greenish-brown skin. It had slit-like eyes and month and looked like a giant frog, they said. It had some trouble walking on dry land; even so, it managed to outpace the witnesses when they chased it.

On 29 June 1988 seventeen-year-old Chris Davis was driving home past Scape Ore Swamp, near the village of Bishopville in

South Carolina, at around 2 a.m., when his car had a puncture. He pulled over and changed the tyre, and was about to get back in the driver's seat, when he saw a figure running towards him across a field. As it drew closer, he saw that it was not human. Over six feet six inches tall and standing upright, it looked like a giant lizard, with green scaly skin, and slanted, red glowing eyes. It had three digits on its feet and hands, each of which had a four-inch-long black claw.

Terrified, Davis jumped back into his car. When the creature reached the vehicle it wrenched the wing mirror off in an attempt to open the door. When Davis drove off, the lizard man leapt on to the car's roof and clung on as the terrified teenager drove through the swampy wilderness at up to fifty miles an hour. Fortunately, the creature eventually lost its grip and fell off.

Davis reported the encounter to the police, and the local sheriff, Liston Truesdale, investigated. 'We checked out his reputation, and he's a pretty clean-cut kid,' said Truesdale. 'He's also agreed to take a polygraph test or go under hypnosis.'

The Lizardman of South Carolina, a strange reptilian humanoid.

Davis's father, Tommy, told the newspapers: 'All I can tell you is that my son was terrified that night. He was hysterical, crying and trembling. It took a while before he was calm enough to tell us what happened.'

In the weeks that followed, numerous other sightings were reported and Scape Ore Swamp became a media circus, with TV crews battling it out for prime filming sites. A local radio station offered a reward of $1 million for the capture of the lizard man. They kept their money. However, a number of three-toed foot-prints, each fourteen inches long, were later discovered in the swamp, and casts were taken. Meanwhile, numerous Fortean researchers stepped forward to offer speculative theories. Others said that Davis had been attacked by a drunken tramp who and crawled out of a ditch, and dismissed the footprints as the work of a prankster. Some later sightings indeed proved to be hoaxes and, soon, the lizard man fell out of the headlines. The enigmatic entity itself was, like so many other anomalous creatures, never identified, let alone captured.

In veteran Fortean investigator Loren Coleman's *Curious Encounters*, he reports encounters with a 'creature from the black lagoon' – named for the 1954 sci-fi cult movie – in Ohio in 1972. At around 1 a.m., on 3 March, police officer Ray Schocke was driving down a riverside road towards the town of Loveland, when his headlights lit up what he initially took to be a dog. But the crea-ture then stood up on its hind legs and he could see that it was a three-foot tall reptilian with leathery skin and a frog-like face. The frog-man looked at him for a moment, then jumped over the guard rail, slithered down the embankment and disappeared into the river. Schocke drove to the police station and returned with fellow offi-cer Mark Matthews. They searched the area. Although they did not find the creature, they did find scrape marks leading down to the river along the course the fleeing creature took.

Two weeks later, Matthews was driving along the same river when he saw what he took to be a dead animal lying in the road. He stopped to move the carcass. When he got out of his patrol car, the creature got up and moved to the guard rail without taking his eyes off Matthews. Matthews took a pot shot at it but missed. The creature climbed over the guard rail and made off. Other witnesses in the area reported seeing a strange frog-like creature.

That same year there were other reptilian encounters at Lake Thetis, near Colwood in British Columbia. On two separate occasions in August 1972, two sets of witnesses saw a humanoid reptile-man with a silver body covered in fish-like scales emerge from the lake. One witness said the creature had a monstrous face, huge ears, and at least one large spike projecting from its head. It was a biped, with three-pronged flippers for feet, a fish-like mouth, and very large fish-like eyes. This description fits other reptoid sightings that date back to the nineteenth century and beyond.

In 24 October 1878 a Kentucky newspaper, the *Louisville Courier Journal,* reported that a strange creature captured alive in Tennessee was on exhibit in Louisville. According to the article, the entity was around six feet six inches in height, had eyes twice as large as a human's and was 'covered with fish scales'.

Sighting reports of these creatures shows such consistency that researcher John Carpenter has been able to piece together a detailed morphology of these scaly creatures and, in MUFON's journal of April 1993, he provided an identikit so that you will recognise one if you see one. These are its characteristics:

- **Height** – six to eight feet.
- **General appearance** – grotesque, repulsive.
- **Skin** – lizard-like scales, smooth in texture.
- **Colour** – greenish to brownish.
- **Head** – central ridge running down to the snout.
- **Face** – cross between a snake and human.
- **Eyes** – cat-like with golden iris and a vertical slit for a pupil.
- **Hands** – four-fingered claw with brown webbing.
- **Chest** – external ribbing often visible.
- **Manner** – intrusive, forceful, insensitive.
- **Behaviour** – intrudes, assaults and rapes.

- **Method of communication** – none.
- **Physical evidence** – large claw marks photographed.

Some researchers have suggested that the reptoids are not new-comers to our planet. While UFOlogists speculate that Greys are a future stage in human evolution who travel back through time to visit us, some have suggested that reptoids may be a remnant of humankind's distant past. Another theory concerns human evolution. Whereas DNA shows that humankind is closely related to the higher apes, the theory of evolution cannot explain the great intellectual and cultural gap that separates *Homo sapiens* from other species. Some suggest this is because human development was spurred on by higher beings visiting our planet from outer space. During his study of reptilian aliens, UFOlogist Dr Joe Lewels turned to the Bible and other, more obscure, religious texts. He found that there are myths and religions from around world that tell of an ancient race of scaly super-beings who descended from the sky to give humankind a helping hand. Take the biblical Creation, for example. An ancient Jewish document called the *Haggadah* says that, physically, Adam and Eve were originally very different from humans today and, when they ate the forbidden fruit from the Tree of Knowledge, it says: 'The first result was that Adam and Eve became naked. Before, their bodies had been over-laid with a horny skin and enveloped with the cloud of glory. No sooner had they violated the command given them than the cloud of glory and the horny skin dropped from them, and they stood there in their nakedness and ashamed.'

The *Haggadah* also says that the snake who tempted Eve was humanoid in form. 'He stood upright on two feet, and in height he was equal to the camel.' Only after Adam and Eve's disobedience was found out was the serpent condemned to crawl on its belly. Indeed, in fifteenth century Christian art, the serpent is depicted standing on two legs and proffering the apple with an extended arm.

So the first two humans were initially covered in a shining, scaly skin, and their punishment for eating the forbidden fruit was to lose their scales. If Adam was created in the image of his maker, then his maker must have been reptilian. Support for this radical theory is found in other early documents. The *Nag Hammadi* texts, a series of ancient scrolls found inside a clay jar in a small Egyptian town of that name in 1945, contains a passage which describes what Adam and Eve did next: 'When they saw their makers, they loathed them since they were beastly forms.'

In his book *Flying Serpents and Dragons: The Story of Mankind's Reptilian Past*, reptilian researcher R.A. Boulay concludes: 'The sad fact is that in the West we have created God in our image and not the other way around. In this way we have hidden the true identity of our creators.'

Numerous researchers have also noted that the Western image of a humanoid creator is in stark contrast to the Eastern beliefs that humanity is descended from reptilian ancestors. Chinese emperors claimed lineage from a race of dragons, and certain noble Indian families claim descent from Indian serpent deities or 'nagas'. Then there is the Dogon tribe of Mali, whose astounding astronomical knowledge came from a race of reptilian extraterrestrials known as the 'Nommo'.

In his book *The Dragons of Eden: Speculations on the Evolution of Human Intelligence* Carl Sagan recalled the pioneering brain studies of Dr Paul MacLean, head of the Laboratory of Brain Evolution and Behavior of the United States' National Institute of Mental Health. MacLean's work led him to propose that the three distinct regions of the forebrain in higher vertebrates – mammals, birds and reptiles – was each acquired during a different phase of evolution. According to MacLean, the most ancient of these regions is the one that surrounds the midbrain and is known as the reptilian R-complex. This, he says, evolved several hundred million years ago and is shared by reptiles, birds and mammals. Surrounding this are the limbic system and neocortex, which both evolved later and are more highly developed in mammals. Humans experience emotions with the limbic system and think with the neocortex. But in his book *The Dreams of Dragons* biologist Dr Lyall Watson suggests that when we dream, it is our long-suppressed reptilian complex that takes over. This archaic portion of human minds might contain memory remnants of the time when, more than 65 million years ago, our ancestors, the first mammals, were tiny, shrew-like creatures that ran around the feet of the dinosaurs. It is unlikely that memories of what it was like to be a tiny creature in a world inhabited by giant reptiles would be entirely lost, even after millions of years of evolution. As our cultural memories of such things were handed down the generations as oral traditions, they would inevitably become distorted. Both Sagan and Watson suggest that this is the key to the intriguing morphological similarities between real dinosaurs and unreal dragons – and why both of these reptilian groups hold such a grip on our imaginations.

A dragon.

Dinosaurs Live

Some researchers believe that the reptilian aliens are not extraterrestrial in origin. They are the descendants of an intelligent race of dinosaurs. One such is researcher and writer John Rhodes. In his book *Dragons of the Apocalypse* he gives a detailed morphology of the reptoids. His researches have led him to conclude that the reptilian race includes a royal elite called 'Draco' – who are also reportedly working at Dulce, according to Thomas Castello. Although rarely seen, Draco are much taller that your average reptoid – up to eleven feet tall. They have cranial horns and leathery wings. He speculates that Draco may be responsible for the outbreak of sightings of 'Mothman' in West Virginia in the 1960s.

On 24 August 1995 Rhodes told the First International UFO

Congress in Mexico City that reptoids were responsible for the recent outbreak of UFO sightings there.

'They may be preparing the way for the prophesied return of the Feathered Serpent god of Mexico – Quetzalcotl,' he said.

Another believer in the survival of dinosaurs is David Barclay. But his theory is slightly different. He points out that, in the fossil records, humankind dates back only a few million years, but during that time we have evolved into an enormously intelligent species. The dinosaurs were around for 150 million years – how much higher might they have developed?

According to Barclay's book *Aliens the Answer?*, a species of humanoid dinosaurs provoked some global catastrophe at the end of the Cretaceous Period some 65 million years ago and wiped out most of its own kind, along with the more familiar species of dinosaur. But some survived. The original human beings were their pets and were bred like we breed dogs. While we evolved into *Homo sapiens* through this process, the humanoid dinosaurs evolved into Greys. This is why, Barclay says, the Greys take such an enormous interest in us.

Alien Motives

Alien abductions are widely seen as the most intriguing twist in the evolution of the UFO phenomenon. Since the first recorded case, involving the forcible abduction of Antonio Villas-Boas in 1959, an increasing number of people around the world have reported being abducted by alien entities and often subjected to humiliating medical examinations. At first their motives were puzzling, but gradually researchers are coming to understand the phenomenon.

One of the first attempts to identify the common features of the abduction experience was made by researcher Dr Thomas 'Eddie' Bullard, who began a comparative analysis of abduction cases from around the world. From his studies, he was able to identify a distinct pattern. Most abductees' experiences, he said, had eight distinct components: capture, examination, conference, tour, other worldly journey, theophany, return, and aftermath.

However, since Bullard finished his initial studies, a wealth of new abduction cases have come in and new components have been identified that may help open the way for a deeper understanding of the abduction phenomenon. One of these new components is the feeling that many abductees have that they are being controlled prior to the abduction itself. Many find themselves being attracted inexplicably to a particular place or destination by an urge they are powerless to resist.

Under regressional hypnosis, Jill Pinzarro recalled an abduction she had experienced at the age of nine in 1958. She was pushing her bicycle home from the library one afternoon, but instead of walking directly home, she found herself drawn inexplicably towards some trees. 'I didn't feel as if I could resist,' she said. Inside the trees, there was a spacecraft with a ladder. She climbed up it into an alien spacecraft where she was stripped and examined.

When she got back to the park bench, it was already dark.

Iguanadon.

She was scared, put her books in the basket on her bike and set off home. It was late and her parents were frantic. They had already called the police who were out looking for her. But when she arrived back, her parents were so relieved that they were not even angry with her.

When she was abducted again, at the age of eleven, the aliens were particularly interested in a scab on her knee she had got after falling of her bike. A tall alien stared into her eyes. She found this reassuring. The alien, she thought, really cared about her and would not let her come to any harm. But for Jill this was not accompanied by any sexual feelings. She thought the alien was a female. However, when the alien touched her on the forehead, she felt calm and had the sensation that she was willing to surrender sexually to the creature.

When she was abducted in 1980 at the age of thirty-two, she was given a baby to hold. It was about two-and-a-half-months-old, she reckoned. It had little hair and its skin was light. The alien nurse-maid said that the child needed nurturing, but they were not very good at it and they needed her to do it. The baby was quiet and seemed to enjoy Jill holding it. When she had to give it back, Jill felt an acute sense of loss. She had bonded with it. She thought this was strange because she did not consider herself a very maternal person. She had only ever wanted one child, which she had – back on Earth.

Many abductions reportedly involve the abductee being taken against their will from their house by aliens who first move them into an open area from which they are lifted at high speed by some extraterrestrial elevator into a UFO hovering overhead. Again the victim has no control over the matter.

In 1982 Barbara Archer was abducted by aliens from inside her own home. She was sixteen. One night, she had just been getting ready for bed when she noticed a light coming in through the window. She drew the curtains, but still the light seemed to illuminate the whole room. She peeked out but could see no source for the light. She checked the other window too, then got the strangest sensation that there was someone in the room with her.

By the closet she saw a small creature, which she took to be male. Although she was puzzled by the light, she was not shocked to see him there. He touched her on the wrist, which reassured her. Then she began to float straight up out of the window.

'When we went out the window, we went straight in between my house and my next door neighbour's,' she recalled. She said it was like being in a lift with no walls. She could clearly see the driveway, her house, then the rest of street, below her. She was scared of heights. It made her feel nauseous and she hoped she would not be sick.

'Up there, I could see everything. I could see all the rows of houses on my street,' she said.

She floated up underneath some sort of flying saucer. It was dark grey, metallic. Then she noticed the light was coming out of it. But the elevation continued. 'We just went right in through the bottom,' she said.

The alien she saw in her bedroom was still with her. More were waiting inside.

She also recalled being abducted when she was twelve. That time she found herself in a room with forty or fifty tables. After the regular physical examination, a tall alien came over to her and looked deep into her mind. This made her feel happy and she lay back. She did not feel sick anymore, just a little cold. Although she was scared of the smaller aliens, she liked the taller one and thought that he liked her. Again there was a very sexual element to this. Although she was only twelve, Barbara suddenly felt very womanly, very grown up. She got the feeling that the alien could read her mind and really understood her.

She was abducted again at the age of sixteen in 1982 when she was suffering from anorexia. This annoyed the aliens because she had stopped menstruating.

When she was twenty-one, Barbara went on holiday to Ireland where she was abducted again. This time the aliens got cross with her because she did not take her clothes off quickly enough. Later she was taken to a nursery on board the spacecraft, where there were about twenty babies in cribs. Some were in nappies. Others were slightly older and dressed in simple smocks. They looked kind of scary. They did not have much hair and their skin was an unnatural grey colour.

The aliens told her she could hold one and picked out a baby girl for her. The child had big eyes. They were shaped like an alien's but they were not as ugly. Barbara remembered feeling very protective and maternal. The alien nurse then told her to feed it and Barbara put the baby to her breast. Afterwards they took the baby away from her. When Barbara was told she had to leave, she felt bad leaving the baby behind. She asked the aliens whether she could see it again. They did not give her an answer.

However, it was in what the abductees observe on board the abductors' craft that researchers find the most consistency. For example, the aliens on board the UFO usually answer to the same description. Often, there is very noticeably a leader, sometimes described as a 'chief doctor' or 'captain', who seems to direct the abduction and who is generally described as a 'he'. The leader is usually described as more cold and clinical or more authoritarian than the other aliens on board. In almost all cases, he is taller than the other creatures. This started way back in 1961 when Betty Hill struck up some rapport with the taller leader.

Almost all abductees describe their captors as having large, compelling eyes. Their impenetrable blackness makes them somehow hypnotic. Some abductees feel that the aliens' eyes are a means of telepathic communication; others fear that the aliens use their eyes to exert control over abductees. However, looking into the eyes of an alien is often said to bring a soothing calmness or diminish any pain the abductee might feel.

Abduction expert David Jacobs believes that when abductees feel they have been profoundly affected by alien eyes in this way, they have, in fact, been subjected to a 'mind scan'. The aliens stare deeply into the abductee's eyes and monitor all their thoughts.

One abductee, Karen Morgan, allegedly felt the effects of 'mind scan' during her abduction in 1981. She remembered entering a UFO and being taken to a waiting area with a number of benches in arched alcoves. She sat in one and there were other men and women waiting in the others. Some wore nightclothes. One young man was slumped, as if he was not at all well. Other women looked very frightened.

They were strapped in. Karen told herself not to panic. She got the curious feeling that she had been through this before. Then the aliens came. There were two per person. The first woman was stripped. The humans were then herded into the examination room. The sick man had to be helped. Karen tried to resist but the aliens push her along anyway.

Karen was last into the examination room. There were four operating tables in the room. A shelf ran around the room with instruments on it. Karen was stripped and strapped to the table. Karen had braces on her teeth at the time and the aliens were fascinated by them. They asked her to take then out, but she refused. Next morning when she awoke, she found them on her belly.

The aliens also cut off a sample of her gum for analysis. This made her fighting mad. She asked how much more of her they were going to take and how long it took to study someone. Their answer was, it could take years.

The tall 'leader' alien asked her to look into his eyes. She did and felt that she was being overwhelmed, as if she was falling into them. Her will power was sapped. She could not look away or fight the alien in any way. It was as if she no longer had a mind of her own.

'Once you look into those eyes, you're gone. You're just gone,' she said.

Later, Karen got angry at the gynaecological procedures the alien was performing on her. She cursed the creature in her mind. The alien read her thoughts and reassured her that she would come to no harm. They performed something resembling a smear test on her, but she believed they were inserting an embryo into her, implanting it in her womb.

She found this idea repulsive and told the alien that he was not going to get away with this. He told her that she had no choice. It was part of a very important programme. But still Karen protested. She said that, back on Earth, she would have an abortion. The alien said that she would not, because she would not remember the embryo being implanted in her. She kept protesting that she would, but felt the alien's hypnotic suggestion that she would forget the incident overwhelming her mind. There was nothing to worry about, the alien said reassuringly, they had done this many times before.

Karen then remembered that she had indeed been through this procedure many times before and felt sick. The embryos, she knew, were hybrids; part human, part alien. She felt like an animal that was being experimented on. Sometimes the procedure was quick. This time it took longer because she resisted. When the alien was finished, he pulled the instruments out and patted her on the stomach. Karen was disgusted and told the alien to take his hands off her. Reluctantly, he did, but shook his head as if bewildered by her uncooperative attitude. In the morning, Karen woke back in her own bed. She found a mysterious gooey substance between her legs, took a shower and washed it off.

There are of course similarities in the events that occur on board abductors' craft as well – especially in reports of sexual and reproductive experimentation. During abductions, orgasms have reportedly been induced in both men and women, and sperm and ova have also been removed. Many female abductees claim to have been made pregnant by their captors, and then forced to carry the human–alien hybrids until the foetus is removed later, during another abduction.

Twenty-one-year-old musician Tracy Knapp recounted an experience of this nature. Knapp was driving from Los Angeles to Las Vegas with two girlfriends in 1978; she was abducted after seeing a light appear above the road and move down on top of her car. As it whizzed by them, the car started spinning. All three of them starting screaming and crying.

The car was being lifted up into the sky. Then Tracy remembered hands coming in through the window. When they touched her, she went limp. Then they lifted her out of the car. From then on, she lost sight of the other women. She did not see them again until they were back on the ground. When she returned home, she found that she was pregnant.

A few months later she was abducted again; she recalls lying down with her legs up. Two creatures were pressing on her and someone cutting her internally with long handled scissors that had very small blades. They doused the wound with a fluid that burned her. The procedure continued for a long time. The aliens seemed to be cutting threads. Then they pulled out their instruments and removed a sac with a tiny foetus in it.

'They removed something out of me. They removed a little baby or something,' she said.

This was put in a small, silver cylinder about three inches wide. The cylinder in turn was put into a drawer in the wall, along with numerous other live foetuses.

While some cases involve physical after-effects, most abductions involve some psychological disturbance. The most common is the sensation of missing time. Many abductees notice a time discrepancy between how long they perceived the encounter to have taken, and how long it had lasted in reality. These periods last maybe just a few minutes, or hours, or even, as in the case of famous abductee Travis Walton, days.

In October 1979, Luli Oswald and a companion were driving from Rio de Janeiro to Saquarema in Brazil when they saw a number of UFOs, which seemed to interfere with their car. Later, when they stopped at a service station, they found that two hours had mysteriously elapsed. Luli suffered some bad after-effects. Regressional hypnosis later revealed that they had both been abducted.

Another element regularly experienced after abductions is so-called 'screen memory'. These were first highlighted by celebrity abductee Whitley Strieber in his book *Communion*. A screen memory involves a disguised version of reality. These are used by aliens to prevent abductees remembering what actually happened. These disguises take the form of false memories or substitute images.

Debbie Jordan, the subject of UFOlogist Budd Hopkin's book *Intruders*, had a catalogue of screen memories as a result of her many abductions. On one occasion, she remembered leaving her house to visit the local store, but she was somehow 'steered' into a UFO which she saw in the store. The sales assistant in the store was a screen memory for the alien, she thought.

Professor Alvin Lawson believes that the abduction experience is a screen memory itself. It is a falsified account of the victim's birth trauma. All the elements are there, he points out. There are foetus-like creatures, obstetrics, medical equipment, even tools such as forceps. Some leave down long corridors; while some are helped out by the aliens or forcibly ejected, which he compares of a forceps birth. He compares some of the more traumatic ejections to Caesarean birth. Professor Lawson also points out the phenomenon of 'doorway amnesia'. Few abductees remember how they got into the alien craft, he says, just as no child could have any memory of how it got into the womb. The problem for Professor Lawson's thesis is that some abductees have a very clear idea of how they were conducted into the UFO.

All the elements described above occur regularly in abductions and researchers have been able establish a consistent pattern to abductions. But what light does this shed on the abduction phenomenon itself?

For some time, it has been noted that the UFO phenomena often echo ancient legends and beliefs. Instead of being abducted by gods or goblins as people were in former time, we are now taken by UFOs and aliens as if this is somehow more in keeping with the technological world that surrounds us. Following this logic, the idea has been advanced that the abduction phenomenon taps into ancient fears and concerns of human beings, expressed in the terms of today's increasingly technology-driven society. A clear parallel here can be drawn between the idea of 'alien implants' and the modern-day fear expressed in films such as *Terminator* and *Westworld* that human beings can be turned into machines.

Researcher John Rimmer argues that the recognition of authoritative figures, the feeling of being controlled and the sexual experimentation that regularly feature in the accounts of abductees all spring directly from the culture in which we live. In his book *The Evidence For Alien Abductions*, he says: 'Abduction cases grow from our own culture and social background and reflect our fears and preoccupations, both on a personal level... [and] a social level...'

Rimmer believes that the abduction experience is psychological in origin. Far from being the result of extraterrestrial intervention, abduction, he says, is a symptom of personal crisis in the life of the individual concerned. However, for abductees it is all too real.

In 1977, Professor Alvin Lawson conducted a unique experiment. He got a number of people who had no reason to believe that they had ever been abducted to write a fictional account of an imaginary abduction. When these were compared to the accounts given by real abductees there was no discernible material difference between them. This led him to conclude that the accounts of the real abductees were also fiction. Others have pointed out that this conclusion is bogus. By 1977, the major elements of the abduction experience were already well publicised and Lawson himself had given the subjects some direction. Even Lawson himself conceded that there was one huge difference between the fictional accounts and the reports of real abductees – the amount of emotion expressed. The abductees truly believed that they had undergone the abduction experience.

Bud Hopkins, who has interviewed hundreds of abductees over more than twenty years of research, performed a similar experiment. He asked subjects to imagine an abduction that involved a medical check-up. Their descriptions were nothing like abductees' reports.

'What we got was ninety per cent their last medical check-up and ten per cent *Star Trek*,' he said.

Hopkins also points out that the medical examinations reported in alien abductions are not a projection of people's health fears. Alien examinations concentrate on the reproductive system and sperm and ova extraction. Surveys show that most people are more concerned with the working of their heart and stomach.

The UFOlogists

Stanton Friedman

Nuclear physicist Stanton Friedman is one of America's leading UFOlogists and has been researching the subject for over forty years, ever since a one-dollar book he bought in 1959 sparked his interest. He co-wrote *Crash at Corona* – the definitive study of the Roswell incident –with Don Berliner. In *TOP SECRET/MAJIC*, he investigated the Majestic-12 documents and US government efforts to conceal evidence of alien spacecraft from the American people. He has lectured around the world. He says that he silenced all but a handful of sceptics who refuse to believe that the Earth is being visited by intelligently controlled extraterrestrial spacecraft.

Curiously, Friedman has never seen a flying saucer himself. Instead he is a critical judge of other people's reports. Nevertheless, he says that seeing UFOs is much more common than most people imagine. At his lectures, he asks people whether they have seen a flying saucer. The hands go up reluctantly, he says, 'but they know I'm not going to laugh'. Typically, ten per cent of the audience admit to seeing a UFO. Then he asks how many of them reported it.

'I'm lucky if it's ten per cent of the ten per cent,' says Friedman. 'Sightings of flying saucers are common, reports are not.'

Friedman became interested in the world of UFOs by accident when he was twenty-four. He was ordering books by mail and needed to buy one more to avoid paying shipping charges. The one he chose was *The Report On Unidentified Flying Objects* by Air Force Captain Edward Ruppelt, former director of Project Blue Book. Friedman read the book and was intrigued. He figured that Ruppelt had to know what he was talking about. So he read fifteen more books on UFOs and spent a couple of years digging up as much information as he could.

His conclusion was that there was overwhelming evidence that Earth is being visited by intelligently controlled extraterrestrial spacecraft. However, he believed that, while some flying saucers are alien space ships, most are not. He believes that since July 1947, when two crashed saucers were recovered in New Mexico along with alien bodies, the government has back-engineered spacecraft of its own. Only a few insiders know that this has been done and he calls the cover-up the 'Cosmic Watergate'.

He began investigating the Roswell incident in 1978 after being put in touch with one of the witnesses. He has now interviewed over two hundred witnesses – of those some thirty were involved with the discovery and recovery of the alien craft and the subsequent cover-up of the two crashes. On top of that he has news cuttings from Chicago to the West Coast newspapers on 8 July 1947 and FBI memos that back the story. He also believes that these show that there was a second UFO crash in New Mexico in 1947, 150 miles to the west of Corona, the first crash site, in the plains around San Augustin. He has found eyewitnesses who saw 'a large metallic object' stuck in the ground there.

He is not convinced by Ray Santilli's alien autopsy film though, seeing nothing in it that was associated with a crashed saucer at Roswell or anywhere else. He is also concerned that Santilli has refused to have the film verified. Nor has he released details of the cameraman so that they can be checked out. Friedman likes to look at the evidence.

Friedman is not flattered by being called a UFOlogist. He says that it is supposed to mean a person who has studied the science of UFOlogy, but there are no standards.

'Anybody who reads two books and carries a briefcase thinks he qualifies,' he says.

A big part of the problem of proving that flying saucers really exist is that people make wild claims that cannot be substantiated by the evidence. But he is more annoyed at the failure of the media to do their job. They have failed to dig into what Friedman considers to be the biggest story of the millennium. He believes that the media pay too much attention to what he calls the 'noisy negativists', none of whose arguments stand up under careful scrutiny, he says. 'They sound good, until you look at the evidence and they collapse of their own weight.'

He points out that there have been five large-scale scientific studies on UFOs, ten doctoral theses have been published and hundreds of papers have been produced by scientists. But most people, especially the debunkers, seem to be totally ignorant of this enormous amount of information. In his lectures he goes through the five scientific studies and asks how many people have read them. Less than two per cent of these people, who are plainly interested in the topic, are familiar with even one of the studies.

Friedman is also invited to speak to government bodies and gets a good response. But he finds that the question-and-answer sessions with the government people are a one-way street. They ask him a lot of questions but they do not reveal anything. He has spoken at Los Alamos National Laboratory and pulled a huge crowd. He has also given testimony to Congressional hearings in 1968 and at the United Nations in 1978.

Friedman finds being trained as a scientist is very useful in his work as a UFOlogist. It has meant that his approach is objective, painstaking, honest and scientific. Much of what he worked on as a scientist was classified. He wrote classified documents and had a security clearance. This gave him the opportunity to find out how security works and was good training for searching government archives for classified material later. Now he now lives in Canada and works on less sensitive science research projects such as pollution control and food irradiation.

He believes that the Majestic-12 documents prove President Harry Truman set up a super-secret group of top people from the fields of science, the military and intelligence to learn about alien spacecraft. He has spent over twelve years trawling through fifteen government archives, checking out whether these documents are real. Repeatedly, he has found confirmation of details in the documents that no one but insiders could have known. Friedman has even collected $1,000 from one critic who claimed one of the typefaces used in one of the MJ-12 documents was wrong.

'It was an absurd challenge, since I'd spent weeks searching through the government archives and he hadn't,' says Friedman, 'It also typifies the intellectual bankruptcy of the pseudo-science of anti-UFOlogy. I've yet to see a good anti MJ-12 argument.'

Friedman has had no chance to check out the data on alien abductions, but believes that every abduction story should be taken on its own merits. He has faith in abduction researchers because of his dealings with them and thinks that some people have been abducted.

According to Friedman's theory the government used five major arguments for withholding evidence from the public. The first is that it wants to figure out how flying saucers work because they make wonderful weapons delivery and defence systems. Secondly, it needs to do this before any potential enemy does. Thirdly, if this information was released, the younger generation would see humankind merely as 'earthlings' – which is what we are from an alien point of view. Friedman thinks this would be a great benefit. The problem with that is that there is no government on earth that wants its citizens to owe their primary allegiance to the planet rather than their country. Fourthly, there are certain religious fundamentalists who maintain humankind is the only intelligent life in the universe – that means that UFOs must be the work of the devil. These fundamentalists have huge political influence and their religions would be destroyed if they were proved wrong.

Finally, any announcement that the aliens were here would cause widespread panic. Some people would believe that were aliens are here to slaughter us. Others would reason that the aliens were obviously more technologically advanced than us and would bring with them new energy sources, new transportation systems, new computers and new communication systems. As a result the stock market would crash and there would be untold economic consequences.

However, Friedman still believes that the public is ready to hear the truth about UFOs. There would, of course, be some people who did not want to know – just as there are five per cent of the American public who do not believe that man has been to the moon. But the evidence about UFOs could be presented honestly and openly.

'I certainly don't think we should put technical data about flying saucers out on the table,' he says. 'But our planet is being visited by intelligent aliens. It's time we grew up.'

Jaques Vallee

Steven Spielberg's movie *Close Encounters of the Third Kind* made Jacques Vallee the most famous UFOlogist in the world. The François Truffaut character is based on the French researcher. Although he became a computer scientist for the Department of Defense, Vallee began his career as an astrophysicist. As a young man, it was curiosity that led him to study astronomy, but that same curiosity led him on into the world of UFOs. He does not find studying anomalous phenomena unscientific, pointing out that Nobel prize winner Niels Bohr said that all science starts with an anomaly.

He was working at the Paris Observatory when he first got interest in UFOs. They had observed a number of 'unidentified satellites'. However, when the scientists there were ordered to destroy the data concerning these 'anomalies' instead of sending it to their colleagues for further study, he rebelled.

This was during the early 1960s when the idea that UFOs were connected to alien intervention was widespread. Back then, he found that the 'extraterrestrial hypothesis' seemed to match witnesses' accounts. But since then, thousands more cases have been reported and statistical models could be used to analyse them. This has forced Vallee to take another, more critical look at the extraterrestrial hypothesis.

Vallee already had a passion for religious history, myths, occultism and parapsychology and, around 1968, he realised that many aspects of the UFO phenomenon were also present in the folklore of every culture. By 1975, he got the idea of combining these disciplines by considering the UFO phenomenon, not as simply a manifestation of extraterrestrial visitors, but as a control system that had been in existence since the beginning of humankind. He points out that UFO sightings did not start with Kenneth Arnold in 1947. Elements of the phenomena existed before. He believes that the wheels of Ezekiel, cherubim and burning bushes seen in biblical times, the flying goblins in luminous chariots of the Middle Ages, the phantom airships of the nineteenth century, the 'ghost rockets' of 1946 and the extraterrestrial spacecraft seen today are all essentially the same phenomenon.

As we learn more about the history and geographical distribution of the phenomenon, the standard extraterrestrial hypothesis leads to glaring contradictions, Vallee says. He believes that objects and beings connected to the UFO phenomenon are symbolic, or even theatrical, manifestations, rather than a systematic alien exploration where abductions are conducted for the purposes of so-called 'biological studies', as other UFOlogists suggest.

'We are also looking at some form of non-human consciousness,' he says. 'However, one must be wary of concluding that we are dealing with an "extraterrestrial race".'

Vallee aims to shatter the assumption that 'UFO' means 'extraterrestrial spacecraft'. He believes that behind these enigmatic luminous phenomena is a form of intelligence capable of manipulating space-time and influencing human evolution. In his best-selling book *Confrontations*, published in 1990, he analysed over a hundred UFO encounters using scientific methods, and concludes that the aliens visiting us come from another dimension.

Vallee is the champion of a bold new speculative physics. He believes that objects capable of gradually appearing and disappearing on the spot are modifying space-time topology. This validates the multidimensional models of the universe that theoretical physicists have been working on in recent years.

But he does not totally reject the extraterrestrial hypothesis, just the hard-nosed American approach to it. He believes that we share our existence with other forms of consciousness that influence the topology of our environment and affect the human mind psychically. Vallee has been accused of contradicting himself, because at times he emphasises the physical and material aspects of UFOs, while at others stressing the psychic and paranormal side. But this contradiction is in the data, he says.

Vallee is a believer in alien abduction, but believes that hypnotising abductees as practised in America is unethical, unscientific and perhaps even dangerous. He has investigated over seventy abduction cases. From his interviews with witnesses he has no doubt that the large majority of abductees have had a close encounter with an object emitting electromagnetic radiation, pulsed at hyper-frequencies. The effects on the human brain of these are unknown, so hypnotising the victims could put them at risk. He points out that UFO encounters are dangerous enough to humans as it is, with large amounts of energy confined to a restricted space.

One of the abduction cases Vallee studied was that of Franck Fontaine, who was abducted on 26 November 1979 from the Parisian suburb of Cergy-Pontoise after seeing a bright light in the sky. Vallee was particularly interested in the case because he was born in Pontoise and went to the same school as Fontaine. Although Fontaine admitted, two years later, that the abduction was a hoax, Vallee does not believe the explanations that have been given. They do not correspond to his knowledge of the area or the psychological state of the witnesses.

'I don't believe it was a UFO, but I do think that Franck was actually abducted,' he says. 'Someone is hiding something.'

The dozen or so 'implants' he has examined have not been mysterious in nature. Analysis showed that many of them were the tips of rusty needles, fragments of insects or other natural material embedded in the flesh. However, Vallee was the first to draw attention to the subject of animal mutilations over twenty years ago in his book *La Grande Manipulation* ('The Great Manipulation'), but he has not published research because he was unable to prove the link between the mutilations and the UFO phenomenon. He does believe that the link exists, though.

Vallee finds the USAF's latest explanation of the Roswell incident – that it was the crash of a balloon carrying a basket full of mannequins – laughable.

'The most recent report from the Air Force is even more absurd than all the other "explanations" given previously,' he says. 'The fact that an extremely strange object came down near Roswell and that the military made every effort to discourage research into the incident and continues to do so is beyond doubt. However, this doesn't mean that the object in question was a UFO.'

For Vallee, the jury is still out on the Roswell incident. He believes that the idea of a crash is only plausible if you believe it to be a deliberate demonstration on the part of an external intelligence. In the meantime he is investigating nineteen other different crash cases.

Vallee believes that every country's armed forces uses the UFO phenomenon to cover up operations involving advanced or illegal weapons. This started in the USSR as early as 1967, when the KGB spread rumours about UFOs in a region where the inhabitants had seen rockets being launched that were carrying satellites in violation of international agreements. UFO rumours also cloak remotely controlled rigid airships that the military use to gather electromagnetic data. An American soldier he knows approached one of these craft standing in a clearing in Germany during manoeuvres before the Gulf War and he has read US patent applications describing them.

Generally Vallee's scientific colleagues are open-minded about UFOs. They have no time for grandiose conspiracy theories, but they do admit the existence of a 'non-standard phenomenon'. During his forty years of UFO investigations, he has discovered that the UFO phenomenon is considerably more complex than he used to think. It cannot be explained simply by an extrapolation of current human technology.

'We are faced with a phenomenon that underlies the whole of human history, manipulates the real world and seems to obey laws that bear no relationship to those we hitherto imagined,' he says. 'I believe we're entering a particularly exciting period in the phenomenon's history, since we now have the opportunity of re-examining all the various hypotheses.'

More recently, Vallee has published a memoir of his years in UFOlogy called *Science Interdite* ('Forbidden Science'). This also examines the validity of the US Army's secret 'Memorandum Pentacle'.

Bob Lazar

Soft-spoken physicist Bob Lazar is one of the most controversial figures in UFOlogy. A man with a strong scientific background, he has been involved in the 'back-engineering' of alien spacecraft at the notorious Area 51 in the Nevada desert.

In 1982 he was a member of a scientific team at the US military's Groom Dry Lake installation. There he worked on a top-secret project to unravel the technology used by alien spacecraft that had been recovered from various crashes. Nine disc-shaped craft were held under armed guard in an underground section of the base known as 'S4'. The job of Lazar's team was to find out what made these flying saucers tick and whether their components could be replicated with materials found on Earth.

Many people have poured scorn on Lazar's story since it was first aired in a TV interview in 1989. As a child he was eccentric. His resumé includes bankruptcy and an association with a Las Vegas brothel. Lazar is easily discredited. Officials at Area 51 deny that anyone named Robert Lazar ever worked there – just as they once denied that Area 51 itself existed. But a salary statement issued by the United States Department of Naval Intelligence proves that Lazar did work in Area 51 for the five months as he claimed.

And when it comes to engineering, it is plain that Lazar knows what he is talking about. He has an impressive list of technical qualifications and is a scientist with a pedigree. In the early 1980s he was employed on several projects at the Los Alamos National Laboratory, New Mexico, where the first atomic bomb was developed. At Los Alamos, he conducted experiments with proton-scattering equipment and worked with high-energy particle accelerators. The work he did there was on the cutting edge of the new physics and could open the way to faster-than-light travel. As a prominent member of the town's scientific community, he earned himself an appearance on the front page of the *Los Alamos Monitor* when he installed a jet engine in a Honda CRX.

Despite the efforts made to paint him as slightly cracked, Lazar's account of what went on in Area 51 is lucid and concise, clearly not the ramblings of a disturbed mind. With his scientific background, his observations have a solid foundation. His specific task at Area 51 was to investigate the propulsion system of a small flying saucer dubbed 'the sports model', which was kept in one of the S4 hangars built into the side of a mountain. He witnessed a brief, low altitude test flight of the disc.

The sports model was some forty feet in diameter and fifteen feet high. It had three levels. The top level was an observation deck nine feet across, with portholes. Below that were the control consoles and seats, which were too small and too near the floor for adult humans to use comfortably. The main cabin had a headroom of just six feet. Also in the central level was an antimatter reactor and, located directly below it on the lower level, were the three 'gravity amplifiers', connected to the reactor by wave guides. He worked on this propulsion system both in situ in the craft and on the bench in the lab.

The power source for the sports model and the eight other discs in S4 was an 'antimatter reactor', Lazar says. These reactors were fuelled by an orange-coloured, super-heavy material called 'Element 115'. This mysterious element was the source of the 'Gravity A' wave as yet undiscovered by terrestrial science. It also provided the antimatter radiation required to power the saucer in interstellar flight.

The flying saucers in S4 have two modes of travel. For local travel, near the surface of a planet, they use their gravity generators to balance the planet's gravitational field and ride a Gravity A wave like a cork on the ocean. During interstellar travel, covering distances that would take aeons even travelling at close to the speed of light, the Gravity A wave from the nucleus of Element 115 is amplified. This bends space and time in the same way it is bent in the intense gravitational field generated by a black hole. As the saucer travels through space, time is 'bent' around the craft. By distorting space and time in this manner, the disc can travel across vast expanses of space at incredible speeds. This is the same principle used by the *Enterprise*'s 'warp drive' in *Star Trek*.

Terrestrial rockets push the craft towards their destination by blasting jets of hot gas in the opposite direct, while alien craft 'pull' the destination towards them. Lazar explains how this works with the analogy of a rubber sheet with a stone, representing the spacecraft, on it. To go to any particular destination, you pinch the rubber sheet at that point and pull it towards the stone. Then, when you let got, the rubber sheet springs back, pulling the stone – or spacecraft-with it.

'In a spacecraft that can exert a tremendous gravitational field by itself,' he says, 'you could sit in any particular place, turn on the gravity generator, and actually warp space and time and "fold" it. By shutting that off, you'd click back and you'd be at a tremendous distance from where you started.'

Although this type of propulsion appears to be the stuff of science fiction, many scientists believe that faster-than-light travel may be possible. Cambridge University's Lucasian professor of mathematics Stephen Hawking has suggested that interstellar travel might be achievable via natural or manmade 'worm-holes' in the fabric of space-time. Understanding how this works in practice is a bit more taxing, of course.

Inside the flying saucers' antimatter reactor, Lazar says, Element 115 is transmuted into another esoteric material called 'Element 116'. This is highly unstable and decays, releasing antimatter. The antimatter then reacts with matter inside the reactor in a total annihilation reaction, where one hundred per cent of the matter–antimatter is converted into energy. This energy is used to amplify the Gravity A wave given off the Element 115 and the heat generated by reaction is converted to electricity via a solid state thermo-electric generator.

The alien craft were saucer-shaped to diffuse the electrical charges generated by the antimatter reactor. In flight, Lazar says, the bottom of the alien craft glowed blue and began to hiss like a high voltage charge does on a sphere.

'It's my impression that the reason that they're round and have no sharp edges is to contain the high voltage,' says Lazar. 'If you've seen a high voltage change system's insulators, things are round or else you get a corona discharge.'

The craft's high voltage makes them hiss when they take off. Otherwise they are silent. And the hissing stops when they have climbed to twenty or thirty feet. 'There are just too many things that Lazar knew about the discs that can't be explained in any other way,' said George Knapp, the TV journalist who first interviewed him.

Lazar says that, at one time, there were Soviet scientists and mathematicians working at Area 51, alongside the Americans there. He did not know whether they were actually allowed to work on the alien craft, but believes that they were employed on the scientific and mathematical theory that underpinned his group's practical work.

They were kicked out after a major breakthrough had been made in understanding how the discs and their propulsion systems worked. They were none too happy about this. Lazar says that in the aftermath of their exclusion, paranoia at the base soared. Employees were issued with firearms, in case the Soviets tried to kidnap them.

During his time at Area 51, Lazar had to read a document the size of a telephone directory, which revealed that the top-secret base at Groom Lake was not the only US government facility back-engineering ET technology. The US government's admission that other secret bases do exist lent weight to Lazar's story. However, what goes on in them is still beyond top secret. Since Lazar's Area 51 security clearance was mysteriously revoked at the end of the 1980s, he has been subjected of intense harassment. His house and car have been broken into and he has been shot at by unseen snipers in an attempt to discourage him from divulging the secrets of S4.

Edgar Fouche

Like Bob Lazar, Edgar Fouche worked at Area 51 and has since spent his time telling the world about what is going on there. Fouche is a true insider who spent twenty-eight years with the US Air Force and Department of Defense. During that time, he was stationed at top-secret sites, including the nuclear test site in Nevada, the Nellis Test Range and the Groom Lake Air Base, home of Area 51. Fouche's work in intelligence, electronics, communications and a number of black programmes has given him inside information on some of America's most classified technological developments, including the super-secret SR-71 and SR-75 spy planes and the TR-3B, which many people believe is sometimes mistake for the 'Flying Triangle'.

However, during the 1980s when President Reagan was in power, he became completely disenchanted with the defence industry. It was full of fraud and abuse of power and he decided that he could not be associated with it anymore. He was suffering serious medical problems at the time and did not think he was going to live much longer. So he decided to speak up.

In this, he was helped by five friends who served with him in Vietnam. One was a former SR-71 spy plane pilot. Two of them went on to work for the National Security Agency. A fourth friend's father had worked for the NSA for twenty years and the fifth worked for the Department of Defense. He also gleaned information about the TR-3B by talking to pilots.

His buddy who was the SR-71 pilot told him that once, when he was flying back across the South China Sea, he saw a shadow fall across the cockpit. The aircraft started to nose down and the avionics went crazy. When he looked up to find out what was happening, he saw a UFO that was so big it completely blocked out the sun. It was oval and surrounded by a shimmering energy field, and he reckoned that it was three hundred feet across.

What really amazed Fouche was that all the pilots he spoke to reported encounters with UFOs. Some had seen circular UFOs, others had encountered plasma balls that seemed to dance around the craft. These reports were all the more impressive because the SR-71 can fly at over 60,000 feet. This gives it enormous visibility. If something is up there, an SR-71 is going to see it.

Fouche's contacts told him that the development of the TR-3B started in 1982 as part of a top-secret project named 'Aurora', whose aim was to build and test advanced aerospace vehicles. He discovered that around 35 per cent of the US government's 'Star Wars' budget had been siphoned off to finance it. The TR-3B is a triangular nuclear-powered aerospace platform and is undoubtedly the most exotic aerospace programme in existence. The designation 'TR' stands for tactical reconnaissance. This means the craft is designed to get to the target and stay there long enough pick up information on the enemy's deployment and send it back. The advantage of being powered by a nuclear reactor is that it can stay aloft for a long time without refuelling.

Its advanced propulsion system also allows it to hover silently for long periods. The circular crew compartment is located at the centre of TR-3B's triangular airframe. It is surrounded by a plasma-filled accelerator ring, called the Magnetic Field Disrupter, which generates a magnetic vortex and neutralises the pull of gravity. The MFD does not actually power the craft; what it does is effectively reduce its mass. Propulsion is achieved by three multimode gas-propelled thrusters mounted on each corner of the triangle. But MFD makes the aircraft incredibly light. It can fly at Mach 9 speeds vertically and horizontally, and can outmanoeuvre anything except UFOs.

One of Fouche's sources who worked on the TR-3B told him that they were working on the possibility of developing the MFD technology so that it not only reduces mass but also creates a force that repels gravity. This would give the TR-3B a propulsion system that would allow it to routinely fly to the Moon or Mars. This anti-gravity system is how UFOs work and Fouche is convinced that the TR-3B has been developed through the back-engineering of alien technology.

Fouche believes that the black triangles tracked by the Belgian Air Force in the late 1980s and early 1990s were TR-3Bs. He has a simple rule: if it is triangular it is terrestrial, if it is circular or tubular it is extraterrestrial. He says that the US government could easily get round treaty agreements that prohibit testing advanced aircraft over Europe. These agreements, he points out, say that they cannot fly an aircraft over a friendly country without that country being informed. It would be easy enough to inform the Belgian government on the sly. After all, the US is not supposed to have nuclear weapons in the UK or Japan, but they do.

Groom Lake's six-mile-long runway is the longest in the world. Fouche says that it was built to accommodate the CIA's latest super-hi-tech spy plane, the 'Penetrator' or SR-75; 'SR' stands for strategic reconnaissance. It can exceed Mach 7 with speeds of over 28,000 miles an hour at an altitude of 40,000 feet and can reach any point on the Earth within three hours. This plane is so secret that the US government does not even admit to its existence. After the SR-71 Blackbird was retired in 1990, the US Air Force said that it would not be replaced because satellites provided all the military's high-level reconnaissance needs. But Fouche's sources say that the SR-75 has been designed to service spy satellites in orbit. It acts as a 'mothership' and launches unmanned SR-74, or Scramp, craft. Operated by remote control, these can place satellites in space, reaching altitudes of 95 miles and speeds of 6,250 miles an hour, or Mach 15.

Fouche was assigned to Groom Lake in 1979 because he was one of the few people who had the necessary top-secret clearance. He was certified to work with particular equipment which, even years after the event, he was not prepared to discuss. He had been working at Nellis Air Force Base at the time and was told that he was being temporarily reassigned, but was given no idea of where he was going to be sent. Some thirty technicians were herded onto a blue bus with blacked-out windows. There were two guards on board, armed with M16 rifles. They told the passengers not to speak unless spoken to. This is how Fouche ended up at Groom Lake.

The conditions were extremely oppressive. He was issued with heavy glasses, like welders' goggles. These had thick lenses that blocked peripheral vision and prevented the wearer seeing further than thirty metres ahead. Everywhere he went, he was escorted by a soldier carrying an M16 who would never talk to him. He could not even go to the lavatory alone.

According to Fouche, the military used sinister mind-control techniques on employees. One of his five collaborators named Sal was a victim of this. A former NSA electronic intelligence expert, he had helped develop Magnetic Field Disruption. After two-years at a top-secret NSA facility, he came down with what he thought was the flu. He went to see the facility's doctor, who gave him some medication and told him to go home and rest. The next day, Sal had no memory of where he worked or who he worked for. When his brother contacted the NSA, he was told that Sal's contract had been terminated. Sal's memory has not returned and the only evidence he has that he worked at the NSA facility at all is a few scribbled notes and his pay slips.

Security at Area 51 was so tight that a key card and a code were needed for every door. Fouche is very sceptical about people who claim to have been at Groom Lake and accidentally stumbled into a hangar with a UFO inside. His twenty-eight years with the Department of Defense and the US Air Force taught him that anything that was top-secret was protected by numerous levels of security.

However, in Area 51 there is a facility on the Papoose Lake site called the Defense Advanced Research Center, which extends for ten storeys underground. It was built in the early 1980s with Strategic Defense Initiative money. The DARC is the centre for what is officially designated 'Foreign Artefacts' – this means alien artefacts. Crashed and recovered alien technology is stored there. The DARC is where all the analysis of 'extraterrestrial biological entities' – alien creatures – and back-engineering takes place.

Fouche says that the reason the US government cannot come clean about what they are up to at Area 51 is because, since the birth of the UFO phenomenon in 1947, it has consistently violated people's constitutional rights. The government considers anything that it cannot control a threat, he says. It cannot control the alien agenda, so it tries to control any information surrounding it. People who find out too much about UFOs or aliens either disappear or have been killed, he says. The government would be held accountable if the facts got out and it could not handle that.

David Adair

Another witness to what is going on at Area 51 is space scientist David Adair. He became involved in the world of UFOs through his lifelong passion for science and rocketry.

Adair was a child prodigy. He built his first rocket at the age of eleven. This was no fourth-of-July firework. He fashioned it from sophisticated alloys, using tools and fuels from his father's machine shop.

Then, in 1968, he set out to build a new type of rocket which used powerful electromagnetic fields to contain and harness the thermonuclear energy from a fusion reaction. Although this sounds exotic, it was not his original idea. He got the plans from the long-range planning division of NASA's Marshall Space Flight Center in Huntsville, Alabama. They had come up with the theoretical designs for fifty different types of engine. Only two of them used conventional liquid fuel or solid propellants, so fusion was the obvious the way to go. The one that Adair decided to build was a remarkable design. At the time he wondered why NASA had never made it themselves. Later he realised that they probably chose not to develop it for political reasons. If you developed an efficient fusion-based propulsion system, oil and gas would be redundant. Nevertheless the fourteen-year-old Adair saw the design's potential and, through Republican Congressman John Ashbrook, he got a $1-million grant to build it.

But the grant came with strings attached. The Department of Defense were involved. He was prohibited from telling anyone about what he was building. And for Adair the outside world ceased to exist as he worked on the rocket day and night for the next three years. In 1971, when Adair was seventeen, the rocket was ready to be tested. General Curtis LeMay, the project manager, decided that the rocket was too powerful to be tested outside a secure military facility, so he scheduled a test at White Sands Missile Range in New Mexico.

When Adair was at White Sands preparing for the test, a black DC-9 arrived. It was carrying Dr Arthur Rudolph, one of the designers of the Saturn-5 moon rocket. Originally Rudolph had worked on the Nazi German V-2 programme, but after the war he had been taken to America. Adair told Rudolph that, proportionately, his rocket was a thousand times more powerful than the

Saturn-5, and Rudolph was furious. When Adair was programming his rocket's guidance system, his military bosses gave him a precise location for the landing. The co-ordinates they gave him specified a place four hundred miles away in an area called Groom Lake in Nevada. This puzzled Adair as all the maps showed there was an empty dry lakebed.

After the rocket was launched successfully, Adair was told to get on board the DC-9. They flew him to Groom Lake and, as they came in to land, he could see the huge runways and a huge base that had not appeared on the map. This, he was informed, was Area 51.

When he arrived at Groom Lake, Adair thought he was there to collect his rocket. But he was bundled onto an electric golf cart and driven over to three large hangars. As he got close to the buildings, he could see that they were new, but they had been painted to look much older. The middle hangar was the area of two football fields. Once he was inside, warning lights began flashing, guard rails sprang up and an area of the floor about seven hundred square feet started to descend. Adair realised they were on a huge lift. It went down through solid rock and, when it stopped, Adair found himself the biggest underground space he had ever seen. It contained a lot of aircraft. Most of them were covered up, but he recognised one as the XB-70, an experimental aircraft. It was huge. But he also noticed a number of craft that were a strange teardrop shape with their surfaces perfectly smooth in all directions. The most peculiar thing about them was that they did not have any of the intake or exhaust ports that are needed by jet engines. In fact, they had no visible means of propulsion, yet they were surrounded by support equipment and looked quite capable of flying. Looking back, he now thinks that they used some kind of electromagnetic or flux-field propulsion.

Still in the golf cart, he was driven over to a big set of doors. The driver jumped out and put his hand on a panel. It flashed and the doors opened. We know these things now as optical hand-print scanners, but in 1971 they were the stuff of science fiction. Inside the air was cold and the lighting was strange. There was plenty of light, but nothing seemed to cast a shadow. He was then shown a huge engine that was about the size of a bus. It looked like two octopuses linked together by their tentacles. When Adair examined it, he realised it was some kind of giant version of the motor in his rocket.

His companions explained that this engine used a fusion reaction similar the one he had designed and they wanted his opinion on the firing mechanism. The whole situation struck Adair as bizarre. Why didn't they ask the people who built it, he enquired. He was told they were on leave. So Adair asked to look at their design notes. This seemed to annoy the people who had brought him there.

'Look son, do you want to help your country or not?' they said.

Adair believes that the engine was extraterrestrial in origin. Although it was huge, he could not see a single bolt, rivet or screw holding it together. The surface was perfectly smooth and, although the room was cold, it felt warm to the touch. Whenever he touched the surface, bluish white waves swirled out from his hands and disappeared into the material. They would stop each time he moved his hand away. He climbed up on top of the engine and looked inside. He saw a large container holding bundles of tubes. These were filled with some kind of liquid. Adair's overall impression was that it was organic – part mechanical, part biological. He realised it had been made using non-terrestrial techniques and materials.

He shrugged his shoulders and told his companions that he had no idea how the thing worked. The manufacturing techniques used were very different from anything he had ever seen before. He reasoned that it could not have been built by American engineers or by the Soviets. As it dawned on him that it must have been built using extraterrestrial technology, he got angry. Flying saucers had landed and the government were keeping it a secret. When Adair expressed his outrage at this, his companions shouted at him to get away from the device.

Adair does not think that the engine was working too well, though they have had three decades to work on it since then and he hopes they have been successful. He could certainly see the potential. Adair's own rocket was puny by comparison but it channelled enormous amounts of energy out of the back of the rocket for propulsion. He believes that the alien engine could have managed to contain all the incredible energy generated by the fusion reaction inside the propulsion system, producing a 'field effect' outside the craft. This would create a huge 'gravitation well' which would break through the fabric of space-time. Space would be folded back on itself, allowing the craft to travel vast distances in an instant, without exceeding the speed of light.

However, he is still angry that this device and other exotic craft are in government hands and all their amazing technology is hidden from the rest of the world. Meanwhile people at NASA are struggling to send small spacecraft to Mars. The fact that the US government are withholding knowledge of their contact with other civilisations he also finds incredible.

'These are ET civilisations we could learn so much from,' Adair says. 'When I think of all the ways that we could advance with this knowledge of ET contact, it makes me sick that this information is hidden.'

Since his visit to Area 51 in 1971, Adair has worked as a technology transfer consultant, redesigning space-programme technology for commercial applications. He has an office in Ventura, California. But he has not forgotten what he saw.

On 9 April 1997, Adair testified to a Congressional hearing in Washington, D.C. as part of the campaign for full UFO disclosure. The hearings were organised by the Center for the Study of Extraterrestrial Intelligence and gave key witnesses, including military personnel and pilots, the opportunity to lobby the US government. David Adair was under oath when he told the Congressional panel what he had seen in Area 51 and, unexpectedly, the Congressmen immediately got confirmation that he was telling the truth.

During his testimony, Adair mentioned that the device he had seen was covering in strange markings. He remembered what they looked like and drew them for the panel. Also giving testimony was an attorney from North Carolina named Steven Lovekin, who had top-secret clearance when he worked as a cryptologist at the Pentagon in the 1950s. As military aide, he had given regular brief-ings to President Eisenhower on UFO activity. In that capacity, he had been shown a piece of metal that he was told came from a downed flying saucer. It was covered in strange markings – the same markings Adair had seen in Area 51.

Wendelle Stevens

Wendelle Stevens' involvement with UFOs began in 1947 when he was assigned to the Air Technical Intelligence Center at Wright Field in Dayton, Ohio, home to the USAF's various in-house UFO study programmes, Sign, Grudge and Blue Book. That year, Stevens was sent from Ohio to Alaska to supervise a squadron of B-29 bombers that were being used to map the Arctic. However, he discovered there was a hidden agenda behind their polar mission. The B-29s were equipped with cutting-edge electronic detection technology and cameras to detect and film 'foo fighters', as UFOs were then known.

Stevens's security clearance was not high enough to allow him to see the footage the B-29s had shot before it was sent to Washington, but the pilots told him of their UFO encounters. Many of his pilots saw UFOs soar rapidly into the sky and fly off as the B-29s approached. In most cases, they caused electromagnetic dis-turbances to the plane's instrumentation, often affecting the engines. On one occasion a UFO approached a B-29 head on. Then, before they collided, it slammed into reverse, manoeuvred itself around next to the wing and stayed there.

Astounded by these revelations, Stevens asked his superiors if he could pursue an investigation into the UFO phenomenon. He was told he could do so only outside of official military channels. So, in 1963, after twenty-three years' active service, he retired and began a new career as a UFO researcher.

He began collecting newspaper clippings of UFOs from all over the world. Where photographs had been printed, he would write to the people who had taken them and ask for a copy. Now he boasts the world's largest collection of UFO photographs – over three thousand images in all – along with a vast library of UFO film and videos.

To establish the authenticity of the photographs, he visits the people who took them and investigates their encounter. He also examines their camera equipment and takes his own photographs from the same spot, so that he can compare relative scale and distances. After these preliminary checks, he subjects the photograph to a series of analytical procedures. Today he uses computer techniques. It was easier in the old days, he says, when all a photographic expert had to do was to make a large-scale blow-up and examine it with a magnifying glass.

Stevens is one of the few UFOlogists who had has made a career of studying contactees. In 1976 he was the first researcher to investigate the claims of Swiss contactee Eduard 'Billy' Meier, who was in telepathic contact with aliens and photographed their spaceships coming into land. At Stevens' behest, Meier submitted his evidence for analysis to scientists at McDonnell Douglas, IBM and NASA's Jet Propulsion Laboratory. Their results were inconclusive. However, computer analysis of one of Meier's pictures reveals a model next to a fake tree and models of flying saucers were found in Meier's home. Nonetheless, Stevens believes Meier is genuine.

Stevens decided to specialise in contactees because they presented a unique opportunity to learn about extraterrestrials and their possible agendas. If possible, he sets up a two-way dialogue, asking contactees to pose questions to the extraterrestrials for him next time they meet. Sometimes he gets an answer.

One of the most important contactee cases he investigated was that of Bill Herrmann, who lived in Charleston, South Carolina, near the Air Force base there. He and his wife repeatedly saw a UFO, which flew in a darting motion with sharp, angular turns, unlike the smooth turns of a plane. One night in 1977, when he was try to get a closer look at it through binoculars, Herrmann was abducted. He was enveloped in a beam of blue light, which drew him up inside the UFO. The extraterrestrials he encountered inside the craft were friendly. They came from one of the twin stars in the Reticulum system. When he asked them questions, he would hear their replies in English inside his head. They told him that the darting movements of their craft were made to avoid any radar lock-on. Radar-guided weapons had previously been responsible for the crashes of three of their ships. They also told Herrmann that they wanted their downed ships back and were prepared to negotiate, but the US government was too hostile to deal with. After this first abduction experience, Herrmann was invited back onto the craft another five times.

When Stevens began investigating the Herrmann case, he discovered that the Reticulans were sending Herrmann vast amounts of information when he was in a trance-like state. He transcribed the transmission in automatic writing. The result was numerous pages of text in a totally unknown alphabet, along with schematic diagrams of their propulsion system. The complex technical information he was provided with was way beyond current human scientific knowledge and Herrmann could never have acquired it from any terrestrial source.

From his work with contactees, Stevens has discovered that there are many different kinds of extraterrestrials. They come from different places and have different languages, morphologies, technologies and agendas. The largest group are the various humanoid species who often tell contactees that they come from the Pleiades star system. The next largest group are the well-known 'Greys', which again comprise a number of different races.

Stevens has also carried out research on Area 51 and tracked down Derek Hennesy, a former security guard who worked on level two of S4, the famous underground complex where Lazar had worked on alien propulsion systems. During his time there, Hennesy saw nine bays for flying saucer bays on level one. There were a further seven bays on level two with three identical alien craft in the first three bays. Hennesy also saw large tubes that contained the preserved bodies of dead Greys. After Stevens first interviewed Hennesy, Hennesy disappeared for a while. When he re-emerged he claimed to have no knowledge of what he had previously seen or said.

However, Stevens had another friend who works as an engineer at Area 51 and says it is engaged in bridging the gap between alien technology and our own. He has built simulators to train human pilots to fly flying saucers. There are two extraterrestrials at Area 51 who can fly alien craft. They have been trying to train humans to do this, but not very successfully. So far they are limited to flights within the atmosphere. They have not yet mastered flight in deep space, but they can hover using some kind of gravity propulsion.

Stevens thinks that there is little chance that the curtain of official secrecy surrounding UFOs will be lifted in the near future. The government have kept what they know a secret for fifty years and he expects them to do so for another fifty. Governments have far too much to lose from any official disclosure, he reckons. The impact on society would be incalculable. The only way the world's governments would admit to the reality of alien visitations is if a group of extraterrestrials makes its presence visible on a massive scale, he says. Stevens believes that there are signs that this may be about to occur in Mexico, where there was an explosion in the number of sightings in the 1990s.

Peter Gersten

For twenty years, New York criminal defence attorney Peter Gersten specialised in murder and drug cases. But then, in 1977, as the lawyer for the UFO group Ground Saucer Watch, he took the CIA to court and won. It was a historic victory for UFOlogy.

The suit was filed under the Freedom of Information Act. Ground Saucer Watch were trying to force the CIA to release just five UFO-related documents the agency had in its possession. But Gersten expanded the case. Under the FOIA it was as easy to create a lawsuit to get the CIA to release all the UFO document it had as it was to get just five. As a result, in 1979, the CIA was forced to release nine hundred pages of UFO-related documents – the first time that any US intelligence agency had ever released previously classified UFO information to the public. A further fifty-seven documents were withheld. But the case showed beyond any doubt that the CIA, which had previously denied any involvement in UFOs, had been studying them for years.

The documents not only confirmed the reality of UFOs and gave detailed descriptions of them, they also gave researchers access to numerous reports from credible witnesses – scientists, military personnel and law enforcement officers. Some of the documents released originated from other agencies. This confirmed that every other US agency had also been studying the UFO phenomenon and that the military had been involved in UFO research even before 1947.

Bolstered by this success, Gersten formed Citizens Against UFO Secrecy (CAUS), an organisation dedicated to breaking down the wall of secrecy surrounding the UFO phenomenon. Its aim is to force the government to come clean on what it knows about contact with extraterrestrial intelligence, and it believes that the public has the absolute and unconditional right to know.

In the early 1980s, Gersten continued his legal assault on the US intelligence community, taking the National Security Agency to court after the NSA refused an FOIA request for UFO-related documents that CAUS knew they had in their possession. In court, the judge asked the NSA's attorney how many documents had surfaced when they had processed the CAUS's FOIA request. He was told that it was classified information. Gersten told the judge that the CIA had told him that the NSA had at least eighteen documents. The judge then insisted that the NSA come up with a figure. The agency finally admitted that there were 135. But that was as far as it went. The NSA invoked the National Security Exemption, one of twelve exemption clauses built into the FOIA. To argue their exemption, the NSA used a twenty-one-page affidavit that was itself classified, and the case was dismissed.

Although Gersten was unsuccessful in obtaining the UFO documents, he did succeed in getting the NSA to admit that they held them. He took the appeal to the Supreme Court and, when it was dismissed, it made headline news. Even though he did not get the documents, he had succeeded in drawing great attention to the issue of UFO secrecy and highlighted the US Supreme Court's role in this cover-up. In further court actions, Gersten succeed in forcing the release of a heavily censored version of the NSA exemption affidavit and, in due course, most of the documents they withheld have been released.

Gersten is not optimistic about the efforts of various organisations – such as Dr Steven Greer's Center for the Study of Extraterrestrial Intelligence – to get the US Congress to hold open hearings on the subject of UFOs. He says that the idea of open hearings is inherently ridiculous because any discussion of UFOs involves a discussion of advanced technology. This is an area that the military keeps secret by invoking national security, while the corporations protect their developments by using patents. The elected officials of Congress are always up for re-election – every two years for Representatives and six years for Senators. They need money and are always vulnerable to the demands of special interests.

Getting Congress to grant immunity to people who may have to break secrecy oaths to testify would not help. Gersten points out the problems: 'Let's say you have a general who wants to testify in a Congressional hearing even though he is sworn to secrecy. He will naturally expect Congress to grant him immunity. However, the military will then question Congress's right to grant immunity and they would then have to fight it out in the courts, which could take years.'

Gersten finds it more effective to work through CAUS, which makes it possible for him to protect the privacy of any informant, through client–attorney privilege, but at the same time get the information out.

He used the Freedom of Information Act to try and pressurise the US Army into releasing documents relating to statements made by Colonel Philip J. Corso in his book, *The Day After Roswell*. Corso was willing to testify that he had seen the bodies of dead aliens in 1947 and that he had read alien autopsy reports in 1961. Gersten was ready to take the issue to court, so he filed an FOIA request with the US Army for the release of any documents they may have had supporting Corso's claims. The Army claimed it could find no documents and Gersten took them to court. But

Corso died and, on 26 April 1999, the case was dismissed. Gersten decided not to take that matter any further. Instead he filed a suit against the Department of Defense over Flying Triangles, in an attempt to find out what these mysterious craft actually are. While Gersten concedes that some of the sighting reports clearly describe advanced US experimental aircraft such as the TR-3B, which researcher Ed Fouche claims was built at Area 51, many of the reports could not possibly be the TR-3B. People have seen triangular craft that are half-a-mile wide. Some are seen at treetop level and over populated areas, shining beams of light on the ground. Witnesses also report seeing orb-shaped lights detach from these craft, fly around and re-attach. None of this can be explained in terms of advanced military technology.

Gersten sued the US government for damages after Betty Cash, Vickie Landrum and her grandson were abducted in Texas on the night of 29 December 1980. Gersten argued that as the UFO concerned was escorted by twenty Chinook helicopters it must have been part of a military operation. The case was dismissed on the grounds that the government denied all knowledge of the UFO and Gersten could not prove that it belonged to them.

Gersten is also bringing an unprecedented FOIA lawsuit against the CIA, the FBI and Department of Defense on the grounds that alien abduction can be viewed legally as a form of invasion. Article 4, section 4 of the US Constitution requires that the Federal Government protect the individual states against invasion, a provision that was enacted to persuade the original colonies to abandon their independent militias and join the Union. However, the Federal government are plainly failing in their duty to protect citizens of the States if those citizens are being abducted.

CAUS and Gersten have even more ambitious plans. As it is unlikely that the President is likely to open up all the files on UFOs in the foreseeable future, they want to find out for themselves. They are planning a privately funded mission to the Moon, to send back pictures from the Sinu Medi regions where some UFOlogists have locateed alien structures. Using existing technology, they estimate that their 'Project Destination Moon' would cost $12 million – small change to the likes of Bill Gates and Ted Turner.

'Think of all the money sponsors would make from the publicity if they funded the first civilian mission to the Moon, especially if alien artefacts were discovered,' says the ever-optimistic Gersten. 'The space programme is in the hands of the government and the military. We are all like virtual prisoners on this planet. This is a project that is just waiting to happen.'

Derrel Sims

Alien implant expert Derrel Sims is a former CIA operative and got involved in UFO research after being abducted himself. He has conscious recollections of multiple abductions between the ages of three and seventeen. He started researching in this field at the age of sixteen and has been at it for more than twenty-seven years. After leaving the world of covert intelligence, he rose to become chief of investigation for the Houston-based Fund for Interactive Research and Space Technology. There he concentrated on collecting physical evidence, as he believes that this is the best way to prove that UFOs and alien abductions actually exist.

He has investigated hundreds of cases of alien implants, some of which have been inside the body for up to forty-one years. Despite being foreign bodies, they trigger no inflammatory response. He says that the devices found are 'meteoric' in origin. Although some labs have said that this is impossible, 'double blind' tests had proved this to be the case.

Dr Roger Leir

For years, people doubted the reality of alien abductions. This was largely because abductees had no physical evidence to back their stories. One man changed all that – Dr Roger Leir. A podiatrist from south California, he was the first doctor surgically to remove an alien implant. Until his first operation in August 1995, they had been seen only on X-rays and CAT scans.

Leir had a long interest in UFOs and was a long-standing member of the Mutual UFO Network, where he gained an investigator's certificate. As an investigator, he attended a UFO conference in Los Angeles in June 1995, when he met Derrel Sims. Sims showed Leir a number of X-rays. One of them showed a foreign object in the big toe of an abductee. Leir was sceptical, but Derrel produced the abductee's medical records, which showed that she had never had surgery on her foot. Leir offered to remove it and this led to a series of operations on abductees.

He selects candidates for surgery by strict criteria, which were developed when Leir was working at the National Institute for Discovery Science. Anyone undergoing surgery had to be a suspected abductee – they had to have experienced missing time or, at the very least, seen a UFO. They had to fill out a form that determined how deeply they were involved in the abduction phenomenon. They also had to have an object in their body that showed up on an X-ray, CAT scan or MRI.

Some of Leir's patients would have a conscious memory of the object being implanted into their bodies during the abduction. But, more often, implants are discovered by accident. Some abductees find unusual lumps and scars that have suddenly appeared and go to their doctors to get them X-rayed. In one case, an implant was discovered during treatment following a car crash.

All Leir's patients are given a psychological examination before and after the implant is removed. Some of them experience a newfound sense of freedom after surgery. One abductee went straight back to her family, saying she wanted nothing more to do with UFOs.

Leir has, so far, operated on eight individuals and removed a total of nine objects. Seven of them seem to be of extraterrestrial origin. Five were coated in a dark grey shiny membrane that was impossible to cut through even with a brand new surgical blade. One was T-shaped. Another three were greyish-white balls that were attached to an abnormal area of the skin. Leir found that patients would react violently if the object was touched and often suffered pain in that area in the week before the implant was surgically removed.

During surgery, Leir discovered that there was no inflammatory response in the flesh around the implant. He found this surprising as any foreign object introduced into the body usually causes an inflammatory response. In this case, there was no rejection. He also found that the surrounding tissue also contained large numbers of 'proprioceptors'. These are specialised nerve cells usually found in sensitive areas, such the finger tips, which sense temperature, pressure and touch. There was no medical reason for them to be found where he found them, clustered around the implant. In two cases, Leir found 'scoop mark' lesions above the implants. In each case, Leir found that the tissue there suffered from a condition called 'solar elastosis'. This is caused by exposure to ultraviolet light, but it could not have been due to sunburn as only a tiny area was affected.

Leir found that the membrane surrounding the implants was composed of the protein coagulum, hemosiderin granules – an iron pigment – and keratin. All these three substances are found naturally in the body. However, a search of the medical literature revealed that they had never been found together in combination before.

The implants themselves would fluoresce under ultraviolet light – usually green, but sometimes other colours. In one case, Leir found that an abductee had a pink stain on the palm of her hand. It could be removed temporarily, but would seep back under the skin. Derrel Sims uses this fluorescent staining, which cannot be removed by washing, to detect implants. Leir believes that it is caused by a substance given off by the implant to prevent rejection.

A wide range of tests have been carried out on the implants Leir has removed. They are submitted to routine pathology tests to see if they are human in origin. When that draws a blank, they are sent for metallurgical testing and they have been examined under optical microscopes and electron microscopes, and analysed using X-ray diffraction techniques that tell which elements they are made of.

When the T-shaped implant that Leir had removed from one patient was magnified one thousand times under an electron microscope, a tiny fishhook could be seen on one end of the crossbar of the T, which Leir believes anchored the implant to the flesh. The other end was rounded off like the nose of a bullet, while in the middle there was a tiny hole into which the shaft of the T fitted perfectly. One of the rods had a carbon core, which made it electrically conductive. The other had an iron core, which was magnetic. An attractive force between them made them cling together. The shaft was encircled by a band of silicate crystals. Bob Beckworth, an electrical engineer who works with Leir, likened this to an old-fashioned crystal set, where a quartz crystal and a copper wire were used to pick up a radio signal.

Specimens were sent to some of the most prestigious laboratories in North America – Los Alamos National Laboratories, New Mexico Tech and Toronto University, among others. The samples were found to contain rare elements in the same isotopic ratios that are found in meteorites. When the labs were told that the specimens had been removed from body tissue, they did not believe it. For Leir, this is the smoking gun.

When you mine an element on Earth, the ratio of the various radioactive isotopes it contains always falls within a certain range. If you mine uranium, for example, it will always contain a certain ratio of uranium 234, 235 and 236. This will be roughly the same anywhere on Earth. But rock samples from the moon or meteorites contain completely different isotopic ratios. The isotopic ratios in the implants showed clearly that they were not of earthly origin.

Leir is not sure what the implants are for. They could be transponders or locating devices that enable alien abductors to track those they have abducted. They might be designed to modify behaviour – some abductees exhibit unexplained compulsive behaviour. They might detect chemical changes in the body, caused by pollution. Or they might be used to detect genetic changes in the body.

'If researchers such as Zachariah Sitchen are correct,' says Leir, 'and the human race is a genetically altered species, then it's possible that this genetic manipulation may still be going on and is something "they" wish to monitor closely.'

But what ever the implants are for, it is quite clear that they are extraterrestrial in origin. As Leir points out, if you find people who have been abducted by aliens and then find implants in them that have an isotopic ratio not found this planet, what other sane conclusion can you draw?

Tony Dodd

Ex-Sergeant Tony Dodd became interested in UFOs after having an encounter with one himself in 1978, when he was a police officer in North Yorkshire, England. He saw an object hovering about a hundred feet away. It had a domed top with four doors it. There were flashing lights around the sides, and three large spheres protruding from the underside. The whole structure was glowing bright white and it was silent. Dodd was sure this strange object was homing in on him, though it eventually floated off and landed nearby.

After he reported his sighting, his superiors told him not to talk to the press. This was standard procedure in the police.

Since then, he has seen seventy or eighty UFOs. Some of them are simply balls of light, anything from a couple of feet to thirty feet across. However, they seemed to contain some kind of mechanical device. He could often see a small, red pulse of light inside them, which created the aura of light. He has received hundreds of reports of these balls of light, which apparently fly in formation. That must mean they have intelligent controls, he reasons.

After retiring from the police force, Dodd took the opportunity to speak out. He devoted himself to UFO research full-time and became Director of Investigative Services for Quest International, one of the world's leading UFO societies, and he oversees the publication of their high influential *UFO Magazine*. For part of his time in the police, he was a detective and he uses police investigation techniques on UFO cases. His police background has taught him which lines of enquiry to pursue and how to encourage witnesses to come forward and talk. It has also given him contacts in intelligence and the military. This is not always an advantage. Dodd's mail is tampered with, even the registered packages that turn up. And the CIA have threatened to kill him, though he remains stoically unintimidated.

Dodd is the foremost expert on animal mutilations in the UK and believes the government know all about it. He also believes that elite forces in America and Britain had adopted a hostile attitude towards a certain type of alien because the aliens out there do not resemble us very closely. Aliens, he points out, do not necessarily have two legs and two arms. Indeed, in human eyes some are quite grotesque. This is the reason the aliens are abducting people and creating hybrids. The aliens, apparently feel the same way about us. When people are abducted, they are treated the way we treat animals on game reserves.

Abductions are never one-off incidents, he says. Dodd has never come across a victim who has been abducted in childhood and never abducted again. Once it has happened, it tends to occur throughout the victim's life. Dodd believes that abductees are being conditioned until they reach puberty. After that the visitors start taking sperm and eggs. Part of the alien's agenda, Dodd believes, is a genetic experiment to create human–alien hybrids. He has investigated cases where aliens have impregnated female abductees. The conception is not natural. It is performed with a needle that it inserted through the navel. Human babies can be conceived using similar methods, but our medical profession is years behind. Three months into the pregnancy, the abductee is picked up again and the foetus is taken from the womb. The resulting 'star children' have thin limbs, large heads and alien eyes and faces, though they have hair on their heads and small human noses.

One woman he knows has been impregnated twice and both times the aliens have taken the baby. When the woman was three months pregnant, she was out walking her dog and a strange light appeared in the sky. She knew they had come to take her baby. She also saw jars containing embryos, which were suspended in liquid, as if in an artificial womb. These jars were all around the walls of the room she was in.

In many of the cases that Dodd has investigated, the abductees seem to have a sixth sense. They get a feeling when they know the abduction is about to take place. However, people generally do not know that they have been abducted. The clue is when they know things that they would not normally know about.

He uses lie detectors in his investigations. But he also uses his knowledge of the subject and his police background to sniff out the hoaxers. He also uses hypnosis and always employs the same hypnotist. This is because the man does nothing more than put the subject under hypnosis. Dodd himself asks all the questions. This is vital because he does not want the witnesses to be led or have them given guides or pointers.

In abduction cases, Dodd also looks for physical evidence. Some abductees have strange marks on their bodies. In one case he investigated, a woman saw strange balls of light in the bedroom at night, and she had an inexplicable burn mark on her arm. The woman had contacted him after he had made radio broadcast about alien abductions and, although many of the things he had mentioned had happened to her, she wanted to be reassured that she had not been abducted.

He has also come across a case where an abductee set off a camera flash near an alien implant in his head. Something under his skin glowed green. It was about a quarter of an inch wide, but it did not seem to cause the man any pain.

On several occasions, Dodd has had a person under hypnosis who has ended up speaking as somebody else – one of the aliens, Dodd believes. When he asked them what right they had to abduct people, the alien voice replied: 'We have every right to do this, you do not understand the nature of things.' Dodd concluded that he was talking to a highly intelligent being.

Dodd has tried to develop this as a method of communication with the alien race and has come to believe that extra-terrestrial beings are involved in a collect-and-analyse experiment to study the human race. He is in regular communication with them, but they only divulge things piece by piece. When he gets impatient, they tell him that they have to take things slowly because the human race is not able to handle the truth. We have to be educated as if we were in infant school. Dodd finds this very spiritual.

This is why they are not communicating with all of us. We are not ready for the knowledge they possess. That is why Dodd himself is here. His role is to disseminate information, to learn from the aliens and to give what he knows out to humankind. His alien contacts have told him that he is some form of teacher. Apparently this was decided before he arrived on Earth as a child and it is why they are making contact with him. They have explained humankind's place in the universe and have told him that we are immortal spirits that go on and on.

'Every flower has its seed and every creature its destiny,' Dodd has been told. 'Weep not for those who have fulfilled their earthly obligation, but be happy that they have escaped that charge of material suffering. As the flower dies, the seed is born and so shall it be for all things.'

Dodd's contact with the aliens has religious aspects. He believes that they are a higher force and that they are responsible for us being here.

A.J. Gevaerd

A. J. Gevaerd is Brazil's leading UFOlogist, editor of the country's only UFO publication, *UFO*, and the director of the Brazilian Centre for Flying Saucer Research, the largest organisation of its kind in the country. He came to international attention in 1996,through his investigation of the famous Varginha case, where two extraterrestrials were captured after their spacecraft crashed in southern Brazil.

According to Gevaerd, there were numerous UFO sightings in the first few weeks of 1996. On the night of 19 January, two people reported seeing a spacecraft which had difficulty flying. At around 7:30 a.m. on the morning of 20 January, a number of people in the town of Varginha reported spotting a humanoid creature around. It had red eyes, a reddish-brown coloured skin and three small bumps on its head. Frightened residents called the Fire Department. They located the creature in an area called Jardim Andere and called the Brazilian army. By 10:30 a.m., army personnel and firemen had managed to net the creature and placed it in a crate. They then took it to the School of the Sergeant of Arms in the nearby town of Tres Coracoes.

Gevaerd discovered that a second extraterrestrial was found later that day. Three girls saw another creature cowering by a wall not far from where the first one had been captured. They told Gevaerd that it had a large head, brown skin, thick veins on its upper body and three protuberances on its head that looked like horns. At 8:30 p.m., a military vehicle with two policemen in it almost drove over a creature Gevaerd believes was the same as the one seen by the girls. One of the officers jumped out of the truck and grabbed it with his bare hands. He held it in his lap until they reached a nearby medical facility. Gevaerd discover that the creature was later transferred to the Humanitas Hospital in Varginha. The capture of the second creature occurred on a Saturday night when everyone was out on the streets. Many people saw the commotion and military trucks pulling up. In all, Gevaerd and his fellow researchers have interviewed over forty witnesses who saw the authorities capture the two creatures.

The aliens' UFO was first detected by an American satellite and the US informed the Brazilian military as part of an agreement between the two nations. So Brazilian radar was on full alert when the craft entered Brazilian airspace and it tracked the craft until it crashed into the state of Minas Gerais. Gevaerd has proof that both the US and the Brazilian government knew immediately that a UFO had crashed and knew roughly its location. Gevaerd tried to get details but there was a complete clamp down in the military. He believes that both extraterrestrials survived the crash, but died within a few hours of capture. The crash seems to have left them badly injured. The crash had occurred at around 3 a.m. When people saw them a few hours later, they were on their last legs.

'It could have been due to the crash,' says Gevaerd. 'Or perhaps the environment was not suitable.'

Gevaerd believes the US was involved from the start. He knows the creatures were later moved to the Hospital of Clinics at the University of Campinas. There were examined by a team of doctors, headed by Brazil's leading forensic scientist, Dr Furtunato Badan Palhares. In all, fifteen masked doctors examined the creatures' bodies, and seven of the team were non-Brazilians – probably US scientists. Gevaerd also thinks that the bodies were shipped to the US. A special US transport plane arrived on 26 January at Campinas, and he thinks that the bodies were taken to an Air Force base in North America.

'Everything indicates US involvement,' says Gevaerd. 'Our government does what it's told to do by the US. They co-operate with the US in return for favours.'

Since the Varginha incident, Gevaerd has consolidated his reputation by his investigation of 'Operation Saucer'. This began in 1977 when hundreds of UFO sightings came from an area along the Amazon river. Many people said they had been attacked by beams of light. Later many of them suffered symptoms of anaemia, although it is not clear whether this was due to loss of blood or to receiving a discharge from a UFO. The state authorities sent in teams of doctors, but they were attacked too. Eventually, the central government took the problem seriously, and, in September 1977, a team of twelve men from the Brazilian Air Force were sent to the area to investigate. They collected reports from over three thousand people who had seen UFOs and had been attacked by balls of light. This inquiry was called 'Operation Saucer' and was headed by Colonel Uyrange Hollanda, who told his story to Gevaerd in 1987, shortly before committing suicide.

The Operation Saucer team were ordered to talk to witnesses, document the evidence and get photographs – they took five hundred photographs of the UFOs in all. Hollanda's team were also ordered to see if they could make contact with the aliens and ask them why they had come. Although he got no direct answer to this question, Hollanda believed that the aliens were here to collect genetic material. Attacks usually took place when victims were alone and isolated. They would see a ball of light moving towards them. It would give them an electric shock, which would put them to sleep for several hours. When they regained consciousness, they would find small scars on their bodies, which Hollanda believed was caused by the extraction of tissue samples. But the damage was not just physical. Many victims suffered trauma and many were terrified. One fisherman who was attacked repeatedly was so terrified that he broke a leg while fleeing, Gevaerd says, but continued running despite his injury.

Hollanda reported seeing the craft associated with the attacks. They were sleek and teardrop-shaped with a large transparent area at the front, like a helicopter canopy, he told Gevaerd. On occasions, alien figures could be seen moving around inside. Towards the end of their investigations, short, humanoid, Grey aliens were regularly seen by the team. According to Gevaerd, the team's presence seemed to attract the interest of the extraterrestrials. Hollanda told Gevaerd that the aliens seemed to know everything the team did before they did it. For instance, if they decided to go up river, they would find the aliens waiting when they got there. Team members felt as though they were being observed. Eventually, the military team themselves fell victim to attacks. All members of the team were abducted. Hollanda himself was subjected to multiple abductions, during which he was examined both physically and psychologically by the aliens. He also told Gevaerd that he had acquired paranormal abilities as a result of his contacts.

However, these abductions caused Hollanda to lose his emotional stability. When Gevaerd interviewed him in July 1987, he broke down and wept. When he described his contact with the aliens he was obviously under great strain and was still plagued by strange phenomena years after he left the Amazon. He committed suicide two days before the first of a series of sessions of regressional hypnosis Gevaerd had arranged for him, thinking this might help.

Operation Saucer concluded that there was no doubt that the UFOs were responsible for the attacks. It also found that people were being abducted; some did not return. Gevaerd does not know why these abductions were happening, or why the aliens had such a special interest in the natives of the Amazon – although it is possible they conducted their experiments in this area because the people were isolated, living far from any protection.

Gevaerd finds the phenomenon of abduction a big puzzle. He has investigated cases where abductees have acquired paranormal abilities, including telepathic and healing powers, as a result. One case that Gevaerd investigated was that of Vera Lucia Guimaraes Borges, who was abducted in the 1960s when she was a teenager. She was living in the house of her grandmother in Valencia, near Rio de Janeiro, when she was woken one night by a noise and was lured into the kitchen. There she was confronted by a ball of light, which hovered in front of her. She promptly fainted. After this incident, Borges acquired remarkable paranormal powers, including the ability to diagnose a patient's illness by simply thinking about them. Under regressional hypnosis, she discovered that she had been abducted by two aliens – one male and one female in appearance – who had subjected her to a medical examination.

Doctors were called in by Gevaerd to test her diagnostic skills. She was 99 per cent accurate. One of the doctors was so impressed that he used her as a consultant. In one case, she told him that a young male patient had been bitten by a poisonous creature and told him which antidote to use.

'I know of many cases where abductees have acquired paranormal abilities,' says Gevaerd. 'Although abductions appear to have no obvious benefits, there are plenty of cases that illustrate we are visited by ETs who can help us do special things.'

However, Hollanda certainly did not benefit from his abduction, and other abductees gain nothing and end up traumatised. Although there are a lot of dedicated UFO researchers in Brazil, only a few are investigating abductions. As a result, Gevaerd is collaborating with the North American alien abduction experts Budd Hopkins and Dr John Mack, who he hopes will teach Brazilian investigators how to do abduction research.

'There is so much new data here that has not yet been seized upon by the media,' says Gevaerd. He believes that it could be the clue to an enigma: 'I'm convinced humanity, in a number of different forms, is spread out all over the universe. We are just a tiny fraction of what exists.'

The World's Greatest Secrets

Acknowledgements

The Publishers would like to thank the following organizations and
individuals for their kind permission to reproduce the illustrations
in this book:

CAMERA PRESS: 19, 111; Alan Whicker 39; MARY EVANS PICTURE LIBRARY: 34;
FRANK SPOONER PICTURES/GAMMA: 117; Tom Kasser 156/Peter Tatiner 101 /
Christian Yioujard 54L&R: JOHN FROST HISTORICAL NEWSPAPER: 128; ROBERT
HUNT LIBRARY: 59, 96; THE KEYSTONE COLLECTION: 132; NOVA SCOTIA
TOURIST BOARD: 143; Taro Yamasaki/PEOPLE WEEKLY © 1986 Time Inc.: 27;
THE PHOTOGRAPHERS LIBRARY: 149; POPPERFOTO: 78; REX FEATURES: 86, 123;
SYNDICATION INTERNATIONAL: 9; TOPHAM PICTURE LIBRARY: 65L&R, 91;
UPI/BETTMAN NEWSPHOTOS: 136, 139; THE WASHINGTON POST: 75.

Frontispiece photographs: Fatty Arbuckle, Group Captain Townsend and
Princess Margaret, two members of the Tonton Macoutes

First published in 1994 by Hamlyn, a division of
Octopus Publishing Group Limited

This 1997 edition published by Chancellor Press, an imprint of
Bounty Books, a division of Octopus Publishing Group Limited,

Endeavour House, 189 Shaftesbury Avenue, London WC2H 8JY

An Hachette Livre UK Company

Reprinted 1999, 2002, 2003, 2005, 2006 (twice), 2007, 2009, 2010, 2011, 2012

ISBN: 978-1-851528-67-7

A CIP record for this book is available from the British Library

Printed and bound by CPI Group (UK) Ltd, Croydon, CR0 4YY

Contents

Chapter One

CRIME SECRETS

Here is a collection of murders most foul – crimes that to this day remain unsolved and where the perpetrators could still be at large – like the A1 murder – did victim Janice Weston have a secret she had to die for? Why did a dashing Guards officer sacrifice everything for the brother he loved? What was the secret of the Christmas child – a boy from nowhere whose death touched an entire community? And finally that greatest psychopath of all – Jack the Ripper – who disappeared into the London fog, never to be seen again and whose identity still remains a secret.

The Fallen Idol

Captain Simon Hayward was a member of two of the most exclusive clubs in the world – the British establishment and the Guards Regiment. Both afforded him a certain social cachet, not to mention a privileged lifestyle and a well mapped-out future. Hayward had served his country well, and the rewards of loyalty were rapid promotion in the ranks, service overseas and invitations to the best debutante balls. His masters at Wellington College in Crowthorne, in the heart of the English countryside, were proud that he had opted for military service; for generations Wellington has swelled the ranks of the British Army officer corps with fine young men. The son of an RAF officer who became a commercial airline pilot, Simon reflected that his father, had he still been alive, would have been proud of his service in the Household Division. He would have been prouder still to have seen his son astride a magnificent cavalry horse guarding the home of the Monarch – Buckingham Palace. Still, even though his father was dead, his mother Hazel had enough pride in her heart for the whole family, and never failed to positively glow whenever she mentioned the achievements of her warrior son.

Simon had two brothers, David and Christopher. David was the youngest of the three and shared Simon's traditional values. Christopher, the eldest, was the exact opposite. At school he performed badly, irrating the very same masters who were impressed by his brother's academic prowess. One classmate branded him a 'flash Harry, a loudmouth, a show off.' He left school in 1968, aged eighteen, and hit the Hippy Trail, trod by thousands of disillusioned young men and women, who walked off to the orient in search of drugs, free love, mysticism – but mostly themselves. He journeyed to Afghanistan, Thailand and India, dabbling in the mind-bending drugs favoured in the 1960s, and finally ended up on the Spanish island of Ibiza. In 1971, the island had not developed into the steel-and-glass holiday resort favoured now by package holiday Britons. Christopher made his first home in the village of Santa Gertrudis, and later near San Carlos, on a remote headland on the north of the island. Here he met a community of hippies and dropouts who had an interest in marijuana. He also found a little work ferrying day-trippers around on a boat he had just bought.

Christopher came back to London in 1972, when, on 12 August, he married Chantal Heubi at Fulham Registry Office. Chantal was a student, a

Captain Hayward in happier days before his arrest.

girl with an impeccable background. She was Swiss-born, and she and Christopher had been lovers for two years. Christopher was then twenty-one and almost became a father the previous spring – but Chantal lost the baby. The marriage was unorthodox, the couple favouring the flamboyant red robes which the mysterious 'Bhagwan' cult members wore. The marriage lasted two years, long enough for Chantal to leave Ibiza to give birth to a son, Tarik, back in Switzerland. Chantal kept the baby, but returned to Ibiza to live and she and Christopher parted but remained friends.

The innocent child could not know that he would become a pawn in a sinister power play that would, eventually, destroy his uncle and force his father into the life of a fugitive.

With the sons carving out their totally different lives, Mrs Hayward was happy that the brothers at least retained a mutual respect and liking for each other. Although worlds apart in the lifestyles they pursued, Christopher was protective of his 'kid' brother, while Simon stuck up for his brother's right to live the way he saw fit. In March 1987, after Simon had completed a long, arduous tour of duty in Northern Ireland – much of his time spent on perilous covert missions with the elite SAS Regiment – he opted for a holiday in the sun in Ibiza.

Simon's days were spent drinking wine and lazing on the beaches his nights partying in the local discos and nightclubs. It was perfect rest and relaxation after the harrowing months in Ulster. But did Simon know that his brother's catamaran *Truelove* was used for more than running idle rich tourists around the islands? Did he know what the police already knew – that Christopher was a lynchpin of a top smuggling organization which dealt in marijuana from Morocco, landed it in Ibiza and processed it in Spain before filtering it out to the lucrative European markets? Was he aware that *Truelove* had sailed for years to the Moroccan town of M'diq, where Christopher loaded its hull with cannabis resin? Simon always claimed he never knew anything of his brother's criminal activities.

Midway through the first week of March, Simon then thirty-three, agreed to do his brother a favour. Sandra Agar, his attractive, well-bred London girlfriend had flown home, so he had time on his hands. He would drive Christopher's XJ6 British racing green Jaguar to Sweden where his brother assured him he had a buyer already arranged to purchase it. The car, he told Simon, was a nuisance, not built for the twisting roads and back lanes of Ibiza – especially the pitted dirt road on the island's northern tip which led to his new home. 'Would you drive it back across the European mainland and sell it for me?', he asked. It was an offer Simon jumped at.

Nearly 1,800 miles away in Stockholm the snow still lay on the ground from the bitter winter. Police officers from the city's narcotics squad and Uppsala, Sweden's main university town fifty miles away, were meeting to discuss details of a drug-busting operation that they had been planning for two years.

Uppsala is outwardly one of Sweden's loveliest cities, but there is also a seamy side to the place – drug peddling. With its 5,000 strong university population – plus all the fringe elements and meeting places which serve that population – there was a ready-made market for narcotics peddling. The narcotics squad in Stockholm had been monitoring the drug organization which smuggled the cannabis in from Spain for two years. Christopher

Hayward did not know it, but he had been under surveillance for months. All the police were waiting for was the chance to catch a courier when the drugs were being delivered, thereby ensnaring him, the consignment and hopefully, at the very least, disrupting the flow of drugs for months. It could also, hoped the detectives, lead to the arrest of further gang members – maybe even to the dismantling of the network. All they were waiting for was the next consignment . . . and intelligence told them that it was due in March.

The Jaguar snaked through the Pyrenees, up through Bordeaux, around Paris, on up through Belgium, Holland, Germany, Denmark and finally purred to a halt to catch the ferry across to Sweden. Simon Hayward was on the final leg of his journey – to meet a man in a railway station at Linkoping, 120 miles south of Stockholm. The rendezvous was at ten o'clock at night and the man he was assigned to meet was called Lokesh – a friend of his brother's from Ibiza whom he had briefly met once on the island. He did not know then, he later claimed, that the man who climbed into the front seat of the Jaguar was actually a long-time drug peddler called Forbes Cay Mitchell. Cay Mitchell told him to drive to a house where they would stay – in reality the 'drop' house for the drug consignment. But waiting in the shadows was an armed squad of the Stockholm narcotics team that had planned the operation to ensnare the organization's courier. It was Friday, 13 March 1987 and the day could not have been more unlucky for Simon Hayward. Inspector Jan Bihlar walked over to the window after Simon's car was pulled over and with full courtesy, told the man who had guarded Her Majesty Queen Elizabeth the Second that he was under arrest.

In Uppsala, where Hayward was first taken, the car was put into a police garage. It did not take the specialized drug-busting team long to discover that hidden in the hollows of the Jaguar's doors were 50·5 kilos of high grade cannabis resin, worth over £250,000 at street value. Pictures taken of Captain Hayward alongside the car with Swedish prosecutor Ulf Forsberg, who would be handling the case, seemed to show a man completely dumbfounded, numb with shock and surprise. Captain Hayward, who flashed his Army identification card at the police when he was apprehended, was charged with being a courier of the drug consignment and charged with smuggling the cannabis in the certain knowledge that he would be paid £20,000 for his trouble. He was then led away to the cells as Fleet Street newspapers despatched reporters to Sweden for the sensational story – the story of a man duped by his own brother; a modern-day Cain and Abel, with a fate worse than death for the officer who now faced disgrace, humiliation and punishment.

11

It was police Inspector Jan-Erik Nilson who first briefed the hungry pressmen with the facts. In an upstairs room of Uppsala police station, usually reserved for lectures and operation planning, he told them how Christopher Hayward had been 'fingered' by another member of the drugs syndicate, Forbes Cay Mitchell. Aberdeen-born Cay Mitchell, a committed marijuana smoker, was netted by the police at the same time, he explained. In exchange for leniency, he told the police that he had been involved in many shipments of cannabis to Sweden; and that he had been in Ibiza when Simon was there with his brother. He heard them talking about the plot to get the drugs into the country via the compartments in the Jaguar. Simon was needed because the regular courier, known only as Macundo, was getting jittery and worn down after one mission too many. Simon, he said, was a willing conspirator, lured into the international drug smuggling network by greed and excitement.

One man would have freed Captain Hayward – but it would of course have ended his own liberty. That man was his wayward brother Christopher. He vanished into Europe, covering his tracks. He has not been seen since. But the manner of his disappearance – and the mysterious death of his ex-wife Chantal three months after Simon's arrest – have led to immense speculation about the whole sinister affair which led to the terrible downfall of an officer and a gentleman.

Police said initially they hoped to make telephone contact with Christopher within days. They believed he might want to cut the same kind of deal that Cay Mitchell had done – leniency in return for co-operation. But Hayward was on the run – a fugitive not only from the law but from the menacing, ruthless figures who controlled the drugs syndicate.

A newspaper managed to confirm that while Interpol was searching for Hayward, he had docked *Truelove*, his 57 feet catamaran in M'diq, where he had a secret reunion with his son Tarik. Later there were phone calls to London from Christopher to his mother – in which he said if he gave himself up for questioning he would be killed. More seriously, so would Tarik. He could not come forward to speak for Simon. For him, there was no hope. Cay Mitchell, at his trial before Hayward's, said it was a plot which the Captain was fully aware of; that it was a challenge to him and that he would be handsomely rewarded for his efforts. For his evidence, Cay Mitchell was given a seven year jail term.

Lawyers for Simon prepared his case – but the circumstantial evidence was incriminating. Why a secret rendezvous in a windswept railway station car-park so late at night? Why was a screwdriver which fitted into specially-designed holes to prise off the door covers from the inside found in the car? What about the overheard conversation testified to by Cay Mitchell in which he alleged Simon was a willing participant in the scheme? All Simon

Hayward could argue was that he was an innocent dupe – a pawn in a power game which his brother had manipulated for greed. He steadfastly maintained his innocence, but a judge and jury found him guilty and sentenced him to five years. Even with the news of the sentence there was still no sign of Christopher anywhere.

Shortly before the verdict, in July 1987 Chantal, Christopher's ex-wife, telephoned from Ibiza to Mrs Hayward at her London home, to say she knew who was behind the drugs run – 'and that it was not Simon or Christopher.' She intended to fly to London and speak with solicitors to give her evidence and testify in the court hearing at Stockholm if necessary. But only days before she was scheduled to arrive, she was found dead – an autopsy had revealed a massive drug overdose, injected into the arm with a needle. What was mystifying was that Chantal had experimented with marijuana, but had never taken hard drugs. There was no evidence on her skin that she was a hardened junkie – just one small pin-prick. And the needle mark was on her left arm – and she was left handed. It raised the question: why did a girl who had never injected herself before use her unfamiliar right hand to pump a lethal cocktail of drugs into her left arm? And why did this occur just days before she was to give evidence to help out her ex-brother-in-law? Christopher Hayward remains on the run. Is he the keeper of a secret which damned his brother? Did he dupe him, or were they partners in crime? What is the terrible power of the organization that he once worked for which has sentenced him, as much as justice sentenced his brother, to a life with no hiding place? Simon Hayward has taken his punishment like a man, although he is stripped of rank, has been discharged from the Army, and had to linger in jail while his mother buried her youngest son, David, who was tragically killed in a car crash in January 1988.

Sweden is a democratic country with decent laws and a judiciary based on equality and fairness. But from his prison cell, Simon Hayward said: 'Ninety-nine per cent of me believes that Christopher stitched me up. Only that other one per cent clings to the fact that he is my brother, that he couldn't have done. But ninety-nine per cent screams out that he did.

'One thing is very obvious; whether he did or he didn't, whether he is genuinely terrified of something or somebody I know nothing about, there *must* have been some way for him to get a message or information through to clear me. He has not done that, and for that I will never forgive him.'

The A1 Murder

Did Janice Weston know a secret that she had to die for? It is a question that has baffled lawmen since the morning of 11 September 1983 when her badly battered body was found dumped in a ditch next to a lay-by on the A1 Great North Road. The frenzied attacker had clubbed her repeatedly around the head with a blunt instrument – police were later to discover it was the jack from her own car – and had thrown her body into the water-filled ditch. David Hurst, a cyclist who had stopped to rest in the lay-by on the northbound section of the road near Huntingdon, Cambridgeshire, raised the alarm, triggering a murder probe which remains unsolved to this day.

Janice Weston was a brilliant lawyer, a product of convent school education who had attained a degree in law from Manchester University. She was well liked, cheerful, pretty, and charming – a woman of the 1980s who had everything to live for.

Janice Weston graduated while in her mid-twenties and quickly landed a plum job in the slect London law firm of Oppenheimer, Nathan and Vandyk. While she was there, Janice met the two most important men in her life – one was Tony Weston, who was destined to become her husband. The other was Heinz Isner, a refugee from Hitler's Germany who had come to London before the outbreak of World War Two and made a fortune from merchant banking. Isner was forty-one years older than Janice, and fell in love with her. But while she remained fond of the old gentleman – who once, in an old fashioned, courteous way, asked if she would be his bride – her affections were for Tony Weston, an ambitious property developer. While he became her lover, she never forgot the gracious old gentleman who settled for being her escort on trips to the ballet and London's West End theatres.

Janice specialized in computer law just at the time that the microchip revolution was thrusting business, financial and industrial life from the Victorian era to the modern age. Word processors would be in every office within a decade and the vast network of computers and their useage would require new laws every step of the way. That was her field and she excelled in it. She was recognized for her talents and employed in 1976 by the top practice of Charles Russell and Company, as a partner.

She was well paid for her work and dealt at the highest levels with clients and management. A year after her appointment the kindly Heinz Isner died.

Janice had realized that he was an amicable old fellow and she had responded to his affections with dignity and courtesy, only too willing to be the friend he was obviously seeking. It was only with his death that she realized the price that he put on her friendship – a legacy of close on £145,000 of paintings, money, stocks and shares and antiques from his vast estate. Janice Weston, was now financially secure in her own right thanks to the legacy and her meticulous attention to detail at work which earned her both promotion and the money which went with it. Her boss Lord Nathan was later to remark that she was 'one of the most brilliant corporate lawyers I have ever known.'

It wasn't until 1982, after Tony Weston was divorced from his first wife, that Janice and he were free to marry. The pair combined business with pleasure – Janice investing some of her money into apartments at a mansion called Clopton Manor in Northamptonshire which property dealer Tony suggested would be a good buy. They used one of the apartments as a weekend retreat when away from their home in London's Holland Park.

Tony Weston was successful too; his business deals brought him an enviable lifestyle as he dealt in property in both England and Europe. When he and Janice were up at Clopton Manor they often drank in the local pubs and were liked by everyone for their quiet, restrained manner.

In 1983 Janice set herself a new task, researching and writing a book on computer law and the latest safeguards for business and commerce in using new technology. In September she was still working on the book when Tony Weston went to France to negotiate the purchase of a Loire Valley chateau. He was never to see his wife again.

On 10 September 1983 Janice was at home doing research on her book. Later that day, at 5.00pm, she turned up at the law offices where she worked – police were later to interview a colleague who testified that she was there. What happened to Janice after that is a mixture of mystery, conjecture and speculation. The next time she was seen was the following morning by the cyclist in the lonely A1 lay-by, fourteen miles from Clopton Manor.

Among the first on the scene on that Sunday morning was Detective Chief Superintendent Len Bradley, Cambridgeshire's head of CID. The first, and most puzzling thing about the appalling crime was: how did Janice get there? For there was no sign of her car. She was not in fact identified for another forty eight hours, when law firm colleagues alerted her sister, who in turn alerted police about her absence. Twenty-four hours after they identified Janice, an alert policeman spotted, abandoned, in the Camden Town area of London, Janice's car – with bloodstains over the window and dashboard. At the scene, a search of the field which bordered the road revealed the car jack – the murder weapon, according to a Home Office pathologist.

Len Bradley, a dedicated, ultra-professional policeman with many years' experience, had to find out why this professional, thirty-six-year-old woman was murdered in an anonymous lay-by on one of Britain's busiest trunk roads; why there was no sign of a robbery at the scene or of sexual assault; why the killer stole her car and drove it to London; why she had driven north in the first place. There were plenty of questions but no answers.

Detectives despatched to the Holland Park address found the remains of a half-eaten meal and a single wine glass, indicating that she had dined alone. They were curious as to why the house had the appearance that she had left in a hurry – the normally fastidious Janice had not done the washing up and had left with her purse, but not her handbag; usually a possession that women never left behind. In the face of too-few clues, the police reasoned this: that Janice Weston was telephoned, or received a message by some other means, that necessitated her driving up the A1 towards Clopton Manor. Was she, then, lured to the lay-by by that person for an appointment with death?

One of the most bizarre aspects of the case, and one which has still not been cleared up, was the mystery of the number plates. Forty-eight hours before the murder was revealed to the Press, a man walked into a car spares shop in Royston, Hertfordshire, and ordered two spare number plates – with the same registration as Janice's Alfa Romeo car. The mystery man has never been traced. Police looked to the car for clues. They discovered that on the Saturday morning before Janice's ill fated journey, she had collected a repaired tyre which had her husband's name and telephone number scrawled on the side in yellow water-resistant chalk. The repairman put it into the boot, leaving the spare on the car. However, when the vehicle was found in London, the repaired tyre was back on the car and the spare was missing. It was, mused police, entirely plausible that Janice had had a blow-out and stopped to change the wheel in the lay-by when her attacker struck her with repeated blows from the jack. But why would the spare wheel be missing?

Tony Weston came back from France and pleaded with the public for information about his wife's killer. To cover all angles, detectives were sent to the Loire Valley to investigate Mr Weston's movements on the weekend that his wife was so cruelly murdered. He was held in custody for fifty-five hours in December and a report was prepared for the Director of Public Prosecutions, but there were no charges.

Police satisfied themselves that Janice Weston was not racing off for an illicit liaison with a lover; she was not given to affairs of the heart. There was no sign that she had picked up a crazed hitch-hiker or any reason to suppose that a madman would lurk in that particular lay-by on a freezing night.

Was she, as one theory suggested 'silenced' because her work in computers touched on high-tech espionage – or worse? Why Janice Weston had to die, when she was at the pinnacle of her career, is still, sadly, a secret.

The Missing Earl

He did it – English law in the form of a coroner's jury decreed that Lord Lucan killed his children's nanny on that dark winter's night. The Edwardian-looking Earl with a penchant for gambling and a disdain for modern life wielded the hammer that killed pretty Sandra Rivett. But what has puzzled policemen hunting for him ever since the murder in November 1974, has been the secret of what happened to him. Is he dead? Is he alive? More importantly, do his friends know his fate? Perhaps even the most outrageous theory of all is that he is innocent and took to the life of a fugitive because no one would ever believe otherwise. What are the secrets of Lord Lucan?

The story starts, of course, with the murder; when a panic stricken Lady Veronica Lucan ran from her home in the pouring rain to a local pub and yelled to the astonished drinkers: 'Murder, there's been a murder. He murdered the nanny.' On Lady Veronica's head was an extremely deep wound which poured blood, mingling with the rain running down her face and into her nightclothes.

Officers forced their way into the home at 46 Lower Belgrave Street where they found the lower half of the mews in darkness. Police Sergeant Donald Baker, directed by the light of his torch, saw, at the end of the stairs leading to the basement, smears of what looked like blood on the wallpaper. Gritting his teeth, he advanced further. The police then made their way upstairs where they found the Lucan children. After comforting them the police officers went to the basement. There, on the hard floor, in a canvas Post Office mailbag, was the body of Sandra Rivett.

The murder weapon was found half-an-hour later – a nine-inch, two and a quarter pound length of lead piping wrapped in medical plaster. Lady Frances Lucan, the eldest child, ten years old, told police that she had been watching TV with her mother in the main bedroom when Sandra went downstairs to make some hot drinks. She was gone twenty minutes when Lady Lucan spoke with Frances and told her to watch the TV alone while she checked on what had happened to the nanny. She reappeared with a wound on her head ... with her husband, Lord Lucan. It was the last time that little Lady Frances ever saw him.

Lady Lucan, in hospital after her ordeal, told police this story; that she found the half-landing in darkness when she went to search for the nanny.

17

She called out Sandra's name and there was no reply, she then heard a noise in the cloakroom behind her. She turned – and then a gloved hand grasped her throat and a rain of blows were delivered to her head. Panicking, she said she grabbed the attacker by his genitals and squeezed hard. The man forced her to the ground and tried to gouge out her eyes – releasing the pressure, as the pain from Lady's Lucan's grip forced him backwards. She said she looked up and saw the face of her husband.

Lady Lucan claimed he told her that he had killed the nanny, mistakenly thinking it was her. She said she saved her own life by reasoning with him that she would help him to get away. They went upstairs to a bedroom and she lay down on the bed while he went to find some wet towels to bathe her wounds. 'While he was gone I got up and dashed out of the house,' said Lady Lucan. That was her frantic dash to the pub which signalled the beginning of one of history's most intriguing murder cases.

Later that first night, 7 November, Lucan's mother, the Dowager Countess Lucan, arrived at the house to meet the police. She said that her son had telephoned, asking her to be there. She told detectives that he had said a 'terrible catastrophe' had occurred, in which his wife Veronica and the nanny Sanda had been hurt by an intruder whom he had disturbed. It was his mother who revealed the first of many secrets about the mysterious Earl. She informed the officers that her son and Lady Veronica had separated and the children were wards of court. Many of Lucan's friends were unaware of this because the outward appearance of a conservative, family man was one he both nurtured and cherished.

Checks at the nearby flat he kept and another mews home which was his did not reveal any clues about his whereabouts or what had gone on earlier that evening. Police found Lord Lucan's passport in his flat together with a suit that was laid out on the bed as if he was meaning to pack it. But from the way the evidence was shaping up, it seemed as if Lady Lucan's story was true; the police began to think that Lucan had bludgeoned the nanny to death after mistaking her for his wife. Sandra Rivett, twenty-nine, died because she did not take the usual evening off – the evening that Lucan presumed she would not be in in the house.

Police began to chip away at the facade of the Earl who behaved as if he belonged in another century. Outwardly he displayed all the signs of a privileged life, with his fine homes, live-in nanny, membership of gentlemen's clubs, a Mercedes car and Savile Row suits in the wardrobe. He was a high-roller on the backgammon and card tables of private gambling clubs where his considerable prowess with the cards earned him the nickname of 'Lucky' among his friends. It was not unusual for 'Lucky' to scoop £5,000 in an afternoon of gambling at the tables of his most exclusive club, the

Lord 'Lucky' Lucan in his ceremonial robes.

Clermont, in London. He held bank accounts in Rhodesia and the Bahamas, and was generally reckoned to be financially sound, having inherited family funds, as well as silver and land in Ireland when he succeeded to the title of Earl of Lucan in January 1964. But Lucan's outwardly affluent lifestyle was, police learned, not quite as financially sound as it seemed.

Lucan had frittered away much of the money. He had a fixed annual income of £7,000 per annum from a trust fund and spent large sums in legal fees in his bid to gain custody of his children in a court case in January 1973. At one stage he was spending £400 a week on a private detective to watch his wife's home as he hoped to find illicit liaisons which might convince a judge that the youngsters would be better off under his wing. Another time, his beloved Clermont club in London's ritzy Berkeley Square once withdrew his credit facilities for a time because he bounced a cheque there for £10,000. In short, Lord Lucan was going broke, and was being eaten away with an almost pathological hatred of his wife which, police surmised, he thought he could exorcise with a swift, clean simple murder.

Police began to trace his movements prior to the killing and the attack on Lady Lucan. The night before he had dined with forty other people at a formal dinner. The day of the murder itself he had lunch with friends at the Clermont, met a literary agent to talk over an article he was planning for a magazine on gambling, and at around 8.30 p.m. phoned the Clermont to book a table for four people for dinner.

He arrived at the club some sixteen minutes later, spoke with the doorman, and then drove off. His guests arrived but he – the host – was never seen again.

On the Saturday morning, 9 November, police discovered that Lucan had posted two letters to his friend, millionaire amateur jockey Bill Shand Kydd. The letters were postmarked Uckfield, Sussex, and had blood on the envelopes. One read: 'Dear Bill, the most ghastly circumstances arose tonight, which I have described briefly to my mother when I interrupted the fight at Lower Belgrave Street and the man left.

'V (for Veronica) accused me of having hired him. I took her upstairs and sent Frances to bed and tried to clean her up. She lay doggo for a bit. I went into the bathroom and left the house.

'The circumstantial evidence against me is strong in that V will say it was all my doing and I will lie doggo for a while, but I am only concerned about the children. If you can manage it I would like them to live with you. V has demonstrated her hatred for me in the past and would like to see me accused. For George (his son) and Frances to go through life knowing their father had been accused of attempted murder would be too much for them.

'When they are old enough to understand explain to them the dream of paranoia and look after them.' He signed himself 'Lucky'.

The second letter carried the heading 'financial matters' and outlined a sale at Christie's he had arranged for family silver.

Finally police spoke with Susan Maxwell Scott at the estate she shared with her husband, Ian Maxwell Scott, on the outskirts of Uckfield – the place where the letters had been posted from. Lord Lucan had told them the same story as the one he recounted to his mother – that he had gone into the home to act as his wife's rescuer and found himself being accused by her of Sandra Rivett's murder. He drove away from her home at 1.15 a.m. in a dark saloon car and has never been seen again.

Or has he? Part of the unanswered enigma surrounding the Earl has been his flight. One theory put forward was that he hopped on a cross channel ferry and threw himself into the cold water from the deck of the Newhaven–Dieppe ship. Another was that he went to a private airfield and flew out of the country with a friend at the controls. Other flights of fancy suggest that he changed his identity, took the small amount of capital he had in a Swiss bank account, and set out to embark on a new life away from justice and the stigma of murder.

But Scotland Yard detectives are never satisfied with untidy ends. One of the toughest nuts to crack has been Lucan's tight circle of aristocratic friends, many of whom seemed bound to Lucan by a code of loyalty and honour rarely found in twentieth century Britain. A code, some policemen think, which may even have transcended society's most heinous crime – murder. One source close to the investigation once said that he believed that up to five of Lucan's friends know that he hadn't taken the coward's way out and killed himself. The obvious suggestion is that Lucan's friends, an elite mafia of the rich and privileged, kept his secret and somehow assisted his flight and bolstered the start of his life as a fugitive. It is only a theory and no one has ever been charged with aiding and abetting the flight of a wanted criminal. But in the minds of detectives who are only happy when the loose ends are tied up, it is one that comes back frequently to haunt them. Until all the answers are known, Lord Lucan's final secret remains safe.

Jack the Ripper

In 1888 the British Empire was at its zenith. The sun never set on this glorious imperial bastion which spanned the globe, embracing peoples of every race, creed and colour. But in London, the centre of this huge domain, there was a place where the sun never shone. The East End was a disgrace to the Empire and to civilized values. People lived in squalor, poverty and filth. Child deaths were double the national average and prostitution and drunkenness, sexual abuse of minors and murders, were rife. It was the sordid environment for a killer whose notoriety lives on unabated to this day. Jack the Ripper made the mean streets of the East End his killing ground. Even now, with most of the crumbling slums gone, the taverns of his day replaced with office blocks and the gas lamps ripped out in favour of electric ones, the East End has become a lurid shrine for Ripper enthusiasts, fascinated by the macabre killer's violent deeds. But the question remains: just who was Jack the Ripper? His crimes were not all that remarkable, given the catalogue of horror which man has learned to come to terms with in the twentieth century. He butchered five women, admittedly in a gruesome manner. It is the question of identity, with all the suspicions that Jack the Ripper may have been someone highly placed in British society, which has made the 'Monster of the East End' a creature of intrigue and has ensured his dastardly deeds are never far from the public's mind.

Jack the Ripper may have gone down as history's most famous murderer but his reign of terror was a short one. He first struck on 31 August 1888. Mary Ann Nichols, a prostitute who haunted the Whitechapel area of the East End plying her trade was found butchered in one of the area's many dark alleyways. 'Pretty Polly' as the forty two year old whore was known, was a chronic drunkard and well-known inhabitant of the gin palaces in the area.

Police think Mary Ann approached a tall stranger with the time-honoured 'looking for a good time, mister?' By the time the man had dragged her into the shadows, it was too late. A hand went around her throat, and in seconds she was cut from ear to ear. 'Only a madman could have done this', said a police surgeon who was to examine the body later. 'I have never seen so horrible a case. She was ripped about in a manner that only a person skilled in the use of a knife could have achieved.'

Murders in that deprived – and depraved – area were not uncommon. Police were happy to put the murder down to a single frenzied attack – until just one week later, on 8 September, 'Dark Annie' Chapman, also a prostitute, was found in Hanbury Street near Spitalfields Market with her few pitiful possessions neatly laid out alongside her disembowelled corpse. Although there was no obvious sign of rape, with this murder as with the first there was every indication that the killer was motivated by some terrible sexual rage as he cut and slashed with grotesque abandon. The dissection of 'Dark Annie', with all her entrails laid out next to the corpse, indicated a knowledge of anatomy or surgery not found in the everyday sex killer.

After the second murder, on 25 September, a mocking letter was sent to a Fleet Street news agency. It read: 'Dear Boss, I keep on hearing that the police have caught me. But they won't fix me yet. I am down on certain types of women and I won't stop ripping them until I do get buckled. Grand job, that last job was, I gave the lady no time to squeal. I love my work and want to start again. You will soon hear from me with my funny little game. I saved some of the proper stuff in a little ginger beer bottle after my last job to write with, but it went thick like glue and I can't use it. Red ink is fit enough I hope. Ha! Ha!

Next time I shall clip the ears off and send them to the police, just for jolly.'

The sick message was signed: Jack the Ripper.

Victim number three was Elizabeth Stride, nicknamed 'Long Liz' because of her height. A policeman found the body of forty four year old Liz in Berner's Street, Whitechapel, on 30 September near some factory gates. Like the others her throat had been cut from behind, but she did not suffer mutilation or sexual savagery. This led police to think that the murderer had been disturbed in his gruesome work – for on the same day they discovered victim number four a few streets away in Mitre Square. Catherine Eddowes, forty-three, was disembowelled and her face practically hacked off.

By the time of this fourth murder, Ripper hysteria had gripped London and was raging faster than the plague in the dark, damp passageways of the East End. Women began arming themselves with knives and whistles to attract the police; the *Illustrated Police News* speculated that well-to-do ladies were arming themselves with pearly-handled pistols in case the Ripper was tempted to move up the social scale in his search for bloody satisfaction.

The Eddowes murder disturbed the police greatly. Her body was by far the most mutilated of all the victims and there was a trail of blood leading to a wall where, scrawled in chalk, was the message: 'The Jewes are not men to be blamed for nothing.' Sir Charles Warren, the head of the Metropolitan Police Force personally removed the notice – and thereby may have destroyed some vital evidence. He was concerned that with the influx into the area of Jews from Eastern Europe – and racial tensions already beginning to bubble – this note could have led to savage reprisals.

The rumours about who the murderer was circulated like wildfire. Some of the frightened wretches who lived in the East End said it was a policeman on his nightly rounds, his job giving him the perfect alibi to be out at night on those cold, dark streets. One suspect was a Russian-born doctor called Michael Ostrog, rumour having it that he was sent by the Tsarist secret police to stir up hatred against the expatriate Jews who fled Russia from persecution; others that it was a mad surgeon, or even Sir Charles Warren himself – a leading freemason who removed the notice to protect a freemason killer.

The final death came on 9 November when Mary Kelly, aged 25 and also a prostitute, was grotesquely mutilated in her squalid rented home. On the morning of 10 November Henry Bowers, her landlord, knocked on her door to collect unpaid rent. The previous evening the attractive blonde girl had been seen approaching strangers asking them for cash. The last one she approached – tall, dark, with a moustache and a deerstalker hat – was her killer. Bowers saw the remains of Mary and later told police: 'I shall be haunted by this for the rest of my life.'

Mary's death was to be the last. One hundred years later, the puzzle of the Ripper's bloody but brief reign has still not been solved. It was with the passage of time that more and more people grew intrigued by the Ripper mystery. One suspect who has continued to cause violent debate was Queen Victoria's grandson Prince Albert Victor, Duke of Clarence. The finger was pointed at him because he was said to be mad, incarcerated in a mental institution after he had committed the murders because the scandal would have been too great had it ever been revealed to the world.

However, Inspector Robert Sagar, who played a leading part in the Ripper investigation, said before his death in 1924: 'We had good reason to suspect a man who lived in Butcher's Row, Aldgate. We watched him carefully. There was no doubt that this man was insane. After a time his friends thought it advisable to have him removed to a private asylum. After he was removed there were no more Ripper atrocities.'

Another prime suspect is one favoured by several authors, namely Montagu John Druitt, whose body was found floating in the Thames a few weeks after the murder of Mary Kelly. In their book *The Ripper Legacy*, authors Martin Howells and Keith Skinner say that this impoverished barrister was the man that the police of the day reckoned to be the guilty party. They point to the fact that after his death there were no more Ripper murders. But those writers who favour the Duke of Clarence are swift to point out that there were no more slayings after he was incarcerated. Nevertheless, Druitt's family had a history of mental illness and he had acquired basic medical skills as a young man. The arguments rage unabated.

John Stalker, who retired last year as Deputy Chief Constable of Greater

Manchester, delved into the Ripper files and declared: 'There is still not a shred of real evidence sufficient for a court of law against anyone. The truth is that Jack the Ripper was never in danger of capture. The police, I am certain, came nowhere near him.

'The Metropolitan Police of 1888 were dealing with something quite new: The first recognized series of sexual murders committed by a man who was a stranger to his victims. And 100 years on those are still the most difficult crimes of all to investigate.'

The Christmas Child

Chuck Kleveland was armed with his twelve-bore shotgun and had his western-style jacket buttoned up against the cold as he stepped out in the frozen morning air to hunt for elusive pheasants in his native Chester, Nebraska. It was Christmas Eve and Chuck, forty-four, who ran a truck-stop diner had closed his business for the festivities. He was actually driving from Chester to nearby Hebron to get his 'holiday haircut' as he termed it, but driving down the back roads afforded him ample chance of potting a bird for the Yuletide table. He stuffed extra ammunition in his fleece-lined pockets, jumped behind the wheel of his pick-up, turned on the engine which belched blue-smoke in the frosty air and lurched down the rutted backroad to Chuck's appointment with the barber.

Chuck Kleveland was scanning the horizon hungrily for the birds that would make a tasty treat for his wife's table, when his eye was caught by a flash of blue. He noticed it because it stood out so starkly in the four-feet high grass, tipped with white frost. Chuck backed up the truck – and then rubbed his eyes in disbelief. At first he thought it was a discarded mannequin, a tailor's dummy tossed in the long grass by a thoughtless adult, or the toy of a child. But it was neither. It was the body of a young boy. Chuck was not to know how deeply this discovery was going to affect him in the days to come.

Chuck scrambled through the long grass to the lifeless bundle that was

25

prostrate just fifteen feet from the cab of his pick-up. 'I thought it was a joke or something' he says now, still reeling in disbelief from those first awful moments when reality was sinking in. 'I thought it was a doll, a dummy. It scared the life out of me when I realized it was a child.'

Clad in a one-piece pyjama suit, the child was lying flat on his back, his face fixed serenely as if he had passed away without pain. One hand was lying flat on his chest, across his heart, almost, said Kleveland, as if it had been placed there in a gesture by the killer. The child was just over four feet in height, with blond hair, a gap in his front teeth and freckles. Altogether, thought Kleveland fighting back the panic rising in him, a rather endearing face.

He ran back to the pick-up. Like most drivers in this back-of-beyond region, he had a CB radio in the cab. Using the emergency channel, he called his secretary and told her to contact the local sheriff. When the emergency summons went out over the police radio, Sheriff Gary Young, initially thought it was a pre-Christmas prank by some rednecks who had partaken of too much good cheer. 'A dead body found abandoned in Thayer County?' he said. 'The prospect just didn't seem real.' As an eight-year veteran of the Sheriff's department he had spent his time in the force breaking up brawls and probing some petty break-ins. Homicide was a big city crime.

Young raced to the scene after being convinced of the authenticity of the call. He was emotionally choked when he bent over and looked at the tranquil features of the little boy. Kleveland saw on a second look that part of the boy's nose and upper lip had been eaten away – probably by mice, he thought. But there was no sign of a violent struggle or a gaping wound; nothing to suggest why the little boy had got into this field, in this way to be discovered on 24 December 1985.

The body of the boy was taken to a funeral home in Hebron where several police investigators from the state capital of Lincoln examined him. Strangely, they found no evidence of foul play. They checked the listings for runaways, local orphanages where children, spurred by a seasonal desire to see their real parents, or try to find them, often made a break. They drew a blank. But many enquiries simply could not be answered – it was Christmas, and like most places the season of goodwill meant that offices were shut and phones rang unanswered. The officials of Hebron decided to wrap the child up in his clothes and attend to his pathetic corpse after the holiday. The little boy was placed in the town mortuary and Hebron settled down to extremely muted Christmas celebrations.

There is no doubt that the dead child haunted Thayer County's Christmas. News of the grim find spread rapidly throughout the rural community and sparked more than one frantic search for a missing child or a son unreturned from a family errand. The close-knit farming communities which made up

'The Christmas Child' is laid to rest.

Hebron and Chester only numbered some 7,000 people, so it was natural that it became the topic of conversation in every home. The locals also gave the boy a name – The Christmas Child.

Chuck Kleveland felt the tragedy more than most. He had found the little boy and it cast a darker shadow over his home than others. His daughter Amy, eighteen, couldn't even bother to fake a Christmas spirit. 'I felt very strange on Christmas day,' she said. 'I couldn't celebrate anything. I felt there was nothing to be cheery about. I thought of this little boy who wouldn't be opening any presents on Christmas morning and that made me cry.' For others, the child's death coming on Christmas Eve signified much deeper religious meanings and sparked many different emotions. The Reverend Jean Samuelson, pastor of Chester's United Methodist Church said: 'There is an aura about it. Why did God send us a child on Christmas Eve?'

For the police, there was nothing quite so metaphysical about it. They had questions to answer, a puzzle to solve. Who was this boy? Why was he here, why was he dead, how did he die? Sheriff Young through that he would have the case solved in a few days. He could not have been more wrong, for in his office to this day the file sits – unsolved. 'I never thought it would turn out as case unsolved,' he says reflectively.

The routine work was done – descriptions of the boy were sent out across the state, then further afield, to social services agencies, police departments and child welfare groups. The autopsy on the child revealed a small one-inch birthmark inside his right calf, and a small circular scar on his right forearm. The FBI computer in Washington was tapped into, cross-checking against all children who had gone missing in the United States for that year and the year before. Over 200 leads and tips of 'possibles' were followed up, but they came to nothing. 'What really bothered me in those first few weeks was that a little child could just vanish, just shuffle off,' said Young.

The autopsy revealed little else, though. Because the boy's body had been frozen in the sub-zero temperatures, the blood tests were inconclusive. The pathologist pinpointed the date of death as 23 December, but he could not centre on the cause. The boy had not died of natural causes – but there were no signs of stabbing, shooting, strangulation or poisoning, apart from a slightly higher than normal trace of carbon monoxide present. The theory which was settled on what that the child was suffocated until he lost consciousness and was then placed outside in the cold with his hand placed over his heart, ready to die in the low temperatures. 'I could never accept that this was anything short of homicide' said County Attorney Dan Werner. 'If I believed the boy died of natural causes after the parents left him I would not be pursuing this.'

So why did the Christmas Child have to die? Slowly it began to circulate that perhaps the boy held some dark secret against an adult – the witness to a murder, perhaps, or the eavesdropper on a criminal plot which had ultimately led to his death. The mystery now obsesses the townsfolk. Thoughts of the boy appeared in the journals of the High School teenagers kept by students at the Chester Hubbell Byron High School. 'Nobody knew this child and yet he has touched all of us', wrote one teenager, Carl Kristienson. 'What had he done that he had to die for it? Is there someone bad in our community? What is the reason – will we ever know?' 'He wasn't just dumped here,' said Sheriff Young, 'he was carefully placed. Someeone picked this spot to be his last. But why, why, why?'

Slowly the people of King County realized that the little boy had become part of their souls. They even gave him a name – Matthew – which means 'gift of God'. An undertaker's firm donated a coffin and another firm supplied a headstone and so on Friday 21 March 1986 the boy was laid to rest in the small Chester cemetery, his marble headstone bearing the inscription: 'Little boy found abandoned near Chester, Neb., 24 December 1985.' The Reverend Samuelson conducted the funeral service, and told mourners: 'We all know the names of little ones who have died, but this one has no name. He haunted us, he haunted me personally. I asked in prayer, "Lord, why do you keep speaking to me about this child? Why should I feel guilt?" The answer: "He has been in your life in other forms, and you have not heard him or seen him because you were too busy trying to prove yourself worth." That is the young boy's message.'

Dan Werner is too long in the tooth as a lawman to pin the reason for the child's death on some spiritual message. He understands that the townspeople's souls have been salved with the word that some form of divine reasoning may have been behind the boy's tragic demise, but he is having none of it. He said: 'Funerals are for the living, and this one makes the people in the area feel better because they have a personal relationship with him; they have kind of adopted him. But his death still tugs at me; I want to solve it.'

The Green River Killer

Police say he could be anyone. He could be a doctor, a lawyer, a car repairer, a shoe salesman. He could be sitting next to you as your read this and he will walk away out of your life without a word passed or a glance exchanged. But his secret is the darkest one yet to be discovered in American criminal history – for he is the Green River Killer, a demonic monster who makes the Yorkshire Ripper look like an amateur apprentice and has, so far, ruthlessly accounted for the lives of at least 42 women. The secret of his success, say detectives, is that he is so ordinary....

It was back in July 1982 that two little boys were out on a fishing trip along the Green River – a stretch of water which meanders slowly near the Seattle–Tacoma Airport in Washington state. The children were bicycling along with their fishing gear, intent on an afternoon of fun by the river, when they made the discovery. One of the boys saw what he thought was a log floating in the shallows, near the iron girders of Peck Bridge. He waded in and rolled it towards himself with his foot before reeling back in horror. He had found the body of sixteen year old Wendy Coffield, the first known victim of the Green River Killer.

Over the next weeks, months, years, Green River's good name – which for generations had signified peace, tranquillity and beauty, was gone forever; stolen by the killer who used it as his grisly trademark.

At first, King County police Lieutenant Jackson Beard thought he was dealing with a straightforward sex killing – a man with too much to drink, picks up pretty girl, is denied what he wants, uses violence, panics, kills, and dumps the body. It was a gruesome crime, but far removed from the kind committed by the most daunting criminal who plagues police forces – the serial killer. He is the most feared of all wanted men because there is no apparent logic, no method or pattern to his madness which could leave valuable clues for lawmen to follow up.

Wendy Coffield was a child prostitute runaway from a nearby town, who had been missing for three months when she was discovered by the boys fishing on 15 July 1982. Five weeks later a one-off sex crime turned into the beginning of the nightmare that has yet to end for the petrified residents of King County. For in a single day three more bodies of young women were found in the river at separate locations.

Over the following years the bodies of women aged between 15 and 36 were found all over King County, in neighbouring Northern Pierce County, and the remains of two were discovered in the state of Oregon, which borders Washington. Police believe that for once the killer deviated from his practice of preying on the small towns and kidnapped his victims to butcher them elsewhere. So far the largest single police operation in US history to capture one man has failed. It has cost in the region of £14 million, involved detectives from seven police forces and the FBI, and has drawn a huge blank. The deck, say police, is stacked hugely in the killer's favour.

Now in the Seattle phone book is a permanent listing for a government agency that did not exist before that bright sunny day in July 1982. It is a seven digit number for the Green River Task Force which waits night and day for new information which could lead to the capture of the killer. Fae Brooks, a spokeswoman for the group which has been formed especially to try to track down the psycopathic sex killer said: 'In terms of statistics, the guy doesn't stop until he is dead or until he's caught. In fact, if anything, it may be that he has gotten more clever over the years.'

Some of the problems the police faced were not in overcoming the ruthlessness or cunning of the killer, but of the attitude of the local population. Although petrified that a killer was stalking the Ivy League fields, mountains and ravines of the communities, police say the local populace developed an unhealthy, complacent attitude towards the murderer because so many of his victims had been involved at some stage of their lives with prostitution. One of the missing girls, nineteen-year-old Tracy Winston, a young prostitute, is now thought to have fallen victim to him in 1983. Her mother summed up the feelings of the grieving parents when she said that attention was being diverted away from catching the killer with the public demanding action against prostitution instead. 'Our kids are being penalized again', she said. 'It sounds silly, but how can you be penalized any more after you've been murdered? We admit freely and openly that our kids had problems but Tracy didn't deserve to die because she wasn't living what was perceived to be a perfect life. The issue was and is this maniac out there, not the lives that some of his victims were leading.'

Lieutenant Dan Nolan of King County Sheriff's Department is a patient man who has been in the police force all his life, and at fifty-two, looks more like a businessman than a policeman. He has worked on every case from traffic offences to first degree murder, and is regarded by his colleagues as a patient, thorough policeman who leaves no stone unturned in his quest for justice. He is second-in-command of the Green River Task Force whose lives have centred on catching this man over the years. He says: 'The man we're looking for is a shade of grey. He is very innocuous, fits right into the community. That is what makes him so very dangerous.'

To protect the investigation the police have revealed little about their suspect, apart from issuing a photofit and these scant details: he is thought to be middle-aged and an outdoors-type who knows the mountains, ravines and streams of the area like the back of his hand. He is remarkably strong, being able to carry the body of a fully grown woman for some distances. On a few occasions witnesses have glimpsed the victims with strange men shortly before they were discovered dead. From these sketchy sightings, police believe that the killer could drive a light-blue pick-up truck speckled with primer paint covering rust spots.

He is a sexual psychopath, his mind tormented perhaps, say experts, by some deep, dark secret from his childhood which induces the terrible anger he vents on his innocent victims. Police will not comment on how he kills his victims, although one psychologist who has worked with them to build up a picture of the death says that the killer probably favours strangulation so he is able to watch his victims suffer as he snuffs the life from them.

The Green River Killer is, above all, very, very clever. He has turned lush meadows and lonely woodlands within a 45 mile radius of Seattle into 'cluster dumps' for his victims. Bodies have been found by mushroom pickers, hunters and joggers, by boy scouts and apple pickers, by bottle scroungers and boys with fishing rods. In one case an amiable psychic said she was drawn straight to the skeleton of one victim after seeing visions of the dead girl over a seven day period. So far there have been 10,000 tips telephoned into the Green River Task Force centre, a handful of bogus confessions from sick glory seekers and 1,000 suspects quizzed – everyone from a devil worshipper to a police officer himself. So far, nothing. Even the faces of two unidentified bodies have been re-constructed by a film expert who worked on the feature film *Gorky Park*. In the film the faces of murder victims in Moscow are re-constituted to help authorities discover their identities. The practice was copied on the two dead women, but it has neither solved their identities nor the identity of the killer.

Lieutenant Nolan, who has been second in command of the hunt for the killer since 1984 says that police officers on the team have learned to live with the disappointment that they have not yet managed to capture the killer. 'The feeling was certainly that we would solve it within a year. When that didn't happen I think we were all frustrated and certainly pretty disappointed. We kind of hit the wall in January 1985. A lot of people started pointing inwardly and saying: "Am I doing my job well enough? Is it possible to solve?" We got clinical psychologists to come out and talk to us about the stress we were going through. We got to a point where we agreed that this was the most difficult investigation that we had ever been involved with and by God, it certainly was worth it and we were going to stay with it until it was solved.'

There is a grudging respect within the Task Force that their quarry is a man who picks his victims well, leaving his hunters with little in the way of witnesses or clues. Unless the police are holding back, apart from the *modus operandi* of their deaths, there is little the killer leaves behind to point them in the right direction. Nolan went on: 'Because he conceals the bodies, because he doesn't want them found quickly, he is clever. Very, very clever. It makes determining death more difficult, leaves no clues.'

The killer has now not struck for three years. Why? Nolan speculates: 'The possibility exists that he's in jail, that he's dead, that he has moved out of the area or out of the country – or that he has quit killing. That is probably the least likely – someone who would commit this number of killings isn't suddenly likely to find his appetite sated.' He added: 'I would love to capture him, to get him to sit down and tell me just why he did this, what drove him. I don't have any idea what this guy's going to tell me, what his secret is. He is still out there, a man with such terrible secrets. . . .'

The Man in the Iron Mask

The great novelist Alexander Dumas immortalized him in his novel of the same name – the story of the wretch kept imprisoned in a mask of iron, his identity shielded from the world, the secret of his crime lodged only with the King and perhaps a few of his trusted advisers. He wore the mask for thirty years, ate with it on, slept with it on. Even at his death the flanged contraption stayed on his face. Who was he? What was the secret of his crime? It is a mystery that has endured to this day with many theories put forward but few concrete answers.

It was on the personal command of the Sun King, Louis XIV, ruler of France, builder of the great Palace of Versailles, that the identity of the man in the iron mask was kept secret – not only from his subjects, but from his court and the jailors. To that end, for three decades, he lived in solitary confinement in different prisons, ending his days in France's most infamous jail, the Bastille. In 1703 when he died, the furniture in his cell was burned, the whitewash on the walls was re-painted to erase any pathetic epitaph to the world and the metalwork of his mask was melted down. Those who had kept his identity secret in life were determined that he should remain anonymous even when he was dead.

The rumours of the man in the iron mask abounded in France before the revolution. Louis was a deity, a divine ruler, whose harsh laws sentenced bread stealers to years of servitude aboard the galleys and death for stealing apples from the royal orchards. Even in an illiterate society as France was at that time, it was no wonder that word of the strange prisoner in the bowels of the Bastille spread across the land. What was he guilty of that spared his life – but condemned him to this living death, trapped in a mask of iron? No correspondence exists between prison officials and court functionaries, but the people had their own fantastic theories. One was that he was Louis XIV's twin brother, who was shut away on the orders of the vain glorious emperor in order to preserve the throne and its privileges for himself. Another theory suggested that he was the illegitimate child of a farm girl, born after a dalliance with the King, and that his resemblance was so close to that of his father that he was imprisoned forever.

Imprisoned for a lifetime.

It was not until fifty years after his death that historians began to probe into the identity of this strange man, and to discover what his crime had been. In 1753, exactly fifty years after he died in the Bastille, a journal kept by one Etienne du Jonca surfaced in Paris. Du Jonca was a lieutenant of the King; literate, educated – and curious. He recorded that in 1698, when the unfortunate man had already spent nearly thirty years behind bars, he was sent to the prison as the King's emissary. He recorded the following: 'Thursday 18 September at 3.00 o'clock, Monsieur de Saint-Mars, Governor of the Château of the Bastille, made his appearance, coming from the command of the Iles-Sainte-Marguerite Pignerol with a prisoner, whom he always caused to be masked, whose name is not mentioned.'

Five days after recording his arrival at the Bastille, du Jonca wrote of the man's death, saying that his removal from the cell and the subsequent burning of his furniture and clothes was carried out with 'great haste'. The King's Lieutenant also noted that the prisoner wore a mask of black velvet and not of iron when he saw him laid out for burial in an unmarked grave. (Whether this was done as a belated attempt at decency by the authorities or not – saving him from burial in the infernal mask – we shall never know.) Etienne du Jonca then testified that the man was buried under the false name of Marchioly. No prison official was allowed to gaze at the face beneath the mask as the corpse was transported from the Bastille under cover of darkness to an unmarked grave somewhere in the vicinity of the city. It is not even known whether or not he received a Christian burial, but it seems likely, for du Jonca also noted that the prisoner received one privilege not usually afforded to inmates of the Bastille – the right to a Bible and Christian worship.

At Villeneuve, in the Bourbonnais region of France, more clues surfaced about how closely guarded the secret of the man's identity was. Peasants there spoke of how, on his journey with the masked prisoner, the governor stopped with his charge at his own château for a meal. Peasants who glanced through the window saw how de Saint-Mars sat opposite his prisoner with two loaded pistols next to his plate, ready to discharge them if the captive made one attempt to reveal his identity to the domestic servants in the château.

Up until the French Revolution in 1789, it was presumed that only de Saint-Mars and the King knew the identity of the prisoner. It was certainly not passed on within the House of Bourbon for neither of Louis' successors knew who he was – and the last ruler of France, Louis XVI, began a frantic search for it at the request of his wife, Marie Antoinette.

When the French Revolution overturned Europe's established order in a tidal wave of change, numerous government agencies were ransacked by rising politicians such as Robespierre. Often the aim was to find information valuable for their own ends; however papers found in the Minister of War's office in Paris shed intriguing light on the secret of France's most celebrated captive. It transpired that for years de Saint-Mars had corresponded with a man named Louvois, a functionary of some kind in the prison service. In July 1669, Louvois wrote to de Saint-Mars: 'The King has commanded that I am to have the man named Eustache Dauger sent to Pignerol. It is of the utmost importance to his service that he should be most securely guarded and that he should in no way give information about himself nor send letters to anyone at all. You will yourself, once a day, have to take enough food for the day to this wretch and you must on no account listen for any reason at all to what he may want to say to you, always threatening to kill him if he opens his mouth to speak of anything but his necessities.' Then another letter, from the King himself, was also unearthed in the War Minister's archives, written to de Saint-Mars, which said: 'I am sending to my citadel of Pignerol, in the charge of Captain de Vauroy, sergeant major of my city and citadel of Dunkirk, the man named Eustache Dauger. You are to hold him in good and safe custody; prevent him from communicating with anyone at all, by word of mouth or writ of hand. So be it.'

Up until the discovery of these letters it was widely believed that the false name he was buried under, Marchioly, was a bastardization of Mattioli, an envoy of the Duke of Mantua who had once incurred the King's wrath. Mattioli did indeed end up in penal servitude in Pignerol, but he and the man in the iron mask were two separate people.

Nineteenth century research into Eustache Dauger proved this: he was one of six brothers, four of whom fell in battle. He came from the northern French fishing port of Dunkirk and was believed at one time to have been a lieutenant in the elite King's Guards – a feat made possible by virtue of his brother's elevation to the nobility.

With his brother circulating in court circles, and himself guarding the heart of the realm, Eustache came close to the wicked Madame de Montespan, the King's mistress and a dabbler in black magic. Those close to the royal circle knew that de Montespan was strong medicine for the King, and that he tolerated her heretical indulgences because he was fascinated by her. It is possible, therefore, that Eustache Dauger became entranced by her, went to a black mass, and was discovered by the King. He could not have him spreading the word that the King's concubine indulged in devil worship. Perhaps that was the reason for the years in jail. Perhaps he was merely jealous, paranoid that a mere soldier was set to steal his sweetheart from him. But why not have him executed? Louis was, after all, a monarch with absolute power.

To this day the secret of the man in the iron mask remains as steadfast as the forged metal which kept his face from the world for over thirty years.

Chapter Two

STATE SECRETS

Spies and spymasters play their never-ending games behind a cloak of secrecy that shields a *mélange* of dirty tricks, blackmail and murder. Read about the spectacular kidnapping of top Nazi Adolf Eichmann by the Israeli secret service; the nightclub dancer whose fatal charms led her into the beds of top military men and ultimately to face a firing squad; and the Rosenbergs, the couple whose twisted allegiance to Moscow made them sell their nation's greatest secret.

Haiti's Voodoo Police

Haiti is one of the poorest countries in the world. Its six million inhabitants exist on an income per head of less than £200 each year. Infants have a one in fifty chance of reaching their first birthday. What little industry there is centres on a few paltry millions made from rum, molasses and tourism. The Haitian people are a bright, sparkling French and Creole speaking nation who struggle in the grip of two terrible forces that have ravaged their land. One is corruption – the other is voodoo.

Haiti is under the spell of voodoo. A popular saying goes that the largely Catholic population worships voodoo gods six days a week – and on Sunday praises Jesus Christ. Haiti's infamous dictator Francois 'Papa Doc' Duvalier realized the sway that voodoo held over his poor blighted land and harnessed it with a vengeance. He created an elite security force which protected him, allowing him to rule over the Caribbean republic like a feudal king. This secret service were the Tonton Macoutes – Haiti's voodoo police. Like the the Gestapo and the KGB, they ruled by fear and kept Papa Doc in riches and power while the wretched masses suffered. The Tonton Macoutes were his praetorian guard, his secret police, his death squads. They controlled every facet of life in Haiti and left behind them a legacy of 40,000 corpses when Papa Doc died in 1971. After him came fifteen years more rule by Jean-Claude 'Baby Doc' Duvalier who, in the fine tradition of despotic dictatorships declared himself President for Life until he had to flee for his life in 1986. Thus ended the brutal reign of the infamous Tonton Macoutes who had probably killed another 20,000 people under the presidency of Baby Doc. What was the secret of their power?

Voodoo is one of the darkest, oldest religions in the world. Even as the people of Haiti starve and succumb to disease, the grip of the religion holds them like a vice. In Port-au-Prince, the capital, there are motor cars and hotels with marble entrances, staffed with polite but restrained natives. But in the hills, when the sun goes down, those same people will offer up blood sacrifices, walk on hot coals and become possessed by demons in their enslavement to black magic.

Voodoo has been in the blood of the Haitian people ever since the late seventeenth century when the French populated their former colony with slaves from west Africa. The religion dwindled through the years in Africa,

Two Tonton members ride past a ceremonial parade.

but remained a potent force on the island. It is a religion which worships the dark side of man's soul, involving summoning up the dead, offering animals for sacrifice and entering into trance-like states.

Papa Doc Duvalier was an evil, corrupt man who knew that harnessing the beliefs and superstitions of the population would, by association, give him great power over them. He came to office in 1957, after Haiti had endured forty years of military rule – first an occupation by the United States and then a military junta. In 1957 Papa Doc took the reins of power and embarked on his voodoo dynasty.

When he was a medical doctor in 1944, plotting his rise to power, he made a study of voodooism because he knew it would make him popular among the superstitious, illiterate peasants. He wrote a book called *The Gradual Evolution of Voodoo* in which he praised the black art as if it were as innocent as a Hans Christian Andersen folk story. He wrote: 'Every country has its own folklore. It is part of its patrimony. It is so in England, Japan and Central Europe.' He then went on to extol the virtues of voodoo as a natural and integral part of the Haitian character. When he became president he wore

Paris suits and English shoes – but the beating of the voodoo drums was never very far from his heart.

Duvalier was a tyrant interested primarily with making life as comfortable and rich for himself as he could, at the expense of the wretched country he ruled over. He promised social reform, education and prosperity. He delivered torture, fear and an iron-fisted rule which ended in death for thousands of his opponents.

When he ruled Haiti, the population lived in fear of his dreaded Tonton Macoutes – the word literally means bogeymen in the Creole dialect. The Tontons were licensed torturers, murderers and robbers. To guarantee the safety of the despot, they took what they wanted from the cringing population, who believed the Tontons were the servants of Baron Samedei – the spirit of death. Many Haïtians believed that Papa Doc was the reincarnation of Baron Samedei on Earth.

Papa Doc changed the colours of the Haitian flag to red and black – the colours of secret voodoo societies – and unleashed the Tontons on their bloody mission. The secret of their power lay in the fear they generated among Haiti's inhabitants. No one was immune from their reach because the president himself had sanctioned their crusade. And the power of the voodoo was with them. In that first year alone, an ex-Tonton later said as many as 600 people died, their throats slit, or their heads bashed in with rocks in remote regions of the island. The world knew little of this wholesale terror for many years – to outsiders Papa Doc retained the image of a philanthropic doctor intent on raising Haiti's poor living standards. To the frightened population he was the voodoo master who, at night, was said to store the bodies of the Tontons in his palace cellar, performing black magic rites upon them until they became Zombies – the living dead. In 1967 when Elizabeth Taylor and Richard Burton starred with Alec Guinness in the screen version of Graham Greene's novel *The Comedians* – a scathing book about life under Duvalier in Haiti – the President was moved to voodoo. Ex-aides reported that he had effigies made of the stars – and stuck them with pins!

The Tontons hid behind the president's power. Armed, hiding behind sinister sunglasses, they displayed none of the sophistication of a secret intelligence service – they were merely the secret police force of a ruthless dictator. They ravaged the land, bartering chickens, flour, jewellery in exchange for lives. In Haitian legend the bogeyman traditionally visited households at Christmas and took naughty children away in his knapsack, never to be seen again. In reality, the Tonton Macoutes carried away thousands of people in their bloody rampage.

While the bogeymen fleeced their countrymen, Papa Doc fleeced the country – creaming off millions in foreign aid to satisfy his lust for fast cars, excellent wines, lavish furnishings. In eccentric gestures he often rode through the presidential gates and threw money from his Mercedes car to the pathetically poor people.

Duvalier went to extremes in his belief in the power of voodoo. He once sent a Tonton Macoute agent to President Kennedy's grave in Arlington Cemetery in Virginia, the United States' most hallowed graveyard for statesmen and warrior sons, to collect a pinch of earth, a withered flower and a vial of air. Papa Doc wanted them for a voodoo rite to imprison President Kennedy's soul and thus control US foreign policy in the area. It is estimated that he built up a personal fortune of some 500 million US dollars, stored safely in Swiss bank vaults.

Duvalier's secret army, dressed in their blue shirts and red scarves, kept the terrified population docile. Through the voodoo priests in the villages, the bogeymen made sure that dues were paid. It was, as one American correspondent observed in 1971, after Papa Doc's death, 'terror by consent'.

After his father's death, Baby Doc Duvalier ascended to the presidency of the embattled republic. Like father, like son, he also exploited and used the terror of the Tonton Macoutes – and if anything he was more ruthless and more greedy than his father.

By the time his father died, the secret of the Tontons was out in the west. Aid from the United States was cut and the Tontons had their name changed to the Volunteers for National Security. It was a name only; they continued with their old ways, murdering, torturing, stealing.

The end came for the tyrant Baby Doc and his servants, the Tontons, in 1986. The President for Life fled for his life after pressure from the United States and internal dissent threatened to engulf him. His departure wreaked a terrible revenge on the Tonton Macoutes whose spell was broken; dozens were dragged out of their homes and butchered with the very machetes which they had wielded against so many helpless victims.

Haiti is still desperately poor and its people the pawns in a never-ending power struggle between politicians and the military. There were two coups in the country this year alone. Newsmen who flooded into the country were shown the graves of the Tontons' victims, Haiti's own killing fields where the unfortunates who couldn't meet their robbing demands or who were deemed undesirables by the Duvaliers, were dumped. The spectre of the bogeyman is lifted – but the voodoo worshippers of Haiti wonder how long the respite will last before another Baron Samedei and his Tontons visit them.

The Eichmann Affair

After the KGB, the CIA and MI5, one agency stands out as the most capable, the most cunning, the most ruthless of the smaller intelligence networks which exist in the world. It is the Mossad, an organization dedicated to the preservation of Israel. In a hostile world, its operatives and agents are more than employees – they are disciples of the state of Israel and understand that the maxim of 'know thine enemy' applies more rigorously to them than to any superpower. The Mossad lives by the creed of a German-born Jewish scientist named Charles Proteus Steinmetz, a pioneering electrical engineer. He once wrote: 'There will come an age of small and independent nations whose first line of defence will be knowledge.' That has become the motto of the Mossad and indeed it could be said to be the motto of the entire Israeli nation. By staying one step ahead of its enemies, Israel has survived and flourished as the spiritual home for the world's Jewish population.

But it was one spectacular act which earned the Mossad the admiration of global spymasters – a top secret operation concerned not with the security of Israel, but an act of revenge, of vengeance, of atonement for the years the Jewish people suffered during the Holocaust. For the Mossad traced, identified and kidnapped one of the most wanted Nazi war criminals. It was a brilliant coup and the forerunner of Israel's policy to this day – that no terrorist is safe, no criminal ever totally free.

Before the kidnapping of Adolf Eichmann in 1960, the Mossad had established itself as the main intelligence agency in the Zionist state. It was born out of the pre-independence days when Jewish guerrillas fought British colonial rule in Palestine. The Haganah, the underground army formed by the Jewish settlers in Palestine, spawned five intelligence branches during the struggle for independence. One of them was the Mossad – in Hebrew, the Institution for Intelligence and Special Assignments. The primary task of the agency, reformed and restructured after the war of independence by prime minister David Ben-Gurion, was to complete Israel's dirty and undesirable tasks, with discretion and success.

Isser Harel was the first chief of the Mossad and most, probably its best. Harel knew no fear, knew no boundaries in his mission to serve the state. He was known as 'Isser the Little' who emigrated from Latvia in 1930; more than any other individual he is credited for making the Mossad the organization it is today. Harel showed cunning and coolness from the first day he landed in Palestine, smuggling a handgun past the stringent British customs, which he had pledged to put to good use in the fight for a Jewish homeland.

After a dedicated war against the British forces, Harel was rewarded with the command of Shin Beth – Israel's second major intelligence service concerned with internal security. Less exciting than Mossad, Harel none the less put his heart and soul into the Shin Beth and within two years, in 1958, he assumed command of all Israeli intelligence operations.

Isser Harel's obsession with secrecy was something of a joke even within the ranks of the Mossad. A popular gag about him was: 'Did you hear about the time Isser jumped into a taxi and the driver asked him where he was going? Isser replied: "Its a secret."' But the apparent frivolity masked a devotion to their boss which was second to none. His height of four feet eight inches was no drawback; only to the public was he 'Isser the Little'. To the agents who knew and worked for him he was Isser the Giant. For a decade he was Israel's chief spymaster, ruling with an autocratic hand. He answered to no one, not even justifying the Mossad budget to the Israeli parliament. Such secrecy guaranteed him the intelligence coup of the century – and earned him a place in history.

Ricardo Klement was an ordinary man. He went to work at the same time each day, bought his wife flowers on her birthday and was nice to his children. In Buenos Aires there was nothing to distinguish him from the countless other foreigners who made up the population of this gracious city, often dubbed 'The Paris of South America.' He was of German extraction, but then so many were; like the British who shopped at the Harrods store in the city, they built their own community, embracing the best of the old world and the new. Only . . . Ricardo Klement had a secret.

Years before, in Germany between 1933 and 1945, he was not Ricardo Klement. He was Adolf Eichmann and his job was mass murder.

Eichman enjoyed the patronage of the highest echelons of the Nazi party. He was a member of the feared SS, rising to the security section of the organization to control the 'Final Solution' – Hitler's euphemism for the extermination of the Jews. Eichmann was the planner. While dregs of humanity may have pulled the triggers and herded the unfortunates into the chambers, Eichmann was the controller – the man who lent intellectual credibility to the monstrous master plan. Six million people died as a result of his planning – the biggest mass murderer in history. What shocked the world was that he had escaped justice at the end of the war.

In 1957 a blind Jew living in a suburb of Buenos Aires heard from his daughter that she was being courted by a man who called himself Nicholas Eichmann. Something triggered itself in the old man's mind; perhaps that this could be the son of the infamous Adolf. He contacted a friend in the German police department – in turn he was put in touch with Fritz Bauer, the public prosecutor of the German province of Hesse. It was Bauer who subsequently delivered to Isser Harel in Tel Aviv the dossier on one of the top ten war criminals still at large. It led to an extraordinary meeting between Harel and David Ben-Gurion. 'I would like permission to bring Eichmann back to Israel,' said Harel.

'Do it,' replied the premier. He had sanctioned the boldest intelligence mission in peacetime of the twentieth century.

Not only was the mission unprecedented in its scope, but the implications of both its successful – or failed – execution were enormous. Harel was not asking for the extradition of Eichmann, trusting to the benevolence or otherwise of the Argentine government. He had known too long that South America was the 'rat run' for fugitive Nazis fleeting from the ruins of World War Two. Harel planned to kidnap Eichmann – a mission so secret that one breath of it would have spelled its end and disgraced Israel in the eyes of the world. No matter that they were after a war criminal – Harel knew that the worst crime in diplomatic and political eyes was the one of being caught.

He assembled a hand-picked team of volunteers within the Mossad ranks and in early 1958 an agent was sent to Buenos Aires on a reconnaissance mission. He checked out the address that the old Jew had relayed to them – 4621 Chacabuco Street, in Olivos, a Buenos Aires suburb. Nothing. The family of Klement no longer lived there, the trail went cold. All the agent managed to gather was that a man whose physical traits resembled those of their quarry used to reside there, but his name was Klement. At the time, that meant nothing to Israeli intelligence.

It was not until 1959, after a Mossad agent paid a discreet visit to the elderly Jewish man, Lothar Hermann, that a detailed dossier was built up on the man they thought was Eichmann. Lother recalled, with the precise attention to detail that blind people have, the speech of his suspect and the physical attributes as they were told to him by his daughter. He also recalled one time when young Nicholas Eichmann had stood in his house and boasted about his father's war service.

A small team of crack Israeli agents, armed with the information supplied by Hermann, stayed on in Buenos Aires. But the budget of the Mossad was not then – and is not now – large enough to expend large amounts of cash without the likelihood of firm results. Harel was on the brink of cancelling the whole operation when in December 1959 an agent picked up a lead. After trailing Nicholas Eichmann from a motor cycle repair shop to a suburb in the

San Fernando district of the city, they were sure they had their quarry. But how sure? The Mossad team had the words of a blind lawyer and a picture from seventeen years ago from SS files. They staked out the suspect house in Garibaldi Street.

The residence was photographed secretly from every angle. More agents were sent in from Israel. The balding bespectacled man did not know he was subject to the kind of scrutiny that once was the domain of the organization he belonged to. But was it him?

The positive proof came on 21 March 1960 when Ricardo Klement got off the bus near his home and walked towards his front door clutching a large bouquet of flowers. From the house came the sound of laughter, the start of a party. A woman greeted him warmly at the door.

One of the Mossad agents scrutinizing the shabby house looked in his dossier and discovered that 21 March was the silver wedding anniversary of SS Colonel Herr Adolf Eichmann. They had found the butcher's lair.

After that events moved rapidly. A team of full-time agents was established in Buenos Aires under the on-the-spot command of Isser Harel. He said he felt had had to take full and personal charge of the operation.

The plan was, in effect, like all the best plans – simple. A travel agency was setup in a European city – still a secret to this day – to process the travel documents and permits for the Mossad team to travel to Argentina. The group's overriding concern was not to be publicly seen to be violating the sovereignty of a friendly nation. There was no other way, however, than a covert mission. Argentina had long given sanctuary to the Nazi war criminals and an official approach, while it might have met with courtesy and public promises of action, would have led to the fugitive escaping into a neighbouring country, or even further abroad. Isser Harel, with the backing of Ben-Gurion, was not prepared to let that happen.

In Buenos Aires, 'safe' houses were rented all over the city. Agents processed by the 'laundry' travel agency flew in from various European cities – no two the same. On 11 May it was decided to snatch Adolf Eichmann.

There were tense moments outside the house on Garibaldi Street that night. Failure meant disgrace in the eyes of the world. Every agent, positioned in their safe houses and outside the home of Eichmann, knew that if the plan was wrong they could count only on their own resources to get clear – and there would be no welcoming committee back home.

Three buses which Eichmann usually caught coming home pulled up. All the passengers disembarked but Eichmann was not among them. On that cold night the Mossad agents prayed that he had not been tipped off and fled as so many other Nazis had.

At 8.00pm another bus arrived and Ricardo Klement, in reality Nazi

Adolf Eichmann, stepped off. The secret mission of the decade was on.

Eichmann wandered, with the same nonchalance that he usually displayed, to the door of his home. He passed a car that appeared to have broken down with two men studying the engine. He did not know that a third man was lying on the floor of the vehicle or that the car parked on the opposite side of the road was positioned to shine its lights directly in front of the parked vehicle he was walking towards. When he got near it he was sandwiched between a wall of light that temporarily blinded him. The man on the back seat of the car jumped out and, with the aid of the accomplices studying the engine compartment, bundled Eichmann into the back seat. With a pistol to his head they muttered: 'Make a sound and you are dead.'

An hour later and Eichmann was in one of the safe houses which the agents had rented. Shackled to a bed, Ricardo Klement was stripped of the identity which had shielded him from justice for fifteen years. The agents checked under his armpit for his SS number, but found only a scar – a crude removal had been attempted. But there was no pretence any longer. The bald man who had devised the timetable for the final solution stood in the pyjamas that the Mossad had bought for him and said: 'Ich bin Adolf Eichmann' – I am Adolf Eichmann.

After the enormity of their capture many of the Mossad agents were overcome with emotion. They had all lost loved ones in the Holocaust which Eichmann had kept running as a smoothly oiled train. Many said afterwards that they expected a monster – what they got was a faceless, balding bureaucrat who recited to them in perfect Hebrew the most holy of Jewish prayers.

Eichmann was kept in the safe house for over a week while phase two of the operation was organized – how to get him out of Argentina.

Harel played a hunch during this period. He thought that the family of Eichmann would go through the usual procedures of checking up where Ricardo Klement had got to – the hospitals, jails, private clinics. But he suspected they would not raise a worldwide hue and cry for a man wanted for some of history's most heinous crimes. And they were right – the secret was safe. Neither did the family set on the tail of the Israeli agents any Nazis who lived in sanctuary in Buenos Aires to pursue the Israelis.

However, soon the Nazi underground whisper was out that something unpleasant could have befallen 'Comrade Eichmann.' That was bad news for Israel and the civilized world too because Harel thought that Dr Josef Mengele, the bestial doctor who carried out grotesque experiments on inmates at the Auschwitz concentration camp was one of those who got away because of the whispers.

But getting Eichmann out of Argentina was the most serious obstacle.

Finally Isser Harel risked all on a simple ploy. He drugged Eichmann, dressed him and his agents in the uniform of El Al, the official airline of Israel, and arranged for a jet to be at Buenos Aires airport. He drove through with the drugged air-crewman, explained that he had sampled too much Agentine hospitality the night before, and asked permission to board the aircraft. 'He's not flying in that state, is he?' asked a customs guard. 'Oh no, we're only the reserve crew,' said Harel. They were through.

Back in Tel Aviv twenty-four hours later Isser the Little walked into David Ben-Gurion's office and said: 'I have brought a little present for you.'

The following day Ben-Gurion made the most moving speech he has ever made to the Israeli parlament, the Knesset:

'I have to announce that a short time ago one of the greatest of Nazi criminals was found by the Israeli secret service. Adolf Eichmann, who was responsible, together with the Nazi leaders, for what they called "The Final Solution of the Jewish Problem" – that is the extermination of six million Jews of Europe.

'Adolf Eichmann is already under arrest in Israel and he will shortly be brought to trial in Israel.'

The rest is history; Adolf Eichmann, who praised his captors from the dock, was found guilty of war crimes and sentenced to death. He was hanged.

The Taking of a Terrorist

The Western world has long groaned at the news of terrorists and their innocent victims for two reasons: first, that the victims are held hostage or killed for beliefs that are alien to them and second, that we seem powerless to do anything about the terrorists themselves. We have all endured the heartbreaking scenes from airports – flashed on to prime-time news reports – as a bundle that was once a human being is pushed from the doorway of a plane to land on the tarmac like excess baggage. In recent years terrorists have dramatically escalated their activities in the air and to a lesser extent at sea. In 1985, a TWA flight from Athens was hijacked shortly after take-off and US Navy diver Robert Stethem was murdered. In October of the same year the *Achille Lauro* ship was hijacked by Arab fanatics and a wheelchair bound US citizen, Leon Klinghoffer, was murdered. In December 1985 a wanton attack at Rome airport killed fifteen people – the massacre sanctioned by terror 'Godfather' Abu Nidal, who was sentenced in absentia by an Italian court to life imprisonment. On the same day Arab fanatics opened up with machine guns and hand grenades at Vienna Airport, killing three and wounding forty-one. The following April a bomb exploded on board a TWA jet as it approached Athens airport. Four US citizens died, and the suspect, a Lebanese woman thought to belong to a Palestinian terror group, escaped. On 5 April 1986 a bomb exploded in a discotheque in West Berlin, killing two US servicemen and wounding 200, including seventy Americans. In September of the same year, in an aborted hijacking in Pakistan, twenty people, were murdered. People groaned uncomfortably in the West – but what was to be done?

No one was more concerned than President Ronald Reagan, a man who put his own personal stamp on the presidency of the United States more than any postwar chief executive since John F. Kennedy. The Reagan years ushered in a new pride in the United States, a new patriotism and belief in the American way. But all that had happened on the international scene pointed to the fact that his citizens – and the citizens of the other 'free' world countries – were easy game for terrorists around the globe. The United States could not stoop to the level of the killers. What could be done? In January 1986 President Reagan signed an order which gave the mightiest nation in the world the right to strike back against the butchers – legally. In doing so he sanctioned one of Western intelligence's most secret operations since the end of the Cold War; a £10 million high-tech kidnapping whose message to terrorists everywhere rings loud and clear: there is no sanctuary anywhere. Reagan put into motion a mission so daring in its concept that it could almost have been penned for the pages of a *Boys' Own* annual. EXCEPT . . . it is true.

Fawaz Younis stood on the tarmac of Beirut airport, clad in a bullet-proof vest and ringed by five murderous looking accomplices who clutched Soviet-made AK 47 assault rifles and, incongruously, Uzi sub-machine guns – the arms of the state of Israel. Younis had just emerged from the cabin of a Royal Jordanian jet where he had overseen fifty-three hours of sheer brutality. The eight Jordanian guards, on his orders, had been tied and beaten senseless, the passengers terrorized in an airborne ordeal which at one time seemed doomed to end in bloodshed and death. However, the terrorists then decided on a course of action that few could have predicted. They released those held prisoner on board the plane and called a press conference. At the end of a rambling speech delivered to waiting cameramen and reporters, the fanatical gunmen on Younis' orders broke the silence of the June morning with the staccato thump of bullets from their weapons into the plane, setting off explosives which destroyed it completely. Then they vanished into the labyrinth of terrorist hideouts in Beirut.

Younis had emerged in the bloody battle-ground of the middle east as a power-player in lethal games. He had access to the top-level leaders of various Shiite militiamen and had been involved in several terror operations before the hijacking of the Royal Jordanian aircraft. He was one of the terrorists on the hijacked TWA flight which resulted in the death of US Navy diver Robert Stethem. More importantly, to US intelligence, he was 'visible', walking openly around Beirut and boasting of his evil trade. In 1986 it was decided to capture him and bring him to trial in the United States.

The mission to seize Younis was spawned at a top-secret meeting hosted by President Reagan in January 1986. Frustrated at the inability of the world's democracies to hit back at terrorism, the President signed a classified intelligence document authorizing the CIA to identify terrorists who had committed crimes abroad and to help bring them to trial in the USA. It gave the authority for Operation Goldenrod to be put into action.

Goldenrod's aim was to capture Younis after he had been 'targeted' by US intelligence agents in Beirut. His crimes were not as heinous as those of the killer aboard TWA Flight 847, or of the Rome or Vienna murderers, but he had broken international law by leading a hi-jack. More importantly, he had not gone to ground. There was a further meeting with the President in October 1986 in which the final sanction was given to capture Younis.

The operation was to be a tri-partisan affair between the CIA, the DEA and the FBI, with the latter's executive assistant director Oliver Revell heading the effort. He told the team: 'This is going to be one of the most important counter-terrorism operations ever staged by the US government.' But the problems facing the team were immense. Reagan did not want the United States branded with piracy over a kidnapping. Nor did he want to run the risk of losing Younis on the long route back home to the United States; this one, he decreed, was for the US alone. It meant that somehow Younis would have to be lured on to a ship or an aeroplane and then taken at all speed, and without stopping, to the United States.

Fortunately for the planners, a bit of good fortune came their way early on with the news that an informer had been recruited by DEA officials in Cyprus. There, on the island that has become a staging post for drug runners and small-time arms dealers, was a disillusioned Lebanese man called Jamal Hamdan. Hamdan used to live in Beirut and was once the driver and right-hand man for a guerrilla leader, with whom he shared an apartment for six months. That man was called Fawaz Younis.

Hamdan agreed to sell information on drug peddlers and other crooks whenever he received knowledge at his home in Larnaca. But Goldenrod's architects saw in him someone far more valuable than a low-level 'grass' on hashish movements. They saw him as the bait to trap Younis. By getting Hamdan to agree to re-establish his friendship with Younis, they set in motion the first steps to getting Younis on to US soil.

The first link was made in March 1987 when Hamdan called Younis from his apartment. They talked about old times, the weather, Younis' two children. It was the first of over sixty calls which led to Hamdan inviting the terrorist to his apartment in July. The bearded terrorist did not know that when he arrived a team of electronic 'spooks' from the three US agencies involved had been there before him, turning the apartment into a giant listening device. Bugs bristled in the bathroom, kitchen, bedroom, even in the toilet. The United States was determined that if Fawaz Younis was going to be tried, he would damn himself with his own evidence.

The listening devices paid off. Younis not only boasted of his role in the Royal Jordanian skyjacking but also his part in the TWA one in which a US Navy diver died. The listeners recording his boasts realized that Younis would be valuable for information about guerrilla factions in Beirut when he let it slip that he had received orders for the hijacking from none other than Nabih Berry, the head of the Amal militia. One of the extracts which the FBI released has Younis talking about the June 1985 hijacking which ended with the plane being destroyed. He said: 'I got inside and I locked the plane's captain in the cockpit. The people were on the floor, their hands on their heads. Everyone, no exceptions. I got a stewardess and asked her about the security men. There were eight. I took their neckties and tied their hands behind their backs. We started beating them. We took four machine guns and eight pistols from them. We kept them tied up for forty-eight hours. We stayed fifty-three hours flying.'

There was a second visit to Hamdan in August, during which the 'friends' went on a five-day bar crawl around the island's clubs. At this meeting Younis had complained that he was short of money. Hamdan, supplied from a special slush-fund set up for the operation, handed Younis US $4000. The news of his cash problems was good for the secret agents. They knew they could probably capitalize on that to their advantage. When Younis visited

Cyprus for a second time that month, the lure of earning big money, tax free, was put in front of him. Hamdan said that a drug dealing friend known as Joseph was willing to pay big money for someone to act as a courier for his illegal merchandise. Would Younis be interested? He said he would.

Once Younis agreed that he would consider any option – as his second-hand car dealing business was bankrupt and he had little money from taxi-driving in Beirut – Goldenrod's controllers put in phase two of their plan; luring him off Cyprus soil and getting him to the United States as fast as possible. There was no way President Reagan would tolerate having Younis' feet touch any soil other than American. The hijackers of the *Achille Lauro*, who murdered a wheel-chair bound American citizen, were forced down in their Tunisian-bound jet in Italy where the authorities insisted on trying them there. Reagan said only US justice was to try Younis – and that was final.

Commander Philip Voss is one of the most experienced pilots in the US forces. He has clocked up over 3,000 flying hours alone on the S-3 Lockheed Viking aircraft, one of less than twenty fliers in the world with as much experience. He was in charge of a squadron of the anti-submarine aircraft aboard the USS Saratoga, an aircraft carrier, when on 27 August 1987, he received a top-level security cleared call from Washington to say he would be involved in a highly secret mission requiring him to fly a great distance. He was told that it would be from somewhere in the Mediterranean to somewhere in the United States. He was told to plan the logistics of re-fuelling and routing, but not to breathe a word about what was being planned. When he drew up a plan he was told to wait and remain silent.

On 7 September FBI officials, together with Pentagon chiefs, decided on the final stages of the plan and the next day it was presented to Attorney General Edwin Meese. He signed it. Goldenrod was on and running.

On 10 September Younis returned to Cyprus for his assignment with the mystery drug runner Joseph. To keep up the appearance of a free-spending pal, more cash was forwarded from the agencies' slush fund for Hamdan to entertain his friend. As the duo lifted their glasses in 'cheers' in a Larnaca nightclub, the ink was just drying on an arrest warrant that had been signed for Fawaz Younis. Hamdan told him that they were to meet with Joseph on the boat he used to transport his merchandise and so the pair stayed the night of 12 September at the Sheraton Hotel in Limassol. The following morning Hamdan's 'brother' – a CIA man – ferried them from the shore to an eighty foot yacht which looked as if it might have a wealthy owner. The trip took ninety minutes, so the yacht was well out into international waters.

Younis dressed as if he were headed for a deck party. He wore beige shorts, a green shirt and sandals, expensive gold rings, necklace and watch. As Hamdan had warned him he would be, he was searched, as Joseph insisted on security aboard his vessel. Then he was given a cool beer and led to the stern where he could talk with Joseph about the job. When he reached the back of the boat, two men nodded at each other in unison. Then acting together they kicked his legs, sending him plummeting to the wooden deck. He hit it so hard that he instantly broke both his wrists. As his hands were bound, FBI special Dimitry Droujinski told him in Arabic he was under arrest by the government of the United States of America and would be sent there for trial. He said nothing, but his look of stunned disbelief spoke volumes.

Within an hour the yacht had met up with the USS *Butte*, a navy ammunition ship which took charge of the wounded Younis and set sail for the Balearic islands to meet up with the USS *Saratoga* and the S-3 plane which would take Younis to the United States.

It took four days to reach the aircraft carrier, during which time Younis was quizzed and admitted his part in the hijackings. Then on 17 September he was strapped into the S-3 plane and catapulted off the deck of the carrier at a speed of 135 miles per hour. The plane then linked up with a circling tanker which replaced the fuel load burned during take-off. 'It's a goer' signalled Voss to the ship and headed his plane on the course for home.

Halfway across the Atlantic he hooked up with the second tanker aircraft for re-fuelling. After that he had just one more hurdle – the civilian air traffic controllers at Andrews Air Force Base in Maryland who had not been told about the operation because the military feared possible security leaks. After a thirteen hour ten minute flight – the longest solo flight in history accomplished from an aircraft carrier – Commander Voss was asked to identify himself before being given permission to land. Luckily officials monitoring the challenge interrupted and told the air traffic controllers: 'Stop him and you explain yourself to the President.' They let him through.

Fawaz Younis was surrounded by fifteen FBI limousines as he stepped from the aircraft in the pouring rain. His trip to meet Joseph had been a one-way ticket halfway across the world into captivity.

He now awaits trial in solitary confinement. A jubilant state department official said: 'We hope this new policy hits home to terrorists everywhere. You can run – but you can never hide. He will be the first of many.'

The Rosenbergs

The date was the 19 June, the year 1953. Old Sparky, the name given to the electric chair in Sing Sing prison, was being tested by Joseph Frankel, who lived near the infamous jail in Cairo, New York. 'Electrician' Joe, as he was known, was due to collect 300 dollars for his night's work – despatching a pale skinny man and his slightly plumper wife to their maker. In his time Joe had plunged the switch and sent the electricity surging through the bodies of countless mafia hitmen, rapists, robbers, nickel-and-dime killers. But tonight was different. Tonight Joe was making history as he threw the switch which would send Julius and Ethel Rosenberg into oblivion. They were spies who sold out their country to the communists at a time when the cold war was at its coldest – in fact the only enemy agents ever to be executed in the United States in peacetime.

Shortly before midnight Joe placed the electrodes on Julius Rosenberg's head, strapped the other electrodes to his chest and arms, and placed a leather hood over his face. Two minutes and forty-five seconds later, with smoke still in the air, he was pronounced dead. After a few minutes to clear the air, his wife was brought in and the ghastly scenario was repeated. After four minutes and thirty seconds she too was pronounced dead. The Rosenbergs, who had made treachery their trade, were no more – two of the Kremlin's most valuable agents, who buried themselves deeply into ordinary suburban life, paid the ultimate price for their actions. This is their story.

Outwardly the Rosenbergs were no different from thousands of other US citizens of Russian–Jewish descent whose forefathers had come to the land of the free to seek a better life. Both were raised in a close-knit community on the Lower East Side in New York, an ethnic melting pot which encompassed people of practically every race on earth. They were poor but, by all accounts, well loved. Ethel, whose maiden name was Greenglass, became a clerical worker after graduating from Seward Park High School. The bespectacled, austere looking Julius, who once nurtured a desire to become a Rabbi, opted instead for an engineering course at the City College of New York in Manhattan. It was at a dance one night that he met the woman who was to become his wife and partner in treachery.

The couple married in 1939, before the outbreak of World War Two, which would see the Germans marching over Europe. Until 1945 Julius was a civilian in the Army Signals Corps and earned fifty dollars a week for

Ethel and Julius Rosenberg.

inspecting electrical equipment. It was a easy job and one which didn't require him to see active service overseas. He lived with his wife in Greenwich Village during the war years and they had two sons, Michael and Robert. Always financially insecure, the Rosenbergs made do like thousands of others and managed to muddle through with the dream that one day things would be better. But they were different from the majority of other people who came to America to earn the mighty dollar and fulfil their dreams. For they were communists who believed that the international socialist doctrine preached from Moscow was the only creed worth adhering to. Julius had been a communist from his earliest days in college. He was clever enough to keep the fact quiet – then, as now, the most stridently anti-communist country was the United States. His covert membership of the US communist party cost him his job in 1945. He was fired when a routine FBI investigation of personnel proved his allegiance to Moscow. With a family to feed, he opened up his own business, Pitt Engine Products, in the same building as a synagogue in down town New York. The venture was plagued by bad cash-flow and poor management. However, Julius struggled on with it and did not have to worry about a knock on the door from the FBI because of his strongly held beliefs. But the knock did come eventually – and it was eventually to cost the doomed Ethel and Julius Rosenberg their lives.

For nondescript Julius Rosenberg, together with his wife and her brother, David Greenglass, sold the United States' most prized secret – the formula for the atomic bomb, to the Soviet Union. It was the most heinous of crimes against a state which had assumed the role of free-world protection.

David Greenglass was seized by the FBI on 15 June 1950 and questioned at length. Greenglass worked at the top-secret Los Alamos site in New Mexico during the war years making 'lenses' – the detonators for the atomic bomb. Everyone within the complex that produced the A-bombs which wiped out Hiroshima and Nagasaki were security-cleared in case of alien loyalties. Greenglass had slipped through the net.

From Los Alamos he stole detailed drawings of the atomic bomb, together with copious notes of how it worked, how it was assembled, what was required to make it. His D-I-Y atom bomb secrets were fed directly through Julius and Ethel to Moscow emissaries in the United States and back to the Kremlin. Greenglass was caught as part of a wide-reaching FBI probe and, to save his own skin, readily implicated the Rosenbergs.

It turned out that a pathetic little Swiss immigrant called Harry Gold, who was the US courier for another major spy, was the go-between for the Rosenbergs and Greenglass. He would meet Greenglass using a code procedure worked out by Rosenberg. At a secret rendezvous point Gold would hand Greenglass the top of a jelly packet with the words 'I come from Julius' written on it. This meant that the coast was still clear and that the Rosenbergs required more information to pass on to their Soviet spymasters.

The United States led the world in nuclear research and had overtaken the Nazis in the race for atomic supremacy. Selling the secrets of their technology was just about the worst crime that they could have committed – especially as it was discovered in the McCarthy Era when the senator of the same name embarked on his witch hunts to root out anything and everyone deemed to be left wing and un-American in their actions, deeds and thoughts.

Gold, who worked as a chemist in Philadelphia before he became embroiled in espionage, was also the courier for top spy Klaus Fuchs. Fuchs was born in Germany and became a communist in his teens. When Hitler came to power he fled to England where he became a citizen. He was part of the British mission given top-level clearance to witness research and tests on the bomb. He too used the services of Gold and confessed to spying in 1950, receiving a fourteen year prison term. To this day it is not known whether he worked independently of the Rosenbergs or with them.

Another person indicted with the Rosenbergs was Morton Sobell, once Julius Rosenberg's classmate at college, who passed on secrets to the couple about the latest radar technology he worked on for the US Navy.

The arrests came in 1950 – Julius first in July and his wife twenty-five days later. The FBI dossier on the Rosenbergs and the others ran to some 40,000 pages and chronicled the information which they had channeled to Moscow in the years 1940 to 1948. At their trial it was claimed that their acts of treason alone had given Russia the Atom bomb – they exploded their first in 1949 when American intelligence had reckoned that it would have taken them fifteen years at least to catch up in the nuclear race. Thanks to the Rosenberg's misty-eyed idealism, the Russian bear was armed, ready for the cold war and the build-up of ballistic missiles.

The fifteen day trial in 1951 was a sensation which riveted the world. Gold's testimony particularly damned the couple as he told of the secret rendezvous he kept with Greenglass. And Greenglass in turned showed no emotion as he poured out the details of the secrets which would send his own sister and brother-in-law to the electric chair. Although he passed the secrets of the bomb on to Julius, he said his sister was a willing co-conspirator who was glad to play her part in ending 'world fascism'. He said she often stayed up late at night and typed up the careful notes which would be passed on to their Soviet controllers.

Another star witness was Elizabeth Bentley, who testified for the government. A Columbia university graduate, she told how she was lured into the ranks of the communists through several disastrous love affairs with Soviet agents. Though without direct knowledge of the Rosenberg's activities, she nevertheless played a crucial role for the state in its conspiracy charges against the couple – testifying that all communists were harmful to the United States because their loyalty lay with Moscow alone.

The jury were convinced and returned guilty verdicts, confirming that the Rosenbergs, who said nothing at all at their trial other than that they were innocent, conspired to commit espionage against the United States in time of war. They were handed down the death penalty by Judge Irving Kaufman, who branded them 'despicable traitors' and, rightly or wrongly, said their actions had led to the Korean war in which 50,000 Americans were to lose their lives. He said Julius had been the 'prime mover' of 'this diabolical conspiracy' and Ethel 'a fully fledged partner'.

Morton Sobell got a thirty year sentence, of which he served sixteen. David Greenglass, who stole the secrets but did not pass them on to the Soviets directly, was treated remarkably leniently, receiving a fifteen year sentence. He is now out of jail and lives under a new name somewhere near New York. Despite twenty two appeals and stays of execution, Julius Rosenberg, thirty-five, and Ethel, thirty-seven, had to die for an administration that demanded blood for the betrayal of its mightiest secrets.

After the switch was thrown that night and the Rosenberg children were adopted by another couple, the doubts and inquests on their guilt or innocence were raised around the world. In Cuba twenty-five years on the Castro regime even issued commemorative stamps bearing their portrait and the legend that they were 'assassinated' by the United States. But those close to the case, even a human rights lawyer who detests the death penalty, remain convinced that the quiet couple who beavered away by day in the machine shop were, by night, agents in a far more murky, more lethal world. 'It is a ghastly and shameful episode' said top Yale law professor Alexander Bickel, 'but I believe they were guilty.' Roy Cohn, the prosecutor, says: 'I feel the guilt was proven overwhelmingly and has stood the test of time.'

Only one man's conscience and heart was not touched by the deaths of the Rosenbergs. For Joe the electrician it was just another job, albeit a celebrated one, among the 137 he carried out before he retired from Sing Sing.

Mata Hari

Mata Hari was the most famous of all women spies, using beauty, seduction, and sexuality to squeeze secrets from men who might have withstood any torture, save that inflicted by a lovely woman's charms.

Mata Hari was born in the Dutch town of Leeuwarden on 7 August 1876 as Margaretha Geertruida Zelle. She led an ordinary childhood, was an ordinary student and made the same moans that most teenagers do when they long to do more exciting things. For her that excitement meant moving to a teacher's college near Amsterdam when she was eighteen.

But Margaretha quickly tired of studying and, a year later, married an army officer who took her off to Java. It was here that she first heard the native name 'Mata Hari', – meaning 'eye of the day' – the name under which she would sell military secrets and the name under which she would die.

For the next seven years of her marriage, Margaretha lived the life of an upper-class colonial woman. But she was a woman acutely aware of her own beauty. In Java she started the dalliances which proved to her that her seductive charms could win her anything she wanted. Her husband found out about her affairs but played the part of a cuckolded husband well. He tolerated Margaretha's infidelity for a number of years before taking her back to Holland where they separated and later divorced.

Margaretha found herself with little money in 1902 and so decided to take up the one thing that had been attractive to her as a teenage girl – dancing. She was a very provocative professional and the dancing was strictly for men only. However, Paris was the place to be in cabaret so, in 1905, she moved to the French capital to continue her dancing – and her affairs.

It was there that she adopted the name Mata Hari, that she had first heard used in Java. History is blurred on her days in Paris, but papers released by French authorities last year showed she had many lovers, most of them military officers. Such dalliances were to damn her when the Great War arrived and the world was divided into armed camps. She stayed in Paris for two years after 1914, as the Kaiser's forces were locked in stalemate with the allied armies on a broad front stretching from the channel ports to the frontier of Switzerland.

In 1916 Mata Hari moved back to The Hague, in neutral Holland, – and it was there that she moved into espionage. She fell into the bed of a German diplomat who asked her for details of the French armies in two vital sectors; one was the Somme front where an Anglo-French offensive was expected. The other was at Verdun, which had been heavily fortified and ringed by steel and concrete constructions. The diplomat promised her cash.

The French were later to allege that Mata Hari gleaned the secrets of the French strengths from her lovers in the French Army. What is known is that she was betrayed to the French authorities in 1917 after she had gone to Paris to pass on some intelligence about French battle plans to a Prussian officer. In a war which was bleeding France, she was tried, sentenced to death by a military court and executed on 15 October 1917 by a firing squad.

What were the secrets that she had passed on? Certainly news of Verdun and the Somme offensive could be deemed to be damaging to the war effort of the allied nations. But European capitals were full of agents, and the Somme offensive was certainly no secret to the Germans who knew about it months before it began. Who was it who betrayed Mata Hari?

Since 1917 historians have been puzzled about the whole affair – particularly the French government's refusal to allow public scrutiny of papers sealed in 1917 about Mata Hari. But in 1985 a US journalist, Russell Warren Howe claimed he was shown the secret papers of the spy lady Mata Hari at the Chateau de Vincennes – the very place where she was executed. He claims that the papers show she was not a German agent, but a freelance 'operative' whose sole espionage effort was in Madrid working for the French. Howe says she seduced a German military attaché there and spent three days in bed

Mata Hari in an unusually demure pose.

with him, but the information she got was stale or inaccurate.

Howe claims she did accept money from German intelligence, but all she gave them were easily culled newspaper reports and old gossip. But France in the Great War was rife with anti-foriegn sentiments and had suffered appalling losses which at one time threatened to break the army. Inept generals were to blame, but a scapegoat in the form of a conniving woman seemed a far better bet, argues Howe. At her trial she was charged with peddling secrets which cost the lives of hundreds of thousands of allied servicemen. And the Germans – who believed that Mata Hari had cheated them as a double agent – sent messages in a code which they knew the French had broken implicating her in the espionage charges.

Whichever story is true – that she was a German spy, a French spy or both – Mata Hari broke the ground rules of espionage in that she was indiscreet and naïve enough to think that her bed-hopping would not alert informers. Who actually informed on her is, to this day, still a secret.

Chapter Three

SECRETS OF THE HEART

Love makes men murder, rulers give up their thrones and has made politicans compromise brilliant careers – read on to find out if the lovely Lady Diana Delves Broughton took the secret of her lover's murder to the grave; were President Kennedy and his brother Bobby bedding the greatest sex symbol of the age?; and why was a King's love affair kept from his subjects for so long...?

The Murder In Happy Valley

There was plenty of belt-tightening and digging for victory in wartime Britain as the embattled island braved German bombers and the threat of all-out invasion. In 1940 in particular, the prospects of the tiny British Isles fighting a prolonged war seemed grim indeed. Merchant ships bringing vital supplies into home ports ran a terrifying gauntlet of U-boat wolf packs which daily inflicted greater and greater losses. Everyone from office girls to shopworkers were engaged in war work. There were no luxuries to be had in the shops, nothing to look forward to except a pitifully small meat allowance and dried eggs.

But over 3,000 miles from Britain's shores there was a place where the war was hardly even a distraction; where living was luxurious, riotous, flamboyant, drunken and debauched. In this place the love lives of the inhabitants were matched only by their unquenchable thirsts for fine champagne and rare brandy. In the beautiful countryside of Kenya, one of Imperial Britain's finest colonial possessions, existed a privileged clique of expatriates who turned one of the country's most splendid regions into their own enclave of hedonism. They were the Happy Valley Set and, until murder most foul interrupted their sordid, cocaine-snorting, sex-filled lives, they caroused and partied with a determination probably unmatched since the days of the Romans.

Happy Valley was situated in the White Highlands of Kenya near to the Wanjohi River, not far from the capital of Nairobi. It was splendid country where tobacco and coffee, along with cattle and sheep, were raised by the wealthy colonials who settled there. But Happy Valley seemed destined to attract more than its fair share of scoundrels and rogues than other Empire outposts. The 'Little England', replete with country clubs like the Muthaiga Club, with its well-stocked bars and spacious bedrooms, cultivated a lifestyle among exiled aristocrats which – while pleasurable – was guaranteed one day to end in tragedy. Act One of that tragedy, which unfolded like a Shakespearean love drama, came with the arrival in Happy Valley of Josslyn Hay, the thirty nine-year-old Earl of Erroll and High Constable of Scotland.

Josslyn Hay dedicated his life to philandering with other peoples' wives and had his very own personal motto: 'To Hell with Husbands!' He dressed in

Savile Row-tailored evening suits and smoked cigarettes which bore his personal monogram. As a thoroughly black sheep – expelled from Eton, cited in a British divorce court where the judge called him 'a very bad blackguard' – Kenya offered this accomplished womanizer and seducer rich pickings. It was also, cynics suspected, a 'cushy' spot for the recently enlisted Hay who landed the post of Military Secretary there – well away from the bombs and deprivations of the home front. Kenya was the focal point for mustering British forces planning the assault on Italian-occupied Ethiopia. Apart from memo writing and answering to higher command, there was little for Josslyn Hay to do except womanize – the thing that he was most expert at.

Hay would probably have sat out the war and died comfortably many years later with a gin in his hand and a woman at his side if a certain Diana Delves Broughton, the beautiful bride of Sir Henry Delves Broughton, had not entered the Happy Valley enclave. Diana, twenty six, arrived with Sir Henry – known as Jock to his friends – in November 1940. Formerly Diana Caldwell, she had married a man thirty years her senior after meeting him at a race meeting in England. He was newly divorced and they married at the end of October and were in Kenya within a week. Sir Henry had opted for life in the colony for several reasons, but mostly because he was struggling financially and planned a last-ditch venture raising cattle there. Everyone who knew him was aware that horse racing was the greatest love of his life – and he embraced it with a passion that cost him untold thousands. He still had money, but not enough to live as wildly as he once had. His savings, though, would guarantee a gracious life in Kenya.

The marriage with Diana was a strange one from the outset. Diana was both beautiful and young and Jock was old – and ageing fast. He knew that for him the marriage was a bond of companionship more than anything else. Those who knew him said they sensed a certain fatalism about him, that it was as if he knew he could not hold on to his ravishing young wife for long. But not even he thought that their marriage would flounder literally within weeks of stepping into the African sunshine.

On 30 November 1940, the sparkling eyes of Diana met those of Josslyn Hay across the bar of the Muthaiga Club – and she fell in love instantly. She had already heard of Josslyn Hay's reputation as a seducer; as a man who derived as much pleasure from seeing the cuckolded husbands squirm as he did from making love to their wives. None the less, there was a genuine sexual chemistry between the two. Josslyn Hay calmly walked over to her and, she was later to recall, spoke these first words to her: 'Well, who's going to tell Jock, you or I?'

Hay, who had been married twice before – his first marriage ending in divorce, his second wife dying from drinking and drugs – courted Diana

The Earl of Erroll and Lady Diana Delves Broughton.

shamelessly in front of the exiled aristocrats. They flaunted their affection at tea dances, dinners, cocktail parties and club banquets. If they tried to keep it from the one person who could claim a right to know – Jock – they didn't make a very good job of it. He knew he was being made a fool of by a younger man, but did little to change the situation. It was even brought to his attention by anonymous letters left in his pigeon hole at the Muthaiga Club. Two months after the affair had begun, on 6 January 1941, an unsigned note left for him read: 'You seemed like a cat on hot bricks last night. What about the eternal triangle? What are you going to do about it?' Some days later a friend who sat next to the elderly Jock as he sipped gin slings at the Muthaiga, watching his wife and Hay dance, whispered to him: 'Do you know that Joss is madly in love with Diana?' It is inconceivable that Jock could not help but know, especially as just twelve days later another anonymous note in his pigeon hole informed him that Diana had spent a weekend with Joss at a friend's home in Nyeri; expeditions which Diana had told Jock were 'girls only' outings to swim and watch big game.

There are conflicting reports about what kind of man Sir Henry Delves

Broughton was. Some say he was an outlandish snob with a contempt of anyone born out of his social sphere; others that he was a kindly old gent who asked for little more than some ready cash to spend on his beloved horses and a wife to give him a little companionship in his old age. An old Etonian – like his rival in love (only he wasn't expelled) – Jock exemplified the stiff-upper-lip attitude of the British everywhere when confronted with an unpleasant situation. He said nothing, perhaps in the misguided notion that his wife's fling with Joss Hay was no more than girlish affection. But on 18 January, the same day as Jock received the second note, Diana went to him and told him she was leaving him for Hay.

In a pathetic attempt to win his wife back he asked her to accompany him on a three month cruise to Ceylon so she could reconsider her decision. Then in a move which showed his utter grasp of unreality about the whole affair, he said she could take Joss with them if it pleased her! Diana had no intention of changing her mind or going on the cruise; she used the pretext that Joss was too busily engaged in war work to go off around the world, and she was certainly going nowhere without her lover. The following day Hay presented Diana with a string of pearls and on 20 January Diana walked out on Jock.

Sombre Jock watched his wife drive out of the estate gates for the last time. If he was upset, he did not show it to the staff, but rather set to work in a bid to erase the pain he must have been feeling.

The following day, 21 January, he telephoned the police to say that burglars had entered the house at night and had stolen two revolvers – both in his possession since his First World War service – some cash and a cigarette case. After completing formalities with police officers, he went to see a lawyer about getting a divorce. Then he penned a letter to a friend in England: 'They say they are in love with each other and mean to get married. It is a hopeless position and I am going to cut my losses. I think I'll go to Ceylon. There's nothing for me in Kenya any longer.'

Two days after that, the few British people of the Happy Valley set who did not indulge in the sordid revels beloved by the majority of the region rallied round 'poor old Jock'. He was invited to tea by a close friend, Mrs Carberry. Unfortunately, Diana and Hay were there too, invited by a third party. But there were no challenges to a duel. Sir Henry Delves Broughton behaved impeccably towards them both. In fact he was such a model of civility and charm that Hay later remarked to a friend: 'Jock could not have been nicer. He has agreed to go away. As a matter of fact he has been so nice it smells bad.'

That evening there was more generosity of spirit from Jock. At a club party where the affair had ceased to be a secret months ago, Jock raised his champagne glass and said: 'I wish them every happiness. May their union be blessed with an heir. To Diana and Joss.' The glasses were clinked and the Happy Valley hedonists echoed the words of Jock as they toasted the lovers.

Three hours later Lord Erroll, philanderer, scoundrel, wife-stealer, was dead – his brains blown out by point-blank pistol shots to the head.

Sir Henry Delves Broughton had staggered to his bed, much the worse for drink, at 2.00 a.m. the morning after the party. Lord Errol had promised that he would bring Diana home to spend one more night under Jock's roof – Jock's last request before Diana walked out of his life forever. He arrived at the mansion in his Buick and delivered Diana safely at 2.15 a.m. At 3.00 a.m. Lord Erroll was found dead, slumped beneath the dashboard of the car which had left the road four kilometres from Delves Broughton's home and had plunged into a pit. He was discovered by two labourers walking along the Nairobi-Ngong road and had been shot at point blank range with a .32 revolver. Two hours later the news was broken to Jock and Diana. The former took it with a look of stunned disbelief – Diana was so distraught she had to be sedated.

But what the police failed to tell them was how Hay died. They let Jock and Diana think that they believed that Hay met his end in a straightforward road accident. The police had already pinpointed Jock as their chief suspect – he had motive, means and willpower to commit murder – and wanted twenty four hours to gather evidence before bringing charges.

The following day Diana, still hazy from the sedatives which had been pumped into her to calm her down, gave a scented handkerchief to Jock and told him to drive to the morgue in Nairobi and place it on Hay's body. Bemused, he did so, handing it to a guard, saying: 'Please place this on his body would you? My wife was very much in love with Lord Erroll.'

In the afternoon there was a bonfire in Jock's garden – numerous articles were consigned to the flames after being doused with petrol. Only one charred artefact survived – a bloodstained Argyll sock. On 25 January, just as Lord Erroll's coffin was being lowered into the ground, the police announced publicly in Kenya that he had not been the unfortunate victim of a road crash, but of a cold-blooded killer. They revealed what they believed was the scenario; that a man had either flagged the car down, or had been sitting next to Hay, when he forced the car to slow down and fired the fatal shots. The car was then pushed off the road with the dying Earl pushed under the dashboard. The implication for Diana was inescapable -- her cuckolded husband had killed her lover. The champagne toast and the wishes of good luck were all a cruel trick. Jock had committed murder.

It was the same conclusion drawn by the police, although Jock was not formally charged with the murder until 10 March. For the most part, there was great sympathy for the aristocratic old gentleman – but also a great deal of surprise, not to say astonishment, when Diana suddenly flew to Johannesburg to hire the best criminal lawyer in Africa to defend him! Jock came to trial in June and it was a sensation for the newspapers. Weary of reporting depressing news about the bombing, blackout and rationing, the steamy scandal was played out in the full glare of publicity for a public hungry for such intriguing revelations.

The case against Jock was this; that he had the motive to kill Hay, that bullets found near his home at a practice shooting range matched those found at the murder scene and that the bonfire, which failed to consume the bloodstained sock, was set to burn clothes which he mistakenly splashed with blood during the killing. The prosecution alleged that the toast to the good health of Hay and Diana was a sham, perpetrated only to hide Jock's real intent – murder. It was alleged that far from being drunk on champagne, Jock had merely feigned his boozy state, slipping out later to intercept the car – knowing that Hay would stop – and then killing him.

Harry Morris, the brilliant South African lawyer hired to represent Jock by his wife, destroyed the most vital piece of police evidence – the gun theory – by bringing in an expert who testified that there was no way the bullets which killed Hay could have been fired from Jock's gun. Moreover, the murder weapon had not been found. As for the bonfire – what was the significance of one blood-stained sock, so badly charred that the blood was unuseable for forensic examination?

For his part, Sir Henry performed magnificently in the witness box. He already had that most valuable ally – public opinion – on his side, and with his gracious manner and stern denial of foul play, won the jury's heart.

On 1 July 1941 Jock emerged into Nairobi's bright sunshine a free man after the jury unanimously found him not guilty.

Whodunnit? Through the years the Happy Valley murder has remained an enigma that could, possibly, have been answered by only one person – Diana herself. But she died in 1987, rich, extravagant and secretive to the last. Did she know who pulled the trigger? Certainly, she patched up, to an extent, her relationship with Jock after the trial. They did take the cruise to Ceylon after all, although halfway through he fell hard on the deck, badly injuring his back. The injury left him with partial paralysis and he returned to England while Diana eventually made her way back to Kenya. Sir Henry commited suicide, in 1942 in Liverpool, leaving notes in which he said the strain of the trial, and ensuing publicity, was too much to bear.

June Carberry, who invited Jock to the tea at her place only to find Hay and Diana showing up too, testified at his trial that she had stayed in his home the night the murder was commited, and believed he could not have done it because he was so drunk. But now, at sixty three, her daughter Juanita has come forward with a claim that Jock confessed all to her when she was a fifteen year old schoolgirl. She said she caught him burning the bloodstained clothing and he told her: 'I hate Happy Valley and its people.' She added: 'I felt a great loyalty to him and I didn't think he was criminal or wicked. I thought he was a lonely distraught man who needed a friend. And I felt very grown up that he trusted me. He killed him.'

But another theory is that one of Hay's ex-mistresses – who killed one of her lovers in Paris five years previously – may have made the journey to Africa to settle an old score. Alice de Janze was known to be consumed by fiery jealousies that could have made such a scheme possible. On the other hand, perhaps the killer was Diana – sensing perhaps that she too could have been ditched by the fanatically unfaithful Earl like others before her.

Whatever she knew, it was a secret that she would take to the grave.

The King and Mrs Simpson

Edward, Prince of Wales, nurtured the secret close to his heart for months. He had fallen for a woman that his position as monarch would never allow him to marry. And yet, hopelessly and obsessively, he could not end the affair – preferring instead to abandon his throne in order to keep the affections of Wallis Simpson. But for the British people, the Prince's love affair was kept secret. While abroad people snickered over the weak Edward's little-boy-lost love for the divorced Simpson, censors and the British establishment combined to keep the very people he reigned over in the dark about their King's lover. It was a calculated move designed to keep an entire nation cut off from reality. It was hardly surprising, therefore, that once the secret was out, it engulfed Edward, Wallis, the establishment and the monarchy like a tidal wave.

Edward VIII was King of Great Britain for 326 days before he abdicated for the woman he loved. But he had been blindly in love for nearly three years with Wallis Simpson. The object of His Majesty's desire in 1936 was the lady who he had met in 1931, a witty but rather plain thirty four year-old American, who had had a childhood and upbringing just about as far as one could get from the House of Windsor. Her father, a businessman from Maryland, had died when she was just five months old and she had been raised in Baltimore by her mother. She married a Navy pilot in 1916, confessing that she found the combination of uniform and derring-do a thrilling combination. But the union with Earl Winfield Spencer was short lived and they were separated in 1922. Her second marriage came in 1928 to Ernest Simpson, a respectable businessman, half British, half American, who headed the London Office of his family's shipping company. It was his arrival in Britain in 1929 that thrust Wallis Simpson on to the London social scene. It had always been an ambition of her mother's that Wallis should elevate herself within society, leaving behind the low social order and poverty of her upbringing. With marriage to Ernest she seemed to have accomplished her goal and established a reputation among the rich and privileged set of the time as something of an amusing and competent hostess. She moved among diplomats, lords and ladies – and loved it. However as Wallis began to enjoy the London social whirl more and more, she began to find her husband staid, dull and uninteresting.

It was in December 1930 that the new first secretary at the American Embassy, Benjamin Thaw, was invited to dinner at the Simpsons'. He came with his wife Consuelo, and her sister Thelma, Viscountess Furness. Lady Furness, a vampish beauty with affected Hollywood starlet looks and manners, had her own secret; she was mistress to the Prince of Wales. A friendship burgeoned between the three women, with Thelma confiding to Wallis about her secret love. Eventually, the Simpsons dined with the Prince and were soon regular visitors to his country retreat. He too dined at the Simpsons' flat off Oxford Street. In January 1934 the Viscountess, at a dinner party, discreetly said to Wallis Simpson: 'I am making a trip to the United States. Please would you look after the Prince to make sure he isn't lonely?' Wallis looked after him all right, rather a little too well for Thelma's liking. By the time she returned in the spring, Wallis and the Prince were lovers.

The secret of the relationship was shared by a small elite group. In the 1930s the Press was far more conservative and did not employ the kind of professional 'royal watchers' of today whose sole tasks are reporting trivia and intimate details of the House of Windsor. Conversely, Edward was being sucked into an emotional vortex which would run directly contrary to his responsibilities as the future King of Great Britain. The secret love letters, which were released after Wallis Simpson's death at the age of eighty nine in 1986, showed the bizarre mother-son relationship which the couple shared – even though Wallis was in fact two years younger than the Prince. His letters are full of infantile pleading, a need to be re-assured, cosseted, adoring in his affections for her. Hers are admonishing, stern, sensible, possessive.

The privileged group of friends who in the early days witnessed them together say that he was completely captivated by her. She, slender, sophisticated, poised, elegant and witty, was the exact opposite of the rather boyish would-be King of Great Britain.

It is not known at which exact date the Prince told the royal family of his love for Wallis Simpson – but they could well have learned from the Prince's indiscreet flaunting of his new mistress on trips to Paris, the French Riviera, Budapest, Berlin and Italy. The foreign press had a field day. Detailed accounts of their trysts in romantic hotels were published in every language from French to Finnish and even the United States press came in on the act – calling Wallis, 'Queen Wally'! Amazingly, Fleet Street printed not a word. The newspapers then were owned by the powerful press barons, men like Rothermere and Beaverbrook, who saw it as their duty to preserve the façade of the British Monarchy – even if their future king were behaving like a playboy. Newspapers coming into the country from overseas had references to the liaison removed and the British public remained ignorant of Edward's behaviour with a twice-divorced woman. The US press in particular went to town with photographs and a story about the couple's visits to Yugoslavia, Greece and Turkey.

Edward became King Edward VIII in December 1935. The affair was at its height and the love letters from Edward to Wallis became ever more sloppy and infantile. But Edward still had the British establishment on his side – that curious creature which is capable of so much indiscretion as long as it is discreet. For Edward and Wallis that turning point was reached when the secret was out on 3 December 1936. Some weeks before then Wallis had finally received a divorce from her husband. Prime Minister Stanley Baldwin, who knew then of the entanglement that Edward had with Wallis, asked the king to persuade Wallis not to go through with the divorce. But Edward told him: 'I have no right to interfere with the affairs of an individual. It would be wrong were I to attempt to influence Mrs Simpson just because she happens to be a friend of the king.' Secretly, it was what he wished and conspired for – knowing that in six months time, before his coronation, he would be free to wed her.

The conspiracy of silence ended when the Bishop of Bradford, Dr Blunt, publicly chastised Edward for his carefree lifestyle which he said was incongruous with a man who was the head of the British Empire. The newspapers construed that the Bishop's outburst was aimed directly at the relationship between the king and Wallis Simpson. The secret was out. Edward was swamped by the public reaction to his affair and naïvely believed that the establishment and the people would understand his affair of the heart. But there would be no sympathetic tears shed for his blighted love. Queen Mary, his mother, was outraged and sent for Baldwin to attend Buckingham Palace. Edward had hoped to move Baldwin into accepting Wallis as his bride and, therefore, as the future Queen. Edward had not yet had his coronation and he believed his popularity with the British people would win through and he would be allowed to marry Wallis. Baldwin told him: 'We will not have it sir. People are talking about you and this American woman. I have had so many nasty letters from people who respected your father and who do not appreciate the way you are going on.'

In the eight days between revelation and abdication, Wallis was subjected to a fearful hate campaign. Stones were hurled through the window of her London home and she received hurtful letters. The children were later to sing in the streets: 'Hark the Herald Angels Sing, Mrs Simpson's pinched our King.' Wallis fled to the South of France while Edward battled against the established order and his own feelings. He was told to ditch Wallis and to assume the responsibilities to which his whole life had been leading, like a man. He tried to sway various influential politicians and press barons, but without much success. One in whom he found an ally was Winston Churchill who, at a lunch with playwright Noel Coward remarked: 'Why shouldn't the king marry his cutie?' 'Because', remarked Coward, 'England does not want a Queen Cutie.' Finally Edward approached the publisher of the *Daily Mail*, Esmond Harmsworth, who suggested the idea of a morganatic marriage – once popular in German royal states – whereby Wallis could become his bride, but would not assume the title of Queen. Her children similarly would have no rights to the throne of Great Britain. Wallis begrudgingly accepted the idea, but it was to no avail; the cabinet would not entertain the idea. If Edward were to remain as king, it would be without Wallis Simpson at his side.

The king, hopelessly, blindly in love with Wallis, decided to abdicate and resolve the constitutional crisis looming over Britain. When Wallis heard that he had stepped down from the throne on 11 December, and broadcast his message to the British people the following night, she wept. Later in her memoirs she wrote: 'I was lying on the sofa with my hands over my eyes, trying to hide my tears.' The King had told the nation that he could not rule without the woman he loved by his side. Edward then left for France, never again to set foot on the shores of his beloved Great Britain.

The couple lived in a splendid white château on the outskirts of Paris for which they paid a peppercorn rent. They married in the Loire Valley and remained as distant outcasts from the Royal family until their deaths – he in May 1972 aged seventy seven, she fourteen years later.

Only at Edward's funeral at St George's Chapel, Windsor, did Wallis come to see the members of the royal family that she so wished to join. She spent one night in Buckingham Palace before returning to her exile in Paris. She ended her days lonely, bedridden, a sad figure whose secret affaire burgeoned into one of the classic romantic tragedies of the century. On her dressing room table she kept a framed message penned by Edward, who assumed the title of Duke of Windsor after his abdication. The touching lines read: 'My friend, with thee to live alone, methinks were better than to own, a crown, a sceptre and a throne.'

Baby Love

In 1986 scandal split the Anglican Church in the United States. It was in the shape of a little bundle of joy named Evan. Evan is now a healthy little girl who plays happily in the garden of her home without a care in the world – and she certainly has no inkling that her birth took place in a storm of publicity. For Evan was born to an unmarried woman priest – a priest, moreover, who conceived her baby not just out of wedlock – but from artificial insemination, from not one but three donors! Now the church hierarchy is threatening that it the mother does not reveal the father's identity she will face excommunication.

The Reverend Lesley Northup was brought up in a religious family in Washington. From her earliest days she attended Sunday school and was fascinated both by the ritual of the Church and the values which its message of love and compassion instilled in her. Lesley Northup's mind was firmly made up; she was going to spread the word of the Lord when she grew up. In 1981 she was ordained by the Bishop of New York, the Right Reverend Paul

Moore. He announced to the assembled congregation that Lesley Northup had the 'qualities and dignity' of a woman well suited to the calling of Christ.

But Reverend Northup had another, equally strong calling – to become a mother. She said: 'I knew that my life was devoted to God and I didn't want a husband because I was so devoted to the Church. But there were feelings within me that I would like to be a mother. To give life, to nurture it and watch it grow. That seemed important to me and did not veer from the teachings of the Bible. I know that the pathway I was considering was not a very romantic one, but it was morally correct. I have no regrets.'

What Lesley did was to enlist the help of two fellow sympathetic male priests and another church worker. They each agreed to provide sperm for artifical insemination. 'I chose them because they were healthy and relatively stable,' said Lesley. 'Good looks didn't count and there was no adultery because they were all single. I was determined that no one, including myself, should know the identity of the father. So on three consecutive nights at my home I artifically inseminated myself. The results are to be found in the beautiful form of my baby daughter.'

Lesley did not foresee the strength of protest and indignation that rose up to meet her when Evan was born. Aside from Church outrage, she was the target of a vicious and prolonged campaign of abuse from the public. Her home was the target of vandals and one letter to her read: 'You have sinned against the Lord. You are an abomination to the church you claim to represent, whore! You will fry in hell.'

Lesley was stunned by the public reaction. She said: 'I did nothing wrong and yet this was happening to me. I didn't want a baby to be the result of a promiscuous act and I didn't want anyone to think that. People said to me: "If you want a baby so badly why don't you just get married?" But you don't just wake up one day and say: "I'll go to the supermarket today and get a husband." And you don't get married just to have a baby. When I got pregnant I didn't want any of the donors to feel responsible individually, but when Evan was born I received christening gifts from all of them. Judging by her looks I have no idea who her father is. She had the bad taste – but the good sense – to resemble a small clone of her mother, so both the donor anonymity and my exclusive parental rights have been protected.'

'Now if I happen to meet one of them, they ask me how she is, but that is all. I couldn't have done this without men but I would point out that I am not a radical feminist. I have gone out with men, I have had relationships with men. I have no anti-male bias whatsoever. I have a quiet, middle-class life and I really am rather conservative in my politics. I chose artifical insemination because it would have been dishonest to get married just to have a baby – plus I devote too much time to God.'

The Reverend Lesley Northup with baby Evan.

Lesley admits that finding the men for the undertaking was a tricky business – especially as she stipulated that they were not to have any involvement with the child's upbringing. But the greatest problems facing her stem from the Church establishment in the United States. She has been the subject of countless debates and the latest dictate from her bishops demand that she reveal the father before they move on to decide what is to become of her. But Lesley is adamant – the secret of the donors will stay just that. Eve the local Bishop who ordained her, has gone against church thinking to declare his support for her. He said: 'There was no adultery and there were no grounds to depose her. So I came out and said: "OK, I am right behind you." I have no intention of criticizing her or condemning her. I couldn't tell her not to have the baby. When you get down to it, she wanted to bring up her own child and I felt she could do a great job. I looked over the Ten Commandments and I didn't see that she had broken any of them."

But his view is not shared by many more othodox, right-wing clerics in the church hierarchy. One of her most outspoken critics, the Reverend John Yates of Vermont, said: 'Her decision to produce a child through artificial insemination is another indicator of the discouraging, dehumanizing drift in our society's perceptions of parenthood and family life. Many in the church do not think she belongs in the cloth and I would support that view.'

Lesley continues to show that she is a force to be reckoned with, declaring: 'I am so proud of what I have done I won't even keep the truth from Evan. How it's phrased will depend on when she asks, but certainly she'll get the whole truth. And she may have a brother or sister to ask as well – because I would certainly have no qualms about doing it again.'

The President and Marilyn Monroe

For almost fifty years the United State's domestic crime agency the FBI was ruled with an iron fist by J. Edgar Hoover, a man possessed by huge prejudice, intense paranoia and an obsession with other people's sex lives. Widely rumoured to be a homosexual himself, Hoover took on a crusading zeal whenever he found what he considered immoral or indecent behaviour in others. Hoover always looked for weaknesses in his real or imagined enemies and built up files which gave him immense potential power over them. For years his twisted brain consumed and collated information ready to be put to use – and no public figure had a bigger personal file within Hoover's office than the President of the United States of America himself – the charismatic John F. Kennedy.

Charismatic Kennedy was anathema to the things which reactionary Hoover believed in. Always hunting communists and liberals, Hoover despised the Kennedy reforms of the racist school system in the southern states and his links with black leader Martin Luther King. Consequently Hoover set out to discover the weaknesses of John F. Kennedy. He found them not in booze, or pornography, bribery, civic corruption or money. Kennedy's weakness was sex.

He had many illicit affairs during his marriage to his wife Jacqueline, both before he stepped into the White House and after. However, unknown to Kennedy at the start of his tenure of office, Hoover had placed many key White House personnel on the FBI payroll as his personal stooges within the President's official residence. Kennedy's telephone conversations were taped, the meetings he had with women secretly watched with times, dates and places being meticulously recorded. Kennedy's attraction to and for other women was something that revolted Hoover. But something that has remained a mystery to this day is whether Kennedy had an affair with the most sexual woman of the age – Marilyn Monroe. And not only him, but his brother Robert Kennedy, was also widely rumoured to have shared the bed of the sex symbol who seemingly killed herself with barbiturates in August 1962 at the age of thirty six. Since her death over a quarter of a century ago, the ghost of Marilyn Monroe has never been laid to rest. Many theories have

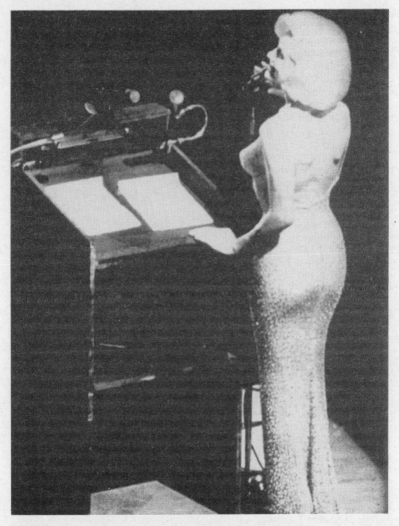

Marilyn singing at President Kennedy's birthday party.

surfaced – ugly stories that the death has not a suicide after all.

Marilyn's affair with President Kennedy was said to have been known by all, but discussed by none. And her death, some allege, was brought about because she intended to publicly expose her affair with the president. There have been other bizarre theories: Did mobsters bug the star's bedroom in a bid to blackmail the Kennedys who were cracking down hard on organized crime? Did Robert Kennedy, then Attorney General in the US, break off his relationship with Marilyn on the very day she died? Did the Kennedys' brother-in-law, the actor Peter Lawford, destroy a suicide note from Marilyn that may have leaked the sensational news that she bedded the two most powerful men in the United States? Was she murdered in a move guaranteed to keep her silent? No serious investiagation has ever placed such a crime at the doorstep of the Kennedys – but several noted journalists who have probed the suicide story believe that mafia bosses – sick of the war waged on them by the Kennedys – may have decided to fake Marilyn's suicide in order to lure Robert Kennedy into a trap.

If the stories are true that both Kennedy brothers indulged in affairs with Marilyn Monroe, the suspicions over her death will continue to linger for many years to come.

Jeanne Martin, ex-wife of singer Dean Martin, is one who claims that Lawford, who was married to Kennedy sister Patricia, played 'pimp' for the Kennedy brothers in fixing up dates with Marilyn. She says: 'I saw Peter in the role of pimp for Jack Kennedy. It was a nasty business.' Jeanne, who does admit never to have actually seen Jack or Bobby Kennedy in bed with Marilyn, added that she does feel 'quite sure' that both men were sleeping with the star.

Other sources say that John Kennedy frequently had rendezvous with Marilyn in a plush New York Hotel. Jane Shalam, the daughter of an influential political family in the city, said she frequently saw Marilyn leaving and entering the hotel by the rear entrance at a time she knew Kennedy was staying inside. Singer Phyllis McGuire, of the McGuire Sisters, says: 'The initial relationship was with John. And there definitely was a relationship afterwards with Bobby. They were seen together at their little hideaways. And, you know, that's very like the Kennedys, to pass it down from one to the other.' Another source claims that President Kennedy 'passed her on' when he grew fearful of Hoover's investigations into his private life – and made sure that Robert always used a false name when speaking with Marilyn on a telephone which was equipped with a special scrambler to prevent wiretapping by Hoover's agents.

Actress Jeanne Carmen, a friend and neighbour of Marilyn's in Holly-wood, claims she was witness to an astonishing episode at Marilyn's Los

Angeles apartment in the autumn of 1961. She said: 'I was at Marilyn's place once evening when the doorbell rang. She was in the tub and she called me to get it. I opened the door and there was Bobby. He had that expression when he saw me of not knowing whether to run, walk or stay. I was stunned and kept saying, "come in, come in". Finally I got out of his way and Marilyn came flying out of the bathroom, and jumped into his arms. She kissed him openly, which was out of character for her.' Carmen also says that Bobby Kennedy and the movie queen enjoyed a naked romp on a nudist beach near Malibu – Marilyn dressed up in a wig and he wearing a fake beard.

One of Lawford's ex-wives, Deborah Gould, said the affair with Jack Kennedy began before he took office in 1961. He broke it off, allegedly because he found Marilyn 'dangerously talkative'. Initially Bobby was just used as the messenger boy, says Gould, but then he found himself spellbound by her beauty and sexuality. But Lawford, who died in 1984, repeatedly and vehemently denied that the affairs had ever taken place. His denial of the secret trysts is not believed by investigative journalist Anthony Summers who, in his book about Marilyn called *Goddess*, speculates: 'It seems that for many months she engaged in intermittent sexual encounters with both the President and Robert Kennedy. For both the brothers and for Marilyn, there had been an initial attraction between stars, each glittering prizes in the interlocking galaxies of politics and show business. The Kennedy brothers, bred to the knowledge that they could have any woman they desired, at first failed to perceive that in Marilyn Monroe they were dealing with a woman who was doubly dangerous.'

Summers says that the nature of the 'danger' lay in the fact that she represented a threat to both of their political lives. She was despondent over frequent miscarriages and abortions – the result of a string of failed love affairs – and her fading movie career. Her grip on reality was ebbing away too.

On the night she died, Summers speculates that Peter Lawford, who was the last person to speak to her on the telephone, came to Marilyn's house before she was dead and, possibly with Robert Kennedy there, took the dying actress to a hospital in Santa Monica. However, when Monroe died, the corpse was rushed back to her home and the death scene was staged before the police were called. His book makes no firm charge, but leaves open the possibility that 'someone else administered the fatal overdose'.

Milo Speriglio, head of a private detective agency in Los Angeles, has been fascinated with Marilyn Monroe, her apparent liaison with the Kennedys and her untimely death ever since she was found in the cold light of day on 5 August all those years ago. He is convinced she was murdered.

Speriglio says he began with a re-investigation of the inquest and police reports. The coroner ruled suicide after hearing that she had swallowed forty-seven capsules of barbiturates. But the autopsy stated that the stomach was almost completely empty except for a small residue of brownish liquid. Also no water was found in her stomach. Did she take forty-seven pills without any water? Sergeant Jack Clemmons, the police officer first at the scene in her home in the LA suburb of Brentwood, noticed that there was no vomit around – usually the first sign that someone has tried suicide with pills – no glass, no water. Jack Clemmons has now left the force and told Speriglio he had recommended an investigation to his superiors. He was told to totally forget about the idea.

Speriglio claims that a friend of Monroe's, Robert Slatzer, first alerted him to the murder theory. Slatzer had known Marilyn for sixteen years and claimed she had told him about her affairs with the Kennedy brothers. Slatzer claimed she showed him a red diary containing the red-hot accounts of her lovemaking liaisons with the brothers and other significant people. He believed that the diary was a reason for her murder. Speriglio says that Monroe actually believed that Bobby Kennedy was going to leave his wife and his large family for her. 'When Robert tried to dump her too like his brother had done, she behaved like a scorned woman,' said Speriglio. 'He had broken up with her in a ruthless way, by having the private phone line on which she called him disconnected.'

Speriglio tried to get copies of Marilyn's phone bills – numbers dialled which would have been listed on the bill – but he found they had apparently gone 'missing'. He tried to find the diary which had been passed into the custody of deputy coroner's aide Lionel Grandison who signed Marilyn's death certificate. Speriglio claimed Grandison told him he had looked through the book and seen references to the Kennedys and some mafia figures in San Diego. But when Speriglio returned the next day with a request to see the diary, the book had not only gone – but had also been struck from the inventory of personal effects turned over to the state.

The private eye also says he had evidence that the Monroe home was bugged – one of his sources was Bernard Spindel, an expert wiretapper who was arrested by the FBI in 1966 and who died in prison before Speriglio could get his hands on the tapes he possessed. But before he died he filed a petition to the Supreme Court citing return of 'a confidential file containing tapes and evidence concerning circumstances surrounding the death of Marilyn Monroe which strongly suggests the official reported circumstances of her demise are erroneous.' Speriglio believed from talking to other informants in the Senate that Marilyn was preparing a news conference to get her own back on the Kennedys – spilling the beans not only on their love affairs but the death plots which, Speriglio claims, Kennedy told her about and which were aimed at Cuban dictator Fidel Castro.

Speriglio charges that the CIA – the sometimes unorthodox intelligence agency of the United States – was involved in Marilyn's death, plotters in the bizarre power-play who may have administered a lethal injection of barbiturates to prevent a scandal from engulfing the White House. Speriglio said: 'In 1980 under the Freedom of Information Act, I petitioned the FBI for Marilyn Monroe's file. Most of the material was blanked out and, under orders of FBI director William Webster, eighteen of the forty-three pages were completely witheld. The reason given for the exempted eighteen pages was national defence and foreign policy. The remaining material was useless.

'But I'd like to know just what in the files of a two-decades-dead movie star still threatens national security!'

Eric Clapton and the Chamber Maid

For months the gossip columns had been filled with the news that buzzed across the Atlantic. Eric Clapton, legendary guitarist, musician extraordinaire, a man who beat heroin and booze addictions to produce some of the best rock music ever, was to be a father again. That fact alone wasn't so startling – it was *who* was going to be the mother. Clapton had already raised more than a few music-world eyebrows when his beautiful Italian mistress Lory Del Santo gave birth at the age of twenty six to the singer's son Conor in August 1986. Patti Boyd, thirty eight, who left ex-Beatle George Harrison for Clapton in 1974, and who married him in 1979, named Lory in her divorce petition. When the rumours started buzzing towards the end of the summer of 1987 that Clapton was going to be a father again, the thoughts were not of *when* but of *who* was carrying his child.

As it turned out, neither Lory or Patty were pregnant by Clapton. But out of the shadows of New York's clubland came a part-time singer, part-time chambermaid with a definite bulge under her dress. Alina Moreni, twenty seven, was carrying Eric Clapton's love child – or so she said.

Fleet Street went mad for her story. The bouncy beauty had an amazing yarn to tell of her secret affair. In both British and American newspapers she boasted how fairytale love had blossomed when she met Clapton at a club in Manhattan one night. She said that she lived in one of New York's smartest streets, Park Avenue, with her wealthy mother, and was an Italian Baroness in a self-imposed exile of luxury in the most exciting city she knew. Her life, she sighed, was a tidal wave of champagne and roses, played out against the backdrop of exciting New York. Her story was the stuff of romantic novels. In one interview she said: 'I knew when I fell in love with Eric Clapton that it was never going to be easy. He has a beautiful heart, but not much brains. He thinks with the most intimate part of his body. But underneath all that he's just a playful, insecure child. That's why I have always liked him – and that's one of the things he always liked about me: my honesty.'

Alina's honesty in her interviews was quite breathtaking. She revealed how she and Clapton had a mad passionate fling which resulted in her pregnancy. She said it was a matter of time before Eric made a statement about their love, and also about the matter of paying maintenance for the child which was due to be born in April 1988.

The publicity was certainly paying off for Alina. She was booked to sing in some of the better-known New York nightclubs and boasted proudly of a hurried love-call to Eric every time she was off stage. 'He makes my heart beat with desire', she gushed in a New York newspaper. 'He is just waiting for the day we can be together forever. He, me and our baby. It will be perfect.' Even though she was heavily pregnant, Alina managed to draw the kind of publicity usually reserved for more shapely aspiring crooners. She was snapped by the paparazzi as she left clubs, snapped as she went in, and droned on about the 'special magic' she shared with Eric. 'I am only revealing the secret of our love because he is soon to break the news to Lory,' said Alina. But the real secret was something quite different indeed ...

Day by day Alina was getting bigger until she resembled a matronly Italian housewife, clasping her hands in front of her to help hold the burden she was carrying. And then one day her manager, Lynne Robinson, who was helping to promote her singing career noticed that the 'pregnancy lump' seemed to move! 'I have seen pregnant women before,' said Lynne, 'and this seemed most odd. The lump definitely shifted – and when I saw her again it seemed to have moved once again.' There was no comment from the Clapton camp about the singer's entangled love life. His management refused to be drawn into the star's personal life.

Then in May, when Alina looked fit to burst, she 'went into hospital to give birth to our darling child'. But while she was away, newspaper men from both sides of the Atlantic began sniffing around what looked like being a very fishy tale indeed. It turned out that Alina was no Italian Baroness. She was a full-time, hard-up maid who last year cleaned the apartment of Eric Clapton. There was no crime in rich and poor getting together in a union of passion, however. Friends rushed to her side to say that the Italian Baroness story was concocted merely to give Eric's friends in the pop world a more favourable impression of his latest love.

But then other cracks began appearing in the saga; Robinson told how she tried to reach out to touch pregnant Alina's stomach, and 'she winced away as if in pain.' She added: 'She wouldn't let me near her. That was when I was convinced that she was a faker and that the whole thing was some kind of calculated sting against Clapton. I said to her: "You are a very, very sick girl and need help." I am a mother of three children and I know how people behave when they are pregnant. There was no way that this woman was carrying anything other than a pillow up her dress.'

Alina's other close friend Rose Genero, who had known her for six years, said Alina telephoned her from a New York hospital on 8 May to say she had given birth to a bouncing baby girl, and that she was going to call her Rosa Lina Clapton. Eric had been on the telephone from London, she told Rose, and everything was fine. 'But I checked back with the hospital and there was no record of her being there or indeed of a baby girl being born that night,' said Rose. 'I think I knew then that the real secret was not her fling with a pop star, but the fact that she had embarked on a Walter Mitty exercise that had only one ending. She was bound to be found out sooner or later. Maybe she did have a fling with Clapton but she sure as hell wasn't carrying his baby.'

With pressure from the media building up, Alina went into hiding with her 'baby' – she still insisted that she had given birth and that Eric was on his way to see her. But then two days later she confessed sobbing to Fleet Street reporters: 'I did not have his baby. I had an abortion because I saw the way he was treating me. When I saw his attitude towards me I knew that he had changed. But I am a woman and I am proud. That is why I pretended for so long that I was carrying his child. It was a very upsetting time all round and now I need lots of therapy for my condition.'

A psychiatrist, John Felton, noted in a US magazine: 'Many girls build up secret love affairs with famous people. They take the pin-up poster adulation one step further and create entire lives and love affairs around them until they finally believe that they are having a relationship with that person. For someone to pretend that they are pregnant is merely taking it just one stage further. The excitement comes from the person who is smitten believing that it is their "secret" – something private and dark and mysterious. Once that illusion is shattered there is nothing left.'

Clapton still refuses to comment on the entire affair. The last word however went to Alina who said 'Dear Eric, I shall always love him ...'

The Princess and the Captain

One way or another, when it comes to affairs of the heart, the House of Windsor has had more than its fair share of anguish and pain. The Prince of Wales, who went on to become King Edward VII, scandalized society with his fling with the exquisite Lillie Langtry. A later successor to his title abandoned the throne for divorcee Wallis Simpson. In more modern times the dalliance between His Royal Highness Prince Andrew and a former soft-porn film star named Koo Stark caused more than just a little concern. But perhaps the saddest secret affair was that between Princess Margaret and Group Captain Peter Townsend; their modern-day love story rivalled anything that Shakespeare could dream up and was eventually to lead to heartbreak for them and strife within the royal family. It started as a schoolgirl crush but went on to become a deeply passionate affair which was kept secret – until a knowing glance gave them away. To this day, there are many people who think Princess Margaret was the hardest done-by royal of all.

She was just an innocent fourteen-year-old schoolgirl when she met the debonair Townsend in 1944. The twenty nine-year-old tall, war hero who had distinguished himself in the Battle of Britain, came to Buckingham Palace as an Equerry to King George VI. The appeal for Margaret was instant; Townsend was good looking, charming, distinguished – and a war hero. For a young woman, increasingly aware of her own blossoming sexuality, he was an incomparable idol. He was also unattainable – married to pretty wife called Rosemary. He was given a house in the grounds of Windsor Castle and assigned to his duties. Margaret adored him and sought him out for – allegedly – fatherly advice and friendship. There was never any question that he would be hers – yet. But in 1947 the king took Margaret and her sister, the Princess Elizabeth, on a three month tour of Southern Africa. The voyage was planned as a test of the love that Prince Philip of Greece held for Princess Elizabeth. Philip had been courting her for some while and the king thought that a long separation would test the feelings of both. Elizabeth's sadness, however, at being parted from Philip, was made up for in feelings of pure joy by Margaret – for it meant the royal party were accompanied by Group

Captain Townsend – while Rosemary stayed at home. Old newsreels of the time testify to the happiness and warmth that the seventeen-year-old Margaret radiated on the visit while she was near to the man she loved. On the visit she stayed up late into the warm African nights, listening to the cultured, witty humour and gentle views of Townsend.

For Margaret, it is almost as if she had a sixth-sense that she would one day be in his arms. She stayed away from the many suitors in society who were attracted to her, waiting for the chance to become Townsend's love. That chance occurred in 1951 when he and Rosemary parted. Their long separations due to his royal tours and other duties put a strain on the union that was too great to bear. She was unfaithful to him and in August 1951, just days after the Princess had celebrated her twenty-first birthday, Townsend told the Princess: 'The marriage is over. We married in wartime and were not right for each other.' The pair were horseriding in the grounds of Balmoral and it was there that Margaret told him for the first time of the burning passion she held for him. It was the start of the affair.

Like her predecessors within the House of Windsor, Margaret underestimated both public interest and her own family's reaction to her 'deep friendship'. The couple were once caught by the king himself as Townsend was carrying Princess Margaret up the stairs as if she were his bride and he were taking her over the threshhold! 'I told him to do it papa, I ordered him,' blurted the embarrassed Margaret who had not breathed a word of her feelings to her father. By this time Townsend was the Deputy Master of the Royal Household and as such had ample opportunity to plan his time around seeing the Princess. They arranged cosy weekends at the homes of discreet friends – a practice later adopted by Prince Andrew when he was seeing Koo Stark – and made sure never to show displays of public affection when the eyes of Britain's press were upon them. They drove away from the Palace in plain cars, Margaret often down in her seat so she would not be spotted by the curious tourists who thronged at the iron railings, craning their necks to catch a glimpse of the inhabitants. Her love for Townsend was deep, genuine – and doomed. Like all secrets, they could never keep it completely and were the subject of a vicious whispering campaign within the establishment. Townsend was accused of being a 'cradle snatcher' – Margaret guilty of foolish child-like emotions that she could neither control or understand. One of the most severe critics of the burgeoning relationship was Prince Philip, who had married Princess Elizabeth. He thought that a divorced 'employee' of the 'family firm' was not a fitting candidate to romance the Queen's sister. But Margaret was determined to share her life with Townsend – even going to see Sir Alan Lascelles, the Queen's private secretary, to enquire whether a divorce on Townsend's part – and for admitted adultery by his wife – would stand in

The early days – Group Captain Townsend and Princess Margaret.

the way of their future happiness together. Lascelles, an independent thinker, said he could see no problems as long as a 'respectable' period of time elapsed before the couple contemplated marriage. Margaret said they were thinking of a period over a year away, and he replied: 'Then I can foresee no problems.' The whole of the royal family now knew that Townsend was courting the Princess as their liaison became less secret. The British public did not. They learned about it when the couple themselves broke their cardinal rule about public displays of affection. The game was up when, shortly after the Westminster Abbey Coronation ceremony for Queen Elizabeth, Princess Margaret was observed by a Fleet Street reporter leaning forward to brush a speck of dirt from Townsend's blue RAF uniform. It was interpreted for what it was – the act of a woman in love, making sure her man looks his best. Captain Townsend's glance into her eyes gave Fleet Street sensational headlines for the next day: 'Princess Margaret's Love For RAF Hero' being one of the more reserved statements.

The couple were treated to a prime display of what Britain excels at – hypocrisy. It was 1953, the divorce rate was soaring and women were on the pathway to determining their own futures. but the establishment balked at what it felt was a constitutional crisis to rival that of the Edward and Wallis Simpson affair of the 1930s. In her role as head of state, the Queen is also the head of the Church of England, defender of the faith and the symbol of all that is sacrosanct in moral behaviour. The idea of her sister first cavorting with, and then marrying, a divorced man, was just too much to bear. Churchill was prime minister and was under great pressure to separate the couple. There were none of the kind words that the young Princess had received from Sir Alan; only a cold warning that their love could never be. Townsend was packed off to Brussels as the air attaché to the British Embassy, and Margaret was sent on a tour of Rhodesia with her mother.

The Princess, still nurturing her belief that they would be allowed to marry, called Townsend on booked international calls twice a day. The lovers plotted future trysts, secret meetings, away from both the pressure of the Palace – where Prince Philip was emerging as a major figure in mustering anti-Townsend sympathies – and the Press which had unleased the news of the couple's love to the world. Remarkably, their romance survived. For the three years that Group Captain Townsend was posted to Brussels their affair was played out in snatched meetings and all-too-brief rendezvous at secret addresses. But shortly before her twenty-fifth birthday, Margaret was summoned by her sister, the Queen, and told that Winston Churchill had communicated to her that Parliament would never sanction a marriage to Townsend. She could renounce her royal status, and go into exile like the Duke of Windsor, but there could be no 'acceptance' into the Royal family.

In October 1955 there came the last week that the couple were to spend together. They dined at the home of friends in London and at country houses, Margaret nurturing a last ditch hope that Parliament would relent; Townsend, the wiser, elder man, knowing their affair was doomed and on its last lap. After consultations with the Archbishop of Canterbury. Margaret met with Queen Elizabeth and told her that she and Townsend had decided to call the whole thing off. On Monday 31 October, a week after crowds outside Clarence House had yelled slogans like 'marry him, marry him!', a statement from Margaret was released to the Press. The moving statement said: 'I would like it to be known that I have decided not to marry Group Captain Peter Townsend. I have been aware that subject to my renouncing my rights of succesion it might have been possible for me to contract a civil marriage. But mindful of the Church's teaching that a Christian marriage is indissoluble, and conscious of my duty to the Commonwealth, I have resolved to put these considerations before any others. I have reached the decision entirely alone, and in doing so I have been strengthened by the unfailing support and devotion of Group Captain Townsend.'

It was over. Princess Margaret went on to marry Anthony Armstrong-Jones, later Lord Snowdon. The initially blissful marriage floundered and in 1978 they were finally divorced. Friends of Margaret say that her heart had never healed from the days of that heady affair with the man who was probably her only true love.

Chapter Four

MILITARY SECRETS

The key to victory or defeat, triumph or tragedy, glory or dishonour can depend on the utmost secrecy – as was the case with Operation Overlord – the secret plan that fooled the Nazis and led to the D-Day landings. However the military mind has a darker side – a side that led to the despot generals in Argentina masterminding a secret war against their own people; and why the evil SS murdered an entire French village in a frenzied orgy of death.

Most Secret Army

The Special Air Services Regiment, or SAS, is Britain's secret army. Its officers and men are, by and large, anonymous, its numbers vague, the areas in which it moves shadowy. Part of the aura which surrounds the SAS is its strict secrecy – and that has only served to enhance its reputation as a military machine par excellence. Indeed, the reputation and rumours surrounding the regiment have become as effective as any weapon which its members include in their formidable arsenal. When the IRA gunmen holding hostages in the Balcombe Street siege in London during the 1970s heard that the SAS were on their way to reinforce police, they surrendered. When Britain entered the Falklands War men of the SAS – and its nautical equivalent the Special Boat Services – were creating havoc behind enemy lines long before the main British Task Force landed to liberate the islanders, and were dubbed 'phantom devils' by Argentine defenders. But the SAS earned a very special place in the hearts and minds of the British public when, televised for the whole world to witness, they stormed the Iranian Embassy at Princes Gate in London in May 1980, and ruthlessly eliminated five of the six terrorists holding hostages. The stark, even frightening, image of men clad from head to foot in black, with balaclavas and gas masks, abseiling from the roof of the building before bursting in through windows told the world what the British Army had long muttered in its ranks: 'Don't mess with the SAS'.

Although now widely regarded as Britain's ultimate anti-terrorist strike force, the SAS, with its motto 'Who Dares Wins', was founded in World War Two. The regiment's first commander was its creator, Lieutenant David Stirling, a veteran of the Western Desert and a man with unorthodox military ideas. In 1941 he penned a detailed memorandum about the possibility of assembling a small, lethal commando force within the British Army to work deep behind enemy lines, practising sabotage, wrecking communications and generally making a thorough nuisance of themselves to the Axis forces. He drove to the Middle East Headquarters of the British Commander in Chief, General Auchinleck, with the express purpose of seeing the chief to put his proposals to him. The British Army at the time was hard-pressed keeping Rommel from winning the desert war and was willing to listen to most suggestions. Stirling was able to present his memorandum to the General's

The SAS storming the Iranian Embassy in 1980.

Chief of Staff and three days later was given the go-ahead to launch his scheme. It was to be called L Detachment of the Special Air Services Brigade. Such a unit did not exist – but like the myths which surround the present day SAS, Auchinleck realized the immense value of propaganda and presumed that the enemy at least would think it real, conjuring up images of crack paratroops and experienced, ruthless commandos.

The success of Stirling's original band of less than 300 men in the Western Desert was real enough. Hundreds of German aircraft were destroyed on the ground by unseen attackers who melted into the desert before their explosives went off. Dozens of tanks, heavy guns, supply columns and fuel tankers were ambushed and destroyed in remote regions of the desert. Apart from an all-round skill in military tactics and weapons, the troops developed the very special skills of thriving in the harshest of climates and terrains, being able to subsist on the smallest of rations while still keeping at a mental and physical peak. That is why today for every fifteen applicants to the SAS from within the regular ranks, fourteen don't make it.

As the allied forces in 1944 and 1945 sped through occupied Europe towards Berlin, the SAS, which had quadrupled in strength, was with them every hard step of the way. But by now it had started acquiring the kind of reputation which the army could only admire. In some of the most ruthless fighting in the war, savage hand-to-hand combat and behind the lines espionage, the regiment acquitted itself with remarkable results. Even the abstemious, sanctimonious Field Marshal Montgomery had to begrudgingly acknowledge the skills of the fighting men, even if their methods and their dress was somewhat unorthodox. The SAS shunned the usual discipline of the parade ground and the barrack hut – theirs was a much more specialized discipline; the need to stay one step ahead and stay alive. They evolved a system of operating which has survived to this day. The SAS men operate in pairs, linking with other pairs numbering between ten and twenty to form 'operational squads'. In the field the officers dispense with the army rule book and everyone refers to each other by their first names. Because of the almost impossible missions which the SAS set out from the start to accomplish, Stirling saw it as reasonable that previously inflexible army rules could be relaxed for fighting men who were being asked to perform beyond the range of ordinary mortals.

It was during the relentless advance through Europe that the SAS perfected its unorthodox skills. The troops became accomplished not only with every weapon in the allied arsenal, but also with those used by the enemy. They developed the skills which up until then were not required for the average British Army footslogger – to think like his enemy. As one ex-SAS man wrote: 'Forged in that iron fire assault on Nazi Germany was a unit so select, so ruthless and so damned efficient, any warlord would have sacrificed five of his best divisions for it.'

At the end of the war with the job done – the total defeat of Nazi Germany and Imperial Japan – the British government had a dilemma to solve. What to do with such an unorthodox unit. Its supporters dubbed it a remarkable band of men – its critics, a bunch of licensed brigands with little regard to legality or rules. It was of course a mixture of both. It was after the war that the SAS entered the grey, shadowy world of government plotting, intelligence and 'covert operations'. It hasn't emerged from it yet.

Initially, in 1945, the SAS was disbanded. Two years later it was re-formed as a Territorial Regiment – staffed largely by the men who fought with it during the war. By 1952 it had once again attained full regular Army status and through the 1950s until the 1980s fought long, bitter campaigns under the blanket of anonymity. A regular soldier in a regular regiment could expect glory, fanfare, a mention in his local paper and respect from the community for his heroism. The SAS man can expect only total secrecy. It is part and parcel of the job. What he can also expect from his government is a denial that he was ever in the place where he carried out his missions for the Crown.

The story of the SAS after the end of World War Two is a chronicle of the downfall of Britain as a great Imperial power. The British Empire was fragmenting at an alarming rate – troops like the SAS were over the Empire to fight against the 'terrorists' in these ugly little conflicts. In Malaya, Oman, Borneo, the Radfan, Aden and the Yemen, the SAS fought its special wars behind the lines. In Malaya, for instance, the guerrilla leaders believed they were safe in their deep jungle hideouts. Getting through the nightmarish jungles in the hope of springing a surprise attack was a naïve hope. The guerrillas killed more British troops hoping to spring surprise attacks than vice versa. To combat the enemy in his lair the SAS devised a tough paratroop training operation to land men in the heart of their territory. The only way this could be accomplished was for the paratroopers to jump straight into the treetops, snagging the parachute canopy on the high branches. Then the soldier could lower himself down on ropes to the ground below. The SAS roll of honour at Hereford, the Regimental HQ, testifies to many men who died while trying to perfect this almost suicidal method of getting to a war zone.

Successive British governments knew that the Empire's end was a foregone conclusion – often they just wanted the withdrawal from their overseas possessions to be as smooth as possible in the face of ruthless guerrillas and terror groups. In Yemen, for example, from 1963 until 1967, the SAS were there trying to aid the pro-British royalists in their fight with the republicans, who received the backing of the strong Egyptian army. It served British interests perfectly to have a royalist regime in power – it did not serve British interests to have it known that the SAS was carrying out covert missions there. Whitehall said that the Britons in action there were mercenaries. They were not – they were SAS regulars learning the ultimate lesson of 'dirty little wars' post-1945: deniability.

The system of recruitment into the SAS today allows the government to still exercise that same level of deniability when it comes to the regiment. Because the SAS is made up of hand-picked volunteers from other regiments – who often return to their 'home' units after a term with the SAS – it is easy for the government to juggle statistics and paperwork to deny the involvement of an SAS team. The 'operatives' could be sent back to their 'home' units within hours of completing a mission and then the government is able to say conclusively: there are no SAS men involved. It is effective and plunges the fighting force further from the military into the secret service. Nowhere has this been more apparent than in Northern Ireland where, for the past twenty years, Britain has been fighting a well-equipped Irish Republican Army with high losses on both sides. The SAS role in Ulster has, and continues to be, a controversial one.

Its first 'denied' operation came in 1969 and was mounted against loyalist fanatics who were smuggling weapons through the Irish Republic to the North. News leaked of SAS involvement and Prime Minister Harold Wilson denied their presence. Nearly twenty years of informed leaks to the press show that the SAS were there, but were attached to other British Army units. The Prime Minister did not lie. He just didn't expand on the quirky ways of covert operations and the need for secrecy.

It was three years after the episode in Ulster that marked a watershed in the future role for the SAS. World leaders saw the writing on the wall – that terrorism was going to be a major, ruthless factor in world power-plays. Would governments have the adequate response to it?

After the massacre of innocent Israeli athletes by terrorists at the Olympic games in Munich the SAS were specifically entrusted with the role of terrorism for the Realm. It could and would be called upon at any time to venture where others had failed and be called upon to win. In 1976 it went back, officially, to Ulster, where in the killing ground of Armagh – 'bandit country' – IRA units had succeeded in wiping out many British soldiers. After five months of 'covert' operations, eleven IRA leaders were dead, in hiding or in jail. The reputation of the SAS was only further enhanced.

Ever since, where there has been trouble, the SAS have not been very far behind. In 1973, when it was feared the liner QE2 was sabotaged with time bombs, the SAS dramatically dropped from helicopters into the ocean to board her; when South Moluccan terrorists seized a train in Holland in 1977, the SAS sent in a team to aid the Dutch forces.

In October of that year Captain Alistair Morrison and Sergeant Barry Davies flew from Britain to lead the crack German anti-terror squad GSG9 in storming a hijacked Lufthansa jet at Mogadishu in Somalia. All hostages were rescued unharmed. In 1980 there came the classic rescue of the hostages from the Iranian Embassy siege, with the loss of just one hostage in a brilliant attack which proved their expertise to the world. In 1982 they were in the thick of covert operations in the Falklands War. In 1984 they were on round-the-clock standby to deal with the Libyan Embassy siege if negotiations were to collapse. In 1988 an SAS squad killed three IRA members, who were on a reconnaisance mission in Gibraltar, plotting a bombing. That operation caused widespread anger from the Republicans in Northern Ireland and led to cries of 'state murder' from IRA sympathizers. But an inquest in September ruled that it was a lawful killing.

Police and military chiefs the length and breadth of Britain, and many from around the world, have been to secret meetings at building sites and dockyards to watch the SAS teams storm everything from a house to a liner. The SAS have developed plans for storming every type of civilian aircraft at every airport in Britain, every nuclear power plant and most high-ranking government offices. Still shrouded in secrecy, the government intends for them to stay that way, and will not publish rolls of officers' names in the Official Army List or release details of their deployment wherever it may be.

After the 1980 Iranian Embassy siege, the SAS men were driven at high speed to Chelsea Barracks in London where their commanding officer Captain Mike Rose made a speech that is now part of regimental history. He produced a pack of cards and told the men who had just made history: 'Gentlemen, this is a big boys' game. The number of cards are the ordinary people, simply wanting to go about their lives in peace. This card is the Knave – the terrorist. This card is the Queen – the one we answer to.

'And this card is the Joker – that's you lot, the wild card the Knave always has to worry about.'

The Odessa

They were destined to be the vanguard of the Thousand Year Reich – the racially pure warriors guarding the Aryan flame as it scorched the world under the doctrine of Nazism. They were members of the SS, the *Schutzstaffeln,* or Protection Squad, formed initially as a praetorian Guard for the Fuehrer, who later became the overseers and organizers of his totalitarian regime. From the concentration camps to the death squads roaming Eastern Europe and Russia, from internal security to the Gestapo, from the Reichsbank to the arts ministry, the grip of the SS was total. By the beginning of war in 1939 it had truly become what Heinrich Himmler had boasted it would – 'a state within a state'.

Apart from a few brilliant tacticians in the fighting arm of the organization, the Waffen SS, the SS was largely made up of Nazi sycophants, sadists, perverts, racial bigots and social misfits. For the appalling crimes it was to carry out, it is no wonder that the bulk of the SS was composed of men without compassion or conscience. The fabric which bound this motley crew together was the unswerving belief in Adolf Hitler and his racial doctrines

Simon Weisenthal – the famous Nazi hunter.

which preached world conquest and the destruction of 'lesser' peoples.

When the going was good for SS men, it was very good. Concentration camp guards were given extra rations, the killers belonging to the 'Action Squads' on the Eastern Front had unlimited alchohol and cigarettes, the men who oversaw them enjoyed the patronage of Hitler and the highest ranking members of the Nazi Party. They were the planners and the perpetrators of the foulest crimes in history – and had the war ended differently, they would have been greatly rewarded by the Reich. Instead, when the good times ended with the collapse of Germany, the SS scuttled like rats from the Fatherland – thanks to the help of one of the most secretive organizations in the world, which still exists to this day – the ODESSA.

The organisation does not take its name from the Russian city. It is an acronym for Organisation der Ehemalige SS Angehoriger – the Organization of Former Members of the SS. But this was no old comrades club. It existed for one purpose only – to get SS men out of Germany – preferably with as much money as possible – when the allies came to exact justice from the Nazi regime and its servants. Its tentacles are spread far and wide in the world, its funds nestling in secret bank accounts beneath the cobbled streets of Zurich and Geneva. Formed by SS members when the tide of war began turning and the enormity of their crimes was being discovered, the SS looked to itself and supporters to save its skin – knowing that Allied scaffolds were the only thing that could be expected after the Holocaust and the ill treatment of civilians in every part of Nazi-dominated territories.

The organization first came to the attention of allied intelligence agencies in 1949. As cries for justice against the SS members echoed throughout the world, a disturbing pattern emerged in their disappearances. They did not just vanish haphazardly from allied detention camps or from under the noses of the very people they terrorized. Rather their journeys into obscurity were well oiled, paid for with huge amounts of cash which furnished their fake papers and new lives. In a bitter twist of irony, the very bankers who withheld information from the Nazis about the funds of Jewish clients when the war started became their salvation at its end. The watchword for Swiss banks is secrecy, and the Jews – and the Nazis – were no exception. Because the war signalled the start of the biggest organized plundering expedition in history, the money to finance a covert organization intent on saving SS members was piled up over nearly six years. Much of it found its way into a reserve bank owned and operated by the *Sicherheitsdienst*, the security arm of the SS, known by its initials SD. From looted art, to gold, silver, diamonds, cash – down to the spectacles stolen from concentration camp victims – the SD deposited billions of pounds worth of loot into the banks of Zurich and Geneva. It was not in marks either, which the ODESSA organizers knew would be worthless when the war was over; the deposits made under false names and companies were in gold and the hard currencies of the allies – dollars and pounds.

But not all the ill-gotten gains were stored in Swiss banks. Billions and billions of marks' worth of gold, silver, tapestries, antiquities, art, bonds and other negotiable artefacts were siphoned off by the SD bankers. The loot was stored in huge salt mines in upper Austria and in caves in the Italian Dolomite mountains. It was this personal fortune which paid for the ODESSA to start operations at the war's close.

Experts calculate that up to £70 billion worth of the loot stolen in history's biggest robbery is still missing. It now resides with the inscrutable men who watch over the vaults of Swiss banks, and also in South American accounts and certain Arab banks. It has all been 'laundered' and is untraceable to the men who stole it. Its probable use in the forty three years since the war ended, has been to grease the pathways to freedom of the SS killers.

One man has spent his entire postwar life in the pursuit of Nazi war criminals hiding from justice. He is Simon Wiesenthal, an Austrian Jew in Vienna who survived the death camps to pursue a lone crusade against the murderers. His intelligence network of unpaid informers around the world has led to numerous arrests of wanted Nazis. But Wiesenthal knew in the very early days after the war that a secret organization existed to keep him from them. He has won considerable victories in bringing fugitives to justice, but has never defeated the machinery which spirited them away in the first place.

His expert knowledge of the ODESSA has been gleaned from secret files kept by the intelligence agencies of the West. Many, including the CIA, have a shameful past when it comes to Nazi war criminals. For when the conflict ended, focus switched from the defeat of Nazism to the new 'cold war' which loomed against the Soviet Union. Intelligence chiefs were only too willing to trade justice for the 'special skills' of wanted Nazis in the new war against communism. One of the men they enlisted was Klaus Barbie – now serving a life sentence in France for his atrocious war crimes. Another was Otto Skorkenzy, Hitler's master commando.

Skorkenzy, however, had more than knowledge about communist agents and spy networks – he was believed to be the first operative head of the ODESSA. During the war he was a gallant soldier in the Waffen SS and pulled off a spectacular glider rescue of the Italian dictator Mussolini from a mountain top. He also dressed his men up as United States soldiers during the 1944 German offensive in the Ardennes, wreaking havoc behind Allied lines.

After the war Skorkenzy traded secrets with US intelligence chiefs – except in one area: the ODESSA. Together with underlings, all using codenames, and never meeting together, they worked out the necessary details to get the

SS fugitives to safety. The favourite place to head for was South America, where the long tradition of right-wing military dictatorships favoured the refugees from a similar regime. Simon Wiesenthal says, 'In South Africa we have the Cape of Good Hope. But in South America we have the Cape of Last Hope for the Nazis. All the circumstances during and after World War Two developed it for the Nazis. About 60,000 members of the Nazi party during the 1930s live in Buenos Aires alone. All over the continent are fugitive SS men who were aided in their flight there by the ODESSA.'

Among the people who fled justice with the aid of the ODESSA were:

Alois Brunner – who designed the mobile gas-wagons to exterminate Jews at the start of the 'final solution'. He was also responsible for the deportation and deaths of 46,000 Greek Jews. Escaped to Damascus at the end of the war with ODESSA money and papers. Still at large.

Josef Mengele, notorious camp doctor of Auschwitz whose grisly experiments at the Polish death camp put him first place on Wiesenthal's most wanted list. He boasted in Buenos Aires to a German citizen several years ago that 'the comrades network', had provided him with his escape. He is widely believed now to be dead.

Joseph Schwammberger – commandant of the Polish concentration camp at Przemysl. Half a million perished under his orders. ODESSA got him to Argentina where he lives in safety.

The list goes on and on. Wiesenthal explains that it was only because of massive amounts of looting that ODESSA was able to accumulate the funds to bribe corrupt officials in the countries where the Nazis sought sanctuary.

Government agencies do not now actively pursue the old, grey men who oversaw Hitler's monstrous plan and did his bidding. Except for Israel, which is always keen to get its hands on the people who tried to exterminate the Jews, most countries are only spurred to action after repeated requests or if the media spotlight falls on them. The ODESSA has managed to keep its secrets over the years because its bank accounts are known only to a few high-ranking members. Those leaders in turn operate in small cells who do not know their counterparts. The cell system, favoured by terror groups such as the IRA, allows for people to be arrested or assassinated without the network being betrayed.

But there is not much chance of that now. Because of advancing years the ODESSA is a now dying organization. But whether or not its captured loot will be passed on to the sons of the fathers is something which Nazi hunter Simon Wiesenthal, and others who retain a conscience concerning those dark war years, want answered.

Oradour-sur-Glane

It was a hot Saturday afternoon in the sleepy town of Oradour-sur-Glane on 10 June 1944 – a town which not only the war, but time itself seemed to have passed by. Four days previously the allied armies had landed at Normandy and were fighting their way forward across Europe in the slow, bloody battle to liberate the conquered lands. True, there was excited chatter in Oradour's little café that afternoon, about the progress of the armies, the progress of their crops, and the summer fête planned for the following month. This small community of less than 700 people had toiled in their little village in the same quiet way that their forefathers had done for 800 years, and the horrors of modern warfare and the brutality of Nazism had, thankfully, passed them by.

In that long hot afternoon war and death came to Oradour. In an afternoon of killing that has long gone down in infamy, the people of the town were butchered in a frenzy of revenge and hatred by soldiers of the Das Reich Panzer division – a hitherto elite unit in the fighting arm of the SS that had distinguished itself on the Eastern Front in combat, but which had also undertaken brutal anti-partisan operations.

The women and children were herded into the village church, machine gunned, torn apart by hand grenades, burned in the ensuing flames which engulfed the building. Several young men in the fields who tried to bolt for it were picked off by SS sharpshooters who were arranged around the village at strategic points. As the smoke and stench of death rose in a grim pall over Oradour on that lazy summer afternoon, 642 people lay dead. Five survivors crawled from the smoking buildings where their fellow villagers had been murdered and were left to puzzle: why?

For years it has been assumed that Oradour was just another massacre, just another piece in the mosaic of appalling crimes perpetrated by the Nazis in all the places which they occupied. It was said that acts of sabotage by the Maquis – the French resistance fighters – had been stepped up in the region and the SS massacre was the ultimate warning to all would-be freedom fighters that the SS were not defeated and that similar atrocious punishments awaited anyone taking up arms against the Nazis. But recently new evidence has surfaced which suggests that the innocent folk of Oradour died because of a secret hoard of Nazi gold, plundered from the conquered territories. Was it this

Oradour-sur-Glane – a town destroyed by greed,

gold that the Das Reich commander was searching for the day he arrived in the town square? Almost certainly the answer is yes.

Major Otto Dickmann, a senior officer in the Das Reich division, was based in St Junien, not far from Oradour, where the remnants of the badly mauled Das Reich division were resting before joining up with the armies reeling back from the allied assault at Normandy. Among the vehicles in the long convoy stationed in the town was a truck which Dickmann referred to as carrying 'special merchandise'. He said it contained the division's records and order of battle, and gave strict orders to an Austrian Lieutenant, Bruno Walter, to double the guard on the truck. He knew that his superior, General Heinz Lammerding, were due into the town soon and he did not want the top brass breathing down his neck if the divisional transport were not well protected from the activities of the growing resistance menace. Since D-Day the Maquis had become more bold in their attacks – events had moved to the stage where SS men were having to put their hands into cow dung on the road to ensure that it wasn't booby trapped. St Junien was a centre of resistance and Dickmann could ill afford the 'special merchandise' coming under threat from the Maquis.

Dickmann, Lammerding and another Major, Helmut Kampfe, had entered into an unholy trinity in those last months of the war in France. They had survived the unbelievable butchery of the war on the Eastern Front and were now looking for some spoils to feather their own nests. All possesed Swiss bank accounts – all knew that unless a political solution was reached with the Western allies the military situation could only deteriorate. They, like countless other murderers among the ranks of the SS and Gestapo, were planning for a future without Adolf Hitler as their leader. But they needed money and the spoils of war seemed the best way of getting it. Dickmann authorized large-scale *ratissages* – looting of French towns under the pretext of searching for Maquis suspects, but in reality looking for gold. The trio had between them collected somewhere in the region of £6 million worth of gold at today's prices. In human terms the cost was beyond comparison – atrocity after atrocity was committed with the kind of barbarity that the Das Reich forces had perpetrated on the Eastern Front – this was a most terrible war, a war where there were no rules.

But the trio were stuck with the gold as they trundled to the battle area to support the flagging regular Wehrmacht forces. They could not ship it back to Germany – over a thousand acts of railway sabotage in the few months they had been in France made it too risky a venture. The three officers crated their booty and disguised it as divisional records. Lammerding decided to take the loot with them, at least as far as the Loire River, where he thought alternative arrangements, perhaps including the use of barges, could be made. It was a terrible worry for the SS men who were sure to be targets for the resistance and allied air strikes on their way.

British intelligence, thanks to the bravery of its network of agents in France, were aware that the greatly despised Das Reich division were in France and on the move with 300 heavy tanks, having swopped its looting and pillaging 'anti terrorist' role to head north to the Normandy battle zone. The resistance were planning receptions all along the route to make the Germans' journey as uncomfortable as possible. The British said that, unhindered, the German division could be in Normandy within three days, making a potentially significant contribution to the Axis forces holding the Allies in the narrow beachead zones. All and any harassment of the division would be invaluable.

At midnight on 9 June the special convoy containing the gold moved out of St Junien en-route for Bellac. Dickmann picked a circuitous route for he was as paranoid as everyone else of running into a Maquis ambush. A staff car preceded the truck, which was sandwiched between that and a half-track full of German soldiers. If all went well the convoy would have been in Bellac in a couple of hours. But all did not go well. A group of young resistance men on their way to another ambush dived for cover as the lights of the car came down the road. Fuelled by eager enthusiasm to do something for their country against the *Boche* they launched an ill-prepared ambush which, against all odds, paid off. The car exploded with a hand grenade through the window, the half track was racked by the searing explosions of several grenades and the soldiers who jumped from it and the truck were cut down in sten-gun fire. Only one German soldier escaped down the road.

Only one young resistance member survived. His six comrades, some as young as fifteen, were all dead, caught in the return fire and shrapnel from the explosions. The lone resistance survivor threw an extra grenade into the back of the truck, expecting to find more German corpses heaped inside. What he found were thirty little wooden boxes, each about the size of a shoebox. When he opened the lids he didn't find divisional records. He found gold, half a ton of it.

General Lammerding, holder of the Iron Cross First Class, decorated hero of the Russian Front, was in a rage that knew no bounds. By the following morning Dickmann felt his life was not worth living. The special convoy had been sabotaged and the gold was gone. On top of that Kampfe, his partner in crime and a longtime friend, had been kidnapped by Maquis and his fate was anyone's guess.

Lammerding had a problem. He was constantly being badgered by Field Marshall Gerd von Runstedt, supreme commander of the western front, to move his forces up to Normandy with all speed. But Lammerding wanted his 'pension' fund gold back – and used the kidnapping of Kampfe as the pretext for staying in the region while he tracked down the terrorists responsible. Kampfe was a high-ranking SS officer and it required investigation and, if necessary ruthless vengeance. But Lammerding only had twelve hours – twelve hours to find the gold which would guarantee him a happy retirement when the fighting was over.

Dickmann was summoned to Lammerding and told to find the gold. The finger of suspicion fell on Oradour – it was the nearest hamlet to the ambush site, just four kilometres away – Dickmann reasoned the only place where a half a ton of gold was likely to be taken. A notorious Captain Kahn, who had distinguished himself by his brutality and utter disregard for human life on the Russian front, was assigned to lead the search in Oradour. But it was likely that he was told it was a retribution raid, a *ratissage*, and not the search for half a ton of gold that was to provide a comfortable living for three senior officers after the war.

There are several theories about what happened in Oradour when Dickmann and 120 SS troopers rolled into the square. Did he mean for them all to die? The answer is almost certainly yes, but not before he had a chance to question them. The most likely scenario is that the hardened SS soldiers started shooting and began torching the buildings before Dickmann, who had travelled to the scene with French-speaking militiamen, could quiz the inhabitants. Either way it doesn't make much difference; there was no gold in Oradour. But the burned out houses, which have been left as they were at the end of that frightful day, are testimony to a frantic search which was carried out by the SS men. They rampaged through the buildings looking for any signs of half a ton of gold. There were none – for the gold was never there.

Robin Mackness, a former successful businessman who ran an investment management company in Lausanne, Switzerland, claims he knows the secret of what happened to the gold. In his book, *Oradour: Massacre and Aftermath*, he claims to have met a man called Raoul, the sole survivor of the ambush. Mackness, whose story about Oradour earned him praise from distinguished historian M. R. D. Foot, claims that he was asked, in 1982, to meet Raoul in France and move some 'black' gold – undeclared gold. It was Raoul who explained to him the secret of Oradour.

Raoul said that he was the survivor of the ambush on Dickmann's special convoy. He said he opened the crates, saw the gold, and carted it to a nearby field, all thirty boxes, and buried it using a shovel from the back of the truck. Then he spread twigs, leaves and grass over the scene and prayed that it didn't look like the ground had been too disturbed. Raoul raided the buried gold after the war and used it to start a small business, but now, as an old man, wanted to get it into a Swiss bank. As some of it it was marked with the initials RB – Reichsbank – he knew he had to get the gold into Switzerland in a no-questions-asked manner.

But Mackness says the deal cost him twenty one months in prison after he was stopped by French customs officers near Lyons airport and found with 200,000 pounds worth of the gold in his car. He says he refused to reveal the identity of Raoul or where he got the gold from.

It is now over forty four years since the massacre and the town has been left just as it was when the last grenade had been thrown and the last round fired – an eternal monument to man's inhumanity to man. Lammerding is dead, Dickmann is dead, Kampfe is dead. And the people of Oradour died in the madness of a totalitarian rage for a secret they knew nothing about.

Overlord – The Great Secret

When Hitler's armies overran the West in 1940, he proved to the world the futility of static fortresses. His armoured units, backed by air support and swift moving infantry, showed the effectiveness of the new kind of warfare, the *Blitzkrieg*, or lightning war. Hitler's tanks had merely sidestepped the most costly land fortress system ever constructed – the Maginot Line, in which France had placed so much faith and tens of millions of francs. It was designed to keep the Germans from forever again breaching French Borders. It was the world's most costly flop. Hitler did not meet it head on – he went around the edge, pushing his armour through the Ardennes forest and completely outflanking the fortifications. The result was the capitulation of France in six weeks.

But although the Fuehrer demonstrated his contempt for the 'fortress mentality', he none the less became a prisoner of it. When his armies were stretched in all parts of the world – in Africa, Russia, Italy, Greece and mainland Europe – he knew that it would only be time before the Allies launched an invasion. To repel such a force Hitler said that any such army was to be 'destroyed on the beaches'. And to do it, the man who showed such contempt for concrete and steel became the greatest fortress builder in history with the construction of the Atlantic Wall in France.

Entire battalions of conscripts and slave labourers were entrusted with the task of turning the French coastline into an impregnable line impossible to be breached. From the Pas-de-Calais, along the Normandy and Brittany coastlines, down the Atlantic seaboard beyond Bordeaux, and into the Bay of Biscay, the coastline was transformed into a giant pillbox, the beaches littered with mines and gruesome obstacles intended to disembowel landing craft as they raced for the beaches. Stretching northwards from France, through Belgium and Holland, through Denmark and Norway, the line zig-zagged upwards – although terrain there did not favour an invasion force.

The German General Staff knew that in order for an invasion to be successful there would have to be a) complete air superiority on the part of the invader, and b) harbour facilities to re-supply the armies at a rate quicker than the Germans could re-inforce the beachheads. If one or both criteria failed,

105

then Hitler's directive would be true and they would indeed die in their thousands on the beaches. As an invasion had to be launched from England, the General Staff calculated problems like flying time for fighters and bombers to protect the beachheads, winds, weather, favourable harbour areas, the shortest sea-distance and supply routes. Everything centred, including intelligence reports, on the Pas-de-Calais. Not only was it the nearest 'heavy-duty' port to mainland Britain, the beaches in place were flat and the tides favourable. For four years, Hitler – despite warnings in his own camp – unswervingly believed that the hammer blow would fall there. Just as unswervingly, he was ready to meet it. It was the great British deception – the secret of Overlord – that was to cost him the war.

Because it was the most obvious choice for an invasion, it rapidly became the most heavily defended region. Strung back from the cliffs were huge batteries, menacing coastal guns with the ability to lob shells into Dover twenty two miles away, and deep underground bunkers for troops that could withstand direct hits from 500 lb bombs. There was barely enough room for rock crabs to manoeuvre between the beach obstacles. Many of these obstacles had mines strapped to their sides for added effectiveness.

But the well protected Pas-de-Calais was not representative of the whole Atlantic Wall. Further down the coast, in the regions where Hitler said no armies could possibly contemplate landing, existed a potential Allied landing point. Down on the Normandy coastline, British planners as early as 1941 had studied maps, aerial photos – even pre-war French postcards – and they came up with a preliminary study which favoured striking where Hitler least expected it – the greatest armada in history would be unleashed after four years of planning to free Europe from the Nazi yoke. It was the biggest job in military history, and only secrecy would guarantee success. The intelligence job was to convince Hitler that Overlord would fall in the Pas-de-Calais – while in reality it would strike in Normandy. How?

It was on 12 March 1943 that British Lieutenant General Sir Frederick Morgan went to a meeting with Combined Operations Headquarters staff, the command run by Admiral Mountbatten. The Admiral himself greeted him warmly and announced to the other top brass members present that Morgan had assumed the role of Chief of Staff to the Supreme Allied Command – COSSAC for short. His brief: to plan for the Allied assault on mainland Europe. One month after the meeting General Sir Alan Brooke, Chief of the Imperial General Staff handed him his orders. 'There it is,' he said curtly. 'It won't work – but you must bloody well make it work!'

The task that Morgan faced was awesome. Not only had he to prepare the blueprints for the greatest invasion in history, he had to keep the plans secret and the Germans fooled. If at any time during the build up to D-Day the Germans switched their attention to the Normandy beaches and away from the Pas-de-Calais, the invasion would be scuppered. In the next fourteen months an inordinate amount of time, energy and resources were put into making the Germans believe that the blow would fall in the Calais region.

Up until 1943, it had been a relatively easy exercise to make German intelligence believe that the Pas-de-Calais was the invasion site. Most of the Nazi espionage network in Britain had been 'turned' shortly after the fall of France in 1940. Those agents who were not executed, fed a continuous stream of disinformation to their spymasters in Berlin. Only after the war's turning point – the utter defeat of the Sixth Army at Stalingrad and the reversal of fortunes on the Eastern Front – did the spectre of a second front loom large over Hitler and his generals. It was vital that new German agents, undiscovered by MI5, were fooled and fooled completely, to keep Hitler from embarking on a massive build-up of defences in the Normandy region.

But by late 1943, the build-up in Britain prior to invasion was proceeding at an almost unmanageable rate. Some two million men of an army, destined to swell to three and a half million were crammed into makeshift camps. The roads and railways systems creaked under the strain of millions of tons of supplies: tanks, heavy guns, aircraft, hundreds upon hundreds of thousands of tons of shells and bombs, millions of gallons of petrol and aviation fuel, the massive 'Mulberry' floating harbours that were being built at British ports ready to be towed to Normandy – each the size of a six storey building – and many other supplies of clothing, food and heavy machinery. General Eisenhower remarked: 'It was claimed that only the great number of barrage balloons floating constantly in British skies kept the islands from sinking under the seas.'

The problem confronting British intelligence was in convincing their opposite numbers that all these were headed for the Pas-de-Calais. Winston Churchill, Britain's wartime leader, well understood the need for deception. He created a central agency, the London Controlling Section, headed by two Englishmen, Colonel John Bevan and Lieutenant Colonel Sir Ronald Wingate, who were entrusted with fooling the Germans.

At first their campaign of disinformation was pretty standard – culminating in a bold plan called Operation Fortitude which must take much of the credit for making D-Day the success it was. It started with thousands of leaked intelligence messages, filtered through Allied-run spy networks, sloppily concealed 'secret' transmissions to Resistance groups in occupied territories, and calculated indiscretions. The Abwehr, Germany's intelligence agency, began collating report after report which signified that the Fuehrer was right – that the blow would fall in the North in the Pas-de-Calais. Espionage acts, too, were carried out all over occupied Europe, masterminded by LCS, and carried out with the aid of Britain's wartime dirty tricks brigade, the Special Operations Executive. The acts of sabotage had no strategic value for Overload – but they kept the Germans guessing and their reserves, particularly their elite Panzer divisions, dispersed over a wide area.

LCS mapped out six principal deception plans, thirty six subordinate ones and many other related strategies. The purpose of Operation Fortitude was to pin down in occupied Europe – away from the invasion zone – some ninety three German divisions. One part of the plan aimed – and succeeded – in bottling up twenty seven German divisions in Scandinavia! By creating a fictitious Fourth Army in Britain – with its command centre in the bowels of Edinburgh Castle – the German High Command was duped into thinking a heavy diversionary assault would fall on Norway. The German intelligence services were flooded with fake messages – one of them being a request from the non-existent 80th Division to Corps Headquarters for the delivery of 1,800 pairs of ski-bindings! Another message transmitted with the express purpose of being intercepted asked for woollen underwear and guides on how to scale sheer rock faces.

Still the deception went on. In neutral European capitals – hotbeds of spying for both sides throughout the war – British agents went around buying up every available Michelin map of the Pas-de-Calais region. Another masterstroke of the subversive war was the Two Generals broadcasts. The broadcasts had started shortly after 1942 and were allegedly the careless conversations of two disillusioned Germany Army officers who spoke to each other on short-wave radios about the state of the war. Germans who listened to the glum, despondent chatter of the men were suprised that there were not more careful or they would be caught. In fact the officers were German speaking actors transmitting from England in a carefully contrived plot to lower morale. In their weekly chats to each other in 1944 they dropped nuggets of disinformation about D-Day – and how they had heard that the invasion was set for Calais.

Perhaps the most brilliant stroke of all was FUSAG – The First US Army Group which was created on paper only. While Montgomery assembled his mammoth 21st Army Group in south-west England ready for the invasion, FUSAG became an army of papier-mache huts, inflatable rubber tanks, cardboard cutout camps, plywood planes and fake ammunition dumps. Fake landing craft made at the Shepperton film studios were moored on the Thames and Brtiain's leading architect, Sir Basil Spence, a professor of architecture at the Royal Academy, designed and constructed an enormous fake oil dock occupying three square miles of the shore at Dover. All of this massive fake army was in the south-east of England and was allegedly under the command of the fearsome US General George S. Patton. The German High Command was so taken in by the nonexistent Army, that they listed it in their documents of British Order of Battle.

The deception paid off – right up until the 11th hour when the strange sixth sense that had made Hitler master of Europe visited him again. In mid April Allied air-reconnaisance photographs showed a military build-up in the Normandy region, coupled with anti-glider obstacles dug into fields earmarked for Allied airborne assault. LCS was frantic that the plan had been discovered – especially when they learned that Russian-front hardened Panzer divisions were lurking in the region. But it seems to have been Hitler's intuition, nothing more, and although Normandy would be a tougher nut to crack than before, the bulk of the German forces remained thinly spread throughout the occupied lands.

By May the greatest task force the world had ever know waited for the orders to attack. A shortage of landing craft put the invasion off until June. Secrecy was at its most critical stage. One careless security lapse could mean years more of war. COSSAC had by this time given way to SHAEF – the Supreme Headquarters Allied Expeditionary Force, led by Eisenhower. A ten mile zone around all coastal areas where the invasion forces were mustered was designated out of bounds to civilians. The British government took the unprecedented step of restricting the diplomatic privileges of all countries, forbidding diplomats and their couriers from entering Britain and censoring previously sacrosanct diplomatic mail. On 25 May transatlantic cable and wireless facilities for American servicemen were withdrawn. A security blanket draped over embattled Britain.

Three weeks before Overlord, Churchill met his commanders. He was told that the great deceit had worked. Germany believed that the invasion, led by the fake FUSAG army, would strike in Northern France.

They met again in June after agonizing deliberations over the foul weather. On Monday 5 June there was talk of disembarking the men from their assault craft and of postponing the invasion until it cleared. But the die was cast by the commanders. 'We go' said Eisenhower.

On 5 June 1944 the armada set sail for the beaches between Cherbourg and Le Havre. Around 5,000 ships, 11,000 planes, and the first waves of three and a half million men plunged through the black night on their mission to liberate Europe. By dawn the next morning the battleships began their bombardment of the coastal positions, thousands of airborne troops dropped behind enemy lines and the infantry were fighting their way up the beaches. Hitler's massive reserves were stirring themselves like a lizard waking up in the sun. But by then it was too late – the Allies were on the road to victory.

The Disappeared

It was given a clinical name. Like Adolf Hitler who called the extermination of European Jewry the 'Final Solution', so the military dictatorship of Argentina which embarked on one of the modern world's biggest witch-hunts did not call it murder, instead they dubbed it 'The Process of National Reorganization'. Whatever the name, humanity in Argentina ceased to exist for millions of citizens between the years 1976 and 1983. Under great secrecy and shielding behind the apparatus of the state, death squads murdered some 11,000 people, now known as The Disappeared. Two million more fled the persecution, hundreds of babies born to The Disappeared while they were being 'processed' by the military junta's servants were sold, bartered or murdered. Of the 11,000 who were butchered, experts now concur that only a handful were the left-wing terrorists who the dictatorship sought to eradicate 'root and branch'. The Process of National Reorganization, like most witch-hunts, took on a momentum all of its own. What happened in the South American nation between those years was the nearest parallel to the years of the Holocaust in the post-war world; a secret plot to eradicate all opposition, the full horror of which was only revealed after Argentina's military defeat in the Falklands War of 1982.

The military has had a long and ignoble history of meddling in the affairs of civilian governments in South America. In Argentina, it began in 1930 and continued until 1976, with the overthrow of Isabelita Peron; there had been no less than six coups and twenty-one years of military dictatorship. No civilian government had lasted its full term, save for that of Juan Peron's first period of office. On 23 March 1976, tanks rolled out on to the streets of the capital Buenos Aires and stationed themselves at the city's vital crossroads and bridges. General Jourge Videla, head of the army, proclaimed a new military junta to oust Isabelita Peron, citing the chronic inflation and massive unemployment as the reason for their intervention. Indeed, the former nightclub dancer Isabelita headed a government which saw inflation in the first quarter of 1976 run at a staggering 800 per-cent; a faster increase than the years of money-madness in post-war Germany in 1921-22. Not only did Videla pledge a re-think on policies, he promised to curb the left-wing violence that had been part of Argentine life since 1966.

110

The Mothers' Protest in the Plaza de Mayo.

Leftist guerrillas had been rampant in the country – kidnapping wealthy industrialists, murdering policemen, sabotaging military installations. To the military big three – Videla, and the heads of the Navy and Air Force – the country was on an inexorable slide into anarchy. The ERP, the Ejercito Revolucionario del Pueblo, the People's Revolutionary Army, and the Montoneros were the two left-wing groups that plunged Argentina into crisis. Had they not created the climate of lawlessness and terror which resulted in thousands of deaths, maybe the military would have stayed in its barracks and on field exercises. Certainly their refusal to recognize the elected government of Hector Campora – elected freely and fairly in 1973 – to continue their bloody revolutionary war was a major factor which prompted the nightmare military response. Videla and his generals were under no illusions what that response would be. It would be total war – carried out not only against the known guerrillas, but against those that they deemed may have a tendency for left-wing action or sympathies. In the dirty war that Videla was about to unleash, thought, association or sympathy with any policy other than that dictated by the junta were crimes punishable under the

111

'Process of National Reorganization'.

After the coup, greeted with calm by most people, sickened of both inflation and the guerrilla war, and with positive joy among the wealthy business community, Videla's government issued a statement to the world pledging full respect for 'law, human dignity, and Argentina's international obligations ... the fundamental objective will be to ensure essential values in leadership, assuring the full development of the country's natural and human potential.' Secretly, the machinery of terror was being assembled. Argentina's military, particularly her officers had long been instilled with a sense of divine purpose – that theirs was a noble cause, protecting Argentina and her strategic place in the world among the great nations, as a bulwark against communism. Now they were told that the final conflict had arrived; that indeed their Third World War against the heretics of Marxism had come.

By 1976, the Argentine officer corps was a different body to the generations that had preceded it. Over 600 Argentine officers had attended a course, started by the John F. Kennedy administration, at the US Army School of the Americans, based in Panama. Although intended by a democratic nation to show South American nations how to defeat communist revolution and maintain the support of the populace, the school taught many gruesome subjects – not the least of them torture. This, coupled with the ceaseless indoctrination in their home country served to equip the Argentinian officers for a covert war against the masses.

Survivors of the terror, those who implemented it and those who were on the receiving end, are among those who testified that the strategy for the 'Process' was worked out at a top secret meeting hosted by Videla in 1975. Accounts, naturally, are sketchy, because no documents testifying to their evil scheme have surfaced. What seems to have happened is this: Videla requested detailed methods of dealing with the guerrillas drawn up by the intelligence chiefs of the three services. Roberto Viola, the general who became Videla's brief successor before General Galtieri in 1981 was there. So were high-ranking intelligence chieftans of the Navy and Air Force. Viola is reported to have argued against the policy which, Videla said, meant the complete and total disappearance of the regime's critics. The state was to act as judge, jury and executioner.

A vivid foretaste of what lay in wait for the people of Argentina was delivered next month, October 1975, when Videla gave a speech in Montevideo, capital of neighbouring Uruguay. He said: 'In order to guarantee the security of the state, all the necessary people will die. A subversive is anyone who opposes the Argentine way of life.'

Only after Britain's victory in the Falklands and the downfall of the dictatorship in Argentina did the misery and wholesale suffering of those years come to light. The terror was directed by the Ministry of the Interior where a master list of those who vanished was said to be kept. But in reality the mayhem loosed on the unfortunate population had little direction or guidance. Each military branch had its own intelligence service masterminding kidnappings, torture and executions. On top of those were the actions of the National Gendarmerie and the police. In addition several government ministries, even the national oil company, held lists of suspects and had security agencies operating for them. The separate arms of state, all vying for the dubious glory of arresting more subversives, caging more innocents, torturing more women, created a system of total mayhem. The kidnappings were done by men dressed in plain clothes. The unfortunate relatives were met with a stone-wall at police stations and government offices. 'How can we tell you what happened, when we have no record of arrest? It must be the terrorists responsible.' It was the stock answer repeated over 11,000 times.

Green Ford Falcon cars became the symbol of the terror, in much the same way as Madame Guillotine had been in the French Revolution two centuries earlier. The four-door cars were packed with men from the *patotas*, the arresting squads. The Falcons cruised down streets keeping a watch for suspects who were then bundled into the boot and oblivion. The *patotas* were heavily armed with pistols and sub-machine guns and used violence at the slightest sign of a struggle during an abduction.

The Disappeared were taken to torture and interrogation centres all over Argentina – places with innocuous sounding names like the Navy Mechanics School on the outskirts of Buenos Aires. A name resonant of research and study; in reality it was a human abbatoir where people were beaten, electrocuted, maimed and finally 'processed' so they were no longer a threat to the right-wing regime which ruled Argentina. The military had long ago decided that ordinary prisons were no solution to terrorism and so set up these sinister, secret detention and torture centres all over the country.

At the Navy Mechanics School was one Lieutenant Alfredo Astiz, a prominent torturer who was responsible for the death of two French nuns among the myriad hordes caught up in the process. Astiz was captured during the Falklands War and spent a short time in Britain before he was packaged back off to Argentina where he now lives freely, unlike so many of his tragic victims.

The military disposed of the bodies of their victims in two ways – in the 'doorless flights' over remote stretches of the River Plate, or by the 'NN' method. The doorless flights were named after the aircraft and helicopters whose doors were either removed or constantly open, allowing the military to dump bodies in remote regions and into the river. As many as 5,000 victims were disposed of in this way.

The NN's were the victims with no-name. Buried in their thousands all over Argentina, the bodies still continue to be found to this day.

Such wholesale disappearances, of everyone from students, university professors, nuns, priests, to clerks and business executives, could not fail to arouse the interest of the world humanity watchdog, Amnesty International. Amnesty first visited Argentina before the end of 1976 and compiled a chilling dossier of life in the state prisons where women told of sexual abuse, torture and humiliation. The Amnesty investigators were shocked – but they hadn't seen all. They still had no knowledge of the secret detention centres which made the prisons look like citadels of decency.

Allen 'Tex' Harris was one of the heroes of the dirty war who saw the Argentinian situation for what it was and relayed it in detail to the authorities in Washington. As a first secretary as the US embassy in Buenos Aires he was entrusted with the task of monitoring human rights violations. He and his assistants chronicled no fewer than 15,000 cases which were sent to the Jimmy Carter administration in Washington. He discovered that it was not a campaign aimed at terror groups and fought between terror groups, but a systematic war against the people of Argentina. He said: 'They killed some real terrorists in shoot-outs early on, sure enough, and they captured some too. But the great majority of the ones they captured were just wine-and-coffee subversives – kids who sat in cafés talking about socialist ideals and how the country should be changed.

'There was a guy from Army intelligence who told me in person that the real tragedy of their operations was that half the people eliminated were innocent even by their own criteria. But it was easier to kill them because it was less risky and less compromising than going through the legal procedures. Easier to handcuff them to a lamppost and just shoot them.'

But governments had little to congratulate themselves on as the toll of human rights abuses continued to mount. The United States made noises on rights abuses and sought guarantees on improvements – but the thinking in Washington was undeniably that a right-wing regime was infinitely preferable to a left-wing one. The Soviet Union, heavily reliant on the United States for grain, did not want to antagonize a potentially major supplier in case Washington turned unfriendly. Britain played a cool behind-the-scenes game with the Argentine junta over the relatively few British people, or those of British descent, who had vanished.

Two things blew apart the secrecy, and it is debatable which was the more powerful. One was the Falklands War in 1982, the other the Mothers of the Plaza de Mayo.

The tactic of making people vanish without trace had proved its effectiveness as early as 1977, one year after the junta took power. There were no martyrs to the cause – indeed, there were no state records of prisoners. There were no demonstrations in the West about Argentina as there had been about Chile and no government had severed diplomatic ties with Videla. But on the afternoon of Saturday 13 April 1977, a small demonstration took place which would become a milestone in Argentine history. Fourteen women, who had lost sons, husbands, daughters, brothers and sisters in the terror staged a solemn walk in the Plaza de Mayo outside the Casa Rosada, the pink palace residence of Argentina's rulers. The walk was formed by Hebe Bonafini and Adela Antokaletz, two women who had both lost loved ones: Mrs Bonafini, her two sons and a daughter-in-law; Mrs Antokaletz her son. The movement grew from a few women pronounced as 'mad' by the Generals, to dozens, who paraded every week despite clubbings, tear gassings and arrests. In the end the military left them alone – the Mothers had won the right to the Plaza and the world bore witness to their silent, noble stand.

In the end, the military became as inept at running the country as the civilians they overthrew. In 1982, in a mad venture, as the economy reeled from the years of murder instead of economic planning, they launched an attack on the Falkland Islands off the southern tip of Argentina. Long a symbol of national pride, *Las Malvinas* were in the hands of the junta for a matter of weeks before a well-trained force from Britain resoundingly defeated them and reclaimed the windswept islands for the Realm. It signalled the total collapse of the junta.

In Argentina in December the following year, Raul Alfonsin came to power as a democratically elected president and the full horror of those years came to light. The graves were discovered the length and breadth of the enormous land, torturers stepped up to confess their crimes and the killers wrung their hands and said they were doing their duty.

So far several hundred Argentine military officers have been sentenced for their crimes, and several hundred more face court hearings. The Mothers of the Plaza de Mayo still tread their weary way in front of the Casa Rosada; those who lost loved ones still wonder how they ever let it happen. But in a volatile land, where the military is never far away from heading for parliament, many fear that justice will stop far short of what they deserve.

'They did it in secret and in silence,' said Mrs Bonafini, who still cries at the thought of the loved ones she lost and has never seen again. 'The world could not imagine our suffering. Let it serve as a warning to other countries not to put faith in military men like we did in Argentina.'

The Manhattan Project

Over forty years have elapsed since the vision of a mushroom cloud of smoke rising over a Japanese city called Hiroshima burned itself forever on the human consciousness. In that split second man unleashed the forces of nature that he had learned to harness in the century's most top-secret research and as a result the nuclear age was born. After that explosion, nothing would ever be the same again. The world now lies split into two camps, each with enough nuclear hardware to make the Hiroshima bomb look like a firecracker. The United States developed the bomb under conditions of amazing secrecy in a research programme called The Manhattan Project. Led by brilliant phycisist Dr Robert Oppenheimer, the Americans were engaged in a frantic race against time – for in a world at war, Nazi Germany was also engaged in its own research to split the atom. Although behind the US effort, the fact that Hitler's scientists were engaged in research made President Franklin Roosevelt aware that, no matter what the cost, the free world had to achieve the first atom bomb and thereby completely ensure its supremacy over the forces of Germany and Japan.

It was the rise of Nazism and the war which caused groups of European scientists, many of them Jewish, to flee to the United States. As early as 1933 these brilliant men and women warned that Nazi scientists had been given huge budget increases to pursue the dream of a controlled nuclear reaction – in effect, a bomb of awesome power. In 1938 US intelligence learned that outside Berlin, in a closely guarded laboratory, the Germans had succeeded in splitting a single atom. They had not harnessed its energy, but they were on the way. It was enough to spur the most eminent phycisist of this, or any age, to write to the President of the United States urging him to push for nuclear research – and quickly.

Dr Albert Einstein, father of the theory of relativity, was one of those banished from Nazi Germany because he was a Jew. He wrote an impassioned letter to Roosevelt, who was still struggling to rebuild the US economy from the days of the great depression which had devastated the United States. The plea from such an eminent scientist shocked Roosevelt and moved him to

Hiroshima – devastated by the atomic bomb.

order research effort on the bomb. Even though the United States was neutral in the war until 1941, Roosevelt and his advisers were of the opinion that the prize of nuclear supremacy should belong to the mightiest industrial nation.

Since the turn of the century scientists had known that the element uranium naturally disintegrated by emitting alpha particles containing neutrons and protons – a process yielding a spectacular million times more energy per atom than ordinary fire. The only problem was – the process took millions of years as part of the natural evolutionary process of earth. What if that process could be speeded up, harnessed – and unleashed? The prospect for scientists was breathtaking and frightening.

Enrico Fermi, an Italian scientist who came to the United States in 1938 from Mussolini's Italy, was awarded the 1938 Nobel Prize for his research into atomic energy and shortly afterwards came to America to take up a teaching post at the University of Columbia. Fermi learned there of the German experiment in Berlin. Together with several eminent scientists from around the world, he began his first experiments into nuclear fission.

Fermi was one of the first scientists to throw a veil of secrecy around the research. In the early days it was an academic project, not sanctioned by the government or military. He had to warn his colleagues – long used to trading information with other scientists and boasting of their progress in scientific journals – to remain silent. The military were later to complain that the security in those early days was 'leaking like a sieve'.

Before building a bomb, the scientists first had to learn how to split the atom and harness its energy. By mid-1938 Roosevelt had authorized the Manhattan Project as a government funded programme for the bomb and, realizing the need for secrecy, decreed that the separate research programmes were to be carried out at sites and locations spaced widely apart. A secret bunker complex was carved out of the Nevada desert in New Mexico, where it was ultimately hoped the bomb would be tested. The research into splitting the atom was carried out under Fermi's guidance in Chicago.

The breakthrough came on 3 December 1942, on a sports field in Chicago. Fermi assembled his research team with the device which would trigger a nuclear chain reaction; the first step to forming the 'critical mass' which becomes the nuclear explosion. The scientists had built a nuclear 'pile', a primitive nuclear reactor designed to test whether nuclear energy could be triggered in a chain reaction and harnessed for energy. The reactor took the form of a spheroid shape, packed with uranium which would be bombarded with neutrons and protons as safety rods inserted into the device were removed one by one. On hand were a 'suicide squad' of firefighters – armed with nothing more than a few buckets of water to put out Earth's first man-made nuclear fire if the chain reaction were so violent that it caught fire!

The sports field had been sealed off for three miles around by police and security agents desperate to shield the experiment that was taking place. Anyone wishing to go near the place was told that soil samples for a new government farming programme were being taken.

One by one the rods were pulled – Fermi witnessed the geiger counters monitoring the berserk levels of radiation as they pulsed through the sphere, triggering the massive chain reaction 'Throw in the safety rods' cried Fermi at the last minute before the sphere looked likely to explode in that most dangerous of nuclear accidents – meltdown. The experiment worked and Fermi celebrated man's arrival in the atomic age with a bottle of Chianti!

However, just as the Manhattan Project got under way properly in 1942 – building the bomb in the Nevada desert complex – some of the physicists engaged became worried about the nature of their tasks. They were concerned with the nuclear destruction that they might be unleashing on the world. It was a question of conscience that caused more than one scientist to leave the project – and gave a security headache to the agencies concerned with keeping secret the most important research of the war. All the scientists involved were required to sign secrecy oaths – but for good measure many were kept under the scrutiny of the military for months afterwards.

The military man in charge of the project was a bluff brigadier-general named Leslie Groves. He was a man used to giving orders and used to having them obeyed. He more than anyone impressed on the men of science the need to keep the project secret. He pointed out that one of the prizes which fell to the German war machine in 1940 during the battle of Norway was the Norsky Hydro Hydrogen Electrolysis plant, which manufacturered heavy water – the most efficient substance, say scientists, for the construction of a chain-reacting atomic pile. Although the plant was later crippled in an Allied commando raid, Groves told the scientists 'Make it quicker, without being caught, and we'll have them. Don't and they will have us.' The work progressed with everyone involved aware of the need for urgency.

The giant Du Pont company was given the government order to manufacture enough plutonium for the bomb. Government contracts everywhere for the manufacture of the weapon were disguised as something else – research into pesticides, research into solar power, research into alternative fuels. The steel delivered for some of the prototype bomb casings was marked down as steel for artillery barrels.

By 1945, a prototype had been developed and, by July, was ready for testing. In the middle of the New Mexico desert Operation Trinity, the code name for the testing, was set for the 16 July. The bomb was called Fat Boy and the site for its testing was ten miles from the Alamagordo Air Base, a complex of underground bunkers and buildings where much of the construction of the bomb had been carried out. A host of military and scientific top brass were assembled to witness the largest explosion ever made by man on Earth. At 5.30 a.m. in the cold drizzle, a ball of fire reaching 41,000 feet, 12,000 feet higher than the tallest mountain, soared above the desert. The thunder from the explosion reverberated across the open spaces, shaking the ground as if an earthquake were about to consume the earth. Oppenheimer, in that fearful moment, recited two verses from Sanskrit, the ancient language of India. One was: 'If the radiance of a thousand suns were to burst into the sky, that would be the splendour of the mighty one.' The second was: 'I am become Death, the shatterer of worlds.'

Three months before the test the most secret airfield ever constructed was built at Tinian, a Pacific island situated near Japan. The inhabitants of the island were completely isolated from the world as teams of engineers and construction workers carved out the forward atomic base from where an elite airwing, the 509th, would be based to carry out the nuclear attack on Japan. President Harry Truman had sanctioned an American nuclear assault on the Japanese mainland in an effort to save American lives as Japanese troops fought fanatically to the death in their bid to hold their ground. The 509th was formed in conditions of such secrecy that even the top ranking scientists and officers on the Manhattan Project did not know that a squadron with the sole purpose of delivering the bomb to Japan had been formed.

The secrecy surrounding the bomb and the delivery of atomic material to Tinian for final bomb assembly had tragic consequences. The cruiser Indianapolis was loaded with the radioactive cargo sailed from San Francisco to Tinian and on its return voyage was torpedoed. Because its mission was so secret the naval command did not know its exact position or whereabouts. As a result nearly 400 men died in the shark infested waters before any rescue vessels were sent to their aid. It was one of the war's prime examples where secrecy overrode every consideration – including human life.

The plane that was to carry the bomb was to be piloted by the United States' top flyer, Captain Paul Tibbets, who named the B-29 bomber the Enola Gay after his mother. On 6 August 1954 Mrs Tibbets achieved fame of a kind when the bomb was dropped on Hiroshima. In the blinding light of the nuclear explosion, equivalent of 20,000 tons of TNT, 150,000 people were incinerated, thousands more suffering the appalling burns of radiation.

The Manhattan Project was successful and Dr Robert Oppenheimer was right; he had become the shatterer of worlds.

Chapter Five

SECRETS OF HOLLYWOOD

In a place where sincerity is as real as a studio backdrop, it is no surprise that Tinsel town's residents have many secrets. Secrets like the sex life of Rock Hudson – the ultimate macho actor whose homosexuality led to his death; or the shocking secrets in film star Mary Astor's infamous diary – a work that made the *Kama Sutra* pale by comparison; and then there were the murders – who killed respected director, William Desmond Taylor?

The Double Life of Rock Hudson

The Hollywood dream factory is a remarkable thing. It can recreate the parting of the Red Sea on a studio backlot, turn a sound stage into a galactic war zone, or make Fred Astaire dance on the ceiling. But in Tinsel Town, where they hand out awards from trickery and deception, things are seldom as they appear.

So it was with Rock Hudson. For almost forty years, this master of the silver screen lived a secret, double life. In public he was the most dashing screen hero of his generation – a rugged, macho love god idolized by women and envied by men all over the world. But in private he was a far cry from the debonair lady-killer of his films. He was a homosexual, whose lusting for taboo love eventually cost him his life ... and shattered the image he had carefully cultivated throughout his career. It was a secret Rock had dearly wanted to take with him to the grave – and probably would have, had he not fallen victim to the disease society has labelled the 'gay plague'.

Even after AIDS was first diagnosed, Rock tried to continue living the lie, and swore his closest friends to secrecy. Eventually, of course, neither he nor they could remain silent, once the devastating effects of the disease became obvious. And so, just a few weeks before his death, the screen giant reluctantly admitted the secret he had kept hidden for so many years.

Back then, Rock Hudson, film star was just plain Roy Fitzgerald, Navy veteran, vacuum cleaner salesman and would-be actor. He worked hard, saving what money he could, and whenever he had a spare moment, would stand outside the gates of the movie studios, waiting to be discovered. It was a lonely time for Roy, as he recalled many years later: 'It was very difficult for me to make friends. People weren't friendly like they were in the Mid-West.'

But by the following year, the struggling actor had made some friends ... friends who would change his life forever: the gay community of nearby Long Beach. It was natural for Roy to feel at home among his own kind. Ever since his days in the Navy, he had preferred the company, and sexuality, of men. But Roy got more than sex and friendship from those he met – he also got his first break on the way to becoming an international sex symbol.

Some of his fellow gays had connections in showbusiness and, at a party in

Rock Hudson at one of his last public appearances.

1948, Roy was introduced to Henry Willson, a fellow homosexual and head of talent for the David O. Selznick Studio. Willson, who could spot that elusive 'star quality' at a glance, signed Roy to a studio contract and changed his name to Rock Hudson.

It was during this time that Rock also met two fellow gays, George Nader and Mark Miller. The three would remain close friends all their lives. Mark, a one-time singer, had given up his career in order to become Nader's business manager. Nader, like Rock, was exceptionally good-looking and wanted a career in the movies. But all three knew that if he and Rock were ever going to make it, they could not allow even a hint of scandal about their sexual preferences to get into print. Rock went to some bizarre lengths. He always made sure he had two phone lines in his apartment, and his room mate was never allowed to answer Rock's, lest someone discovered that Rock was living with another man. He and George also developed code-words to talk to each other in public. 'Is he musical?' was a code for 'Is he gay?'

In 1953, Rock, who had already appeared in several films, though was not yet considered a star, met Jack Navaar, a twenty-two-year-old friend of Nader's. The two hit it off immediately and within a few weeks, the dynamic-looking couple were lovers and room mates. But Rock could never publicly show any affection for Jack, and even when his first big film, *Magnificent Obsession*, premiered the following year, he was forced to bring a script girl from the studio as his date. Jack, who arrived in a separate car, was also given a female escort. Studio bosses knew they had a potential superstar on the rise, and they didn't want the press to get a whiff of scandal. 'Universal invested a lot of money in Rock, and it was important for his image to remain that of a lady-killer', said Mamie Van Doren, a friend of Rock's.

Unfortunately for Jack, however, fame soon went to Rock's head, and the once-happy couple began to argue bitterly about anything and everything. To make matters worse, Jack couldn't even go out to dinner with his lover anymore, because *Magnificent Obsession* had made Rock a huge celebrity. Inevitably, within twelve months, the affair was over – and Hudson, his career booming, would not live with another man for a decade.

But in 1955, despite Rock's intricate precautions, the Hollywood scandal sheet *Confidential* was threatening to write an exposé on his taboo love affairs – which would destroy not only his career, but financially cripple the studio as well. To kill the story, the studio and Rock decided that he should get married, which he did on 9 November.

The hastily arranged nuptials, to his agent's secretary, Phyllis Gates, saved his career. Unfortunately for Phyllis, she was never told the marriage had been planned by the studio bosses, or that Rock was gay. Many years later, she recalled that Rock had managed to keep his homosexuality from her until the very end of the relationship, which lasted almost three years.

By 1960, Rock was the world's number one box office attraction, and had just completed his first comedy, *Pillow Talk*, with Doris Day. It was about this time that he began to be driven more by sex, than his career. After all, he had now made it to the top, and all those years of self-sacrifice and self-discipline were about to be abandoned. Rock even confided to friends that he thought about having sex all the time during this period, even while driving his car or rehearsing his lines.

In the next ten years, he had numerous lovers, but still managed to keep his secret from the public, thanks to loyal friends and discreet colleagues within the industry. It was a precaution he had to take. Even a malicious gag could almost end a career, as Hudson found out in the early 1970s. A vicious hoaxster sent out invitations to gossip columnists, inviting them to the 'wedding' of Rock and good friend Jim Nabors. The tasteless prank ruined Nabors' career, whose prime-time variety series was cancelled soon after, even though he and Hudson were never more than friends.

The experience left Rock even more paranoid about his secret life, and he avoided Hollywood night life more and more. Instead, he would entertain guests at his Beverly Hills mansion, where a string of handsome young men would lie around the pool waiting to offer their services.

In 1973, Rock again took a full-time housemate and lover – Hollywood publicist Tom Clark, whom he'd met ten years earlier. Clark, a far cry from the pretty boys that had walked in and out of Hudson's bedroom over the years, would become the most important person in the actor's life. They were inseparable for many years, and spent wonderful times doing things they both loved – drinking, cooking, travelling, watching football and making love. But in Tom, Rock also found something very special. For the first time in his life, he had a man with whom he could walk down the street, take to restaurants and studio parties. Tom, you see, had become Rock's personal manager and publicist . . . a legitimate connection.

'I can take him anywhere,' Rock confided to friends. 'I can even introduce him to Princess Margaret.'

In 1975, Rock turned fifty – and Tom threw him the 'prettiest party we ever had.' As the guests mingled in the party room, the hired band struck up *You Must Have Been a Beautiful Baby*. Down the staircase came the birthday boy, wearing only a nappy, as the guests whistled and cooed.

Of course, there were many other parties at Rock's mansion over the years. Once, in 1977, just before he returned home from a three-month tour, he called secretary Mark Miller and said: 'I want a beauties' party when we get home. Could you arrange it? Have a party waiting for me at the house.'

Miller obliged. He invited ten of Rock's closest friends, and fifty handsome young men! One of the guests later recalled: 'There were some of the best-looking men I'd seen in my life.'

But the pleasures of the party were short-lived. That same year, Rock hit bottom, drinking all day, worrying about his age and sliding career and even took to touring homosexual clubs in San Francisco where anything went. Ironically, it was at about this time that the AIDS virus was taking a foothold within the gay community. Rock's sex and drinking binge lasted almost four years, until, in November 1981, he was forced to undergo by-pass surgery on his heart. It was, quite literally, a sobering experience.

'He woke up from the drunkenness of the '70s,' said old friend George Nader. 'The meanness and sniping fell away, and he was returning to the Rock we had known in 1952 – a warm human being who laughed and played games.'

But he was no longer devoted to Tom Clark. In 1982, Rock began to have a lusty affair behind Tom's back with a much younger, more virile man, Marc Christian. Within a year, Tom was tossed out of the house, and Marc moved in. It was to be Rock's most passionate, and final relationship.

In 1984, Rock was invited to a White House dinner, where he gladly posed for pictures with President and Mrs Reagan. A few weeks later, the photographs arrived at his office, personally signed by the First Couple. As he and secretary Miller looked at the photos, they noticed a red sore on Rock's neck. It had been there for over a year, but it had become bigger.

Under Miller's constant nagging, Rock eventually decided to see a doctor about the sore ... and on 5 June 1984, he received the news he had dreaded. It was AIDS. But Rock still wasn't about to let his secret out; not yet, anyway. Those few friends he did tell were sworn to secrecy, as the dying actor vainly sought a cure. Marc Christian didn't know Rock had AIDS until February 1985, even though they continued to have sex; and Linda Evans, the actress whom Rock kissed on an episode of *Dynasty* didn't know until the world did. Rock had lived a lie for so long, that he couldn't even bring himself to tell the truth to those close to him. It wasn't until the end was near, when death was certain, that he finally revealed his dreadful secret.

Fans around the world were understandably shattered, and yet they responded to his plight with sympathy and renewed curiosity about this mystery disease. Suddenly, AIDS was on the front pages of newspapers around the world; research funds were set up; the United States Congress vastly increased efforts towards finding a cure; the United Nations hosted conferences on it; everywhere, people wanted to learn more about the disease which had taken their idol.

Ironically, the secret Rock felt he could never share with the world has spurred that same world to action. Rock's defeat may become his victory.

Death of a Hollywood Director

On the morning of 2 February 1922, celebrated film director William Desmond Taylor was found lying on the floor of his Hollywood bungalow, a diamond ring on his finger, a smile on his face – and a bullet in his back.

Today, more than sixty-five years later, the identity of his murderer remains one of Hollywood's most tantalizing secrets, a 'whodunnit' in the greatest traditions of the cinema.

It had everything: sex, drugs and scandal; an evil, exploitative stage mother; a sexy young starlet; an affable, handsome director who happened to be bisexual, and a studio that was prepared to go to any lengths to cover it all up.

But what makes the Taylor case even more fascinating is that several people either saw the murderer enter or leave the house, and yet no one was ever charged with the crime! The moguls of Hollywood, it seems, had influence over more than just the movie world, and they knew a trial would only further scandalize an industry still reeling from the Fatty Arbuckle rape trials in San Francisco.

Indeed, when the police were finally called to Taylor's residence that sunny afternoon, they found no fewer than eleven of his friends and colleagues scurrying about the house in an attempt to 'sanitize' the murder scene. Studio heads were trying to erase any signs of homosexual misconduct, while comic star Mabel Normand was hunting for love letters she had written to Taylor. Sweet-faced Mary Miles Minter, the nineteen-year-old *ingénue* who also shared the director's favours, was doing likewise.

In spite of the impromptu house cleaning, however, police still discovered a hoard of scandalous material which the intruders hadn't had time to destroy.

According to accounts of the time, authorities found a stack of pornographic pictures of Taylor with various women of the stage and screen, as well as a collection of fine silk lingerie, including one rose-coloured nightie bearing the initials MMM. Police also found some of the love letters which had eluded the two actresses' frantic search.

Subsequent investigations revealed even more disconcerting facts about

127

William Desmond Taylor in army uniform.

Taylor. He was really William Deane-Tanner, a New York antiques dealer who had walked out on his wife and family fourteen years earlier, and that his mysterious butler, Sands, was really his brother. Sands, a dubious figure who had been in trouble with the law a few years earlier for passing bad cheques, vanished shortly after the murder and was never seen again.

To say Hollywood was in shock is an understatement. It was reeling, for not only was Taylor one of the most respected film-makers in the business, but he was also a social figure of some standing, and had even been the president of the Screen Directors' Guild. Further, the newspapers of the time hinted that Taylor had been the reason screenwriter Zelda Crosby, with whom he had also been intimate, committed suicide.

But there was still more scandal when it was learned that on the night of the murder, Mary Miles Minter, followed by Mabel Normand, had separate trysts with Taylor – his reputation as a Lothario was apparently well-founded.

According to a neighbour, Mrs Faith MacLean, about ten minutes after Mabel left, she heard what she described as a small explosion. She went to her door and in the shadows saw a man running from Taylor's house. The man, seeing her, hesitated, and returned to the bungalow, as if he had simply forgotten to tell the director something. His cool reaction convinced Mrs MacLean that nothing was amiss, and that the noise she'd heard had been a car backfiring.

But Mrs MacLean had indeed seen the killer, and yet her description of the suspect only deepened the mystery.

'It was dressed like a man,' she later recalled, 'but you know, funny-looking. It walked like a woman – quick little steps and short legs.'

Her description fuelled speculation that the killer may have been a woman – and indeed, just two years ago, author Sidney Kirkpatrick announced he had solved the murder and named Mary Minter's domineering mother, Charlotte Shelby, as the long-sought killer.

Kirkpatrick claimed that Mrs Shelby, an evil woman who made the young starlet's life a misery, had forbidden Mary from seeing Taylor. When she learned they were having a torrid affair behind her back, the enraged Shelby killed her daughter's lover.

Other writers and investigative reporters also suspected Shelby, but they say jealousy, and not a mother's outrage, was the motive. According to these amateur sleuths, Shelby and Taylor were also locked in a torrid relationship and she killed him when she learned he had also been bedding her daughter.

Kirkpatrick's information came from the memoirs and artefacts of the late director, King Vidor. In 1967, Vidor claimed he had finally solved the mystery of Taylor's death, and had planned to make a film based on the extraordinary case to herald his comeback to the big screen. Unfortunately for Vidor – and crime buffs everywhere – he died before he could reveal his secret. Kirkpatrick says he stumbled across what he claims to be proof that Mrs Shelby was the killer while doing research for a biography on Vidor.

However, according to other crime historians, both Kirkpatrick and his colleagues who named Shelby as the murderer, overlooked the fact that the person Mrs MacLean saw leaving the Taylor house after the shooting was the same person other witnesses said had earlier asked for directions to the director's home. And they had no doubts that person was a man.

Also, it must be remembered that Mary Minter hated her mother to her dying day, and if there was ever a hint Mrs Shelby had shot the director, the young actress would have gladly accused her publicly.

Could then, the killer have been Taylor's brother, the shadowy butler, Sands? Unfortunately, that too, appears unlikely. Given Sands' dark past, surely he would have ransacked the house for the money and jewels which lay untouched by the murderer. No, this was a crime of passion.

Maybe it was an irate husband, who had learned of Taylor's dalliance with his wife. Just one year after the murder, police had already compiled a list of 200 possible suspects! However in the end no one came to light as the culprit, as the identity of Taylor's murderer remains a mystery.

Sadly, Taylor was not the only victim of this bizarre mystery. Hollywood may have felt the wrath of an indignant public once the lurid details of the directors' secret life hit the newspapers, but it was Mabel and Mary who became the scapegoats for the powerful film moguls.

During the investigation, it became known that Mabel had a heavy cocaine habit, the kiss of death for actors back in the 1920s. The two-faced 'puritans' who ran the studios took her films off the market, forever destroying her once-brilliant comic career.

As for poor little Mary, she also became too much of an embarrassment to the movie world. At Taylor's funeral, she approached the coffin and kissed her lover's corpse full on the lips. She then caused another sensation by telling the congregation: 'He whispered something to me. It sounded like "I shall love you always, Mary."' One newspaper called it 'her greatest performance'.

That little outburst – together with the juicy details of her affair with Taylor, which by now had been blasted all over the pages of Hollywood's racy tabloids – forced Mary into a hasty retirement and a life-long battle with obesity. She died in 1984.

Fatty Arbuckle – King of Comedy

Roscoe 'Fatty' Arbuckle was every child's favourite clown. Parents loved him too as the champion of good clean fun; an affable, roly-poly star of the silent screen who would do anything to make a youngster smile, whether it be by taking falls in the mud or custard pies in the face.

But unknown to the millions of film-goers across the United States who lovingly called him 'The Prince of Whales', Fatty's good-natured buffoonery before the cameras masked a sinister – some would say diabolical – lust for booze and women. It was an explosive mix that one fateful night would cost him his career . . . and a young starlet her life.

What actually happened in that San Francisco hotel room remains a secret to this day. Only Fatty and pretty Virginia Rappe knew the real story. He never talked. She couldn't. But one thing is certain – it was the night Hollywood lost its innocence forever.

The weekend had begun innocently enough. It was early September, still summer in Los Angeles, and Fatty was looking forward to three days of rollicking fun far away from the harsh lights and demanding directors. On a morning like this, it felt good just to be alive. But as Fatty left his Tudor-style mansion that day he knew he had more to be thankful for than most. He had friends, money and fame. Only eight years earlier he had been a plumber's assistant, cleaning out drains for a few dollars a week.

But this was 1921, and Fatty was the king of comedy. He'd just signed a contract with Paramount Pictures to prove it. Three million dollars for three years – an incredible amount of money for those times.

The thirty-four-year-old star couldn't wait to celebrate his good fortune with friends and the ever-present throng of showgirls. He'd been planning this weekend for a long time. It was going to be special. Virginia, his adorable Virginia, would be there. Fatty had had his eye on her for some time, and with good reason. She was a stunning brunette from Chicago who didn't mind using her ample charms to get the break she craved. For Fatty, it was an irresistible combination.

Arbuckle had chosen San Francisco as the site for the revelry and on this

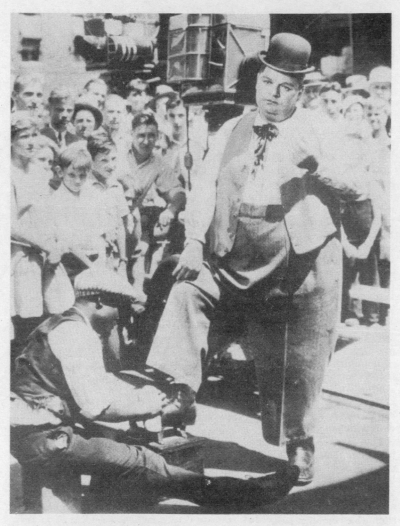

Fatty Arbuckle on set.

morning, Saturday, 3 September, he and his friends loaded themselves into two cars for the 450 mile journey to the bay city.

Arriving late that night, Fatty took three adjoining suites at the plush Hotel Saint Francis. As soon as the crates of bootleg liquor arrived, the comic star turned on the radio, fiddling with the dials before settling on the swinging sounds of a local jazz station. The party was under way.

For the next forty-eight hours it continued to pick up pace and, by Monday, there were as many as fifty revellers, in various states of undress. They toasted the good health of their boozy host, who stumbled about the room in his pyjamas and bathrobe swapping jokes and spilling drinks.

Eventually, Fatty made his way over to Virginia, who'd been throwing back her fair share of gin, and persuaded her to join him in the bedroom of suite 1221. As they left the room, the balloon-bellied comic winked to his friends and said: 'This is the chance I've waited for for a long time.'

Everyone laughed and wished him well.

Minutes later, above the merriment and music coming from the adjoining room, Virginia Rappe screamed for her life. An uneasy silence fell over the party, as guests strained to hear the ugly sounds coming from the bedroom. Suddenly, Virginia let out another blood-curdling scream. The revellers froze. Then the moans began. Loud, agonizing moans.

A laughing Arbuckle, by now a grotesque caricature of the jolly screen clown, walked back into the party room, his pyjamas ripped and torn.

'Go in and get her dressed ... She makes too much noise,' he laughingly told his stunned friends.

As Fatty swayed by the bedroom door, Virginia screamed again. This time, his smirk turned to a sneer. 'Shut up or I'll throw you out of the window,' he yelled.

Two of Virginia's friends, Bambina Delmont and Alice Blake, went into the bedroom. What they saw haunted them for the rest of their lives. The once-bubbly beauty lay almost naked on the bed, writhing in agony. Her clothes, which had been brutally torn from her body, were scattered about the floor. As they tried to comfort her, Virginia sobbed: 'I'm dying, I'm dying. He hurt me.'

Five days later, the twenty-five-year-old starlet was dead. Before she died, however, she managed to speak one more time, whispering to a startled nurse: 'Fatty Arbuckle did this to me. Please see that he doesn't get away with it.'

But Fatty and his powerful Hollywood friends did their best to hush the sordid story, and if it wasn't for an incorruptible coroner, Michael Brown, they may well have succeeded. Instead, Brown launched a full-scale inquiry into the bizarre death after examining the dead girl's body. He found that her female organs had been severely traumatized, causing death from peritonitis.

Following a police investigation, Arbuckle, who never showed any remorse over the girl's death, was formally charged with rape and murder. Hollywood, indeed the entire United States, went into shock. Was the king of comedy really a perverted Jekyll-and-Hyde monster?

The tabloids of the time believed so, and they had a field day publishing the lurid 'details' of the infamous weekend. During Arbuckle's first trial in November 1921, one of the most frequent rumours to find its way into print was that Virginia had been ravaged by a champagne bottle. Others claimed that she had been fatally injured when the 266-pound actor leapt on top of her in frenzied passion. But that's all they were ... rumours. And the jury, which had been constantly reminded by defence attorneys that the dead girl was no angel, needed proof Arbuckle had indeed caused Virginia's death. After forty-three hours, they voted ten–two for acquittal. A mistrial was called. The second trial, which this time ended ten–two for conviction, was also declared a mistrial.

In April 1922, Fatty had to face his peers yet again. It was third time lucky for him. Not only did the jurors take just one minute to find him not guilty, but they also apologized to him, saying 'there was not the slightest proof to connect him in any way with a criminal wrong doing'!

As he left the courtroom, an obviously relieved Arbuckle, who went broke paying for his three defences, said in a solemn voice: 'My innocence of the hideous charges preferred against me has been proved ... I am truly grateful to my fellow men and women. My life has been devoted to the production of clean pictures for the happiness of children. I shall try to enlarge my field of usefulness so that my art shall have a wider service.'

He never got the chance. In the eyes of twelve jurors, Fatty was innocent. In the eyes of the United States, however, he was guilty. Ironically, the three million dollar film contract which had indirectly led to his downfall, was torn up, and Arbuckle went into an enforced, drunken retirement.

What really did happen that late summer night? Two years before his death in 1933, Fatty was arrested for drunk driving by Hollywood police. As the officers approached the car, the fallen idol threw a bottle from the car, laughing in their faces: 'There goes the evidence!'

Was he somehow, through the murky haze of alcoholism, thinking back to that warm San Francisco night, of another bottle sent hurtling out of the twelfth storey window?

It was a secret Arbuckle took with him to the grave.

Thelma Todd – the Ice Cream Blonde

On the night of Sunday 15 December 1935, bubbly comedienne Thelma Todd attended a lavish party at the swish Hollywood nightclub, the Trocadero. It was one of the hottest tickets in town and fittingly, the beautiful comic star was the guest of honour – however this was to be the last party the so-called Ice Cream Blonde would ever attend. The next time her friends would see her, there would be no laughter, no Christmas cheer, no clinking of cocktail glasses . . . only the quiet murmurs of sadness as they filed past her coffin.

What actually happened in the eight hours between the time the effervescent Thelma left the party and the time her limp body was discovered in her garage, one can only guess. There were many clues and contradictory stories, as well as whispers of drug trafficking, gambling and even the possible involvement of Charles 'Lucky' Luciano, the first Godfather of organized crime, and a man feared by studio bosses and politicians alike. And yet, the case of the Ice Cream Blonde remains shrouded in secrecy. It is a mystery Hollywood never solved – or forgot.

According to initial police investigations at the time, Thelma was chauffeured home following the swinging evening at the Trocadero. She had walked up the long stairway to the apartment she shared with her lover, director Roland West, while her driver watched to make sure she entered safely. The next time anyone saw her for certain – apart from her killer – was slumped behind the wheel of her chocolate-coloured Lincoln convertible, the blood dripping from her mouth on to her silver-and-blue evening gown and expensive mink coat. The ignition switch was on, but the motor was dead. So too was the delicious comedienne, whose flowing blonde locks and light-headed antics in film comedies with such superstars as the Marx Brothers and Laurel and Hardy had won her a legion of fans. She was just thirty years old.

Following a lengthy police inquiry, which uncovered a baffling array of contradictory evidence, the grand jury which investigated the death delivered a curious verdict – death by asphyxiation due to carbon monoxide poisoning. The conclusion, which left many questions unanswered, suggested that Thelma may have committed suicide. Yet why would Thelma want to kill

135

Thelma Todd lies in state.

herself? She had everything to live for – a successful career, scores of friends, money. In fact, actress Ida Lupino, a close friend who had been at the fateful Trocadero party, said Thelma seemed on top of the world that night, even gleefully telling her closest friends that she had taken a new lover, a San Francisco businessman, behind West's back. And if she had committed suicide, as implausible as that was, why was blood found on her mouth and clothes? And, strangest of all, why had several credible eye-witnesses claimed to have seen Thelma very much alive driving through Hollywood with an unidentified man beside her, after the party? Who was this dark stranger? Could it have been West, or maybe even the murderer? Were they the same person? Where were he and Thelma going at such a late hour? None of these questions was ever fully answered, despite the grand jury investigation and the lengthy police inquiry.

However, later it was revealed that West, who together with Thelma co-owned a smart neighbourhood restaurant favoured by movie stars, did eventually admit to the authorities – but only after a lengthy grilling – that he and the actress had a blazing row after she returned home from the party. But West told investigators he threw Thelma out of the apartment, and did not kill her. Other residents in the neighbourhood backed up West's story. They told police they heard a screaming Thelma pounding and kicking on front door of the apartment – leaving fresh kick marks which were later verified – before storming off into the night. West, it seemed, had an airtight alibi. But amateur sleuths always suspected that the director had staged the whole scene – just like one of his movies. According to them, West used a look-alike Thelma to play out the row in front of startled neighbours – while inside he quietly knocked out the real Thelma before stuffing her in the car and turning on the ignition. Supporters of this scenario claim West had long wanted to end the often-stormy affair, and keep the prized restaurant for himself. (Alas, like all the other theories, it was never proven, though in 1976, Pat Di Cicco, the once-powerful Hollywood agent and Thelma's former husband, said that he always believed West was behind the killing. (West was never to make another picture and died a forgotten man in 1952.) Meanwhile, not long after Thelma had been laid to rest amid much publicity, her lawyer was demanding a second inquest which he claimed would prove what he always suspected: that the happy-go-lucky comedienne had been bumped off by professional hit men working under orders from 'Lucky' Luciano. Luciano, the most powerful New York gangster of his day, had been expanding his empire into bars, clubs and restaurants up and down the Californian coast, setting up illegal gambling dens in back rooms. And it was no secret that emissaries from the evil Luciano had once approached Thelma seeking her permission to open a casino on the top floor of her restaurant. Luciano believed Thelma's rich, carefree friends would flock to the den. She refused, however, and Luciano was not known for giving people second chances. According to the lawyer, the moment Thelma turned 'Lucky' down, she became a marked woman, and it was only a matter of time before she was killed. As plausible as this theory was, the Luciano connection hardly saw the light of day, let alone the inside of a courtroom. Before any real inquiry had begun, the investigation was unceremoniously dropped. It seems the studio bosses, who wisely feared the all-powerful mobster and his ties to the film industry, eventually persuaded the lawyer to let the matter rest in peace.

And so the investigations into the mysterious death of Thelma Todd, the one-time grammar school teacher who found fame and fortune among the bright lights of Hollywood, were consigned to the massive scrap heap of criminal history.

It was a sad ending for the vivacious woman with the turquoise blue eyes who had thrilled movie-goers in films as warm hearted, vital and gay as she herself had been.

137

Mary Astor's Diary

Unlike so many of her contemporaries, actress Mary Astor not only survived the public airing of some of her most intimate secrets, she actually fared much better after her love life had been exposed. Such are the vagaries of a fickle public.

Mary, the fluttery-eyed murderess in the 1941 mystery classic, *The Maltese Falcon*, had one life-long friend – her diary, in which she faithfully confided every day. Now this may be a harmless hobby for a starry-eyed young girl growing up in the wheat fields of Illinois, but for a lust-filled screen siren it could, and would, prove to be dynamite. Newspapers of the day didn't call it 'the little blue book' because of its colourful binding, and its contents became 'must reading' in tabloids across the nation. The public just couldn't get enough and, as its revelations came tumbling out, newspaper circulation managers reached heights of ecstasy not unlike those Mary wrote about.

Eventually, the diary would become the most talked-about book of its time, causing a delicious uproar from Hollywood to New York. Guessing the likely 'stars' of Mary's prose became a national past-time, as did filling in the asterisks which covered Mary's sometimes 'colourful' language.

But the identities of all but two men remain secret to this day – and so does the whereabouts of the diary itself, which has become as elusive as the legendary Maltese Falcon. Yet if it hadn't been for a pair of misplaced cufflinks, the world may never have even known about the diary's existence . . . let alone its incredible contents.

It was 1935, and Mary, a delicate beauty with a sophisticated grace, was involved in a torrid extramarital affair with playwright George S. Kaufman, whom she had met during a trip to New York. Following every one of their encounters, Mary would rush home to her diary and begin writing furiously about that day's love-making in rhapsodic detail.

Despite its explicit contents, however, Mary inexplicably took no pains to hide the book, and instead kept it in a drawer of her bedroom – the bedroom she sometimes shared with her husband, Dr Franklyn Thorpe. It was a careless mistake Mary would come to rue dearly.

One day, as the good doctor was looking around for his errant cufflinks, he came across the diary and, being the inquisitive type, decided to take a peek at his wife's innermost secrets. The contents wounded what hurt most – his pride. It didn't take Dr Thorpe long to realize that he was not the Casanova

The seductive Mary Astor.

being written about. As he continued reading, he discovered the superman to be none other than Kaufman, a witty, though otherwise bland New Yorker. One can imagine how the poor physician felt as he sat on his bed, poring over Mary's exquisite memories.

In one very descriptive passage, Thorpe learned that his wife's affair with Kaufman had continued even after Mary got home to Hollywood from the visit to New York. Kaufman, not wanting to be far from the action, had conveniently set up his winter headquarters in nearby Palm Springs, and Thorpe soon found that all those trips Mary had made to the studio for 'costume fittings' were actually ruses to meet with her lover.

Dr Thorpe soon discovered that Mary's affair with Kaufman had been bubbling away merrily for over a year. But there were other names in the book as well, including a list of the best lovers in Hollywood – a list Mary had compiled from personal experience – including screen legend John Barrymore. Just who else was included on the list was never revealed, but it sent shock waves throughout the movie industry and allegedly sent some very prominent actors running for cover.

Of course, to Dr Thorpe, one name was more than enough to send him into a frenzied jealousy. He demanded Mary end the affair, but the defiant actress, unable to do without Kaufman's considerable charms, promptly told him what he could do with that suggestion. Not surprisingly, the doctor, who had wisely held on to the diary, demanded and was granted a divorce. He then went after custody of their four-year-old daughter, Marylyn. While Mary may not have contested the divorce proceedings too strongly, she was prepared to fight all out to retain custody of the child.

In the down-and-dirty struggle which ensued, Dr Thorpe began leaking selected passages of the saucy diary to the press, while Mary sat on the witness stand in tears. The public was agog, but Astor's lovers were aghast lest they be named. Kaufman's friends reported that he tore his hair out and cried that he was being crucified as the revelations about him and Mary came tumbling out, while John Barrymore vanished into an asylum. In addition, a deputation of Hollywood tycoons, some of them rumoured to be in the book, visited Astor and begged her to withdraw her claim to Marylyn.

Astor refused, risking her reputation and career, and so the scandal continued, as Thorpe leaked more and more pages, until Judge 'Goody' Knight, who was presiding over the custody battle, ordered the diary impounded as 'pornography'. The public, to say nothing of the newspaper editors, was dismayed.

But with his most explosive ammunition now in the hands of the court, Thorpe, whose own philandering was no secret in Hollywood, was fighting a losing battle. Indeed, his maid testified that on four successive nights, he had four different showgirls share his bed. The court, which by now had had about all it could take of bedroom antics, decided that Thorpe was no saint himself, and ordered that the child spend nine months of the year with Mary, and the three-month summer vacation with her father. However, much to Mary's dismay, the judge steadfastly refused to return her beloved diary.

What actually became of the diary is still a mystery. In 1952, it was reportedly burned, but stories persist to this day that it still exists, as phantom like as the Maltese Falcon.

According to the late New York journalist Howard Teichmann, the diary was never destroyed as reported by the wire services, but was locked in an underground vault of the *Daily News* newspaper which mysteriously acquired it many years ago. After Mary's death in 1987, a team of reporters from the newspaper scoured the files looking for the lost legend, but found only some correspondence between editors of the paper and Astor's ex-husband. Unfortunately, the editors who might have had first-hand knowledge of the diary's whereabouts and therefore be able to shed some light on one of Hollywood's most enduring mysteries are now dead.

The diary's final resting place, and the identities of Mary's many lovers, remain among Hollywood's most vexing mysteries.

Chapter Six

SECRETS OF THE PAST

What is the secret of Stonehenge, the great circle of gaunt stones which stand as lonely sentinels on Salisbury Plain? Who constructed the baffling Money Pit which man has been trying to excavate for 200 years? and what happened to an entire population who mysteriously vanished from an ancient Mexican city?

The Money Pit

Buried treasure is the stuff of boyhood dreams – doubloons, sovereigns, gold ingots – buried in the sand by pirates or plunderers, waiting to be discovered centuries afterwards by intrepid explorers. Sadly for most it remains a dream. But on a tiny island in Mahone Bay, off the coast of Nova Scotia, is a huge hole in the ground where just such treasure may have been buried. Trying to discover the secrets it holds has cost the lives and fortunes of men obsessed with the thought that within its confines lies untold riches. The Money Pit of Oak Island is one of the most enduring mysteries of all time . . .

It is in 1795 that the story of the Money Pit begins, when Daniel McGinnis, a sixteen-year-old farmer's son, gently paddled his canoe across the placid water to the hour-glass shaped Oak Island – so named because of the dense growth of mature oak trees which flourished across it. The island, crossed by a stretch of stagnant swampland, is just one of many in Mahone Bay which McGinnis, intent on a picnic and a spot of solitary fishing, alighted on by chance. The boy went ashore, gathered his picnic basket and rod and moved inland to deposit them under the shade of one of the oaks. He found, in a small clearing, a gnarled old tree with the tell-tale grooves in its bark indicating where a block-and-tackle system for hauling or lowering had been in place. Below the tree was a circular impression in the earth, an indentation which seemed to the boy as if a hole had been dug and then filled in rapidly. The replaced earth had not been stamped down hard enough to conceal all signs of digging. Daniel was convinced that he had hit on a clearing where buried treasure had been hidden away!

The lad forgot his fishing expedition and paddled back to the mainland to breathlessly tell his pals about what he had seen. Gathering picks and shovels, he and friends Anthony Vaughan, thirteen, and John Smith, twenty prepared for a return visit the following day.

Digging into the earth was testimony that McGinnis had been right. They found themselves burrowing down into some kind of chamber, the sides bearing pick and shovel marks of long ago. When they had gone down just over a metre they struck a smooth-faced flagstone. Scraping away across the floor of the pit they realized that they had discovered an entire floor of such stones. Underneath, they dreamed, must be the treasure. But when the heavy stones were prised from the clay, there was nothing but more earth. Over the

The Money Pit in recent years.

course of the following week they continued digging and at three metres, six metres and nine metres hit a flooring of closely packed logs, the gaps between filled with coconut fibres. By nine metres the disillusioned but intrigued youngsters decided to abandon their venture. In the way of all excited young men, they pledged an oath to return – and unlike most of these hastily made, hastily broken pledges, one of them kept their word, returning to the island nine years later for a more thorough, scientific excavation of the pit. Nothing had dented John Smith's certain knowledge that deep in the shaft lay treasure.

Smith secured the financial backing of a syndicate, comprised of local businessmen, but funded chiefly by Simeon Lynds, a well-to-do local landowner. When they got back to Oak Island the shaft looked much as they had left it all those years before. Using the money from the syndicate, a workforce was raised among local farm labourers and work began in earnest, digging deeper and deeper towards the glittering prize which Smith knew was there. More oak platforms with their coconut fibre matting were struck at twelve metres, fifteen metres and eighteen metres – the latter having putty as well as the fibre between the cracks in the logs. At just over twenty one metres they hit a covering of plain oak, at just over twenty four metres another platform of putty-sealed oak and at just over twenty seven metres a stone – not of indigenous Nova Scotia rock – which bore an inscription that could not be made out. Smith, a successful businessman in his own right by then, had actually purchased the whole island. He took the stone and put it in pride of place over his hearth, the significance, if any, of the almost illegible script completely lost on him.

After the stone was wrenched free, another layer of wood lay underneath. Finally, although there was no reason to suggest why, the syndicate thought that under this wood lay the caskets of treasure. They resolved to rest for the night for a final surge in the morning which would make them wealthy. They were all of the mind that twenty four hours would not make any difference to riches which had lain there for so long.

In fact the men left the pit for forty eight hours – the following day was Sunday, and Smith declared no work on the Sabbath. On Monday morning the men returned to the pit – to find it flooded to within ten metres of the top. They frantically began bailing using an outmoded pump bought by the syndicate from an old oilfield. Their efforts were in vain; no matter how hard they pumped or how furiously they bailed, the water stayed a constant ten metres below the lip of the shaft entrance. It was defeat bitter enough to make them abandon the shaft for a year.

The following spring they hit upon a new idea; burrowing a separate shaft alongside the original to a depth of thirty-three-and-a-half metres. Then they planned to break through and release the water into the surplus pit and then resume work on the treasure hunt. All went well until the final stages when the walls of the new hole suddenly caved in, hurling tons of water and earth on to the diggers. They were lucky to escape without loss of life and injury. That pit too flooded to a depth of ten metres from the top. Smith and his partners finally conceded defeat to the forces of nature, reasoning that an underground spring of such force lay beneath the site that they were never likely to reach their goal.

The next assault on the Money Pit came in 1849 when a new consortium of wealthy businessmen was formed. Called The Truro Syndicate – taking their name from the Cornwall district once rich in tin mines – they included in their ranks Anthony Vaughan, who had once again become intrigued by the treasure island he first dug on all those years ago. Dr David Lynds, a relative of Simeon Lynds, was also one of the backers.

The first shaft was drained using more modern, powerful pumps and cleared out completely. There seemed to be no problem with water or clearing out the debris from the caved-in second shaft to a depth of just over twenty six metres. But again, after calling a halt on Saturday night and returning on Monday morning the syndicate found that the shaft was completely flooded – again just ten metres from the top. After several more pumping and bailing methods, the syndicate decided to use a drill that was driven by a horse which would bore through the different layers below. Borings from the drill produced clay, gravel, mud and sand. To the east of the pit, at a depth of thirty two metres, they discovered fragments of oak, fifty six centimetres of metal, more oak and finally a bed of spruce before finally hitting the clay bed again. A faint jarring motion on the drill as it went down made the searchers believe they had brushed past two treasure chests.

Next occurred one of those puzzling episodes for which a completely satisfactory answer has never been found. The drilling foreman, James Pitblado, was accused by one of the tough labourers of taking something shiny from the drill bit as he ran his calloused hands through it after it was brought to the surface. The labourer who witnessed this incited the other men to believe Pitblado had pocketed a jewel of some kind and they demanded that he produce the gem at a meeting. Pitblado refused, saying he would announce his discovery, whatever it may have been, to the directors of the syndicate the next time a meeting was held. Pitblado then tried to buy the entire eastern-end of Oak Island, away from the Money Pit. He was unsuccessful in his venture and vanished shortly afterwards – the riddle of what he pocketed still unanswered.

In 1850 a new shaft was dug. That too flooded – but this time a curious labourer tasted the water on his hands. He was curious about the popular underground-stream theory because the heavy clay, like that on his farm, was impervious to water. Tasting the water gave the searchers the clue they were seeking about the flooding pit – it was seawater. On a nearby beach the syndicate unearthed another of the amazing secrets of the Money Pit.

'As the tide receded the sand seemed to suck the water down, like it was thirsty,' noted one syndicate member James Bolton. They excavated the sand to discover a truly remarkable engineering feat. Whoever had originally dug the money pit had ensured its safety by an intricate system designed to flood it if intruders came close to penetrating its secrets. A tunnel of stones, sealed over with kelp grass and coconut fibre, led in a slanting direction from the beach to the money pit. The grass and fibre kept out sand which would have clogged the tunnel but allowed the water to run freely through it. The stone tunnel led straight back to the pit, entering the shaft at a depth of thirty metres. As long as the pit stayed full of earth, the water would be kept out. But as soon as the diggers reached it, the water burst through as high-tide was reached, keeping the secrets of the pit safe. Smith had not been beaten by nature but by a carefully designed and built man-made security system.

At first the prospectors tried damming the tunnel, a solution that failed when it was smashed by an unusually high tide. Then they tried to block the tunnel completely by digging yet another shaft near to the site of the original. Water flooded in at a depth of just under eleven metres after the labourers had dislodged a boulder. The party thought they had intercepted the tunnel from the beach, but they were not deep enough and should have realized it. Wood was driven into the soft earth to stem the flow of the water and yet another shaft was dug. At thirty six metres they tunnelled sideways into the original shaft – and the whole thing collapsed, again miraculously without loss of life. Another nine years passed before the syndicate returned – again with no success. More shafts were sunk and flooded. And the Money Pit claimed its first victim – a worker scalded to death when a steam pump blew up.

After the Truro Syndicate abandoned its operations, hopeful treasure hunters spurred on by the lure of great wealth arrived like locusts on the island. Soon the area around the pit resembled a pock-marked moon surface with countless shafts and holes. One man even attempted to swim to the bottom of the flooded original shaft using primitive diving apparatus!

The next assault on the secret was made in 1866 by the Halifax Syndicate which ascertained that the water entered the shaft at a depth of thirty three metres and that the mouth of the tunnel was just over one metre high, and just under one metre wide. One of the Halifax team, said: 'I saw enough to convince me that there was treasure buried there and enough to convince me that they will never get it.' Blair was right. The Halifax Syndicate folded after investing £20,000 in an effort to pump out the water which stood as sentinel to whatever lay at the base of the pit.

In 1891 the search passed on to the Oak Island Treasure Company which was headed by Frederick Leander Blair. He organized one assault on the original shaft but when that failed, the pit lay dormant for seven years as the syndicate struggled to raise more money. It wasn't until 1897 that the excavation began again at the mouth of the flood tunnel. Nearly seventy kilogrammes of dynamite was lowered into the mouth of the tunnel and detonated to prevent further flooding. They drained the pit, came back the next day – and found it flooded again! Then, using a drill encased in piping to ensure smoother operating, a bore was lowered into the murky depths. At thirty eight metres it bit into a sheet of iron. A smaller drill was passed down and this drilled through the obstruction to a depth of forty six metres, passing en-route through some soft stone. Fifty three centimetres below that it hit some oak, then hit more metal, and a fragment of parchment. When the parchment was examined on the surface it contained the letters V.I. When the engineers attempted to insert piping down the length of the drill to obtain further samples, the bit was deflected, and water rushed up the bore pipe at enormous pressure. Blair, thinking that he had struck yet another water-barrier that the ingenious mind behind the construction of the Pit had devised, poured in red dye and ordered labourers to watch the sea. Sure enough, red dye seeped into the sea in three different areas, confirming more water barriers constructed to keep the pit from the reach of man. The syndicate sunk fourteen more shafts in a bid to block the tunnels, failing in their plan and turning the area around the pit into a maze of holes and swamps. The syndicate bankrupted itself soon after.

The next plan came in 1909 when rich engineer Captain Henry Bowdoin invested £30,000 in a new drill. He failed. Then in 1912 a madcap boffin tried a scheme to freeze all the water in the pit and hack it out with picks. He too failed. For the next twenty years the D-I-Y prospectors picked over the ravaged site, the original shaft barely discernable from the countless other pits and holes which dotted the area. In the 1930s several schemes were formulated by wealthy businessmen. One involved rigging up a system of steel pylons ringing the site to keep out the water, another sending divers in a diving bell to the water's depths. Only one explorer distinguished himself from the others with their madcap schemes – an adventurer called Gilbert Hedden who found a large triangular pile of stones on a deserted beach near to where the original tunnel was located. There was also an arrow pointed towards where the Money Pit lay. Hedden, using a chart he claimed was printed in a book called *Captain Kidd and his Skeleton Island*, which chronicled the exploits of one of history's most infamous pirates, said his discovery proved conclusively that the treasure was the property of the infamous pirate. While many subscribed to Hedden's theory, others poured scorn on it.

Hedden was followed by engineer Edwin Hamilton who drilled the deepest shaft of fifty five metres, and discovered that the second tunnel entered the pit at forty six metres on the opposite of the original flood tunnel. In 1963 the next casualties of the mystifying hole occurred when on 17 August Robert Restall was overcome by the exhaust fumes of his water pump, killing him, his father and two other men who tried to rescue them. In 1965 a geologist, Robert Dunfield, squandered £120,000 in digging more new holes, without any success.

To this day the secrets of the Money Pit have not been penetrated. One author, Rupert Furneaux, in his authoritative account of the island entitled *Money Pit: the Mystery of Oak Island*, speculates that the British Army buried the treasure there during the American War of Independence. But there are no records of such an undertaking. The secret lies intact in the mud and clay of that lonely little island.

The Secret City

No traveller to Mexico City can fail to be awed by both its achievements and its ghastly pollution. Sitting in an enormous bowl in the earth, the smoke and fumes belched out by its millions of citizens and their cars, factories and fires makes for an acrid haze which hangs over the city like an impenetrable screen. Only when it rains does the haze disappear momentarily. In such an environment it is no wonder that most visitors 'escape' from Mexico City to another metropolis – the secret city of Teotihuacan.

In this magnificent place there is no pollution – for the simple reason that it is a dead city, abandoned mysteriously by its people centuries ago. The race which built Teotihuacan on the plains outside modern-day Mexico City displayed a skill equal to that of the pyramid builders of ancient Egypt, and brought a level of culture to the Americas that was undreamed of in Europe at that time. But the great edifices of the pyramids of the Sun and the Moon which stand at the top of its broad cobbled avenues, its intricate carvings and ornately decorated palaces, leave no clue to the people who built and inhabited it – a people who left without a trace, twenty centuries ago. Just what the secrets of Teotihuacan are is a puzzle which has fascinated and confounded historians ever since the city was first discovered.

The builders of the city of Teotihuacan – the name given to the place by people who inhabited it long after its founders had disappeared – were highly religious and raised the massive structures in reverence to ancient gods. They treated their dead with a respect that Christians would admit was civilized and created magnificent artefacts which have been unearthed over the years. At its peak, some quarter of a million people lived in Teotihuacan over a vast plateau which stands some 2,250 metres above sea level. Indeed, even though the broad-sweeping avenues and tall pyramids give an impression of a great city, archaeologists estimate that nine-tenths of Teotihuacan lies buried under the dirt and shifting sands blown over its structures through the centuries. At its height it stretched over twenty three square kilometres!

It was the Aztecs, that other great Mexican civilization, who, stumbling on the ruins of Teotihuacan a thousand years after its decline, named it. In their language Teotihuacan means 'The place of those who have the road of the Gods'. The Aztecs, although they adapted the ruins of the city for their own purposes and way of life, were just as baffled as to who the mysterious race

148

The secret city of Teotihuacan.

was which originally had constructed the city of Teotihuacan.

Teotihuacan's main thoroughfare is called The Avenue of the Dead which leads up to the mighty Pyramid of the Sun. There is another pyramid at the northern end of the Avenue called Pyramid of the Moon; both structures signifying the great importance the founders placed on paying homage to the two great forces ruling their lives. Of the two, the Pyramid of the Sun is the tallest, aligned on an east-west axis that reflects the path of the sun across the sky. It is generally believed that the pyramid was constructed to symbolize the universe, with its four corners representing the points of the compass and its apex representing the 'heart of life'. Its sides measure 225 metres at the base and it is seventy metres high. Experts estimate that there are some two and a half million tonnes of dried brick and rubble constituting its body – and that it would have taken 3,000 men thirty years to complete!

The Pyramid of the Moon is smaller, some forty three metres high, and faces an open space which was called The Plaza of the Moon. Here, ancient rites in praise of the dark forces were performed, although there has been little evidence unearthed over the years to suggest that the people practised human sacrifice. Archaeological exploration has revealed several layers of the city, built during the eight hundred or so years it flourished.

For historians, the most striking constructions are the palaces, particularly the Temple of the Feathered Serpent God. The temple, situated off of the Plaza of the Moon, would have been reached by the way of the Avenue of the Dead, the thoroughfare on which stood the houses of the city's elite; the priests, craftsmen, minor functionaries and the leaders themselves. The remainder of the population lived in the surrounding areas – testified to by the huge numbers of wattle and daub hut remains found under the earth.

At the height of its power, the walls of the city shone with beautiful frescoes which testified to the artistic development, even genius, of the population. Other items found there include a tripod vase, graceful eating bowls and implements, and numerous figures depicting fertility, the seasons and death. The inhabitants developed a system of writing – which, unlike hieroglyphics – still has to be fully understood, and also a system of numeracy. Aztec, Toltec and Mayan cultures in Mexico did not use systems similar to those discovered in the ruins of Teotihuacan.

Researchers think that the wattle-and-daub hut remains could have been there much longer than the city itself – suggesting that there was a settlement of primitive people there in prehistoric times whose labour was harnessed by a cultured, more intelligent race to build the magnificent edifices which remain to this day. Frenchman Desiré Charnay, credited with being the first European to stumble across the site in 1880, believed it to be a Toltec ruin. But exploreres after him have ruled out the Toltecs – they merely adopted 'squatters' rights' over the buildings when they arrived around the first century A.D.

Mexican scholar Jimenez Moreno argued that the city was built by a priestly autocracy, the like of which has not been witnessed in other parts of Mexico. He argues that the numbers of buildings erected to religious figures, coupled with the pyramids of the Sun and the Moon, point towards an educated priest-class who ruled over workers who toiled in the surrounding fields on the fertile plain. Remains of maize, wheat, barley, beans and other vegetable produce found on the different layers of the city testify that it was once a huge market area as well as a great metropolis. Jimenez says the Temple of the Feathered Serpent God signifies the union of heaven, earth, land and water and suggests that the whole city may be one gigantic monument to the gods – thanking them for blessing the surrounding region with abundant crops, water and wildlife. Another Frenchman, Laurette Sejourne, concurs, stating that religious symbols and artefacts found in most of the buildings indicate that it was a giant 'cloistered' city, with the workers and artesans living in the hut villages on the outskirts.

Nobles in the city lived in separate complexes, off the Avenue of the Dead. One of these complexes, called Zacuala, covered an area of some 3300 square metres and had its own private temples. The casual visitor to these gracious buildings is reminded that they were flourishing at a time when the Huns, Goths and Vandals were turning Europe into rivers of blood! Like the Romans, the original inhabitants of the city invented a drainage system which provided fresh water, but which could be plugged if supplies ran low. Beneath the houses were found human remains, burned, wrapped in linen shrouds, presumably placed in these home-made crypts after being blessed by the priests. The inhabitants placed great significance on the death ceremony, garnishing the burial area with statuettes and tools for the deceased's life.

One professor who has devoted much of his academic life to the study of Teotihuacan is Rene Millon of the University of New York at Rochester. He thinks that the hut dwellers eventually left the outskirts of the city to seek the sanctuary of the stone dwellings within. He bases his findings on evidence of a withdrawal from the plain around about A.D. 150. But what he and others have been unable to ascertain is the reason for the mass exodus of the city's population. There have been no signs of a great fire, no evidence of a plague, no sackings or mass killings. One author in the 1950s put forward the theory that the priests were overthrown by the peasantry in a year of famine.

The truth is, the secrets of Teotihuacan are as safe now as they were when the mysterious race who built this most incredible city vanished forever.

Secrets of the Standing Stones

They stand as mighty symbols of a time that modern man barely comprehends. The scant knowledge gleaned of ages when the massive stones were formed, has been unearthed through archaeological studies and examination of artefacts left behind. No records exist to tell us what made the ancient inhabitants of Salisbury Plain build the circling stones which are the enduring legacy of not-so-primitive man. And no pot, pan or flint head, valuable though they are, can express the brooding, dark secrets of that age when the most famous of all the megaliths that span western Europe was constructed. Centuries on, the giants of Stonehenge still keep their secrets.

The ancient monument itself is but one of a number of megaliths – the word is Greek meaning great stones – which cut across Europe in a giant swathe. There are sites in Brittany, Malta and Spain, and 900 in the British Isles alone, the northernmost ones situated on the windswept Shetland Isles. But Stonehenge has come to symbolize the age of the megaliths, with all its sinister and mysterious connotations of human sacrifice, sun worship and pagan ritual. The monument itself was built in three distinct phases spanning a period of over 1,300 years. Each group that embarked on the mammoth task of hauling, carving and placing the stones, did not quite manage to complete their work – leaving the job to be finished by their successors.

Historians agree that the first builders were neolithic, beginning the original construction around 2700 B.C. These first hunter-warriors excavated the encircling ditch and erected the so-called heel stone, which is aligned so that the first rays of light from the sun on Midsummer's Day strike it and the central point of the inner stone circle. The same men dug the Aubrey Holes – the fifty six shallow pits which form a ring near the banked earth surrounding the structure at Stonehenge. When the pits were excavated earlier this century they contained a wealth of burned objects and charred bones – giving rise to one theory that the stones constituted a holy cremation ground for early man.

Eight hundred and fifty years after man began the first steps towards creating Stonehenge, the race called the Beaker People moved in to finish the massive stone legacy. The Beaker People – the name derived from their habit of burying their dead with ornate pots and vases – accomplished amazing engineering feats which have baffled and bemused modern technicians. Theirs is truly one of the great secrets of Stonehenge – for the Beaker People, equipped with flint head axes and without the use of the wheel – quarried rock from Wales and dragged it to Stonehenge! Over 480 kilometres from the hills of South Wales, to the plateau of Stonehenge, were dragged the enormous stones; eighty in all, each weighing more than four tonnes, the stones were assembled into a double circle. Just how the Beaker People accomplished such a feat with such primitive tools has baffled researchers.

No less impressive a feat occurred around 1500 B.C. when the Beaker People – who failed in their bid to finish the construction – were themselves succeeded by another, unamed generation, who harnessed the labour of an estimated 1,000 workers or slaves to drag quarried stones from the downs near modern-day Marlborough to the Stonehenge site. Historians can only concur that primitive sledges were used to haul the stones in an operation that would have taken months to complete. Once at the site, they were fashioned into the giant stones that exist as the Stonehenge we know. And these same craftsmen, who had devised no system that we know of to read, write or perform mathematics, created a system to lever into place the giant lintels which crown the upright stones. The means by which they did this is unknown, but Stonehenge man shared something in common with his fellow megalith builders in Europe and other parts of the British Isles; all the monuments are constructed using the same unit of measurement which has since become known as the Megalith Yard, a distance of 0.83 metres. How or why this common unit of measurement came to be used by these 'primitive' people is something that has not been satisfactorily explained.

The cult of Druidism is espoused by the heirs to the ancient Celtic priests, who lay claim to Stonehenge and each Summer Solstice are allowed access to the jealously guarded national monument to practise their ancient rites. But experts concur that it is too old to have been built by their forefathers, the original Druids.

The most widely accepted theory about the origins and construction of Stonehenge is that propounded by Oxford University professor Alexander Thom who, after a long days sailing on Loch Roag on the Isle of Lewis, off Scotland's bleak western coastline, stopped to gaze at the standing stones of Callanish, often dubbed Scotland's Stonehenge. He went ashore and, standing in the centre of the stones, checked the position of the Pole Star. By this he was able to determine that the structure was aligned due north-south. But because this monument was prehistoric, and was built in a time when the Pole Star's constellation had not reached its present position in the galaxy, Professor Thom reasoned that its architects must have had some other means

153

of determining the alignment of the stones. Excited by his discovery, Professor Thom embarked on a journey throughout Britain and Europe to examine more than 600 standing stone sites. And they all proved his theory was correct – that the stones were, in fact, crude space observatories. All were built on the north-south axis, marking the moments throughout the calendar when the sun and moon rose and set.

In 1963, another professor, Gerald Hawkins, the professor of Astronomy at Boston University in the United States, took the Thom theory one step further and announced that Stonehenge was, in fact, a massive prehistoric computer, capable of complex calculations based on the heavens. 'The men that built it proved they were not primitive by dint of their architecture' he said. The published works of C.A. Newham followed on by stating that a caste of highly evolved astronomer-priests would have stood in the centre of the stones and tracked the path of the sun and moon by using the stones as a guide. Dr Euan Mackie of Glasgow's Hunterian Museum took the 'elite' caste system theory further along when he announced that he had found the stone-age 'university' where these priests may have lived and trained. Artefacts of woven cloth, remains of a rich diet and other objects found at Durrington Walls near Stonehenge were proof of the higher quality of life among a select few that distinguished them from their fellow men.

If what the academics say is true, then the widely held belief that Stonehenge was a place of pagan worship is inaccurate. It also means that, in a time when there was no numeracy or literacy, an intellectual elite existed within the stone age communities and, somehow, gleaned the knowledge to measure the megalithic yard and to chart planetary movements. Professor Sir Fred Hoyle, one of Britain's foremost astronomers, also supported the theory that Stonehenge was a giant observatory. He agreed with Hawkins' speculation that the stones could be used as markers to gauge the moon's activity as it passed through its lunar cycle. The Aubrey Holes, dug by the first workers on the site, were significant, said Hoyle; their number, fifty six, representing almost exactly three times the 18.6 years of the moon's cycle. When he fed this into a computer he found out that the stones could predict eclipses of the Sun! 'The construction demanded a level of intellectual attainment greater than the standard to be expected from a "primitive" community,' he said.

As to other theories about the mysterious stones, the enthusiast for mystery can choose any one of a number; that the site was a marker for aliens from outer space to land their craft; that it was a place where infertile women went to be blessed; that it was a temple for human sacrifice, an altar to the gods who saw over the harvest, or a forum for a primitive parliament.

Only those massive, immoveable stones know the true history of Stonehenge – and they can never reveal their secrets.

154

Secret Societies

The Ku Klux Klan

Of all the world's secret societies that have their origins in the past, few are more hated than the dreaded Ku Klux Klan.

Founded on Christmas Eve 1865, by former confederate General Nathan Forrest and five other Civil War veterans in Pularski, Tennessee, the Klan was originally formed to relieve the boredom of the post-war era by intimidating 'niggers'.

The General and his friends gave themselves preposterous titles, such as Grand Dragon and Imperial Wizard, and dressed themselves in white, hooded robes to shield their identities.

Within two years, the group, which by now comprised of hundreds of former slave owners and soldiers, was waging an all-out terror campaign against blacks across the southern states of America – intimidation of Jews and Catholics was soon to follow.

Using violence and threats, the KKK played a key role in shaping the beliefs and customs of the post-war deep South, using its considerable clout to influence elections and derail any legislation it considered detrimental to its aim of total white supremacy. The KKK also killed on a huge scale without fear of ever being caught, largely because no one knew the identities of the members, and those who did were sworn to secrecy. The penalty for breaking the Klan code of silence was death.

According to historians, more than 3500 blacks – men, women and children – were murdered in the Klan's first ten years of existence, as the shadowy organization spread its tentacles further and further across the defeated and demoralized southern states.

By the 1920s, at the height of its popularity, the Klan had about five million members, including doctors, lawyers, police officers, judges and other pillars of white society. Even the so-called 'liberal' northern states fell victim to the scourge, as Klan groups appeared in the industrial cities where there was a dwindling number of jobs and increasing local resentment at the number of immigrant workers. The Klan's burning crosses and hateful rhetoric struck fear in minority groups across the nation, and more than 900 blacks alone were lynched in the decade.

During the 1960s the Klan was also at the forefront of attacks on civil rights

A Klan member gives a menacing salute.

groups during a time when southern states were ordered by the federal government to desegregate their schools, hotels, bars and restaurants. Claiming they were going to protect 'the old way of life,' the KKK embarked on an all-out campaign to block the inevitable changes in civil rights. They lynched local blacks, bombed churches and burned down minority-owned farms and businesses. In 1964, Klansmen brazenly killed three civil rights workers as they drove across Mississippi trying to rally support for their cause.

As civil rights in the U.S. have improved over the years, membership of the Klan has dwindled – latest Government estimates put the number of Klansmen at about 7000 – however the KKK still has not forsaken its violent tactics. Its members still attack black families, peace activists and Jewish communities, and as recently as 1981 the Klan lynched a teenage black man.

Of most concern today, to law enforcement groups and civil liberty organizations, is the growing alliance between the KKK and the neo-Nazi movement. According to FBI reports, neo-Nazi attacks on minority groups have more than tripled in the past two years, and the group has been blamed for several racially-motivated murders.

The thugs, who have become virtual storm troopers for the older Klansmen, were brought into the racist fold by Tom Metzger, a long-time KKK operative and avowed white supremist. The neo-Nazis act as bodyguards at Klan rallies, and recently gained national notoriety when they started a studio brawl on a television show which was probing the re-emergence of hate groups in the United States.

The neo-Nazis have also learned the value of secrecy. Two years ago, when one of their comrades decided to leave and speak out against the group, he was nailed to a plank as a warning to any other would-be traitors.

As long as people hate simply because of a person's skin colour or religious beliefs, the white-robed Klansmen and the evil neo-Nazis will always be a blot on U.S. society.

The Mafia

From its humble beginnings many, many years ago in the small towns and villages of Sicily, the modern-day Mafia is probably the most feared – and dangerous – secret organization in the world. During its incredibly violent history, it has carved out a multi-billion dollar criminal empire dwarfing even the assets of the largest legitimate corporations, protecting its ill-gotten gains with murder, bribery, extortion and a code of silence: the *omerta*, which if broken is punishable by death.

Few men have ever lived to break the *omerta*, but in 1985, Tommaso Buscetta, a Mafia chief, revealed to a hushed New York courtroom the most secret rituals of the underworld crime Tzars.

'I was given a "saint" (a wallet-size picture of a saint with a small prayer printed underneath) and then my finger was pricked and I had to rub blood from my finger onto the saint and then set fire to it and I had to say the oath. After ... I was to say that if I should betray the organization, my flesh would burn like this saint.'

Buscetta also revealed that the mobsters regard themselves as 'men of honour,' who are sworn under penalty of death not to touch another Mafioso's wife or lie to another member.

According to law enforcement officials, the Mafia or Cosa Nostra – Italian for 'This Thing of Ours' – is made up of just a few thousand members, but has tens of thousands of associates. The Mafia gained a foothold in the United States when Italian immigrants arrived *en masse* during the early 1900s. In run-down areas of cities like New York and Chicago, young packs of hoodlums would extort money from their hard-working countrymen.

The rise of the Mafia, in the form we know it today, began with the murder of one of the first major syndicate bosses Nicholas Morello, leader of the Sicilian gangsters in New York, who was shot to death in September 1917. Following his execution, the two warring Mafia factions, those of Sicilian and Neapolitan descent, merged for the first time and operated under the leadership of Guiseppe 'Joe the Boss' Masseria for nearly a decade. Eventually, Masseria was executed by one of his top henchmen who, just five months later, was himself killed. The next day, forty old Mafia mobsters were murdered by killers loyal to a 'rising star' on the Mafia scene Charles 'Lucky' Luciano – the man credited with establishing the Mafia 'family' system in the United States.

Luciano carved New York City up into five criminal families, all headed by men he could trust – other cities across the nation soon followed suit. Within a decade, Luciano was known as the *Capo di tutti Capi* – Boss of All Bosses and the first Mafia Godfather. He also created 'the commission' – a mob board of directors made up from the heads of the families which decided who could become members of the clan, which family got what share of business and, when another mobster had to be executed.

The Prohibition years of the early 1930s fuelled the mob's financial coffers and political clout, as the nation turned to the bootleggers for its booze. Thugs like Al Capone and Frank Nitty rose to incredible heights of power during those violent days, when the Mafia families virtually controlled the cities in which they were based. It was said that Capone ruled every senior politician, judge and police officer in Chicago during Prohibition.

After Congress repealed Prohibition in 1933, the Mafia began to look at new ways to make money, and quickly became more involved in drugs and gambling. Las Vegas, it has been said, was built by mob money.

During the 1940s, 1950s and 1960s, scores of mobsters were ordered to be 'taken out' by rival gangsters as the battles for new sources of revenue heated up across the country. Leadership succession was shaped to a large degree by assassinations. One of the most ruthless hit men of the period was Albert Anastasia, who headed the infamous 'Murder Incorporated' which hired itself out to whoever could afford the 'special' services it offered. Anastasia, like many of his peers, was himself eventually murdered. He was shot to death in October, 1957, while he sat in the barber shop of a New York hotel.

Although the family system of Mafia rule has survived to the present day, federal prosecutors and law enforcement officials have scored recent successes against the organization, and have put four of the five heads of the New York city families in jail. However, authorities predict a new breed of leaders will soon emerge and fear a new wave of battles, as mobsters fight for power.

The only New York City family boss still active in the day-to-day operations of his syndicate is John Gotti – head of the Gambino family – and the modern-day 'boss of all bosses'. He controls an estimated 250 hard-core members and hundreds more associates. Police believe Gotti was behind the execution of Paul Castellano, his immediate predecessor. Castellano was gunned down in December, 1985, as he pulled up outside a Manhattan restaurant. To no one's surprise, the three killers have never been identified.

The Masons

Not all the world's secret societies are committed to crime, violence or other forms of chaos. In fact one of the oldest and largest of the secret groups, the Freemasons, was originally formed to protect the professional and religious interests of a particular group of craftsmen – the stonemasons.

In spite of what some masons may proclaim however, the beginnings of Freemasonry do not go back to the Biblical days of King Solomon. On the contrary, the organization was founded in London, in 1717, at the Goose and Gridiron Tavern. Throughout the previous century, membership in guilds of men actually working as stonemasons, began to decline rapidly. To bolster their dwindling membership, the masons opened their doors to honorary members, who became known as Freemasons.

The exact origins of the name 'freemason' is shrouded in mystery, although it has been in use for several centuries. Some scholars believe the word stems from the fact that masons were free from feudal serfdom, while others believe it points to a worker who fashioned freestone. Regardless, within sixteen years, borrowing rituals and symbols from many ancient sources, the number of freemason 'lodges' had grown to 126, and soon the secret order of

159

the Brotherhood was spreading throughout Europe and the New World.

In fact, Freemasonry became so acceptable in the United States, that there is ample evidence to suggest that it was a highly influential force in framing the Constitution, even in designing the Great Seal of the United States, which is full of masonic symbols such as the All-Seeing Eye set within a triangle and the unfinished pyramid, which represents the unfinished temple of Solomon.

In recent years however, the freemasons or 'brotherhood', as they are sometimes known, have come in for a certain amount of criticism. This has arisen from growing suspicion about the continued intense secrecy surrounding the society's rituals and aims and a feeling that freemasons may put the interests of the society and their fellow members before that of say, the organization they work for. For instance there have been recommendations by a number of senior police chiefs, that policemen should not be members of any masonic lodge as this could present them with a conflict of interest in the course of their policework.

To become a freemason, a candidate must undergo a series of highly-secret ceremonies and tests. If an applicant is accepted by the lodge – and the vote must be unanimous – he must submit himself to the three-degree rituals.

Firstly, his head is covered, he is stripped of his clothes save for his underwear and shirt, and made to repeat numerous, often bizarre oaths. For the first degree of membership, 'the Entered Apprentice', the applicant's left breast, shoulder and arm are then bared and a rope is tied around his neck. For the second degree of membership, 'the Fellow Craft', the man's right breast, shoulder and arm are exposed. The rope is tied around his upper right arm. The third or 'Master Mason' degree also requires the candidate to be disrobed and blindfolded. The rope is then placed around the man's body three times.

In all three instances, the candidate must go through this procedure before he takes the oath for each degree. The Master Mason obligation, for instance, offers a blood-curdling penalty for violating the oath and failing in one's duties. It reads, in part, that a candidate 'will promise and swear that I will not write, print, stamp, stain, hew, cut, carve, indent, paint or engrave (masonic secrets) . . . binding myself under no less penalty than to have my throat cut across, my tongue torn out by the roots, and my body buried in the rough sands of the sea at low water mark.'

Freemasonry, if nothing else, has a sense of the dramatic, but members insist it is a just society with secrets, not a secret society. But of all the fraternal groups, freemasons see the rituals and rites of their brotherhood as the essence of the organization's very being.